MW00423657

THE FILMS OF JESS FRANCO

Contemporary Approaches to Film and Media Series

A complete listing of the books in this series
can be found online at wsupress.wayne.edu

General Editor

Barry Keith Grant
Brock University

Advisory Editors

Robert J. Burgoyne
University of St. Andrews

Caren J. Deming
University of Arizona

Patricia B. Erens
School of the Art Institute of Chicago

Peter X. Feng
University of Delaware

Lucy Fischer
University of Pittsburgh

Frances Gateward
California State University, Northridge

Tom Gunning
University of Chicago

Thomas Leitch
University of Delaware

Walter Metz
Southern Illinois University

THE FILMS OF JESS FRANCO

EDITED BY
ANTONIO LÁZARO-REBOLL AND IAN OLNEY

WAYNE STATE UNIVERSITY PRESS
DETROIT

© 2018 by Antonio Lázaro-Reboll and Ian Olney. Published by Wayne State University Press, Detroit, Michigan 48201. All rights reserved. No part of this book may be reproduced without formal permission.

ISBN 978-0-8143-4316-6 (paperback)
ISBN 978-0-8143-4493-4 (hardback)
ISBN 978-0-8143-4317-3 (ebook)

Library of Congress Cataloging Number: 2018942076

Wayne State University Press
Leonard N. Simons Building
4809 Woodward Avenue
Detroit, Michigan 48201-1309

Visit us online at wsupress.wayne.edu

CONTENTS

PART III: The Cult Reception of Franco

AN EDITORIAL NOTE ON FILM TITLES AND DATES

As readers familiar with the director will already know, Jess Franco's filmography is famously tangled and hotly contested. Apart from there being no consensus about the total number of movies he made, there is little agreement about the official titles and release dates of many of his films. And no wonder: some of them have been released (and rereleased) in a variety of different cuts, under disparate titles, in diverse markets, and on assorted formats over the years. The reasons for this—including Franco's fast and loose working methods and the fly-by-night nature of the European exploitation film industry within which he operated for much of his career—are examined in more detail in the introduction. The challenge such uncertainty poses for a volume like ours is obvious. Which titles and dates should we and our contributors use when referring to Franco's films? How can we ensure that readers are able to track the discussion of his films across the essays that make up this book? For the sake of consistency and clarity, we have adopted the approach outlined here. Each time a Franco film is introduced in the chapters that follow, it will be with its original title and release date. In cases where the movie has received an American release, either theatrically or on home video, the title under which it is most widely known or available in the United States today will also appear. All subsequent references to the film will be made using this American title. In cases where a Franco film has received no American release, the original title will be used throughout. We have elected to use the original titles and release dates listed in the three-part filmography included at the end of Stephen Thrower's authoritative (if not definitive) *Murderous Passions: The Delirious Cinema of Jesús Franco* (2015), supplementing it where necessary with information found on the *Internet Movie Database*. This system is far from perfect—especially since some of the director's films are better known outside the United States under titles other than the American ones we favor—but it does lend a sense of shared focus and uniformity to the essays that follow, creating a thread we hope will help readers find their way through the labyrinth of Jess Franco's cinema.

INTRODUCTION

The Many Faces of Jess Franco

Antonio Lázaro-Reboll and Ian Olney

avid J. Khune. Clifford Brown. Candy Coster. Jess Franck. Manfred Gregor. Frank Hollman. Lulu Laverne. Franco Manera. A. L. Mariaux. Dave Tough. Over the course of his astonishing fifty-year career as a director of popular European cinema, Jesús Franco (1930–2013) worked under dozens of assumed names, including the one by which he is most widely known today: Jess Franco. Adopting these aliases was largely a matter of practical necessity; indeed, in Franco's heyday many Western European filmmakers used Anglicized pseudonyms as a production and marketing strategy. As a Spanish filmmaker working in genres that for much of his career were widely considered "non-Spanish" both in Spain and abroad—horror, science fiction, noir, pornography—his foreign-sounding pseudonyms gave his movies a credibility (and bankability) they would have otherwise lacked. As a transnational filmmaker working in countries across Europe, rechristening himself "Jess Franck" in Germany or "Franco Manera" in Italy enabled him—and his independent producers—to avoid taxes levied against non-native directors and enhance the appeal of his movies for local audiences. And as an exploitation filmmaker working at a frenetic pace—turning out more than half a dozen movies a year at the peak of his productivity in the 1970s, when he reportedly developed the strategy of shooting two or more at the same time (though he later denied this)—his false identities helped him disguise a prolificacy that likely would have struck many of his business partners as disreputable.

Practical necessity aside, however, one wonders whether the sheer number of aliases Franco used was also his way of slyly suggesting something slippery about himself as a filmmaker, for, more so than most directors—cult or mainstream—he is tough to pin down. His work presents us with many different, often conflicting, faces. It seems, simultaneously, to be the product of a marginalized artist and a commercial hack; a horror specialist and a genre agnostic; a Spanish national and a rootless exile; a feminist eroticist and a misogynistic pornographer; a relic of the grind-house era and an apostle of the digital age. Multifaceted and paradoxical, it is a body of films at war and obsessed with itself. As such, it resists the interpretive frameworks typically brought to bear on cinema, complicating any attempt at classification or categorization. While many of Franco's detractors (and not a few of his admirers) have called his work perverted, it can thus more accurately be described as perverse: eccentric, unruly, and rebellious. His movies are difficult, not in the sense that they are abstruse or demanding—in fact it is hard to imagine cinema more committed to visceral pleasure—but in the sense that they stubbornly refuse to submit to the discipline of film criticism and theory. Even the auteur theory, which might seem to offer a straightforward and obvious way of taming Franco's oeuvre, fails to fully curb its perversity: his movies (and his attitude toward them) challenge some of our most basic assumptions about film authorship.

Following Franco's death in 2013, obituaries published in the United States, the United Kingdom, and his native Spain coincided in noting some of the trademarks associated with his films: his distinctive approach to filmmaking and his love of cinema, his prolific filmography and the impossibility of ever fully cataloging it, and, above all, the cult auteur status bestowed on him by fans. In their attempts to summarize his life and career, the Spanish national dailies painted an extraordinary trajectory, that of "a unique cineaste" (Weinrichter 69, our translation) whose body of work was impossible to fully grasp, as "labyrinthine and unmanageable" (Costa, our translation) as it was "unclassifiable" and "incommensurate"

(Palacios, our translation). U.K. obituarist Stephen Thrower remarked upon the "cumulative density" of Franco's output, a "rippling borderless continuum, with individual films less important than the wider trends and currents passing through [them]" ("Jesús 'Jess' Franco" 19). Spanish commentators emphasized his cinephilia and his fondness for lowbrow art forms, and noted how, in his films, he parlayed "a genuine love for popular culture—pulp fiction, comics, horror and mystery films, eroticism, noir serials—into his own shrewd and deconstructive auteurist look" (Palacios, our translation). For *Variety*, Franco placed "sex, blood and gore at the front and center of his motion pics" (Fitz-Gerald), while tributes in the *Guardian* and *Sight & Sound* hailed him as the author of "a distinctive brand of psychedelic Gothic horror" (Newman) and as a "creator of erotic horrors who had a unique cinematic vision" (Thrower, "Jesús 'Jess' Franco" 19), respectively. *Fangoria*'s tribute confirmed that "[b]eyond the sex, sleaze, microbudgets, meandering narratives and zoom-lens addiction lay profound poetry both intentional and inadvertent. Franco should never be forgotten. He was an auteur" (Alexander 5). *Sight & Sound* portrayed him as a "voracious cineaste [who] pursued a boundless love of film, on his own recalcitrant terms, to the very end" (Thrower, "Jesús 'Jess' Franco" 19).

With a career spanning the second half of the twentieth century, Franco's filmic trajectory runs parallel—in a very self-conscious way—to the emergence of auteurism and its various reformulations, from its initial expression in the late 1950s, coalescing around the Cinémathèque Française, New Wave cinephilia, and the construction of *la politique des auteurs* in *Cahiers du Cinéma*, to cult-based critical approaches linked with the home video generation of the 1980s and 1990s and the surge of horror film fanzines. Indeed, over the last three decades the impact of new technologies (VHS, DVD, and Blu-ray) has thrust the director into the notorious canon of "sleaze artists." The "commerce" of his auteurism, to borrow from Tim Corrigan, opens up further the legibility of Franco the auteur as a "commercial strategy for organizing audience reception, as a critical concept bound to distribution and marketing aims" (46) that identify and capitalize on the potential cult status of an auteur. Mail-order video and DVD companies such as Redemption, Image Entertainment, European Trash Cinema, and Severin Films have exploited Franco's reputation as a cult auteur in the circulation of his films on home video. And Franco himself, in turn, sought strategically to adopt the auteurist mantle from the beginning of his professional career. As a critic for *Film Ideal*, a journal that courted cinematic auteurism in the early 1960s, he penned an essay on John Ford's *The Man Who Shot Liberty Valance* (1962) playfully titled "J. F. Writes on J. F."—an early example of his *insistent* forging of a self-mythologizing narrative that would link him with the origins of auteurist film culture. Over the course of his career, in "a biographical template which [was] told and retold in interviews, recollected in his autobiography *Memorias del tío Jess* (2004), and, in turn, reproduced by journalistic film criticism, fans and—lately—academics" (Lázaro-Reboll, "Jesús Franco" 168), Franco relived such "biographical" moments as his regular visits to the Cinémathèque Française in the early 1950s and his meeting with Henri Langlois, then director of the French Film Institute, who apparently arranged special screenings for Franco "on his last day in Paris" (Lázaro-Reboll, "Jesús Franco" 170). Similarly, Franco constructed a pulp auteur past by claiming that under the pseudonym David Khune he wrote pulp novels (detective fiction, westerns, and horror) in the 1950s, an unverified claim since research into the pulp production of "David Khune" yields no traces. These and other well-touted biographical snippets and authorial identities were regularly invoked by Franco to frame his entry into film culture. The numerous interviews he granted to alternative publications and recorded for DVD extras over the last two decades of his life, in particular, allowed Franco to cultivate and perform an auteurist persona, contributing to the making of what we editors call here the "many faces" of Franco: the cinephile, the pulp auteur, the horror auteur, the transnational auteur, the cult auteur.

While fan and cult appreciation of Franco's distinctive approach to filmmaking was common in the world of horror film fanzines and film festivals on both sides of the Atlantic from the 1980s onward, official recognition by film institutions did not come until the very end of his life. In the context of fan reception and consumption, his work has often been discussed in auteurist terms, especially by devotees of Euro horror, trash, or cult cinema. It was first cataloged as such in reference publications such as *The Psychotronic Encyclopedia of Film* (1983), *Re/Search #10: Incredibly Strange Films* (1986), and *Immoral Tales: European Sex and Horror Movies, 1956–1984* (1995), and, subsequently, in the pages of newsletters and fanzines like *European Trash Cinema* (Craig Ledbetter, 1988–98), *Eyeball* (Stephen Thrower, 1989–92), *Video Watchdog* (Tim Lucas, 1990–2016), and *The Manacoa Files* (Alain Petit, 1994–95), which cemented Franco's auteur standing. The "video nasties" crackdown in the United Kingdom in the mid-1980s did much to bolster this reputation. Equally, the first works devoted solely to Franco emerged from fan-based contexts: *Obsession: The Films of Jess Franco* (Lucas Balbo, Peter Blumenstock, and Christian Kessler, 1993), or *Jess Franco: El Sexo del Horror* (Carlos Aguilar, 1999). More recent iterations of the long-standing fan and critical obsessions with Franco's cinema return to and supplement the studies of the 1990s and include such volumes as Carlos Aguilar's *Jesús Franco* (2011), Alain Petit's *Jess Franco ou les prospérités du bis* (2015), and Stephen Thrower's *Murderous Passions: The Delirious Cinema of Jesús Franco* (2015), all of which provide reams of painstakingly documented information about the films of Franco. Other books such as Jack Hunter's *Pornodelic Pleasures: Jess Franco Cinema* (2014) satiate the appetite of Franco fans for illustrated filmographies and (rare) lurid visual material from the director's films.

Mainstream recognition of Franco's auteur status was comparatively belated and, when it finally came, qualified. With the exception of a showcase of certain Franco films organized at the Filmoteca Española (Spanish Film Institute) by Carlos Aguilar in April/May 1993, the retrospective—as an institutional marker and maker of auteurist reputation—did not happen for Franco until 2008, when the Cinémathèque Française acknowledged his work in "Fragments d'une filmographie impossible." While this high-profile and amply resourced event—involving the screening of sixty-nine films from across his career at the Espace Cinéphile, an interview with Franco himself at the Salle Henri Langlois, a twenty-page press dossier curated by the Cinémathèque's director of programming,

Jean-François Rauger, and accompanying lectures—was a watershed moment in his wider reception as a significant filmmaker, it nevertheless positioned his oeuvre as problematic for the auteur theory, maintaining that "the frenetic pace at which Franco worked (he wrote more than ten films in 1973, for example) and the conditions under which he worked, disrupted the status of the filmic work as it had been established at a 'modern' juncture in cinema, the one which affirmed the absolute symbolic power of the 'auteur'" (Rauger, our translation). Indeed, for representatives of "official" film culture, Franco's work posed a challenge not only to auteurist production practices but also to readings of his work as a cohesive whole. When the Spanish Academia de las Artes y las Ciencias Cinematográficas (Spanish Film Academy) awarded Franco a lifetime achievement Goya in February 2009 for his "long, rich and varied filmography, and for his absolute dedication to the film profession," it did not strictly recognize Franco as an auteur within the Spanish film canon, where authorship has long been associated with art-house and dissident (read anti-Francoist) cinema. And when the Filmoteca Española ran a posthumous retrospective in April 2014 with a total of only fourteen Franco films, it fell short of the more comprehensive and grand overview curated by the Cinémathèque Française. At first glance, therefore, Franco appears to be a prime candidate for canonization as an auteur, and yet any argument for his auteurism must take into account the development of auteurist film cultures, as well as the different historical contexts of exhibition, circulation, reception, and consumption in which he worked, since Franco operated in a variety of industrial contexts and embraced international ventures as a mode of production throughout his career. It must also take into account the sheer perversity of his work.

The Case for Franco as a Cult Auteur

When one thinks about cinematic authorship, the name "Jess Franco" may not spring readily to mind. And yet, as Thrower observes, "when a filmmaker is as prolific as Jesús Franco, it's natural for the viewer to seek patterns" (*Murderous Passions* 31), both thematically and stylistically. The typical codes of auteurism can certainly be located in Franco's cinema: the writer of most of his scripts, he is a director with a distinctive mode of self-expression and visual style, as well as a characteristic tendency toward experimentation. At the narrative level, his movies advance a distinctive brand of erotic horror. They combine sex and violence, creating a hybrid that Tim Lucas, an early champion of Franco's work and advocate for his recognition as an auteur, has dubbed "horrotica" ("Horrotica!"). In these films, mad doctors fondle their patients' breasts before operating, wicked wardens subject their prisoners to sexual torture, vengeful assassins seduce their hapless targets before dispatching them, and female vampires drain their male victims via fellatio. Horror and eroticism share the screen equally, defying the conventions of both the horror movie, where sex is usually subordinate to violence, and the erotic film, where lovemaking normally takes precedence over bloodletting. Indeed, they are frequently indistinguishable: in movies like *Gritos en la noche* (*The Awful Dr. Orlof*, 1962), *Miss Muerte* (*The Diabolical Dr. Z*, 1966), *La Comtesse noire* (*Female Vampire*, 1973), and *Greta—Haus ohne Männer* (*Ilsa, the Wicked Warden*, 1977), sex *is* violence and bloodletting lovemaking. One could say the same of other European horror films of the postwar era, a period when "the boundaries between sex and horror became blurred," creating "a new type of cinema that blended eroticism and terror" (Tohill and Tombs 5). They owed much to Franco's pioneering brand of erotic horror, however. As Cathal Tohill and Pete Tombs note, it was in his early horror movies that sex first "sizzled into the foreground, changing the face of Euro horror for the next twenty years" (77). It is also the case that Franco took this fusion of terror and eroticism further than almost all of his contemporaries. In the mid-1970s, he was practically alone, for instance, in mixing hard-core pornography with horror in films like *Exorcismes et Messes noires* (*Exorcism*, 1975) and *Die Marquise von Sade* (1977). While Franco may not have been the only Euro horror director synthesizing sex and violence, then, his mode of "horrotica"—virtually unprecedented and rarely matched—can stand as a defining feature of

The monstrous Morpho (Ricardo Valle) embraces a beautiful female victim (María Silva) in *The Awful Dr. Orlof*, an early example of Franco's trademark "horrotica." (Hispamer Films, Ydex/Eurociné, and Plaza Films International. Courtesy of Photofest.)

his movies. (Franco's enduring horrotica is covered extensively in part 2 of this volume.)

In true exploitation fashion, Franco's narratives also privilege spectacle and excess over unity and logic. His is a cinema in which plot takes a backseat to elaborately choreographed scenes of sex and violence designed to engage the audience at a visceral level. Such an emphasis on spectacle is, of course, common in horror, pornography, and other "body genres"—genres that, to quote Linda Williams, "sensationally display bodies on the screen and register effects in the bodies of spectators" (4). More specifically, it is a central characteristic of postwar Euro horror movies, which are regularly punctuated by explosive jolts of sex or violence designed to satisfy the original audience for these films: distracted, thrill-seeking viewers of the sort who frequented West Germany's inner-city *bahnhofskinos* (shabby cinemas located near train stations), Italy's provincial *terza visione* (third-run) theaters, the United Kingdom's sex cinemas, or Times Square's all-night grind-house cinemas. In Franco's films, however, the "numbers"—to borrow a term coined by Cynthia Freeland for scenes that "stop the action and . . . capitaliz[e] on the power of the cinema to produce visual and aural spectacles of beauty or stunning power" (256)—unspool for minutes on end, completely derailing the narrative. This is the case, for example, with the eight-minute lesbian sex scene that opens *Lorna . . . l'exorciste* (*Lorna the Exorcist*, 1974), delaying the beginning of the story proper, and the drug-fueled, murder-capped orgy that brings the plot to a halt for an astounding fifteen minutes in the middle of *Mil sexos tiene la noche* (*Night Has a Thousand Desires*, 1983).

Franco's narratives are further decentered by their predilection for excess in the form of story elements with little or no connection to the main plot. Episodic and digressive, they have an improvisatory feel, a jazz-like spontaneity. This "wayward quality" (Tohill and Tombs 95) is evident in Franco's first feature, *Tenemos 18 años* (1961), a road comedy about two free-spirited teenage girls embroiled in a series of unconnected adventures, which was conceived by the director himself as "a film without continuity in its narrative. Something I could film with a very small technical crew . . . a van, a limited group of actors and a small electrical generator" (Cobos, Martialay, and Pruneda 520, our translation). It is also on display in *Necro-nomicon* (*Succubus*, 1968), an erotic horror film "setting in motion a willed drifting apart of the components expected in commercial genre cinema" and "evoking a morbid, dreamlike atmosphere in which rational thought gives way to defocused reverie as an end in itself" (Thrower, *Murderous Passions* 124). This commitment to narrative "drift" signals a trademark disregard on Franco's part for the rules of mainstream storytelling.

This is not to say that Franco had no interest in plot; on the contrary, he wrote or cowrote most of his films and returned to certain characters and narrative motifs obsessively over the course of his career. Thematically, his work circles around a cluster of distinctive concerns: sexual sadism, surgical horror, mind control, erotic obsession, uncanny femininity, staged performance, revenge murder, and exotic adventure, to name a few. It shuffles these themes like a deck of cards, combining and recombining them to generate a fairly limited number of narrative "hands." Indeed, Franco himself claimed that "his entire, sprawling filmography could probably be condensed to as few as eight recurring plots" (Lucas, "Jess Franco's Declaration" 19). Consequently, working one's way through his oeuvre can often feel like watching one long film. This impression is heightened by the fact that many of Franco's films are part of larger series or cycles, like his Orloff, Fu Manchu, Frankenstein, Dracula, and Sade movies. Repetition and seriality are also endemic in Franco's work more generally. He draws upon the narrative strategies, genre practices, and modes of reception and consumption associated with serial filmmaking, mobilizing the narrative principles of seriality—such as the repetition of limited story plots and the inclusion of stock characters—in his appropriations from pulp novels and comics, in his work within and against the conventions of lowbrow genres, and in his intensive cultural production. In Whitney Strub's words, "you learn to watch not for the plot . . . nor even for the standalone value of a single film, but rather for the densely intertextual, all-consuming constellation that his body of work forms." The impression of narrative interconnectedness given by Franco's films is also heightened by the characters in them. His work is full of recurring figures: mad scientists, secret agents, avenging angels, lesbian vampires, sadistic libertines, women in prison, bloody judges, lustful Amazons, alligator ladies, and killer Barbys. Even character names are recycled. In any given Franco film, one is bound to encounter a Lorna, a Linda, a Tanner, a Radek, a Morpho, a Melissa, a Wanda, or a Eugenie. Moreover, as Lucas notes, these character names are often attached to specific character types, so that Tanners tend to be heroes, Radeks villains, Morphos henchmen, and Lornas demonic women ("Jess Franco's Declaration" 19–20). Narratively speaking, then, there are good reasons to consider Franco an auteur.

There is also a case to be made for Franco as an auteur at the formal level. Although Franco's style was frequently compromised by shoestring budgets, brutally short production schedules, and low production values, leading many critics to dismiss him as a hack director, he was nevertheless a gifted and idiosyncratic stylist who managed to imbue his movies with a distinctive look. To be sure, Franco's films must be located within the specific contexts of their production. One cannot ignore the stylistic impact of the differences in the production values between an early film like *The Diabolical Dr. Z*, which had a fairly respectable budget of ten million pesetas and was shot across two months, May and June 1965, and a later film like *Killer Barbys* (1996), shot in four weeks with the support of Spanish fan investors, or the "home movie" *Paula-Paula* (2010), shot in the living room of Franco's own Málaga apartment in a matter of days. At the same time, one should also question the facile critical generalizations that have been repeatedly made about Franco's directorial style (or lack thereof) in reference books that define his films as among the sleaziest movies ever made. For example, the *Aurum Film Encyclopedia: Horror* (Hardy, 1985) fixates upon "his relentless use of the zoom lens" (253) as a marker of his utter lack of craftsmanship. Likewise, *Re/Search #10: Incredibly Strange Films* (Morton, 1986) emphasizes Franco's "notorious" overuse (194) of the zoom, and *Immoral Tales: European Sex and Horror Movies, 1956–1984* (Tohill and Tombs, 1995) describes him as a "zoom hound, someone who uses this brain jarring device repeatedly and without mercy" (101).

There is unquestionably something unique about the style of Franco's movies. His approach to cinematography over time and across various platforms (film, video, digital) was particularly inimitable. Often operating the camera himself, Franco crafted images that are unmistakably his, developing a trademark aesthetic defined by painterly abstraction. His films favor cinematic impressionism over hard-edged realism, eschewing visual precision, clarity, and coherence for fragmentation, ambiguity, and changeability. Watching them—even his most explicit hard-core pictures—one is struck by the extent to which they traffic in suggestion and indirection, preventing the eye from fully absorbing or lingering too long on any one image. His is a cinema that caters not to the gaze but to the glance.

His adoption of the zoom lens was to some degree a practical measure, enabling him to save time and money by reducing the number of camera setups required on a shoot. It was also, however, an artistic choice that serves his films in a number of ways. Their air of freewheeling spontaneity, for example, owes in part to his habit of employing the zoom shot to "pick out details or move in quickly to capture interesting, accidental happenings, unplanned images, and events that could add atmosphere to the finished film" (Tohill and Tombs 123). He frequently uses camera zooms to underscore his favorite narrative motifs as well—particularly the theme of erotic obsession. Chris Fujiwara observes that in *Des Frissons sur la peau* (*Tender and Perverse Emanuelle*, 1979), a film about an enigmatic concert pianist and her sexually possessive husband, Franco's "repetitive zooming implies the impossibility of movement and development" in their relationship. Most strikingly, Franco exploits the zoom lens as a means of capturing his mise-en-scène in a uniquely abstract fashion. Perpetually pushing into and pulling out on the image, alternately breaking it down and blowing it up, he flattens cinematic space, robbing it of verisimilitude. He also renders it mutable and volatile, prone to sudden expansion or contraction. The result is that films as varied as *Der Teufel Kam aus Akasawa* (*The Devil Came from Akasava*, 1971), *Diamants pour l'enfer* (*Women Behind Bars*, 1975), and *La mansión de los muertos vivientes* (*Mansion of the Living Dead*, 1983), all prime illustrations of Franco's zoom-laden approach, share a characteristic look—one predicated on the plasticity of the moving image. As Fujiwara puts it, "In Franco's films, zooming is so compulsive, so pervasive, at times seemingly so random, that it serves as a formal imperative that justifies the existence of the film. Franco represents cinema in decomposition." The zoom, therefore, is to be regarded as "an essential part of his style, a vital contribution to the grammar of his cinema and an aesthetic fingerprint of considerable eccentric charm" (Thrower, *Murderous Passions* 22).

Other cinematographic devices are equally important to Franco's aesthetic of visual decomposition. Slow motion plays a crucial role. Its use is perhaps to be expected in films as dedicated to spectacle and excess as Franco's, but the manner in which it is deployed is far from ordinary.

While it often appears, unsurprisingly, in violent or erotic scenes—like those devoted to natives feasting on human flesh in *La déesse des barbares* (*Cannibals*, 1981) or lesbian go-go dancers having sex in *Paula-Paula*—it is applied much more extensively (and repetitively) than is the norm in horror or porn. In many of Franco's films, slow motion is utilized as liberally as the zoom lens. Like the camera zoom, it serves as a means of representing the circular, hermetic nature of obsessive desire. Moreover, it serves as a means of pushing the image toward abstraction—in this case, via deceleration. The same is true of camera focus. Franco routinely racks in and out of focus in his films, blurring, then clarifying, then blurring the image again. At these moments, frequent in such movies as *Les Nuits brûlantes de Linda* (*The Hot Nights of Linda*, 1974) and *Sinfonía erótica* (1980), he flirts with purely nonrepresentational cinema, threatening to dispense with the diegesis altogether. He employs filters and photographic effects like solarization in much the same way, playing with color tones in scenes from *Paroxismus* (*Venus in Furs*, 1969) or *Lust for Frankenstein* (1998), for example, in order to detach them from reality. Even his approach to lighting and camera placement emphasizes visual decomposition. Although it has sometimes been described as expressionistic—largely because of the chiaroscuro lighting and oblique camera angles that feature in his early, black-and-white noir and horror movies—it typically tends toward impressionism. Franco lights and photographs his subjects to seem on-screen as though they are always on the verge of disintegration, as in *Eugenie . . . the Story of Her Journey into Perversion* (1970), where the title character's ravishment at the hands of a Sadeian cult is lit in a flood of crimson that makes it difficult to distinguish figure from ground, or *Sadomania—Hölle der Lust* (*Sadomania*, 1981), where a sexual encounter between a female convict and the governor's wife is filmed mostly in the reflection of a mirror whose segmented glass fragments the actors' bodies. Here, as elsewhere, his cinematography privileges the fugitive, the half-glimpsed, and the abstract.

Franco's signature visual style also owes much to his frankly odd methods of montage. The editing in his movies, which he sometimes cut himself, has a ragged rhythm to it, oscillating choppily between takes that feel truncated and takes that feel far too lengthy. And the links between scenes often seem tenuous at best, lending a random, even surreal, quality to the assemblage. To some extent, this raggedness is the result of the cuts made by censors in different contexts of exhibition—the Spanish Junta de Clasificación y Censura de Películas Cinematográficas (Board of Classification and Censorship) in the 1960s or the British Board of Film Classification in the 1970s and 1980s—as well as cuts motivated by the needs of the local market (namely, more or less "spice"). According to Franco, for example, *99 mujeres* (*99 Women*, 1969) was "mutilated [by] twenty-four minutes [by the Spanish censors]," the dialogue was changed, and the "ending [in the Spanish version] differed from that in other countries" (qtd. in Olano: 10, our translation), whereas *Die Säge Des Todes* (*Bloody Moon*, 1981) was cut in theatrical release by almost two minutes, banned as a video nasty in July 1983, and rereleased in its cut and uncut versions by Interlight Video in 1992. Nonetheless, leaving aside the role of censors, producers, and distributors, as well as video and DVD companies, the disconnected editing in Franco's films is often deliberate. It is the primary way in which Franco achieves the narrative "drift" characteristic of his films. Abandoning the principles of coherence and causality that govern classical montage in favor of radical discontinuity, he gravitates toward editing techniques that give his stories a strong centrifugal spin. For example, in films like *Les Cauchemars naissent la nuit* (*Nightmares Come at Night*, 1970), a psychological thriller involving an exotic dancer who may or may not be slipping into homicidal madness, he jumps unpredictably between fantasy and reality, leaving the viewer unsure which is which. Similarly, he often confuses past and present, as in *Le Journal intime d'une nymphomane* (*Sinner: The Secret Diary of a Nymphomaniac*, 1973), whose complex flashback structure is loosely modeled after that of *Citizen Kane* (1941). He uses ellipses to create plot holes in such movies as *El secreto del Dr. Orloff* (*Dr. Orloff's Monster*, 1965), which opens with a montage of still images hinting obliquely at the film's backstory. And he employs long takes and repeated images to impede narrative progress (yet another means of underscoring the inhibitive power of obsessive desire): the ten-minute takes of the ménages à trois in *Gemidos de placer* (1983) or the frequent shots of scorpions, kites, and moths in *Vampyros Lesbos* (1971), for instance. In each case, Franco's editing shapes our experience of the story in an entirely distinctive way.

For all their visual abstraction and discontinuity, Franco's movies are firmly rooted in place. Not surprisingly, given their recurrent narrative concerns, they return to the same settings again and again—nightclubs, hotels, castles, crypts, laboratories, jungles, prisons—but they also feature very specific, and often exotic, real-world locations. Over the course of his career, Franco filmed in countries across Europe, Asia, and Latin America, including Spain, Portugal, France, West Germany, Italy, Turkey, Brazil, and Honduras. He had a discerning eye for unusual landscapes and architecture, and often wove into his work what he encountered on location. Thus *Die Sieben Männer der Sumuru* (*The Girl from Rio*, 1969) highlights the imposing Museu de Arte Moderna in Rio de Janeiro, *Succubus* showcases the white-walled Torre de Belém in Lisbon, and *Macumba Sexual* (1982) prominently features the vast sand dunes of Maspalomas in the Canary Islands. No doubt these settings appealed to Franco as an inexpensive means of creating visual interest in his low-budget films; he turned to them as "cheap locations that would add the necessary flavour and suggest the proper emotions" (Tohill and Tombs 105). They serve as more than just colorful backdrops, however. The environments in Franco's work often function as characters in their own right, sculpting his stories in crucial ways. For example, the Byzantine design of Istanbul's Hagia Sophia museum, where the climax of *Venus in Furs* takes place, reflects the labyrinthine, inescapable nature of the musician hero's relationship with his ghostly mistress. Likewise, the Aztec-inspired architecture of the French port city of La Grande-Motte suggests the ancient, pagan power of the titular witch in *Lorna the Exorcist*. In Franco's cinema, place takes on an outsize narrative significance.

Franco's films are notable for their performances as well. In the first place, they repeatedly feature the same actors. Over the years, Franco built a company of players from which he drew in film after film. Of his regular actors, the most famous are undoubtedly a pair of female stars he "discovered": Soledad Miranda and Lina Romay (whose real names were Soledad Rendón Bueno and Rosa María Almirall Martínez, respectively). Miranda, celebrated by fans for her air of mystery and penetrating "black stare" (as the title of Lucas's essay on the actress has it), appeared in half a dozen of Franco's most well-regarded early films embodying "the very epicenter of Spanish horrotica" (Lucas, "Soledad Sang") before her untimely death in a car accident in 1970. Romay, renowned for her feverish intensity and fearless exhibitionism, acted in over a hundred of Franco's movies between 1972 and her passing in 2012, becoming his romantic partner (and later his wife), as well as his frequent codirector, cowriter, and coeditor. Both Miranda and Romay have achieved cult status for their performances for Franco, but they are not the only actors closely associated with his work. Others include Howard Vernon, Diana Lorys, Janine Reynaud, Jack Taylor, Maria Rohm, Paul Muller, Alice Arno, Monica Swinn, and Antonio Mayans. His films also feature appearances by such established stars as Christopher Lee, Jack Palance, and Klaus Kinski. And Franco himself frequently turns up in supporting roles, playing a rogues' gallery of jazz musicians, perverted journalists, sleazy doctors, creepy hotel clerks, and gay slave traders. Aside from regularly showcasing the same faces in his films, Franco coaxes a distinctive brand of acting from his casts. Stylistically, it is quite physical. Franco's work contains remarkably little dialogue (and what there is tends to be spoken in voice-over rather than on-screen), so his players must create their characters largely through movement, gesture, body language, and facial expression; the acting is stylized and iconic, not unlike that of the silent era. Tonally, it stresses emotional intensity. While such intensity is typical of performances in genres like horror and porn, it is not only unusually pronounced in Franco's films but also strangely bipolar; his actors are made to swing between unrestrained frenzy and languorous ennui, sometimes in the space of a single scene. The memorable acting in his movies, then, is a product of both casting and coaching.

Finally, Franco distinguishes himself as a director through his singular approach to film sound, especially where the use of music is concerned. As a trained musician and composer with a deep affinity for jazz (reflected in the improvisatory spontaneity of his filmmaking), he wrote the scores for some of his movies and worked closely with longtime collaborators such as Daniel White to create the soundtracks for others. It is no surprise, therefore, to find that music figures prominently in them. On a nondiegetic level, it is almost omnipresent, shaping rhythm and mood in important and often surprising ways—as with José Pagán and Antonio Ramírez Ángel's eerie, atonal soundtrack for *The Awful Dr. Orlof*, which orchestrates cacophonous drums, blaring horns, and mournful woodwinds to lend the Gothic story of surgical horror a decidedly edgy, modern feel. Nondiegetic music also works across Franco's oeuvre to signal specific shifts in narrative register, so that "samba music leads into introspective stories, psychedelic music leads into delirium and madness, and films of similar intentions sometimes share the same musical cues" (Lucas, "Jess Franco's Declaration" 25). This is the case, as Lucas notes, with a haunting melody from *La mano de un hombre muerto* (*The Sadistic Baron Von Klaus*, 1964) that resurfaces in *Exorcism*, another film that explores the psychopathy of a deranged killer ("How to Read a Franco Film" 28). Music frequently factors into Franco's movies at the diegetic level as well. Indeed, many of the "numbers," or spectacle-driven scenes, in his work are *actual* numbers—that is, musical interludes. This is to be expected in *La reina del Tabarín* (1960) or *Vampiresas 1930* (1961), musicals Franco directed early in his career. It represents a striking departure from genre norms in most of his films, however. Consider the nightclub set pieces that stop the plot in many of his horror movies: Soledad Miranda's erotic dance with a mannequin to "The Lions and the Cucumber" by The Vampires' Sound Incorporation in *Vampyros Lesbos* or Lina Romay's striptease in a giant spiderweb to "Raga" by The Lazy Sundays in *Mari-Cookie and the Killer Tarantula* (1998). Diegetic music also serves the story in Franco's work, of course. Repeated phrases, for instance, become one more means by which he suggests the power of erotic obsession in movies like *Venus in Furs* and *Female Vampire*. Thus, in sound and in image, in narrative and in form, Franco's films appear to offer ample support for his canonization as an auteur.

Franco's signature use of music to evoke erotic obsession is on display in *Venus in Furs*, the tale of a jazz trumpeter (James Darren) tortured by his masochistic love affair with a dead woman. (Terra-Filmkunst GmbH, Cineproduzioni Associate, Commonwealth United Productions, Inc., and Towers of London. Courtesy of Photofest.)

FRANCO AND THE LIMITS OF AUTEURISM

And yet Franco's work also poses a significant challenge to the auteur theory. The issue is not his standing as the director of low-budget exploitation movies. A number of "B" (and even "Z") directors have achieved auteur status in the horror genre alone, including Edgar G. Ulmer, Jacques Tourneur, William Castle, Mario Bava, Terence Fisher, Roger Corman, Jean Rollin, José Ramón Larraz, Lucio Fulci, and John Carpenter. Nor is the issue the fact that, as even his most passionate champions will concede, many of Franco's movies are—by all objective measures and accepted standards—terrible. After all, compelling cases have been made for the canonization of such "bad horror" auteurs as Ed Wood, Al Adamson, Claudio Fragasso, and Uwe

Boll. The problem, rather, is threefold: (1) the amorphousness of Franco's filmography, (2) the contradictory nature of the movies themselves, and (3) Franco's famously ambivalent attitude toward his own work.

First, any claim for Franco as an auteur is complicated by his filmography, which is notoriously sketchy and hotly contested. The most basic details of many of his films remain unsettled: titles, release dates, production credits. There is not even consensus regarding how many movies he made. Franco himself was unsure, hazarding "more than 200" (Mendíbil) in an interview conducted shortly before his death. The few books on the director to appear during his lifetime do not agree. Balbo, Blumenstock, and Kessler's *Obsession: The Films of Jess Franco*, published in 1993, credits Franco with directing or codirecting 150 released feature films up to that point, for example, while Tohill and Tombs's *Immoral Tales*, first published by Primitive Press in the United Kingdom just a year later—an interval during which Franco completed no new movies—credits him with 156. The director's death in 2013 did not settle the question. In his obituary for *Sight & Sound*, Thrower puts the final count at "more than 180" (19), while Lucas's tribute in *Fangoria* disputes the *Internet Movie Database's* tally of 194 without offering one of its own ("Jess Franco" 47). Constantly updated and collaboratively compiled, the *Internet Movie Database* and other online resources might seem to offer us the best chance at finally arriving at a definitive number, but so far they do not agree either. As of this writing, Franco's *IMDb* page records a grand total of 203 movies—9 more than it did at the time of Franco's death—but cautions that 14 of these titles are "uncredited" or "unconfirmed," giving us a (provisional) net total of 189. Meanwhile, the *Wikipedia* page devoted to Franco catalogs 171 completed, released films for which he is the confirmed director or codirector. The fact is that the true number of movies he directed may, in the end, be unknowable.

There are two main reasons for the amorphousness of Franco's filmography, both of which have to do with the exigencies of low-budget exploitation filmmaking in postwar Europe, the business practices of distributors on both sides of the Atlantic, and Franco's own less-than-scrupulous working methods. One is the uncertain provenance of a number of the movies credited to him. Among them are *Le Lac des morts vivants* (*Zombie Lake*, 1981), a Nazi zombie film attributed to Franco for years but now thought to have been directed by Jean Rollin, and *Les Amazones du Temple d'Or* (*Golden Temple Amazons*, 1986), a jungle adventure film likely made not by Franco but by Alain Payet. Franco is often credited as Rosa María Almirall for movies apparently directed by Lina Romay as well, including *Una rajita para dos* (1984) and *Las chicas del tanga* (1985). To some extent, such confusion is typical of postwar "Eurotrash" cinema. Franco was part of a fly-by-night industry devoted to the rapid manufacture of cheap cinematic knockoffs—movies designed to cash in on big hits and popular trends. Made on a handshake and essentially thrown away after playing in theaters, they did not usually leave much of a paper trail; when they did, it was frequently tangled. No wonder, then, that there are questions surrounding Franco's credits. In his case, though, those questions are amplified by an extremely fast and loose approach to filmmaking. His habit of using pseudonyms, his penchant for working in different countries, and his alleged practice of surreptitiously shooting footage for two or three movies at once with the same cast and crew all make it exceptionally difficult to track his activities as a director. Consequently, putting together an accurate filmography represents a special challenge. One simply cannot be sure that Franco really made all of the movies attributed to him; furthermore, one cannot be certain that he has received credit for all of the movies he actually made.

The other principal reason for the amorphousness of Franco's body of work is that many of his movies exist in multiple different versions, none of which are clearly definitive. For example, *La Comtesse noire*, an erotic horror film from 1973 featuring Lina Romay as a mute female vampire who survives on the sexual potency of her victims, was also released as a more traditional vampire movie under the title *La Comtesse aux seins nus* and as a hard-core pornographic movie under the title *Les Avaleuses*. Likewise, *Exorcismes et Messes noires*, an S&M horror film from 1975 starring Franco himself as an unhinged ex-priest who tortures and murders sex show performers, was also released as a hard-core pornographic movie under the title *Sexorcismes*, and, recut with additional footage shot years later, as a thriller about an escaped mental patient under the title *El sádico de Notre-Dame* (*The Sadist of Notre Dame*). To complicate matters more, both films have been released in still other versions on home video: *La Comtesse noire* as *Erotikill* and *Female Vampire*, for instance, and *Exorcismes et Messes noires* as *Demoniac* and *Exorcism*. In all, some of Franco's movies have been released under a dozen titles and in as many versions in various markets and formats over the years.

Again, this has much to do with the nature of the industry in which Franco worked and the way he operated as a filmmaker. It was common practice for "Eurotrash" directors in the postwar era—especially those laboring under Spain's repressive dictatorship—to prepare at least two separate cuts of their movies: a censored version for socially conservative

Lina Romay as the title character in *Female Vampire*, one of many Franco films that has been released in a bewildering variety of versions in disparate markets and on different formats over the years. (Eurociné and Général Films. Courtesy of Photofest.)

markets and a racier version for socially liberal markets. After these "official" cuts were exported, moreover, they were frequently subject to further re-editing by distributors to satisfy the specific requirements of local censorship boards or appeal to the particular tastes of local audiences. The result was that a single movie might appear in several slightly different iterations. In Franco's case, though, the iterations are more numerous and the differences between them more significant because of his methods as a filmmaker. Partly because he catered to a myriad of markets (horror, soft-core, hard-core) and partly because he tinkered endlessly with his work (recutting, reclaiming, reselling), he produced far more versions of his films than his fellow directors. And given the differing interests of the audiences he served, as well as his need to disguise his creative recycling, his variants tend to be more than usually divergent: as much as a full half hour of footage can distinguish one from another, practically making them different movies. Consequently, with any given Franco film, we are confronted with the task not only of sorting through a bewildering array of conflicting versions but also of deciding which (if any) is definitive—and which may "count" as a separate movie. This makes it, once more, exceedingly difficult to draw the boundaries of Franco's filmography, leaving us with a body of work in flux. Blogs such as Robert Monell's *I'm in a Jess Franco State of Mind* zealously attempt to steady this flux, dedicated as they are to "the archaeology of Jess Franco's films." As Geoffrey O'Brien neatly observes, "an entire subculture [has been] required simply to keep track of his activities" (183). It has become increasingly apparent, however, that the excavation of Franco's filmography is a hopelessly quixotic task—a notion to which Will Dodson returns in the concluding chapter of this volume.

The amorphousness of Franco's filmography complicates the claim that he is an auteur. An auteur must demonstrate a consistent style across a body of work that is both substantial and well defined. The body of work must be substantial because it is challenging to make a case for stylistic consistency on the basis of a small group of films. The body of work must be well defined because it is challenging to make a case for stylistic consistency on the basis of an uncertain group of films. Franco's cinematic output clearly qualifies as substantial, but it is not well defined. As we have seen, there is not even consensus regarding how many movies he made, thanks to the doubtful provenance of some of them and the manifold nature of others. This presents a problem for the auteur theory. To begin with, how can we come to definite conclusions about Franco's directorial personality when those conclusions may be based in part on movies not made by him—or arrived at in the absence of movies he made but that have not been properly credited to him? In a widely quoted line meant to indicate the level of viewer immersion necessary to discern Franco's auteur signature, Lucas has claimed of the director's films: *"You can't see one until you've seen them all"* ("How to Read a Franco Film" 23). But can one see them all—or know when one has? Franco's filmography leaves us with more questions than answers, as Lucas himself notes: "Which are the true Franco films, and which ones are false? Which films were announced but never made? Which were begun but never completed? Does anyone know the true answers to these questions?" (Introduction 14). There are, of course, more than enough "true" Franco movies for us to make assumptions about his directorial personality, but without a definite sense of his oeuvre, assumptions are all we can make, and we must accept the possibility that at least some of those assumptions are wrong.

Moreover, we are confronted with the fact that many of the "true" Franco movies exist in multiple versions, raising further questions. On which of these versions do we base our conclusions about him as an auteur? One? Some? All? The auteur theory presumes that an auteur's films exist in unique form. In Franco's case, they do not, making him closer to an "anti-auteur" like Orson Welles, one of his cinematic heroes. Jonathan Rosenbaum has argued that Welles represents an ideological challenge to film criticism (and to Hollywood) in part because many of his movies exist in multiple versions that cannot be ranked "in terms of authenticity" (281), making it "impossible to speak of a 'definitive' . . . version" (281). Ironically (considering the massive gap in cultural status between Franco and Welles, as well as Rosenbaum's contempt for Franco as the man responsible for the "disastrous" [319] assemblage of Welles's unfinished *Don Quixote* screened at the Seville Expo and the Cannes Film Festival in 1992), we might say the same of Franco: that his working methods pose a challenge to film criticism and the auteur theory in particular because they deny the importance of the unique form of artistic works, making it impossible to evaluate them in a conventional way. In the absence of definitive or authoritative versions of Franco's movies, we are forced to guess which might be most representative of his directorial personality—or to embrace them all and attempt to reconcile the (sometimes significant) differences between them. Either way, our estimation of his identity as a filmmaker will fall short of the clarity demanded by the auteur theory.

Second, Franco's seemingly solid standing as an auteur is undercut by the contradictory nature of his films. They demonstrate a problematic incoherence both individually and as a whole. Taken as a whole, they are far less uniform than the pioneering auteur studies of Franco by Lucas, Tohill and Tombs, and others might suggest. This is perhaps nowhere more apparent than in their narrative focus. As previously noted, Franco is closely associated with the distinctive brand of horrotica he pioneered early in his career; indeed, reading much of what has been written about him, one would be forgiven for thinking that he directed only erotic horror films. Actually, nothing could be further from the truth. Over the course of his career, he made many different kinds of movies, including documentaries, comedies, musicals, mysteries, spy movies, science-fiction films, action-adventure pictures, and pornographic flicks. Altogether, over seventy-five of the films he is thought to have directed could be described as non-horrotica; assuming he made around two hundred movies in all, that is 40 percent of his total cinematic output. It would thus almost be as accurate to call Franco a mystery or porn director as it would be to label him an erotic horror director. As Franco himself said, "I don't think I have a definitive film. Such a thing is not possible for me" (O'Neal). The general lack of agreement between his films is thrown into relief by the rather tortured attempts made by several Franco aficionados to bring order to his work through periodization. Lucas, for example, sought to establish an underlying logic to Franco's oeuvre over the course of several early essays, adopting and discarding various groupings like "The Pop Art Years (1965–1967)" (Introduction 18–19) and "The Porno Holocaust Years (1976–1981)" ("How to Read a Franco Film" 21–22). With "the greater availability of Franco films from all the periods of his career" ("Jess Franco's Declaration" 17), Lucas again revisited, reorganized, and renamed these categories in 2010, focusing particularly on the early years of the director's career between 1959 and 1967 ("Jess Franco's Declaration" 17–49). Inevitably, such systemization only partially captures the character of the director's work at a given moment in his career, underscoring for us in falling short of the full picture just how riddled with contradiction that picture is.

A similar kind of incoherence can be found in the individual films making up Franco's oeuvre. Critics have often observed that his movies are uneven, not simply in terms of quality but in terms of effect. In the average Franco film, as Tohill and Tombs put it, "Some sequences are great, others look thrown together, and seem jarringly dull compared to the good stuff" (107). As a result, his work is marked by "annoying fluctuations," ricocheting "from feverish intensity to half-baked ordinariness and back again" (107). Tohill and Tombs chalk this unevenness up to Franco's lack of discipline as a director: "He's not constant, he has a problem focussing attention on things that don't stimulate him" (107). Whatever the reason, the consequence is that his films have the same fractured quality individually that they do as a whole. Again, this quality is perhaps most noticeable narratively, particularly where tone is concerned. Tonally, Franco's movies shift wildly from one moment to the next in swings that are hard to predict and seem at times to be completely divorced from the story. For instance, as Hawkins writes, "Horror sequences bottom out in farce or melodrama, so that the affect level of terror or shock (or even suspense) is hard to maintain" (99). The same inconsistency apparent across Franco's work as a whole is manifest in each separate part. His films are as contradictory at the micro level as they are at the macro level, displaying little or no unity at either end of the continuum.

The contradictory nature of Franco's films presents a problem for the auteur theory, which is partly predicated on the notion of artistic unity. At every level, the work of an auteur is expected to demonstrate harmony: the perfect integration of its disparate parts into a unified whole. Thus while an auteur may make many different kinds of films, there should be an underlying logic that ties them together into a coherent oeuvre. For example, the celebrated director Howard Hawks, working in the classical Hollywood studio system, made movies in just about every genre imaginable, including comedies, musicals, westerns, war movies, detective films, and gangster pictures. Yet he demonstrates in all of them a core concern with what Robin Wood calls "the absence of family, or the substitution for it of the ad hoc group with its freedom of membership, its lack of rules other than personal (and provisional) commitment and reliability" (xxiv). In Franco's work there is no such unifying factor. The issue is not that he directed movies other than the erotic horror films for which he is renowned, ultimately, but rather that there is no organizing principle binding his diverse output into a harmonious whole. This means that the auteurist practice of sifting through a director's films in search of a thematic Rosetta stone, the key to unlocking the meaning of the entire oeuvre, is bound to fail in Franco's case. So, too, is the auteurist practice of determining the director's intent in a particular film through a careful analysis of its overall effect. The arbitrary fluctuations of a Franco movie make it difficult to draw conclusions about its general meaning and therefore to discern his artistic purpose in it. Contradictory in part and in whole, his work stymies both approaches, rendering it that much more opaque from the perspective of the auteur theory.

Third, Franco's attitude toward his own films complicates claims for him as an auteur. He was famously dismissive about his work, frequently professing his dislike of his movies and his astonishment that anyone would bother watching them. In particular, he seemed acutely uncomfortable with the suggestion that there might be anything exceptional about his films; certainly he did not class himself with his own cinematic heroes. As he put it simply in one interview he gave toward the end of his life: "No, I don't like my movies. I prefer John Ford's movies" (O'Neal). There are a number of possible explanations for Franco's disregard for his own work. Tohill and Tombs speculate, for example, that it was a product of his frustration over his inability—whether because of the meagerness of his resources or the failure of his technique—to realize his films the way he envisioned them, noting that, "When he talks about his own films he gets agitated. They hardly ever turn out the way he planned, he's nearly always dissatisfied with them. Maybe this is why he keeps reworking the same ideas" (91). Another possibility is that he was embarrassed by the "discovery" of his movies, which were never intended to be widely known, much less celebrated—that as a filmmaker who "chose to work in the shadows and turn out marginal little films . . . [he] willfully courted obscurity" (Tohill and Tombs 122), ultimately making movies only to please himself. A final possibility is that Franco did not take the notion of film art very seriously. He often expressed doubt about whether directors—even extraordinary ones—should be considered artists like novelists or playwrights, stating in the same late interview quoted previously: "I think it's a mistake to consider the movie director as if they were great artists [*sic*]. . . . A film is a film. It's something to entertain you a couple hours. Not to be considered as if it were Shakespeare" (O'Neal). Likely, Franco was cavalier about his movies for all of these reasons. In fact, they essentially boil down to the same thing: that he viewed filmmaking in terms of process rather than product. Instead of attaching value to individual films, he prized the work of making movies itself.

This presents yet another issue for the auteur theory. The problem is not the "paradox" that Franco, who devoted his life to making movies—movies whose value his champions have gone to heroic lengths to establish—"[didn't] like his films!" (Tohill and Tombs 126). After all, it is not necessary for a director to have a high opinion of his or her own work to be considered an auteur. The canonical filmmakers of the Hollywood studio era, for instance, generally saw themselves as craftsmen rather than artists. Franco's preferred director, John Ford, routinely described movies like *7 Women* (1966) as just another "job of work" (McBride 663). The problem is that Franco was interested not in films but in filmmaking—that the meaning of his career lies not in the movies he made but in the way he made them. In this respect, he is once again similar to Welles, whom Rosenbaum tells us was in love "with process rather than product" (74). "Because [Welles] loved to work . . . and because for him all work was work-in-progress" (Rosenbaum 282), his career has been difficult for critics to quantify. Franco presents a comparable challenge, especially from the perspective of the auteur theory, which dictates that directors be evaluated by the works they produce, not the manner in which they produce them. How would one assess a filmmaker who privileges process over product? The very notion runs counter to auteurist thought. Yet Franco is precisely such a director. In his philosophy of filmmaking, as well as in his filmography and in his films, he represents a perverse challenge to auteurism. Notwithstanding the apparent strength of his stylistic signature, as well as his persistent, career-long identification with and invocation of early auteurist filmmakers and film culture, Franco is therefore at best an incomplete auteur. Or, to put it another way, the auteur theory can offer us only an incomplete picture of Franco as a filmmaker.

Franco's ambiguous standing as an auteur is by no means the only way in which he defies the discipline of film criticism and theory. His perversity as a filmmaker also poses a challenge for genre studies. Unlike "some directors [who] developed their vision within a particular genre such as Ford with the western [or] Fuller with the war film" (Grant 5), Franco did not just work in a myriad of genres, he also mixed and matched different genres within his movies, creating new hybrids like horrotica and blurring the boundary that separates popular film from art cinema with pictures "poised between high and low genres, belonging to both of them simultaneously" (Hawkins 101). Consequently, any discussion of his work as straightforward "horror" or "trash" is problematic. His cinematic "crossbreeds and mutants" subvert the notion of "generic purity" (Altman 16) central to genre criticism and theory. Likewise, Franco's films present a problem for national cinemas studies. At first glance, his movies seem characteristically Spanish. It is tempting to argue, for example, that like other films of the Francoist era, his early works use "eroticized violence . . . to expose the legacy of brutality and torture that lay hidden beneath the surface beauty of the Fascist and

Jess Franco, a director who until the end of his career valued the process of filmmaking over the product, with Silvia Superstar on the set of his 1996 movie *Killer Barbys*. (Civic Producciones S.L., Emilio-Miguel Mencheta Benet, and Jacinto Santos Parrás. Courtesy of Tomás Cimadevilla.)

neo-Catholic aesthetics" (Kinder 138). This reading, however, ignores the fact that he spent the formative years of his career outside Spain, developing an international brand of cinema that might be more accurately labeled "European" than "Spanish." He can be seen, like his fellow countryman Luis Buñuel, as an "exile who problematises the very idea of the national in his films" (Russell). Franco's films are troubling from an ideological perspective as well—especially that of feminist criticism and theory. On the one hand, they feature women prominently and often revolve around formidable female characters, playfully subverting gender expectations. In *Tenemos 18 años*, for example, "hybridism in his style (horror, road film, thriller) entertains as it enhances the plurality of gender possibilities that he constructs" (Pavlović 110). The irrepressible heroines of this film, María José and Pili, became "the archetype for his famous women detectives such as Diana and Regina from the Red Lips agency" (Pavlović 110). On the other hand, Franco's films undeniably objectify the female body, fetishizing it through the use of copious nudity and devices like the genital zoom; they also suggest a "graphic association of the monstrous with the feminine body" (Creed 37) through their frequent depiction of violent or uncanny femininity. In short, it is never a question of "either/or" with Franco's work, but always of "both/and." Multifaceted and contradictory, it is cinema at its most perverse. Consequently, it is, as Lucas writes, "perhaps impossible for anyone to speak with perfect authority about the phenomenon of Jess Franco" (Introduction 13).

READING FRANCO'S PERVERSE CINEMA

Our goal in this volume, then, is to offer a range of different ways of looking at this fascinating filmmaker, rather than reductively insisting on a single approach. *The Films of Jess Franco* does not avoid the methodologies most commonly used in the past to analyze Franco's work—auteur criticism, genre criticism, national cinemas criticism, and cult film criticism. It does, however, show how Franco's films complicate these critical approaches in the manner discussed above. It also seeks to open up fresh avenues for academic inquiry by featuring a dozen original essays that consider his oeuvre from a number of new angles, including star studies, adaptation studies, spectatorship studies, and cinephilia studies. Collecting these innovative perspectives and others on Franco, our book effectively meets the challenge of his multifaceted cinema with multifaceted criticism that supplements current Franco scholarship and suggests exciting new directions for its further development. Building on the Franco criticism emerging out of a network of alternative publications, the valuable knowledge accumulated by Franco connoisseurs (among them, Tim Lucas, Stephen Thrower, Tim Paxton, Craig Ledbetter, Robert Monell, Carlos Aguilar, and Álex Mendíbil), the broader access to Franco's movies via the new technologies of video, DVD, Blu-ray, and the internet, and the critical-academic conversation surrounding Franco's cinema (see Hawkins,

Pavlović, Olney, and Lázaro-Reboll), *The Films of Jess Franco* contributes to the ongoing process of understanding a significant and provocative body of work.

The first three chapters of the book share a commitment to placing Jess Franco's films within the wider industrial, generic, and aesthetic dynamics of popular European cinema and its cultural histories. Andy Willis discusses Franco's early films before and after *The Awful Dr. Orlof*, examining how the director built a series of pivotal working relationships with respected professionals, some of whom would become an important part of a critically acclaimed, oppositional Spanish cinema in the late 1950s and early 1960s. Rather than focusing on his early output as a critical operation to validate subsequent films, Willis explores the historical milieu in which Franco worked vis-à-vis contemporary debates around film aesthetics and film culture within Spain and beyond to reveal a Franco who wanted to be perceived as a serious artist, a cinephile, and an auteur. While they might appear at first glance to be completely unrelated, Ian Olney argues in the next chapter that sixties cinephilia and Franco's cinematic "sleaze" are, in fact, deeply interconnected. Olney investigates how Franco's filmmaking in the 1960s was defined by that decade's intense cinephilia, which was pervasive in European cinema and culture, and proposes that the films Franco made during this period are expressly about and for cinephiliac pleasure. Olney discerns in Franco's '60s cinema a desire to cater to cinephiles by privileging the "cinephiliac moment" and detects in fan writing on this work a unique cinephiliac gaze that reclaims such moments from the cultural dustbin to which trash cinema is often consigned. Franco's films also catered to the low genre market characterized by international coproduction formulae and transnational imagination. In his chapter, Nicholas G. Schlegel focuses on Franco's *Kriminalfilms* (or *"Krimis"*)—two Edgar Wallace adaptations, *The Devil Came from Akasava* and *Der Todesrächer von Soho* (1972), both West German-Spanish coproductions released by Artur Brauner's internationally minded Central Cinema Company—to examine how these films participated in larger international networks of production and distribution reaching audiences across Western Europe.

Although Franco's contributions to the German *Krimi* cycle were made late in its evolution, when the genre had entered a parodic stage, Franco added his distinctiveness to the Wallace series and stamped it as uniquely his own.

The next four chapters of the book address the intersection of horror and eroticism in Franco's cinema from a variety of theoretical and methodological angles. Tatjana Pavlović looks at one of Franco's major contributions to European exploitation cinema: his "horrotica." Drawing on Walter Benjamin's notion of the "translatability" of an artwork—that is, the essential quality that enables its renewal or "new flowering" (Benjamin 72)—Pavlović considers the latent durability of *The Diabolical Dr. Z*, *Sie Tötete in Ekstase* (*She Killed in Ecstasy*, 1971), *Vampyros Lesbos*, and *Female Vampire*. For Pavlović, the durability of these films can be located in their transnationality and transmutability, in their rejection of the art cinema's hierarchical supremacy and its institutional contempt for the genres in which he was working, and in their transgressive emphasis on sex and eroticism in a very straitlaced era. Glenn Ward explores Franco's representations of "female pleasure" within the conflicted discourses of sexual modernity and libidinal revolution between the late 1960s and the early 1970s, placing the fantasies and fascinations exhibited in Franco's films within a historically specific conjuncture. Ward discusses the ideologically ambivalent terms in which Franco's notions of "permissiveness" and "erotic liberation" are articulated within an intertextual, cross-media space that draws on contemporaneous sexological theories and "discoveries." For Ward, Franco's "Gothic sexology" responds to many ideas about female desire, pleasure, and orgasm as they circulated in the discourses of the sexual revolution, and, at the same time, echoes the reactionary—or at least neurotic—constructions of "nymphomania" and "frigidity" that can be found in the advice manuals, sexological studies, and other "factual" literature of the day. Aurore Spiers argues for the transgressive quality of Franco's work through an analysis of two of his female vampire films, *Vampyros Lesbos* and *Female Vampire*. Beyond their explicit and evocative eroticism, their transgression relies on gender reversal and the depiction of women as powerful figures and sexual subjects. Spiers considers them in relation to Jean Rollin's *Le Viol de vampire* (*The Rape of the Vampire*, 1968) and *Le Frisson des vampires* (*The Shiver of the Vampires*, 1971) and perceives certain similarities between the "counter-cinematic" imagining of gender in the directors' work that sets it apart from contemporary cinematic traditions in their respective countries: just as Franco was an anomalous presence in between the official cinema of the dictatorship and the dissident cinema of the auteurist-driven *Nuevo Cine Español* (New Spanish Cinema) and *Escuela de Barcelona* (Barcelona School), Rollin was caught between commercial filmmaking and the *cinéma militant* that followed the *Nouvelle Vague* as a result of the events of May 1968, when politically minded filmmakers revolted against the French film industry. Alberto Brodesco's chapter explores the Marquis de Sade-Franco connection by analyzing the ways in which Franco "adapts" Sadeian figures, leitmotifs, and topics across his filmography. In the same way that Franco draws upon and transforms pulp novels and pulp movies, he also reworks and rerehearses his contradictory and shifting approach to the literary works of Sade. Through a discussion of the director's appropriation and rearticulation of Sadeian tropes—sadomasochism, voyeurism, isolation, performance, masks, taboo—the chapter maps the affinities between Franco and Sade.

The final four chapters bring to the analysis of Franco's films theories of spectatorship and of cult receptions, contexts, and critical debates. Finley Freibert engages with Franco's late work from the perspective of discourses on and conceptualizations of queerness. Freibert considers Franco's collaboration with individuals involved in American shot-on-video "Z"-grade horror and scream queen fandom in the late 1990s, focusing on how *Mari-Cookie and the Killer Tarantula* and *Lust for Frankenstein* foster what he calls queer monotony and queer zoning-out—transgressive modes of spectatorship unique to the movies the director made during the final, underappreciated years of his career. Antonio Lázaro-Reboll zooms in on the discursive constructions and fan-canonizations of Franco as an exploitation and cult auteur in Anglo-American contexts of reception and consumption from the late 1980s to the present date, with particular attention to Tim Lucas's *Video Watchdog* and Stephen Thrower's *Eyeball*. These magazines are the two most prominent products of the subculture devoted to a cult appreciation and connoisseurship of Franco, carving out a niche on the study of the director that deserves critical attention. The chapter considers their archival, critical, and curatorial work, examining the reasons that bring Lucas and Thrower back to Franco time and again. While Freibert and Lázaro-Reboll examine the international dimension of Franco's status as auteur in the transatlantic cult fan nexus, Rodríguez Ortega and Romero Santos investigate the legitimation and cultification of Franco in the Spanish underground scene of the late 1980s and early 1990s. As they argue, Franco's cult filmmaking and cult auteurism in this specific historical and geographical context were part of a wider cross-media phenomenon wherein diverse players from different media and disciplines (alternative publications, the indie music scene, popular journalism) converged. Cult stardom is the subject of Xavier Mendik's contribution, in particular the figure of Franco's cinematic muse Soledad Miranda, who prior to her violent death in a car crash in 1970 had established herself as a "dark star" of European exploitation cinema. Mendik explores the extensive collaboration between Franco and Soledad Miranda and the roles in which she was cast in order to assess the fluid boundary between the fictional and fatal performances undertaken by the actress, and to consider the dead star's subsequent reception by film critics and movie fans.

By way of conclusion, Will Dodson offers a metafilmographic take on Franco's perverse body of work. Contemplating the quixotic task of making sense of Franco's oeuvre, Dodson constructs a sort of reader-response filmography, suggesting a personally experienced approach to apprehending the director's movies, or an improvisational encounter between film viewer and filmmaker. But Dodson also returns to many of the questions raised in this introduction, among them the impossibility of cataloging or ordering Franco's corpus, and the ongoing and unique interaction between Franco's fans—Francophiles—and his movies. Dodson dives into two "immersion points": Franco's brief but legendary involvement with Orson Welles early in his career and Franco's microbudget and digital film production from the mid-1990s to his death, on the one hand to revisit cinephiliac experiences of Franco's filmography, and on the other to open up alternative understandings of his recursive cinema. Like the other contributions that form this volume, Dodson's offers fans and scholars alike new ways of reading a uniquely multifaceted, paradoxical cinema, revealing a few more of the many faces of Jess Franco.

Works Cited

Aguilar, Carlos. *Jess Franco: El Sexo del Horror.* Ed. Carlos Aguilar, Stefano Piselli, and Riccardo Morrocchi. Florence: Glittering Images, 1999. Print.

———. *Jesús Franco.* Madrid: Cátedra, 2011. Print.

Alexander, Chris. "First Rites." *Fangoria* 325 (Aug. 2013): 5. Print.

Altman, Rick. *Film/Genre.* London: BFI, 1999. Print.

Balbo, Lucas, Peter Blumenstock, and Christian Kessler. *Obsession: The Films of Jess Franco.* Ed. Lucas Balbo and Peter Blumenstock. Berlin: Graf Haufen and Frank Trebbin, 1993. Print.

Benjamin, Walter. "The Task of the Translator." *Illuminations.* Trans. Harry Zohn. Ed. Hannah Arendt. London: Fontana, 1973. 71–72. Print.

Cesari, Francesco. *Il caso Jesús Franco.* Venezia: Granviale Editori, 2010. Print.

Cobos, Juan, Félix Martialay, and José Antonio Pruneda. "Entrevista con Jesús Franco. El largo camino de los que empiezan." *Film Ideal* 103 (Sept. 1962): 520–24. Print.

Corrigan, Tim. "The Commerce of Auteurism: A Voice without Authority." *New German Critique* 49 (Winter 1990): 43–57. Print.

Costa, Jordi. "Muere Jesús Franco, símbolo del cine como juego y arrebato." *El país.* 2 Apr. 2013. Web. 14 Apr. 2013.

Creed, Barbara. *The Monstrous-Feminine: Film, Feminism, Psychoanalysis.* New York: Routledge, 1993. Print.

Du Mesnildot, Stéphane. *Jess Franco: Énergies du fantasme.* Paris: Rouge Profond, 2004. Print.

Fitz-Gerald, Sean. "Cult Filmmaker Jess Franco Dies at 82." *Variety.* 2 Apr. 2013. Web. 14 Apr. 2013.

Franco, Jesús. "En el cine, sinceridad, honestidad y claridad." *Film Ideal* 46 (Apr. 1960): 11. Print.

———. "J. F. escribe sobre J. F." *Film Ideal* 107 (Nov. 1962): 636. Print.

———. *Memorias del tío Jess*. Madrid: Aguilar, 2004. Print.

Freeland, Cynthia. *The Naked and the Undead: Evil and the Appeal of Horror*. Boulder, CO: Westview, 2000. Print.

Fujiwara, Chris. "Zooming through Space." *HiLoBrow*. 5 Jan. 2012. Web. 28 May 2015.

Grant, Barry Keith. Introduction. *Auteurs and Authorship: A Film Reader*. Ed. Barry Keith Grant. Oxford: Blackwell, 2008. 1–6. Print.

Hardy, Phil, ed. *The Aurum Film Encyclopedia: Horror*. Vol. 3. London: Aurum, 1985. Print.

Hawkins, Joan. *Cutting Edge: Art-Horror and the Horrific Avant-Garde*. Minneapolis: U of Minnesota P, 2000. Print.

Hunter, Jack. *Pornodelic Pleasures: Jess Franco Cinema*. London: Glitter Books, 2014. Print.

"Jesús Franco." *The Internet Movie Database*. Web. 15 June 2015.

"Jesús Franco." *Wikipedia*. Web. 15 June 2015.

Kinder, Marsha. *Blood Cinema: The Reconstruction of National Identity in Spain*. Berkeley: U of California P, 1993. Print.

Lázaro-Reboll, Antonio. "Daring Cycles: The Franco-Towers Collaboration, 1968–1970." *New Review of Film and Television Studies* 11.1 (2013): 92–110. Print.

———. "Jesús Franco: From Pulp Auteur to Cult Auteur." *A Companion to Spanish Cinema*. Ed. Jo Labanyi and Tatjana Pavlović. Oxford: Wiley-Blackwell, 2012. 167–71. Print.

———. *Spanish Horror Film*. Edinburgh: Edinburgh UP, 2012. Print.

Lucas, Tim. "The Black Stare of Soledad Miranda." *Obsession: The Films of Jess Franco*. Ed. Lucas Balbo and Peter Blumenstock. Berlin: Graf Haufen and Frank Trebbin, 1993. 183–96. Print.

———. "Horrotica! The Sex Scream of Jess Franco." *The Francofile*. 30 Nov. 1997. Web. 12 July 1999.

———. "How to Read a Franco Film." *Video Watchdog* 1 (1990): 18–35. Print.

———. Introduction. *Obsession: The Films of Jess Franco*. Ed. Lucas Balbo and Peter Blumenstock. Berlin: Graf Haufen and Frank Trebbin, 1993. 13–30. Print.

———. "Jess Franco: The Undying Legend." *Fangoria* 325 (Aug. 2013): 46–48. Print.

———. "Jess Franco's Declaration of Principles: How to Read the Early Films, 1959–67." *Video Watchdog* 157 (2010): 16–49. Print.

———. "Soledad Sang." *Video Watchdog Blogspot*. 20 Dec. 2007. Web. 1 June 2017.

McBride, Joseph. *Searching for John Ford*. New York: St. Martin's Griffin, 2001. Print.

Mendíbil, Álex. "Franconomicon interviews uncle Jess (English version)." *El Franconomicon/I'm in a Jess Franco State of Mind*. 30 Oct. 2009. Web. 21 June 2015.

Monell, Robert. *I'm in a Jess Franco State of Mind*. Web. 21 June 2015.

Morton, Jim. *Re/Search #10: Incredibly Strange Films*. Ed. V. Vale and Andrea Juno. San Francisco: Re/Search Publications, 1986. Print.

Newman, Kim. "Jesús Franco obituary." *Guardian*. 5 Apr. 2013. Web. 14 Apr. 2013.

O'Brien, Geoffrey. *The Phantom Empire: Movies in the Mind of the 20th Century*. New York: W. W. Norton & Company, 1993. Print.

Olano, Antonio D. "Entrevista a Jesús Franco." *Cine en 7 días* 619 (17 Feb. 1973): 9–12. Print.

Olney, Ian. *Euro Horror: Classic European Horror Cinema in Contemporary American Culture*. Bloomington: Indiana UP, 2013. Print.

———. "Spanish Horror Cinema." *A Companion to the Horror Film*. Ed. Harry M. Benshoff. West Sussex: Wiley-Blackwell, 2014. 365–89. Print.

———. "Unmanning *The Exorcist*: Sex, Gender and Excess in the 1970s Euro-Horror Possession Film." *Quarterly Review of Film and Video* 31.6 (2014): 561–71. Print.

O'Neal, Sean. "Jess Franco Is Not the Devil." *A. V. Club*. 24 Sept. 2009. Web. 21 June 2015.

Palacios, Jesús. "Jess Franco, la otra cara del cine español." *El mundo*. 2 Apr. 2013. Web. 14 Apr. 2013.

Pavlović, Tatjana. *Despotic Bodies and Transgressive Bodies: Spanish Culture from Francisco Franco to Jesús Franco*. Albany: State U of New York P, 2003. Print.

Petit, Alain. *Jess Franco ou les prospérités du bis*. Alignan du Vent: Artus Films, 2015. Print.

Rauger, Jean-François. "Fragments d'une filmographie impossible." *La Cinémathèque Française* (June 2008): n. pag. Web. 18 July 2008.

Rosenbaum, Jonathan. *Discovering Orson Welles*. Berkeley: U of California P, 2007. Print.

Russell, Dominique. "Luis Buñuel." *Senses of Cinema* 35 (Apr. 2005): n. pag. Web. 23 June 2015.

Strub, Whitney. "Francomania Exposed! *Murderous Passions: The Delirious Cinema of Jesús Franco* by Stephen Thrower." *Senses of Cinema* 80 (Sept. 2016): n. pag. Web. 17 Oct. 2016.

Thrower, Stephen. "Jesús 'Jess' Franco (1930–2013)." *Sight & Sound* 23.6 (June 2013): 19. Print.

Thrower, Stephen, with Julian Grainger. *Murderous Passions: The Delirious Cinema of Jesús Franco*. London: Strange Attractor, 2015. Print.

Tohill, Cathal, and Pete Tombs. *Immoral Tales: European Sex and Horror Movies, 1956–1984*. New York: St. Martin's Griffin, 1995. Print.

Weinrichter, Antonio. "Muere Jesús Franco, cineasta irrepetible." *ABC* 3 Apr. 2013: 69. Print.

Weldon, Michael. *The Psychotronic Encyclopedia of Film*. New York: Ballantine, 1983. Print.

Williams, Linda. "Film Bodies: Gender, Genre, and Excess." *Film Quarterly* 44.4 (1991): 2–13. Print.

Wood, Robin. *Howard Hawks*. New ed. Detroit: Wayne State UP, 2006. Print.

I

FRANCO IN CONTEXT

1

BEFORE AND AFTER
THE AWFUL DR. ORLOF

Constructing a "Respectable" Jess Franco
Andy Willis

he films that make up the majority of Jess Franco's enormous directorial output, many of which were made on what can only be described
as microbudgets, and many of which exist in multiple international
versions, are often distinguished by their high level of explicit sexual content, leading them to be dismissed out of hand as cheap pornography. His
work has appeared in a variety of genres that accommodate such overt
material—the women-in-prison film, the lesbian vampire movie—and in
exhibition contexts, such as the grind-house exploitation circuit of the
1970s and 1980s and the VHS boom in the early 1980s, that are known
for their associations with explicit content. The dominant perception of
Franco's work is confirmed by the 2013 on-set documentary *A ritmo
de Jess* (Naxo Fiol), which shows the then eighty-two-year-old director
shooting a series of loosely connected sex scenes with a skeleton crew in
and around a large hotel near Málaga in Southern Spain.[1] The improvisatory nature of the shoot, the ultralow budget, and the seeming lack
of a finalized script all contribute to the legend of Jess Franco as an
unstoppable, quality-averse, and unapologetic purveyor of Euro-sleaze.
One scene even shows the director encouraging his young cameraman to
"zoom in on the actress's pussy." After decades behind the camera, Franco
remained as willing as ever when it came to utilizing one of the trademarks of his visual style, the zoom lens, another trait of his work used to

dismiss him as something of an incompetent technician. It is these aspects of his work that have led to Franco being regarded as a director of poorly executed trash cinema. At the same time, however, others revere these idiosyncrasies, seeing them as factors contributing to his status as a renegade, underground auteur. But such binaries are all too neat. This chapter argues that Jess Franco was not always so easy to pigeonhole, whether as an exploitation auteur or as a filmmaker so mired in sleaze that his reputation cannot escape the stench.

In opposition to the marginalization that both poles might suggest, I want to make a case for an early-career, "respectable" Jess Franco, and in doing so reveal a filmmaker who was associated with a number of figures who would become the backbone of progressive Spanish cinema in the 1960s, and a director whose work was in dialogue with, and would have a profound influence on, developments within Spanish (and European) popular cinema during the 1960s and 1970s. Franco remains one of the most widely known directors associated with Spanish horror cinema, and his first foray into the genre, *Gritos en la noche* (*The Awful Dr. Orlof*, 1962), would predate the wider revival of the genre in Spain by a number of years. The film laid important foundations for other filmmakers to later build upon, establishing a number of tropes that would become staples of the Spanish horror boom of the early to mid-1970s. Following this genre debut, Franco later made numerous horror films—within and outside Spain—that established him as one of Europe's most productive exploitation filmmakers. However, the decade that concerns us reveals a director forging a flourishing career during a period when the division between "respectability" and "sleaze" was far from clear-cut.

Franco on the Margins

For many commentators on the horror genre, Franco remains a rather vexing persona. For example, Jim Morton, writing in the *Incredibly Strange Films* edition of *Re/Search*, states that Franco is "known for his prolific output and deviant sensibility" (152). He goes on to argue that he is "one of the most prolific and controversial directors working in exploitation today," one who "makes his films quickly and seemingly with little regard to production values," and whose films are "usually heavily dosed with sex, though most of his films are in the horror genre" (193–94). The clear frustration many mainstream observers feel when faced with Franco's films is further reflected in the *Aurum Film Encyclopaedia: Horror*, edited by Phil Hardy, where his work is described, in a discussion of *The Awful Dr. Orlof*, as "lazily filmed" (148). It would seem then that there is a widely held assumption that Franco is unquestionably a low-grade filmmaker. Alongside these often ill-informed critical dismissals there are those writers, often emerging from fan cultures, such as *Video Watchdog* editor Tim Lucas, who have argued that the director be reclaimed as significant through the application of auteurist approaches to his work (73–101). For Lucas, the very reasons that others dismiss Franco's films are part of the reason for celebrating them. He puts it thus: "For many years, I was unable to see past the hasty surface of Franco's work and hated it. Today, in a climate of insultingly mild horror product tailored to fit the MPAA straitjacket, I can't get enough of it. Franco's defiantly uncommercial, acutely revealing, taboo-busting stance is like a breath of fresh scare, even when his movies are clumsy, which is (let's be honest) most of the time" (74). Lucas, and Franco's other defenders, such as Stephen Thrower (*Murderous Passions: The Delirious Cinema of Jesús Franco*) and Carlos Aguilar (*Jesús Franco*), passionately engage in extensive, very well informed, debates about the minutiae of the director's output, often championing films others have forgotten or dismissed. Indeed, until recently, it had been left to the world of fan publications and internet websites to identify, study, and explore, as well as simply celebrate, Franco's work.

While Franco has some of his staunchest defenders in fan culture, the director's reputation in mainstream academic writing about Spanish film has been, for the most part, rather more negative—if he is mentioned at all. For some of the most influential writers of the history of Spanish cinema, Jess Franco's filmography is seemingly not worthy of consideration. Important studies that encompass the 1960s—one of Franco's key periods—such as those by Peter Besas, John Hopewell, Núria Triana Toribio, and Sally Faulkner, find no need to discuss the director. Meanwhile, Barry Jordan and Rikki Morgan-Tamosunas, in a book focusing on the period of the 1980s onward, one of Franco's most prolific periods, limit him and his work to a brief mention of *Killer Barbys* (misspelled as "*Killer Barbies*"), which they refer to simply as a "trash movie" (109). Refreshingly, more recently studies focused on Spanish genre cinema have found space to discuss Franco's output seriously. Within this body of work, one might argue that the initial fan-generated reconsiderations of Franco have now fruitfully begun to slowly bleed into academic writing. For example, Joan Hawkins significantly draws on the groundbreaking work of Cathal Tohill and Pete Tombs for her exploration of the work of Franco and Georges Franju (87–113). More recently, Tatjana Pavlović has analyzed the use of the body in Franco's work, relating it to wider social and political transformations within Spain, while Antonio Lázaro-Reboll discusses the director's work systematically throughout his *Spanish Horror Film*.

RETHINKING THE EARLY FRANCO

In *Despotic Bodies and Transgressive Bodies*, Pavlović argues that Franco was a director somewhat out of step with the dominant trends within Spanish cinema of the 1950s and early 1960s. In suggesting the filmmaker was something of an outsider, she states that:

> In Spain of the 1950s, when Jesús Franco started his career, there was, on the one hand, saturation by historical epics, musicals, and melodramas intended to inculcate traditional moral and religious values, sponsored officially by the Francoist government. On the other hand, there was the dissident cinema, grounded in the neorealist tradition, that dealt with social problems that the "official" cinema would never acknowledge. The uniqueness of Jesús Franco is that he did not make either type of film even though his career began in those turbulent years. He was an anomaly not fitting in any of these camps. (108)

While it might be tempting to see Franco as something of a renegade outsider from the outset, if one looks closely at his initial forays into the film industry, this reading of the director as an anomaly, something of an anarchic maverick, becomes questionable. This is particularly so when one looks at the formative years of his career. In this early period, Franco, rather than existing outside the binary opposition that Pavlović sets up within Spanish cinema, can be identified as a figure who straddled it.

I would argue that, focusing on the period immediately before and after Franco directed his most famous early work, *The Awful Dr. Orlof*, it is possible to trace the career of a filmmaker with a perfectly respectable reputation, and one with a string of creative associations with film personnel who would become very much a part of a critically acclaimed, oppositional Spanish cinema of the late 1950s. As with many directors who progressed to feature film directing in Spain during the late 1950s, Franco had attended the national film school, the Instituto de Investigaciones y Experiencias Cinematográficas (IIEC), although, like a number of others before him, he did not graduate. Significantly, this period at film school meant that, as Pavlović notes, Franco had connections "with a group that would produce the film magazine *Objetivo*, whose debates on film culminated in the Salamanca Congress but whose political and aesthetic preoccupations he never shared" (109). While Franco is often dismissed as having always been merely a commercial director, and even then something of a hack, these links begin to suggest a rather different and more nuanced picture. Franco was concerned with and involved in the contemporary debates around film culture within Spain, and as such was an associate of key figures such as Juan Antonio Bardem and Fernando Fernán Gómez. Furthermore, instead of being an outsider, or an anomaly as Pavlović suggests, Franco was an acquaintance of those involved in producing the type of "dissident cinema" she mentions.

One of his acquaintances, the writer and director Juan Antonio Bardem, had, like Franco, failed to complete his degree at the IIEC. But he had gone on to be one of the most high-profile figures involved in setting up the magazine *Objetivo* in 1952. Bardem also contributed heavily to the

Salamanca Conversations that took place over four days at the city's university in May 1955. This event brought together a range of perspectives from both right and left regarding cinema and culture and was to have a significant impact on subsequent developments and government policy regarding film in Spain. As Besas notes:

> Despite the moderate tone of the Conversations, a hue and cry was raised by conservative circles who denounced them as "Communist infiltrations" in Salamanca. The magazine *Objetivo* was banned, but the Conversations had been successful. They had formulated and expressed the concerns and aspirations of a whole new generation of filmmakers, so much so that after the four days were over there was talk of the "spirit of Salamanca." (42)

Whatever one's reading of the events at Salamanca, Jess Franco's connections with those heavily involved suggest someone closer to the key debates within Spanish film culture than both Pavlović and his later reputation might suggest. Indeed, his connection with both Bardem and those around him had already been solidified in 1953 when Franco worked as an assistant on the production of the director's feature *Cómicos*, which was selected for the Cannes Film Festival in 1954. In fact, Franco's work on the film even went so far as a contribution to elements of the score. His close association with the Bardem family during this period would extend to his casting Rafael, Juan Antonio's father, in his first feature, *Tenemos 18 años* (1961). These links clearly suggest that Franco was very much part of the aesthetic and political changes that were beginning to stir within Spanish cinema in the 1950s, something supported by his working relationship with one of its major dissident figures, Bardem. It is difficult, then, to sustain a picture of Jess Franco during this period as isolated from these facets of Spanish film culture.

Franco's initial work as a director also intersected with this period of Spanish film history. His directorial debut, *Tenemos 18 años*, which was produced by Auster Films and credits Bardem's close associate and another key oppositional filmmaker of the period, Luis García Berlanga, as associate producer, was made in 1959. While it begins as a light comedy about two young women who, turning eighteen, embark on a fantasy-inspired road trip around Andalusia, it eventually turns into something much graver and more in line with the veiled critique inscribed in the oppositional films of the period. *Tenemos 18 años* opens with colorful animated credits accompanied by a traditional jazz score by Don Parker and his Jazz Orchestra with piano solos by Franco himself, no less. This sequence suggests a light-hearted, modish, youth-focused film typical of those made across Europe in the late 1950s and early 1960s. This impression is enhanced by Franco's use of direct address to the camera in the opening sequence, where María José (Isana Medel) writes in her a diary and introduces the viewer to Pili (Terele Pávez), her cousin and best friend, and her other cousin Mariano (Antonio Ozores). María José is presented as a romantic dreamer who longs for the kind of love she reads about in romantic novels and who has a tendency to embellish the truth. These early scenes mock youthful types of the period. For example, early on Pili says she likes a young man named Castro whom she compares to Kirk Douglas and whom the film shows as a rather ridiculous, angst-obsessed youngster dressed in a black roll-neck sweater who tells another girl, "If I wasn't so troubled I'd love you." What follows is a series of adventures around Andalusia in a broken-down old car that are related with a romantic tinge by the girls. What marks *Tenemos 18 años* as a film closer to other oppositional works of the period is the attempt to offer an element of social criticism amid its more popular and modish trappings. The key sequence in this regard occurs toward the end of the film and involves María José retelling the story of how the young women found a man who had collapsed outside their tent one morning. When he comes round, they realize he is armed, and when, exhausted and hungry, he falls down again, they prepare to make their escape. Crucially, just as they are about to leave, their humanity comes to the fore and they decide they must help him. When he regains consciousness, he explains that he is a bank robber on the run. On the surface—and as far as genre convention is concerned—he would seem to be the type of character from whom the protagonists need to free themselves. However, the scenes that follow show the man explaining sympathetically why he is as he is due to particular historical and social circumstances. He explains that he grew up during the Spanish Civil War (1936–39), and the trauma of that experience meant he could not easily fit into postwar society. During this period, he says, he got used to guns, violence, and death and had no choice but to turn to crime. His antisocial behavior, therefore, is reframed as his attempt to survive in a post–Civil War context. Affected by his story and the reasons for his actions, the women assist in his escape by taking him to the border. The change in tone toward the end of the film shows Franco attempting to address social issues of the day within the formulaic template of the youth film. The young women believe they have done the right thing by helping the man and feel positive about their actions. As they are about to leave, sounds of border guards shouting "halt" introduce a further change of mood that is confirmed shortly after when gunshots are heard offscreen. It is at this moment in the narrative when reality crashes back into the story being retold by María José and shifts it from being a fantastical tale of freedom and adventure to a harsh story of death and crushed hopes. The oppression of the Spanish state of the time shatters any romanticism they may still harbor. The last shot of the film confirms as much: when María José is asked by her potential boyfriend, who has also acted as the interlocutor of her story, "You have changed now?" she simply replies, "Yes." The attachment to the fantasy world of romantic fiction that shaped her worldview at the beginning of the film is now presented as ideologically conservative and is forever swept away by her experiences on the road in the Spain of General Franco as she scatters on the wind the pages of her diary.

Franco's subsequent work in the early years of the 1960s also reveals a director working much closer to the mainstream of the Spanish film industry than his later reputation might suggest, further challenging Pavlović's picture of him. This is evidenced by the fact that during this part of his career, Franco, in fact, made two period musicals for Hispamer Films and the producer Serge Newman, contributing to the cinematic genres that had saturated Spanish screens, namely historical epics, musicals, and melodramas. Potentially responding to the success of Juan de Orduña's

El último cuplé (1957) in Spain and Richard Pottier's *Tabarín* (1958) in France, these films, as Stephen Thrower has noted, were reasonably well received by the press at the time. For example, *La reina del Tabarín* (1960), which is set in 1913, was praised in the pages of *ABC Madrid* as "proficient, accurate and also expressive. The atmosphere is right and the composition of the images, as well as their rhythm, is felicitous" (qtd. in Thrower: 58). *Vampiresas 1930* (1961) is a self-reflexive musical piece set in the backstage world of entertainment in a rather cosmopolitan Paris, coproduced with CIFESA, the state production company associated with musicals and historical epics throughout the 1940s and the 1950s, another fact that—in terms of funding—further challenges the assumption that Franco was a marginalized outsider figure during this period.

The above factors would indicate, then, that by the time he directed *The Awful Dr. Orlof*, the first of his films to be widely labeled as a horror film, Franco's status within the Spanish film industry was not quite as low as subsequent narratives of Spanish cinema would present it, and his name did not yet have the exclusively negative connotations it would later evoke. A detailed look at *The Awful Dr. Orlof* reveals Franco to be a craftsman of some skill, and, as I argue, the film is certainly a thoughtful and highly accomplished piece of work with moments of great sophistication in terms of its cinematic construction.

THE AWFUL DR. ORLOF

Given the preceding discussion of Franco's status within the Spanish film industry, *The Awful Dr. Orlof* might appear to be a sharp change in direction and one that would thrust him more clearly into the arena of European exploitation cinema. It seems that while Franco and his producers, Serge Newman again and Marius Lesoeur of Eurociné, were awaiting approval from the censors to begin work on another film project, they stumbled upon the inspiration for what would become *The Awful Dr. Orlof*. Interviewed for Andy Starke and Pete Tombs's *Eurotika* documentary, *The Diabolical Mr. Franco* (broadcast on the U.K.'s Channel 4 in 1999),

Franco suggests that one of the economic stimuli for the film came from an awareness that at that time horror produced in other parts of Europe, particularly the United Kingdom and Italy, was becoming a highly marketable commodity. He states that while preparing to work on an eventually unmade project called *Los colgados*, they passed a cinema that was screening Hammer's *Brides of Dracula* (Terence Fisher, 1960) and that, upon his suggestion, he and the producers returned that evening to see the film. In the *Eurotika* documentary, Franco claims that at the time the producers had little experience with this more adult version of the horror genre and that he urged them to attend the screening to "show them the possibilities [offered by the genre]," since for Lesoeur and Newman, "horror films were some shit they saw when they were children, that's all." His proposal proved highly successful. As he recalls, "they saw that film, then coming out they said: beautiful, fantastic, very commercial too. They said: 'Why shouldn't we make a film of this kind? Very good idea. Let's do it. Prepare a synopsis.' . . . I prepared Dr. Orloff." While the resulting film retains the commercial, adult-orientated focus of its Hammer inspiration, even outdoing its model in certain regards, at least in the French version of the film, which includes a number of shots of naked female breasts, it also connects to the formal spirit of innovation that was more widely present within various trends in European cinema of the period. In order to develop this point, I will now offer a close reading of *The Awful Dr. Orlof* that incorporates a consideration of its narrative and stylistic traits with focus on the film's relationship to other European films, in particular Georges Franju's *Les Yeux sans visage* (*Eyes without a Face*, 1960) and cycles of production such as the West German *Krimi*.

The strange, off-kilter world of Dr. Orlof, the lead character of *The Awful Dr. Orlof*, is set up early on in the film by Franco and his collaborators, cinematographer Godofredo Pacheco and musicians José Pagán and Antonio Ramírez Ángel. Together they combine a discordant, jarring jazz score with odd, unsettling camera angles to create an eerie setting and atmosphere. The film opens with a woman arriving home on a dark and dank night, clearly slightly drunk as she staggers toward her door.

When she enters her room, she is attacked and overcome by a mysterious man with a face scarred around the eyes who has been hiding in her wardrobe. As the woman screams, Franco cuts to shots of various neighbors, none of whom come to her assistance, looking out of their windows and doorways. The scarred man, who appears to be blind, carries the woman from the building, guided by the sound of a cane being tapped against a wall in the street. The attacker joins the shadowy figure with the cane, and the pair leave down a rain-soaked street as the scene fades to black. It is, then, the visual style and the aural arrangements that combine to create the disconcerting world of *The Awful Dr. Orlof*, marking it as something more aesthetically striking than simply a copy of its cinematic inspirations, such as Franju's *Eyes without a Face*.

This sequence is followed by one that is more conventionally shot and edited. It introduces two of the film's other main characters, police inspector Edgar Tanner (Conrado San Martín) and ballet dancer Wanda Bronsky (Diana Lorys), who have recently met while the former was on holiday. When the inspector returns to his office, he is given the case of the missing woman, which, along with four others, makes up file 3253. Many of the police procedural elements of the story are shot in a very conventional, even flat, visual style, often using shots that simply frame the actors as they speak, and with minimal editing. These scenes contrast sharply with the stylistic inventiveness of the opening sequence and create a clear sense of difference between the everyday normality of the world inhabited by the police—and, by extension, the wider society—and that of the abductors.

This opposition is maintained in the film's next sequence, when we are properly introduced to the character of Dr. Orlof, who is shown wooing a singer at a nightclub. Here, Franco chooses to emphasize the dark side of Orlof by continually keeping the actor playing the part, Howard Vernon, in the shadows. This is the case even when he is framed in the same shot as the singer; the object of his seduction remains well lit throughout. This contrast is further emphasized when Orlof leans forward, yet remains in shadow. Orlof plies the singer with drink and gives her a distinctive necklace, which will ultimately be the source of his downfall. Like the woman in the film's opening sequence, the singer is shown staggering as if drunk from the nightclub to Orlof's waiting carriage. Now, in the private interior of the vehicle, there is finally a fully lit shot of Orlof's face. The shadowy nature of the character, however, is quickly reinforced when they arrive at their destination and Orlof steps out of the private arena of the carriage into a public space, the street, and pays the driver. Franco now reverts to showing the doctor in shadows and half lights, here with the brim of his hat casting a shadow across his eyes and upper face. Once inside the building, Orlof's victim realizes it is, in fact, empty and she is now alone with her suitor. As she shouts, asking where she is, Franco intercuts shots of the victim's face with another series of off-kilter shots of the Gothic interior of the building—empty hallways, stairs, and rooms. This sequence confirms once more the differences between the blandness of the "normal" world of the police and that inhabited by Orlof by visually emphasizing the environment associated with him as an exotic and mysterious place of darkness, shadows, and strange music; the contrast is made all the more concrete by a score that utilizes an offbeat and discordant organ and cymbals.

Franco's careful construction and manipulation of mise-en-scène is further revealed in the following sequences, particularly those capturing Orlof's arrival at his actual, almost castle-like, home. In these sequences, we see the continued use of distorted camera angles and the constant framing of Howard Vernon's face in shadows, which prevents a clear view of him. When Orlof is finally shown, Franco emphasizes the sinister aspects of the character by using a lighting setup that reveals the craggy details of his face. Here, the casting of Howard Vernon contributes greatly to this sinister character, as his somewhat gaunt visage, combined with Franco's lighting and framing, highlights the otherworldly, unreal, and almost unknowable aspect of Dr. Orlof.

The contrasts between the lighting, set design, and camera angles across the scenes that include Dr. Orlof and his assistant, Morpho, and those that contain Tanner and the other police officers show a clear attempt to create difference through visual style. Taken out of context, the scenes involving the police might be considered rather perfunctorily and unimaginatively put together. However, once they are placed alongside the scenes that include Orlof, a clear system of opposition and contrast begins to appear. Franco is effectively deploying a varied visual style to assist in his creation of meaning on-screen. A detailed examination of the film's mise-en-scène reveals that Franco at this time in his career was far from the sloppy film-maker he would later be caricatured as; instead, it suggests that the director was operating as a consummate craftsman who knew how and when to harness the visual and aural potential of cinema.

In addition to Hammer's *Brides of Dracula*, *The Awful Dr. Orlof* had a number of antecedents within the European cinema of the period. As noted by Joan Hawkins, among others, Franco was heavily influenced by Franju's *Eyes without a Face*. Images and plotlines inspired by that film would appear not only in *The Awful Dr. Orlof* but also in many other films

Dr. Orlof (Howard Vernon) and Morpho (Ricardo Valle) in *The Awful Dr. Orlof*, a film that demonstrates Franco's directorial style and consummate craftsmanship at this early point in his career. (Hispamer Films, Ydex/Eurociné, and Plaza Films International. Courtesy of Jerry Ohlinger's Movie Materials.)

throughout his career. In the particular case of *The Awful Dr. Orlof*, the idea of Dr. Orlof stalking young female victims in order to use their skin to graft onto his disfigured daughter is clearly drawn from Franju's earlier film. Like Franju's film, *The Awful Dr. Orlof* might also be considered to exist in the space between exploitation and art, although, for instance, the scenes that show the surgical skin removal are shot and edited quite differently by Franco, lacking the unflinching gaze of Franju's camera and creating an impact of their own. Kate Ince has noted that *Eyes without a Face* was widely seen as something of an homage to German expressionism in general and Fritz Lang in particular (51). This influence may also be traced onto *The Awful Dr. Orlof*. Franco's film utilizes the same shadowy lighting techniques and characters, such as the driven, demented doctor, that are found in both Franju's work and those that Ince suggests influenced it. Significantly, segments of *Eyes without a Face* are devoted to the rather incompetent police investigation of the missing girls. Ince sees this as evidence that the film was intended as a combination of the horror film and the *polar* or French crime film. Yet another sign of the influence of Franju on Franco is the way in which *The Awful Dr. Orlof* combines horror elements with those drawn from the crime film, although his detective is much more focused on solving the crime than those in *Eyes without a Face*, even if Tanner does conveniently miss the message sent by his girlfriend revealing Dr. Orlof as the perpetrator of the abductions he is investigating.

Tohill and Tombs suggest that the presence of the codes and conventions of the crime film leads to another, less commented upon, influence on *The Awful Dr. Orlof*: the West German *Krimi*, in particular the series of Edgar Wallace adaptations that were being made by the production company Rialto at this time and that had proved very popular across Europe. This also points to the fact that Franco was working much more closely to the established norms within European film production than his detractors, or those who want to present him as an outsider, may wish to admit. As Tim Bergfelder has outlined, versions of Edgar Wallace's crime fiction had been produced in Germany since 1927, and Rialto had acquired the rights to these literary sources in 1959. It then embarked upon what would become a very successful series of adaptations, producing their first two *Krimis*, *Der Frosch mit der Maske* (*Face of the Frog*) and *Der rote Kreis* (*The Crimson Circle*), that same year (148–50).

Indeed, the name of the policeman who is pursuing Dr. Orlof—Edgar Tanner—is perhaps a direct acknowledgment of that influence for those familiar with European crime cinema. Furthermore, Franco's utilization of the type of imagery found in these films, particularly the shadowy look of alleyways and the domestic environments of the master criminals, itself drawn from earlier German expressionist films and from those Hollywood films that incorporated their iconography, further reveal Franco's awareness of popular cinema from across the continent and, indeed, the world. The willingness of Franco to accommodate such a wide range of influences also projects forward to his later works, which would be criticized for being too open to the influence of commercial necessity at the expense of overall narrative coherence. In the case of *The Awful Dr. Orlof*, the incorporation of mild nudity indicates that Franco and his producers were already becoming willing to shoot extra material for non-Spanish audiences. Here, the nude shots would be inserted into the version of the film released in France as *L'Horrible Docteur Orlof*. However, this should not simply be taken as a clear indication that he was already a marginal figure; he was, rather, one responding to changes in European film production and using those changes to create commercial films that also incorporated experimental touches drawn from the developing European art cinema. *The Awful Dr. Orlof*, then, may be seen as a film that straddles the mainstream, in its clear commercial bent, and a more artistically ambitious style of cinema, in its concern with form and meaning; it is a far more accomplished work than Franco's critical reputation might suggest.

QUESTIONS OF "QUALITY": POST-ORLOF PROFESSIONAL ASSOCIATIONS

The attempt to work within commercial styles and cycles and also produce work that was formally engaged and interesting would continue after *The*

Awful Dr. Orlof. It is my argument that even though this film is one of Franco's most emblematic works, it did not represent a descent into mere exploitation. Franco continued to operate as a "respectable" filmmaker, now forging links with creative personnel of some standing not just within Spain but across Europe. These included the likes of Fernando Fernán Gómez, Jean-Claude Carriére, and Orson Welles.

In the immediate post-*Orlof* period, Franco maintained and further developed his working relationship with Fernando Fernán Gómez, a figure who was also closely associated with both Juan Antonio Bardem and his close collaborator and fellow "dissident" filmmaker Luis García Berlanga. An actor and director who would become one of the most respected figures within the Spanish film industry, Fernán Gómez played the lead in Franco's post-*Orlof* 1963 release *Rififí en la ciudad.* A brief consideration of Fernán Gómez's film *El extraño viaje* (*Strange Voyage*, 1964) reveals that these links also extend to their approaches to filmmaking, in particular the way in which Fernán Gómez's film blends a murder story with the trappings of other genres, including the old dark house horror story. As Alberto Mira has noted, "The scriptwriters and Fernán Gómez reworked the basic murder plot into a baroque narrative structure and mise-en-scène, alternating conventions of the thriller, the horror film, the sex comedy and the comedy of manners" (120). Alongside this, like Franco's film, *Strange Voyage* also utilizes a jazz-heavy score that helps create its slightly unhinged atmosphere, and also has a strong sense of its characters' sexual repression. Perhaps most emblematic of all, when it comes to the working relationship of the pair, Fernán Gómez cast Franco in the significant role of Venancio. A decade later, Franco would be immersed in the world of European exploitation cinema, directing the likes of *Vampyros Lesbos* (1971) and *Des Frissons sur la peau* (*Tender and Perverse Emanuelle*, 1979). However, along the way he would also find a number of prestigious and "respectable" collaborators.

Franco's move into more international filmmaking can in part be explained by the pressures and constraints imposed on filmmakers who were trying to make challenging and innovative work within the context of the restrictive Spanish film industry of the 1960s. For Franco, these restrictions would become too limiting and help explain why the director would increasingly seek to continue working on coproductions across Europe. These were films that would allow him to continue exploring his increasing interest in cinematic form, since experimentation was allowed in European exploitation cinema if commercial demands were also met.

During this period, within the wider context of European popular cinema, Franco was once again able to find collaborators that suggest his status within the film world was not what his detractors suggest. Primary among these collaborators was screenwriter Jean-Claude Carriére, who worked with Franco on the scripts for *Miss Muerte* (*The Diabolical Dr. Z*, 1966) and *Cartas boca arriba* (1966) at the same time as he was beginning his partnership with that other Spanish iconoclast, Luis Buñuel, on *Le Journal d'un femme de chamber* (*Diary of a Chambermaid*, 1964), and with Louis Malle, on films such as *Viva Maria!* (1965) and *Le Voleur* (1966). Even Howard Vernon, who so often played Dr. Orlof for Franco and who would go on to become one of Franco's closest collaborators, came with an impressive acting reputation at this time, forged by his appearances in works by the likes of Jean-Pierre Melville and Fritz Lang. If these professional collaborations suggest a more respectable Jess Franco than subsequent writers have acknowledged, there was an even more prestigious collaborator that Franco himself was happy to discuss. That was Orson Welles.

This professional association is another key factor in the construction of Jess Franco as a respectable and "serious" filmmaker during this period. As Tohill and Tombs explain, in 1963 Welles was seeking personnel to work on *Chimes at Midnight* (1966), and one of the key roles that needed filling was that of second-unit director. According to the story, which has been repeated in numerous interviews with Franco, Welles took a fancy to working with the Spanish director after he had seen Franco's *La muerte silba un blues* (1962). Welles's producers, however, were not impressed by his choice and in an attempt to dissuade him screened *Rififí en la ciudad*, thinking it would put him off. In fact, Welles was equally impressed by

The eponymous Dr. Zimmer (Antonio Jiménez Escribano) and an unfortunate victim (Marcelo Arroita) in a visually striking scene missing from many versions of *The Diabolical Dr. Z*, a film scripted by longtime Luis Buñuel collaborator Jean-Claude Carrière. (Hesperia Films, S.A., Speva Films, S.A., and Ciné Alliance. Courtesy of Photofest.)

this work and Franco was hired (Tohill and Tombs 87). This story is often cited as a means of showing that the two directors were both marginal figures who had some sort of symbiotic maverick streak. However, another explanation might also be read from these events, which is that at this stage in his career Jess Franco was seen as a very competent professional whose admittedly low-budget films were well constructed and contained some visually striking sequences. Orson Welles was able to see this, and identifying him as an equally creative and ambitious filmmaker, hired him.

Certainly, a closer look at another horror-tinged film that Franco made just after *The Awful Dr. Orlof* reveals further evidence of the director's impressive use of mise-en-scène. *La mano de un hombre muerto* (*The Sadistic Baron Von Klaus*, 1964) utilizes specific visual motifs in its combination of various codes and conventions drawn from the crime and horror film. In particular, the use of lighting from the outset is significant. The first meeting of the investigators—a detective, a journalist, and a psychologist—in a village inn following the discovery of two bodies is shot in deep focus with all three men clearly visible in the frame and all equally well lit. This shot emphasizes a strong sense of unity in their desire to discover who the killer is. Here, then, through the use of frame composition and lighting as well as the fact that each remains in focus as they discuss the murders, Franco establishes visually their closeness, revealing cinematically that the three men want to work together to achieve their shared goal. The audience's suspicion will soon fall on the character of Ludwig, whom Franco again defines though lighting. Like the brightly lit inn in which the detectives are shown, Ludwig's space is carefully and thoroughly conveyed: we are shown the basement of a family mansion in a semi-lit darkness full of foreboding shadows that prevent the audience getting a clear look at the character. The fact that he is constrained by his family legacy, initially represented by the mansion, is further enhanced by the placing of objects within the foreground of the frame that work to hamper a clear view of the character. Franco creates a visual contrast between the two sets of characters, the detectives and the person under suspicion, rather than using dialogue. A consideration of sequences such as these reveals that during this period Franco was a director who was very capable when it came to creating and utilizing visually striking images on the screen. This, in turn, further suggests a filmmaker who was very far from the poverty-row hack he would later be portrayed as being.

Franco the International Filmmaker

It was within the period that followed *The Awful Dr. Orlof* that Franco became associated with international rather than national cinema production. As Pavlović has argued, one of the most significant things about the career of Jess Franco is the way in which he challenged the idea of national cinema. In fact, many of the films he worked on immediately after *The Awful Dr. Orlof* confirm this in relation to both his career and the critics' perception of him as a filmmaker. According to Pavlović, "Jess Franco's opus . . . while probing questions of gender and problematizing boundaries of genres with which he worked, also disturbs the boundaries of national film production" (119). She goes on to argue that the "international production and circulation of Franco's low-budget, cult, trash, B production, and sexploitation films have transnational implications posing questions about co-productions, market, and movement across national borders" (119). These factors, in turn, meant that Franco could no longer be understood as part of the oppositional cinema that had developed within Spain during the 1960s. Indeed, by the mid-1960s, Franco had become an international filmmaker who more often than not chose to absent himself from shooting in Spain. Tohill and Tombs discuss this shift in terms of the rationale for his use of so many pseudonyms, something with which Franco would famously become associated, but that would also contribute greatly to his dismissal by more seriously minded critics:

> When he began making films outside Spain he was forced to use an assortment of *noms de plume*. Filming in Europe can be a complicated business, with all sorts of red tape. For example, if you direct a French film you get heavily taxed if you are not a French national—Franco got around this by having his French producer register himself as Clifford Brown. This meant that the producer could pick up the royalties for him and, more importantly, Franco was free to direct under the name Clifford Brown. (85)

Franco's distance from the Spanish film industry was also driven during this period by his desire to delve into ever more erotic and sexual subject matter, material that would stand no chance of being passed even by the most liberal censors operating in Spain during the late 1960s and early 1970s. This almost self-imposed exile meant that, while Jess Franco's name is perhaps the first that comes into most people's minds when they think of Spanish horror cinema, his interaction with the country's film industry during the period when directors took up the horror genre was nevertheless both sporadic and limited. This marginalization due to the content of his work, however, does not mean he was simply an exploitation filmmaker. Indeed, others whom Tohill and Tombs celebrate in their work, such as Alain Robbe-Grillet and Walerian Borowczyk, have recently had their outputs during this period reassessed and deemed to be examples of a radical, taboo, category-busting, and artistically challenging cinema.[2]

Like these figures, Franco needs to be rethought, reconsidered, and potentially repositioned within European cinema of the period. He was certainly, as a close look at his work reveals, an ambitious director who was consistently willing to stretch and interrogate the codes and conventions of popular genres. This often resulted in works that reflected on their construction and status as "cinema." In liner notes to the 2000 DVD release of *The Awful Dr. Orlof* by Image Entertainment, Lucas states that Franco later called the films he made during this period "museum pieces," perhaps referring to their kinship with a 1960s European art cinema he felt he had left behind. Indeed, as the decade progressed, the director would increasingly distance himself from what he saw as his more conventionally made work and embrace a more expressionistic, less narratively coherent style of cinema. The modish techniques that swamped the industry as the decade ended and the 1970s began quickly found their way into his visual style. Perhaps the most notorious of these would be his use, or overuse, of the zoom lens, a device that became emblematic of what many saw as his lazy, slipshod style. Ultimately, whatever one may think of Franco's later, more sexually explicit, even pornographic, works, it would be wrong to read history backward to reinvent him as a perpetually sex-obsessed, technically poor filmmaker. His early works and associations certainly show that during the period before and after *The Awful Dr. Orlof* he was far from that—perhaps something that ardent fans who desire to simplistically celebrate his "bad" cinema do not wish to acknowledge. Indeed, one cannot understand Franco's later films without grasping that they are a continuation of experiments he began in the 1960s, when he was a "respectable" director working within both commercial and "dissident" traditions of filmmaking.

Notes

1. Naxo Fiol is a writer and filmmaker who since the early 1990s has been associated with the Spanish fanzine culture that was at the forefront of rediscovering and celebrating Franco and his works. *A ritmo de Jess* was made by the production companies Pellicules et essai and Subfilms and has been released by Cameo on DVD in Spain.
2. Recent rereleases of Borowczyk's work, such as the Arrow Films 2014 collection *Camera Obscura: The Walerian Borowczyk Collection*, have been accompanied by detailed booklets reassessing it—in this case by Daniel Bird and Michael Brooke. A similar collection, *Alain Robbe-Grillet: Six Films 1963–1974*, was released by the BFI in 2014 and contained audio commentaries by *Video Watchdog's* Tim Lucas as well as an extended essay by David Taylor.

Works Cited

Aguilar, Carlos. *Jesús Franco*. Madrid: Cátedra, 2011. Print.

Bergfelder, Tim. *International Adventures: German Popular Cinema and European Co-Productions in the 1960s*. Oxford: Berghahn, 2005. Print.

Besas, Peter. *Behind the Spanish Lens: Spanish Cinema under Fascism and Democracy*. Denver: Arden, 1985. Print.

Faulkner, Sally. *A Cinema of Contradictions: Spanish Cinema in the 1960s*. Edinburgh: Edinburgh UP, 2006. Print.

Hardy, Phil, ed. *The Aurum Film Encyclopedia: Horror*. Vol. 3. London: Aurum, 1985. Print.

Hawkins, Joan. *Cutting Edge: Art-Horror and the Horrific Avant-Garde*. Minneapolis: U of Minnesota P, 2000. Print.

Hopewell, John. *Out of the Past: Spanish Cinema after Franco*. London: British Film Institute, 1986. Print.

Ince, Kate. *Franju*. Manchester: Manchester UP, 2005. Print.

Jordan, Barry, and Rikki Morgan-Tamosunas. *Contemporary Spanish Cinema*. Manchester: Manchester UP, 1998. Print.

Lázaro-Reboll, Antonio. *Spanish Horror Film*. Edinburgh: Edinburgh UP, 2012. Print.

Lucas, Tim. *The Video Watchdog Book*. Cincinnati: Video Watchdog, 1992. Print.

Mira, Alberto. "El extraño viaje." *The Cinema of Spain and Portugal*. Ed. Alberto Mira. London: Wallflower, 2005. 119–27. Print.

Morton, Jim. *Re/Search #10: Incredibly Strange Films*. Ed. V. Vale and Andrea Juno. San Francisco: Re/Search Publications, 1986. Print.

Pavlović, Tatjana. *Despotic Bodies and Transgressive Bodies: Spanish Culture from Francisco Franco to Jesús Franco*. Albany: State U of New York P, 2003. Print.

Starke, Andy, and Pete Tombs. *Eurotika! The Diabolical Mr. Franco*. Boum Productions, 1999. Film.

Thrower, Stephen, with Julian Grainger. *Murderous Passions: The Delirious Cinema of Jesús Franco*. London: Strange Attractor, 2015. Print.

Tohill, Cathal, and Pete Tombs. *Immoral Tales: Sex and Horror Cinema in Europe, 1956–1984*. London: Titan Books, 1994. Print.

Triana Toribio, Núria. *Spanish National Cinema*. London: Routledge, 2003. Print.

2

SLEAZE AND CINEPHILIA

Jess Franco in the Sixties

Ian Olney

> Although I no longer see fifty films a month, I am still a cinephile. I get many
> cinephiliac pleasures not only from some of the recognised masters but also from
> watching the films of Terence Fisher, Koji Wakamatsu, Jose Mojica Marins,
> 1950s and 60s German Edgar Wallace and Mabuse films or even downright
> sleaze movies like those of Jesus Franco. I am enough of a cinephile still to won-
> der about cinephilia.
>
> —Paul Willemen

This essay takes as its starting point the above lines, which form a
curious coda to the final chapter of Willemen's 1994 book *Looks and
Frictions: Essays in Cultural Studies and Film Theory*. Briefly, the chapter, an interview with Noel King titled "Through a Glass Darkly: Cinephilia Reconsidered," advocates for a critical approach to film rooted in
the desire for cinema. For Willemen, this desire, cinephilia, expresses itself
in the "serialisation of moments of revelation" (233). The cinephile cher-
ishes and collects fragments of film—isolated scenes, gestures, looks—that
are "subjective, fleeting, [and] variable, depending on a set of desires and
the subjective constitution that is involved in a specific encounter with a
specific film" (236). The cinephiliac moment, importantly, is not "strictly
programmable in terms of aesthetic strategies" (237). In other words, it
is not simply the filmmaker's creation. Rather, it is coproduced by the
cinephile as a highly personal, revelatory experience. As Willemen puts
it, "what is being seen is in excess of what is being shown" (237). Also
important is the fact that the cinephiliac moment demands expression.

It "spark[s] something which then produces the energy and the desire to write, to find formulations to convey something about the intensity of that spark" (235). While cinephilia has incited passionate discourse on the pleasures of cinema, however—especially in France, where it fueled disquisitions on *photogénie* in the 1920s and *la politique des auteurs* in the 1950s and 1960s—it has not generally inspired film theory and criticism. In Willemen's view, this is partly because, as a mode of engagement with film "premised on notions of revelation, on the notion of excess," cinephilia "escape[s] rationalised, critical-theoretical discourse" (237–38, 233). The challenge for such discourse lies in determining: "How is that moment of revelation talked about?" (236). Although Willemen offers no definitive answer to this question, his thoughtful reconsideration of cinephilia has become a touchstone in contemporary cinephilia studies, guiding the work of scholars like Christian Keathley and Rashna Wadia Richards, who have proposed various approaches to analyzing film through the lens of cinephilia.

I call the closing lines of Willemen's piece curious because in suggesting that cinephiliac pleasure might be found in "B," trash, or exploitation cinema, they run counter to the rest of the chapter, which associates such pleasure almost exclusively with classical Hollywood films made at the end of the studio era. For Willemen—and, one might add, for many of the cinephilia scholars who have followed in his footsteps—the "privileged object of cinephilia" is "Hollywood cinema between the Korean war and the Bay of Pigs" (234). The reason is twofold. The production of these films coincided with the "heyday of cinephilia," which ran "roughly from the early 1950s to the late 1960s" (227). Moreover, cinephilia "operate[s] particularly strongly in relation to a form of cinema that is perceived as being highly coded, highly commercial, formalised and ritualised. For it is only there that the moment of revelation or excess, a dimension other than what is being programmed, becomes noticeable" (238). No surprise, then, that Willemen's chapter focuses on cinephiliac moments from late classical Hollywood films: Marlon Brando playing with Eva Marie Saint's glove in *On the Waterfront* (1954), Ava Gardner walking barefoot in *The*

Barefoot Contessa (1954), the cascade of diamonds in the opening credits from *Imitation of Life* (1959) (234–35, 245). What is surprising is that it ends with a paean to the cinephiliac pleasures of "downright sleaze movies" (256) like those of Jess Franco. This raises all sorts of intriguing questions, among them: Exactly what sort of cinephiliac pleasures do such movies offer? Are they the same pleasures afforded by more conventional objects of cinephilia? Are they coproduced by cinephiles in the same way? Do they provoke the same kind of writing? In short, what is the relationship between sleaze and cinephilia?

Tantalizingly, Willemen's chapter hints at answers to these questions. Its fleeting references to Roger Corman (245), Riccardo Freda (236), and Raffaello Matarazzo (236) suggest that while there may be general agreement about the sort of moments privileged as cinephiliac, "people might not agree on the films within which they occur" (235–36). In fact, citing surrealist cinephile Ado Kyrou, who celebrated the sublimity of "bad" movies, Willemen goes so far as to state at one point that the cinephiliac moment is "unstable": one cannot predict which moment the cinephile will find revelatory or what type of film will contain it (236). It may even be the case, he concedes, that "B," trash, and exploitation films offer greater opportunity for cinephiliac pleasure than the late classical Hollywood movies widely venerated by cinephiles:

> A lot of pleasure can be derived from minor programme fillers made by nonentity Hollywood directors, the *Hollywood Confidential* sort of thing. Some early Roger Corman films are badly scripted, atrociously acted, not well shot. And partly because of that lack of polish and the cavalier attitude toward shooting, some of these revelatory dimensions come along more than they do in highly rehearsed films that had twenty different takes in order to get [it] right. (242)

The fascinating implication here is not only that sleaze might be a source of cinephilia but also that there might be a special kinship between the two. Regrettably, Willemen does not pursue this idea further. It remains little more than a provocative footnote to his discussion of cinephiliac pleasure. And it has received scarcely more attention in the field he helped to establish; over two decades later, cinephilia studies remains focused on a relatively narrow canon of "traditional" cinephiliac texts—from classical Hollywood movies to European art films—neglecting those at the cultural and cinematic margins.

The pleasures of cinematic sleaze have, of course, been explored elsewhere in film criticism and theory, perhaps most notably by Jeffrey Sconce. In a landmark essay on the cult appeal of "paracinema"—his catchall term for "'badfilm,' splatterpunk, 'mondo' films, sword and sandal epics, Elvis flicks, government hygiene films, Japanese monster movies, beach-party musicals, and just about every manifestation of exploitation cinema from juvenile delinquency documentaries to soft-core pornography"—Sconce argues that such movies offer fans the opportunity to practice a "politics of excess" (372, 391). Employing an ironic reading strategy that "renders the bad into the sublime, the deviant into the defamiliarized," the aficionados of paracinema "cultivat[e] a counter-cinema from the dregs of exploitation films" in order to "explicitly situate themselves in opposition to Hollywood cinema and the mainstream US culture it represents" (Sconce 386, 381). The notion that pleasure derived from "B," trash, and exploitation cinema is primarily "renegade, [and] neo-camp" (373) in nature has proven highly influential—especially in the realm of cult film studies, where it has been taken up and elaborated on by Joan Hawkins, Matt Hills, and others. Such pleasure is, however, very different from the cinephiliac passion for sleaze hinted at by Willemen. Indeed, it is in many respects the inverse of cinephilia. Willemen gestures toward a pleasure in sleaze that is personal, not political; sincere, not ironic; and revelatory, not calculated—in other words, a cinephilia very like that lavished on such Hollywood classics as *On the Waterfront* and *Imitation of Life*. Instead of turning elsewhere for answers to the questions about sleaze and cinephilia posed by Willemen's chapter, therefore, I want to try to pick up where it leaves off, to follow the train of thought it suggests. In doing so, I ultimately hope to demonstrate that although the connection it makes between sleaze and cinephilia might at first seem curious, each, in fact, has something important to teach us about the other.

This is nowhere more apparent than in a consideration of the cinema of Jess Franco, whose "downright sleaze movies" Willemen enthusiastically invokes at the end of his meditation on cinephilia. There is a special kind of cinephiliac pleasure to be found in Franco's films—particularly those he made in the 1960s, cinephilia's golden age. To begin with, they are clearly themselves the work of a committed cinephile. The passionate love for movies pervasive in European cinema and culture during the sixties—the formative period in Franco's career—profoundly shaped his filmmaking. Surveying Franco's diverse cinematic output from the time, one finds him in conversation not only with the classical Hollywood movies worshipped by cinephiles, but also with other cinephiliac films emerging from Europe, like those of the French New Wave. Furthermore, his work engages the cinephiliac gaze in a unique way. Cheap, ragged, and often just bad, it compels the cinephile to watch with a selective eye, editing out the uninspired in favor of the revelatory—a mode of cinephiliac spectatorship reflected in the writing it has stimulated. In the pages that follow, I explore the unique pleasures Franco's sixties cinema holds for the cinephile, concluding with a close reading of *Necronomicon* (*Succubus*, 1968), which I see as the epitome of his cinephiliac style of filmmaking during this period and a supreme example of the kinship between sleaze and cinephilia.

Looking at Franco's movies through the lens of cinephilia, one immediately notices two things. First, there is a powerfully cinephiliac dimension to the films themselves. They reflect a passionate commitment to cinema on Franco's part. The sheer number of them is telling: between his debut as a filmmaker in 1959 and his death in 2013, he directed some two hundred movies in Spain and across Europe. At the peak of his productivity, he turned out as many as half a dozen a year. Also telling is the diversity of his work: although he is best known for his horror films, he operated in just about every genre imaginable, including comedy, science fiction, film noir, action-adventure, and pornography. In accounts and interviews, his collaborators invariably describe how his "mad love for film" manifested as an "unstoppable urge to keep shooting" (Tohill and Tombs 126, 124). The actor Howard Vernon, who appeared in dozens of the director's movies, has written that "Franco without a film in progress is absolutely unthinkable! As I used to watch him working, with his camera on his shoulder . . . I would get the impression that here was a very strange being indeed, a creature with two heads and three eyes, the inseparable union of the mind and the art of cinema" (11). Karl-Heinz Mannchen, a producer on a number of Franco's early films, puts it more simply: "Jess Franco *is* cinema" (qtd. in Tohill and Tombs: 90).

Franco's work not only demonstrates his love of cinema as a filmmaker, it also reflects his cinephilia as a filmgoer. Cathal Tohill and Pete Tombs note that his movies are "shot through with . . . affectionate nudges or jokey references—what Franco call[ed] 'a little wink at the audience'" (84). Sometimes these allusions are to literature, painting, poetry, or music, but more often than not they are to cinema. His pictures pay elaborate homage to a wide range of movies, weaving what Laura Mulvey, in a reading of Jean-Luc Godard's *Le Mépris* (*Contempt*, 1963), calls a "fabric of quotations" (235–36). And as with Godard, whom Franco frequently cited as his "favorite director ever" (Mendíbil), the "unifying thread that ties these oblique references together is the world of *cinéphilia*" (Mulvey 225). The cinematic allusions in Franco's work are to movies that shaped him as a cinephile and as a director. As Tim Lucas writes, "Franco had grown up adoring the movies. . . . His appetite for cinema was . . . voracious. He loved Fritz Lang, F. W. Murnau, Carl Dreyer, Robert Siodmak, John Brahm, and Orson Welles . . . but he also loved Universal horrors, MGM musicals, Republic serials, and Jean-Luc Godard" ("Jess Franco's Declaration" 29). Consequently, his films are "like a glorious junk shop, spilling over with references to all he has absorbed" ("Jess Franco's Declaration" 29). Through these references, he is telling his own story, but he is also telling a story about the cinema, employing quotation as a way of "mediating between [film's] past and present" (Mulvey 225). For the cinephile, part of the pleasure of watching Franco's movies lies in identifying in them the signs of the filmmaker's own passionate engagement with cinema.

Although the cinephiliac dimension of Franco's filmmaking is apparent across his oeuvre, it is most obvious in his movies from the 1960s. The passionate love for cinema that defined the decade clearly informs his work as a director at this early stage in his career. In fact, the initial arc of his career uncannily mirrors that of other European cinephiles who began making films in the sixties, especially those associated with the French New Wave. Like Godard, François Truffaut, Éric Rohmer, and Jacques Rivette, who famously worked as critics for *Cahiers du Cinéma* before directing their first films, Franco wrote for the Spanish magazine *Film Ideal*, "champion[ing] directors like Robert Siodmak, Joseph Lewis, Phil Karlson, John Brahm, Raoul Walsh, John Ford, and Douglas Sirk" prior to picking up a camera (Tohill and Tombs 91). He also attended the prestigious Institut des Hautes Études Cinématographiques in Paris and frequented screenings at the Cinémathèque Française—so often, reportedly, that Henri Langlois admitted him for free (Tohill and Tombs 80). He learned the craft of filmmaking at the feet of Hollywood legends on location in Spain, serving as an (unconfirmed) assistant to King Vidor on *Solomon and Sheba* (1959) and Nicholas Ray on *55 Days at Peking* (1963), as well as a (confirmed) second-unit cameraman for Orson Welles on *Chimes at Midnight* (1966). He also benefited from the tutelage of such Spanish New Wave luminaries as Juan Antonio Bardem and Luis García Berlanga. When he began directing films, his first projects, like those of Godard and Alain Resnais, were short documentaries. He graduated to narrative features in 1959, the same year as Truffaut and Resnais, and then, like the leading lights of the French New Wave, embarked in the sixties on a series of movies that pay homage to classical Hollywood genres—the musical, science fiction, horror, film noir—while at the same time thoroughly deconstructing them, essentially "inventing a new form of genre cinema, informed by European art cinema of the period" (Lucas, "Jess Franco's Declaration" 18).

These films were, to quote Lucas, "as post-modernist as any titles then coming out of the French New Wave" ("Jess Franco's Declaration" 17). That is, they demonstrate the same textual playfulness, reflexivity, and—above all—referentiality. They are full of allusions, both narrative and formal, to classical Hollywood cinema and European art cinema of the postwar era. Franco's first horror film, *Gritos en la noche* (*The Awful Dr. Orlof*, 1962), draws heavily on the aesthetic of classical Hollywood horror, particularly in its gothic sets, chiaroscuro lighting, and oblique camera angles. Lucas identifies the John Brahm thrillers *The Lodger* (1944) and *Hangover Square* (1945) as especially important influences ("Jess Franco's Declaration" 32). *Vampiresas 1930* (1961), a musical comedy concerning the transition from silent to sound cinema, is obviously inspired by *Singin' in the Rain* (1952). And the noir thriller *Rififí en la ciudad* (1964), whose title recalls Jules Dassin's celebrated heist film *Du rififi chez les hommes* (*Rififi*, 1955), is replete with references to the work of Orson Welles, including an aquarium scene straight out of *The Lady from Shanghai* (1947) (Lucas, "Jess Franco's Declaration" 40). Other allusions are to contemporaneous European art movies. In addition to its literary source, Edgar Wallace's 1924 crime novel *The Dark Eyes of London*, *The Awful Dr. Orlof*'s tale of a mad scientist driven to restore his daughter's ruined beauty through illicit face transplants owes much to Georges Franju's *Les Yeux sans visage* (*Eyes without a Face*, 1960). The opening lines of *Miss Muerte* (*The Diabolical Dr. Z*, 1966)— "It's Bresson. . . . A convicted criminal has escaped!"—are a tongue-in-cheek nod to Robert Bresson's *Un Condamné à mort s'est échappé ou Le vent souffle ou il veut* (*A Man Escaped*, 1956) (Tohill and Tombs 92). Meanwhile, the opening sequence of *El secreto del doctor Orloff* (*Dr. Orloff's Monster*, 1965), a flashback composed entirely of still images, pays homage to Chris Marker's experimental science-fiction short, *La Jetée* (1962). Even Franco's casting in the sixties was influenced by art films of the period: he borrowed Eddie Constantine, the star of Godard's *Alphaville* (1965), for the lead in *Residencia para espias* (1968); Françoise Brion, the enigmatic "L" in Alain Robbe-Grillet's *L'Immortelle* (1963), for a part in *Cartas boca arriba* (1966); and Howard Vernon, the repentant Nazi officer in Jean-Pierre Melville's *Le Silence de la mer* (1949), for a dozen roles over the course of the decade, beginning with the titular villain in *The Awful Dr. Orlof*.

The second thing one notices in looking at Franco's films through the lens of cinephilia is that they invite a special kind of cinephiliac gaze.

Christian Keathley writes that there are "certain stylistic approaches that [have] facilitated or . . . [been] related to the appearance of cinephiliac moments" (112). One is the highly codified filmmaking of classical Hollywood cinema, the regimentation of which throws the rare revelatory moment into sharp relief. Another is what Keathley calls "sketched" film: film "composed automatically, instantaneously, out of a desire to register the image as near as possible to the moment of its existence" (74). As "unfinished" cinema open to the unplanned and the accidental, sketched film—Keathley points to the movies of Jean Renoir and Roberto Rossellini as examples—fosters cinephilia by deliberately leaving room for cinephiliac moments. In some respects, Franco's cinema resembles sketched film. He approached filmmaking spontaneously. Like his cinematic idol, Godard, he often worked with the barest outline of a script, arriving on set in the morning with new pages written the night before (Tohill and Tombs 95). He also frequently improvised with the camera, using it to "pick out details or move in quickly to capture interesting, accidental happenings, unplanned images, and events that could add atmosphere to the finished film" (Tohill and Tombs 123).

Generally speaking, however, Franco's movies are more "sketchy" than "sketched." They are famously uneven, ricocheting "from feverish intensity to half-baked ordinariness and back again" (Tohill and Tombs 107). In the average Franco film, as Tohill and Tombs put it, "Some sequences are great, others look thrown together, and seem jarringly dull compared to the good stuff" (107). This unevenness is partly a product of the circumstances under which Franco worked: as an exploitation filmmaker, he shot his movies very quickly, on shoestring budgets, for less-than-scrupulous producers. Consequently, they often feel shoddy and slapdash, like other exploitation movies. And like other exploitation movies, they privilege moments of affect and excess, treating the scenes in between with a decided lack of interest and care. The result is a cinema that tends toward the imbalanced, with long, plodding stretches of plot development occasionally interrupted by explosive jolts of eye-catching spectacle. In Franco's case, this tendency is exacerbated by "a problem focussing attention on things that don't stimulate him" (Tohill and Tombs 107). Depending on his level of interest, some scenes in his films "are shot with quirky precision and painstaking attention to detail, while others are cobbled together cheaply" (101), making for cinema that is, Tohill and Tombs write, "as restless as he is, constantly on the prowl for that inspired moment, that elusive instant when the old rules are shattered and something compelling and unexpected hits the screen" (108). The sketchiness of Franco's cinema is obviously different than the sketched quality of a Renoir or Rossellini film, but I want to suggest that as a stylistic approach, it, too, fosters cinephilia. It does so not only through its openness to the unplanned and accidental—a byproduct of the fast and loose, fly-by-night nature of exploitation filmmaking, as well as Franco's personal predilection for spontaneity and improvisation—but also through its radical inconsistency, which calls attention to the revelatory amid the insipid, inviting a unique cinephiliac gaze.

This gaze is not identical to the one associated with sketched film. Keathley tells us that sketched film prompts a "panoramic" gaze that "sweep[s] the screen visually in order to register the image in its totality, especially the marginal details and contingencies that are the most common source of cinephiliac moments" (8). The panoramic gaze finds expression in standard cinephiliac discourse as the detailed recounting of a film's "contingent, aleatory, ephemeral element[s]," usually in tandem with "an articulation of the director's recurring theme or an attempt at a description of his style" (127, 82). Franco's sketchy cinema invites a different kind of cinephiliac gaze and inspires a different sort of cinephiliac dialogue. Its unevenness means that "the inevitable reaction [to it] alternates elation with irritation. Elation at sampling something unique and unheralded. Irritation at the slipshod and the mundane" (Tohill and Tombs 101). Deriving cinephiliac pleasure from it requires a discriminating gaze that overlooks the "slipshod and the mundane" in favor of the "unique and unheralded." In other words, Franco's movies demand a cinephile with a selective eye—one that does not so much sweep the screen as forage the film for revelatory moments, separating the gold from the dross. This gaze is reflected in the cinephiliac discourse surrounding Franco's films, which celebrates such salvaged moments and submits them as proof that the director should be considered a bona fide auteur despite his low cultural status as an exploitation filmmaker and the frequently mediocre quality of his work. Like standard accounts of cinephilia, then, it has a dual focus: "the moment as evidence of authorship, and the moment as revelatory encounter for the spectator" (Keathley 85). Unlike those accounts, however, which find meaning and pleasure in "scan[ning] panoramically beyond what has been ordered and organized for viewing and locat[ing] instead the unorganized" (Keathley 127), it revels in rehabilitation, rescuing trash from the dustbin of culture and finding cinephilia in sleaze.

Once again, although the special cinephiliac gaze motivated by Franco's films functions across his entire oeuvre, it operates particularly strongly in connection with his work in the 1960s. That work has sometimes been described as being fairly consistent, even conventional, compared to his later filmmaking. Lucas goes so far as to call it "classical" (15–16) in his introduction to the 1993 book *Obsession: The Films of Jess Franco*. Actually, Franco's sixties films are every bit as inconsistent as his later movies—a fact Lucas acknowledges in a recent reconsideration of the director's early cinema, writing that it "was more traditionally produced but is . . . anything but traditional or classical in content" ("Jess Franco's Declaration" 17). Indeed, one could argue that they are more uneven, given that their gestures at conformity to the standards of mainstream filmmaking (gestures that are largely absent in his later movies) only serve to highlight the places where they fall decisively short of cinematic norms.

This is the impression, at any rate, that one gets from the criticism they have engendered, which repeatedly draws attention to their sketchiness. For instance, Joan Hawkins notes of *The Awful Dr. Orlof* that, "The sheer amount of time spent on police business in the film, as well as the lengthy development of [Detective] Tanner's relationship with his fiancée, tends to give *Orlof* a curious rhythm. Horror sequences bottom out in farce or melodrama, so that the affect level of terror or shock (or even suspense) is hard to maintain" (99). Geoffrey O'Brien characterizes *Paroxismus* (*Venus in Furs*, 1969) as a paradoxical "vortex of artistic sleaze defined by inexplicable narrative ellipses, distended zooms, soft focus dissolves, slow motion pursuits, red and purple filters, a score by Manfred Mann, and overheated voice-overs by James Darren" (182). Similarly, Phil Hardy, writing in the volume of *The Aurum Film Encyclopedia* devoted to horror, calls *The Diabolical Dr. Z* a "picture poised between nightmare and crude sensationalism," its "beautifully stylized imagery" and "coldly disturbing sensuality" compromised by the "mechanical stringing together of exploitative scenes" (171); of *Dr. Orloff's Monster* he says: "Combining clichés and ponderous dialogue with flamboyant bits of gothic *mise-en-scène* and a decided tendency to slip in to sexploitation . . . Franco here concocts a mixture characteristic of his work until the late sixties" (166). Hardy's assessment of *Dr. Orloff's Monster* neatly captures the critical consensus around Franco's cinematic output in the 1960s: again and again, unevenness is cited as a defining characteristic. As Danny Shipka puts it, this period in the director's career offers a distinctively "weird hodgepodge of classy stylings mixed with exploitation that leaves the viewer feeling slightly disoriented" (188).

It may also leave the viewer feeling more than a twinge of cinephilia: the extraordinary unevenness of these films acts as an especially powerful catalyst for the cinephiliac gaze generally associated with Franco's work. This becomes clear in surveying the writing they have inspired, particularly online. On blogs like *I'm in a Jess Franco State of Mind* and forums like *Latarnia: Fantastique International*, the dialogue surrounding Franco's sixties cinema insistently privileges moments over movies. Instead of celebrating the director's films, which they readily acknowledge are deeply flawed, Francophiles (as Franco's fans often refer to themselves) single out specific scenes for commemoration, promoting the part above the whole. Even their "Top Ten" lists tend to be compilations of their favorite moments rather than their favorite movies—as is the case in a series of posts on *I'm in a Jess Franco State of Mind* that share readers' picks for Franco's best scenes, including the moment in *The Awful Dr. Orlof* when "Howard Vernon plac[es] the necklace around Maria Silva's neck, [and] the light from the jewels illuminat[es] his face for the first time" (qtd. in: Monell, "Favorite Franco Scenes/Moments: Tim Lucas"), and "the long scene of Eugenie's sexual initiation, ending with the blind guitarist playing near the sea" (qtd. in: Monell, "Favorite Franco Scenes/Moments: Francesco Cesari") from *Eugenie . . . the Story of Her Journey into Perversion* (1970).

In such privileged moments, the discourse devoted to Franco's sixties cinema locates opportunities for revelation and signs of authorship that serve to redeem the films containing them. Responding to a thread on Franco's spy movie spoof *Lucky el intrépido* (1967) in the "Franco Lounge" at the *Latarnia Forums*, for example, one forum member rhapsodizes that the "scene where Lucky and pal chase Beba Loncar across the rooftops in Rome to the accompaniment of [Bruno] Nicolai's 'Spy Chase' theme is 2 and a half minutes of pure eurocult bliss!" (Poveratti), while another sees the film's "funny, silly, witty" moments as proof of Franco's "filmmaking genius" despite the fact that the movie is never "credible in the least" (Barnett). Likewise, a review of *Dr. Orloff's Monster* on *Castilian Crimson*, a branch of *Latarnia: Fantastique International* dedicated to Spanish horror cinema, argues that although the film is no masterpiece, it "spark[s] more fascination and yearning that any polished and perfect product," especially in its final moments:

> The climatic ending, a must-see for anyone serious about international horror, is a graceful tour de force of direction and cinematography at the service of a perfectly delineated idea, and can be watched again and again with no diminution in impact or feeling. This exhilarating sequence of fate and existential ache proves that when Franco has a good script and tries, he is a director of the first order. (Lipinski)

The cinephilia on display here is typical of the dialogue inspired by Franco's sixties films, online and elsewhere. While registering the imperfections of these films, it finds in them redemptive moments of meaning and pleasure. Indeed, because of the wildly uneven character of the movies Franco made in the 1960s, it is exceptionally alive to such moments. Carefully winnowing them from the surrounding chaff and enshrining them in writing, it gives definitive expression to the special cinephiliac gaze invited by the director's work.

The highly cinephiliac nature of Franco's sixties cinema is perhaps most evident in his 1968 film *Succubus*. Originally titled *Necronomicon*, an allusion to the apocryphal book of the occult cited in the fiction of H. P. Lovecraft—which Franco claimed to have actually read and used as inspiration for the film ("From *Necronomicon*")—*Succubus* focuses on Lorna Green (Janine Reynaud), the star of a Grand Guignol–style show featuring acts of sadomasochistic violence and simulated murder at a nightclub in Lisbon. She is happily in love with her American producer, Bill (Jack Taylor), but plagued by dreams that suggest she has led past lives as a supernatural succubus, seducing and killing unwary victims—perhaps at the bidding of the devilish Pierce (Michel Lemoine), who shadows her every move and may be controlling her actions as well. It becomes increasingly difficult for her to distinguish between past and present, fantasy and reality, as people she dreams she has murdered turn up dead in her waking life. Unsettled by her erratic behavior, Bill runs off to Berlin to produce another show; when Lorna follows him there, he arranges with Pierce to have her killed. In the final scene, however, she returns—apparently from beyond the grave—to exact revenge, first seducing Bill and then almost ceremonially plunging a dagger deep into the back of his neck.

Succubus was a pivotal film in Franco's early career. It was the first movie he shot without Spanish financing, meaning that he enjoyed a creative freedom in its production that he had never experienced with his earlier projects, all of which were funded at least in part by companies in Spain and therefore subject to strict censorship under the country's Fascist regime (Shipka 186). Working with producers in West Germany, he was able for the first time "to make a film the way [he] wanted to make it" ("From *Necronomicon*"). This shows in the movie itself, which is not only more explicit than his films to that point in its depiction of violence, nudity, sex, and drug use but also more experimental in both narrative and form. Moreover, thanks to an infusion of cash from millionaire investor Pier A. Caminneci, *Succubus* had the highest budget of any film Franco had yet made (Tohill and Tombs 95), as its relatively lavish production values—including a score by jazz composer Jerry van Rooyen and costumes by fashion designer Karl Lagerfeld—attest. Finally, the movie enjoyed greater commercial success than any Franco film had to date, including in the United States, where it rode a late-sixties "wave of sexually explicit international films [that] allowed American audiences to experience a sex-and-violence scenario without feeling 'dirty'" (Shipka 187). It even garnered high praise in some corners. No less an eminence than director Fritz Lang is supposed to have extolled the film after a screening at the Seventeenth Berlin Film Market, saying that it was the first erotic movie he had watched all the way through because it was "a beautiful piece of cinema" (Hardy 191).

Its special place in Franco's sixties filmography notwithstanding, however, *Succubus* is very much of a piece with the other movies the director made over the decade. In the first place, it is a prime example of the kind of cinematic sleaze in which Franco specialized at the time. Catering to viewers who "trawled art-houses in the 1960s . . . looking for a sex kick they could pass off as 'thoughtful' or 'challenging' or 'radical' rather than simply 'hot' or 'kinky'" (Thrower 129), it offers "all the hallmarks of a dangerous, decadent European film: S&M nightclub scenes, beautiful women who kiss and kill for lust, spooky dream sequences, strange word games that end in death, mad hedonistic parties, lesbianism and mannequin terror" (Tohill and Tombs 94). As Tohill and Tombs comment, it left audiences wondering: "Was it art or was it pornography?" (94). More importantly, *Succubus* is the epitome of Franco's cinephiliac style of filmmaking in the sixties. It is clearly the work of a committed cinephile, shot through with allusions to classical Hollywood movies and European art films alike—a tapestry of quotation representing a meditation on cinema's past and present. Its extraordinary unevenness also invites a special cinephiliac gaze, one alive to moments of brilliance amid the banal that can serve as occasions for revelation and evidence of authorship. Intriguingly, the film can even be read as a sort of allegory of sixties cinephilia, a metaphor for the way in which movie lovers of the time obsessively pursued their ghostly object of desire.

To begin with, *Succubus* offers perhaps the ultimate example of the cinephiliac referentiality running through Franco's sixties cinema. It is brimming with allusions and homages to the kinds of movies beloved by cinephiles in the 1960s. Some of these references are to classical Hollywood cinema. Hitchcock is mentioned by name, for example, and as Stephen Thrower observes, the narrative conceit of a mysterious femme fatale haunted by her past lives is borrowed directly from *Vertigo* (1958)—Lorna even recalls visiting San Francisco at one point (125). Franco also alludes to the history of classical Hollywood horror, prominently displaying in one scene a row of Aurora monster models (the Creature from the Black Lagoon, Dracula, Frankenstein, the Phantom of the Opera), next to which he positions his movie's monster, Pierce.

But most of Franco's cinephiliac references in *Succubus* are to contemporaneous European art films, many of them directed by fellow cinephiles. Characters earnestly debate the relative merits of movies by Godard, Lang, and Luis Buñuel. The decadent jet-set party that Bill and Lorna attend, where the guests drop acid and crawl toward Lorna on all fours, barking like dogs, recalls the debauched revels at the end of Fellini's *La dolce vita* (1960), which culminate with Marcello Mastroianni riding a drunken blonde like a horse. As I have noted elsewhere, the scenes of Pierce driving Lorna around in a black Cadillac pay homage to Heurtebise's chauffeuring of the deathly Princess in a Rolls Royce in Cocteau's *Orphée* (*Orpheus*, 1950) (*Euro Horror* 162). Lorna's denials when confronted with strange men claiming a past association with her echo those of Delphine Seyrig in Resnais's *L'Année dernière à Marienbad* (*Last Year at Marienbad*, 1961). And most crucially, the dark tale of romantic obsession told in *Succubus*—a beautiful, mysterious woman who may in fact be dead, an exotic seaside setting, a sadomasochistic love affair fraught with repetition and compulsion—owes much to Robbe-Grillet's *L'Immortelle*.

Cataloging his cinematic passions and influences, this network of references tells Franco's personal story as a cinephile and a filmmaker, but like the fabric of quotation Godard weaves in *Contempt*, it also tells a story about the cinema. It represents a meditation on the medium's past and present, offering "an elegiac commentary on the decline of one kind of cinema while celebrating [the emergence of] another" (Mulvey 227).

A story of erotic obsession with ghostly overtones set in an exotic, seaside locale, *Succubus* is a cinephiliac valentine to such contemporaneous European art films as Robbe-Grillet's *L'Immortelle*. (Aquila Films Enterprises and Trans American Films. Courtesy of Jerry Ohlinger's Movie Materials.)

Through homage and allusion in *Succubus*, Franco declares his solidarity with the Buñuels, the Langs, and the Godards—directors whose movies have something "new" to offer, as one of his characters puts it—and furthers their work, demonstrating a cinephiliac faith in the future of film.

Succubus also acts as an especially powerful catalyst for the cinephiliac gaze prompted by Franco's sixties cinema. More so than most of the movies he made during the decade, it exchanges consistency and coherence for a "misty abstraction, a dreamlike acid haze" (Tohill and Tombs 95). Indeed, Shipka writes in an overheated but not inaccurate review that while "evocatively filmed," the movie is "horrendously, perhaps consciously, slow and feels like what I think a bad trip would feel like" (221). And yet many Francophiles rank the film as one of the director's most compelling, pointing to his "willingness to sacrifice [narrative] progression for an obsessive dwelling on the moment" as precisely the source of its power (Thrower 44). As Stephen Thrower puts it, *Succubus* can be "coy and irritating," but it is also a "beautiful and imaginative work which demonstrates its creator's erotic daring, his sophistication and his sardonic sense of humour" (129). For fans, these qualities inhere in the film's intermittent flashes of brilliance, illustrative both of cinema's epiphanic potential and of Franco's filmmaking genius.

Such moments are almost invariably the focus of writing on *Succubus*, which seizes on them in spite of the movie's failings to reframe it as a cinephiliac object. Thrower himself picks out a scene in which Franco films Lorna and Bill making love through an aquarium. Describing the "subtle flicker of light on water, the flitting of fish as they dart to and fro with vague lovemaking figures glimpsed in the background, the tendrils of music curling like elegant seaweed, the deep rich colours lubricating the eye," he argues that its surface "texture and sensuality" capture the "marvel of the moment" and reflect Franco's "skilled manipulation of mood and his careful sculpting of our awareness of time and place" (129). Another commentator, also noting that the film is "unusually elegant and even poetic in spots," similarly contends: "Smaller visuals, such as the way bare trees shade a conversation about the emptiness of love, are . . . prevalent and reveal Franco's capacity for subtlety" (Gallman). A third reviewer takes pleasure in scenes featuring Lorna at Lisbon's white-walled Torre de Belém, where "the strong primary colors, the gorgeous flat planes of sky and sea with the ancient castle in the background" represent evidence of "wonderful, just masterful filmmaking" (Standridge). The commonly held view among Francophiles that *Succubus* is one of the director's masterpieces, then, is actually not in spite of but because of its lack of coherence and consistency. Wildly uneven, even compared to the other movies Franco made in the 1960s, it invites a cinephiliac gaze by bringing attention to the moments where it transcends its own limitations. Casting these moments as occasions for revelation and evidence of authorship, writing inspired by the film does not seek simply to salvage it, but to exalt it within Franco's oeuvre—and the annals of cinematic sleaze—as a cinephile's dream.

Finally, *Succubus* can actually be read as an allegory of the cinephilia that defined the sixties. Scholars working in the field of cinephilia studies have frequently noted that film, because of its uniquely indexical relationship with reality, has an ambiguous, even eerie, ontological status. Images on a movie screen are simultaneously present and past, here and absent, alive and dead. To quote Keathley, "in the film frame, objects are both themselves and something new, living and not living, real and magical" (71). Consequently, cinephilia, the passion for this uncanny medium, is itself uncanny. In fact, Willemen suggests that "cinephiliac" is a good description of the cinephile's relationship with film "because of its overtones of necrophilia, of relating to something that is dead, past, but alive in memory" (227).

It is this notion that Franco seems to explore in *Succubus*—largely through the character of Lorna Green, who can be read as the embodiment of cinema as a deathly but desirable medium. She is, first of all, repeatedly presented as an object of the gaze. From her opening performance onstage in front of a rapt nightclub audience to her private striptease for Bill in his apartment to her autoerotic play with her own reflection in a mirror at the ancient castle where she resides, she is defined by her to-be-looked-at-ness—not just as a woman, displayed for the male gaze, but as a cinematic object. Like the cinema, Lorna confuses the usual distinctions made between past and present, dream and reality, life and death. Judging from her running voice-over, she has apparently led many lives, in various parts of the world and at different times; moreover, the border separating these lives seems porous, allowing her to slip easily between past and present. She also slides effortlessly between dream and reality, often making it difficult to tell which is which. There are scenes in which her dream life seems to bleed into her waking life, as with her murder of the mysterious Admiral Kapp (Howard Vernon). Lastly, she transcends the boundary between life and death, reappearing in Bill's Berlin flat moments after he has had her killed.

Lorna Green (Janine Reynaud) as a cinephiliac object of desire in *Succubus*. (Aquila Films Enterprises and Trans American Films. Courtesy of Photofest.)

And like the cinema, Lorna is framed as an object of universal desire, pursued by virtually everyone in the movie, male and female, yet possessed by no one. Bill's obsession with her, figured as a kind of *amour fou*, persists after he leaves her to go to Berlin; he is completely in her thrall. The same is true of the other characters orbiting around her: her psychiatrist, Ralf Drawes (Adrian Hoven); Bill's playboy friend, Hermann (Pier Caminneci); even Pierce, who considers himself her "creator" (and also serves as her "director"). Lorna emerges in *Succubus* as "an oneiric creature condensing desire and death into a single figure" (Hardy 191). Like film itself, she is "something that is dead but alive, past but present" (Keathley 38)—an "enigma and elusive object of desire" (Mulvey 236). It is possible that Franco's conception of Lorna was inspired by an icon of sixties horror cinema: Barbara Steele. As I discuss in a recent article, Steele emerged as a cinephiliac figure fusing death and desire in a series of gothic horror movies filmed over the course of the decade ("Haunted Fascination" 12–24). In any case, through Lorna's character, Franco is able to capture the passion for cinema that reached a fever pitch in the 1960s, a time when cinephiles haunted the movies and were, in turn, haunted by them.

Franco's sixties cinema, then, has something important to teach us about sleaze and cinephilia—that, as curious as it might seem, the two share a deep affinity. Each illuminates key facets of the other. To be sure, the cinephiliac gaze activated by the sketchy films Franco made in the 1960s differs from the one mobilized by classical Hollywood movies and European art cinema. It finds pleasure and meaning not in an appreciation of the unplanned and accidental in filmmaking, primarily, but in the recovery and rehabilitation of cinematic trash. For Francophiles, cinephiliac spectatorship is a salvage operation. Sifting through the director's imperfect work and seizing on the parts worth celebrating, they effectively reclaim it from the dustbin of culture.

This difference aside, however, their passionate attachment to Franco's "downright sleaze movies" is very similar to traditional cinephilia. Both involve the fetishization of cinematic fragments in highly personal, revelatory encounters with film. And both involve the expression of these privileged moments in writing that frames them not only as occasions for revelation but also as evidence of directorial authorship. In fact, Francophilia is arguably cinephilia at its purest. Antoine de Baecque and Thierry Frémaux make clear that cinephilia's "definitive essence" is to root through the "culture of the discarded" in an attempt to "find intellectual coherence where none is evident, to eulogize the non-standard and the minor" (137). As James Morrison puts it: "Anyone can spot a masterpiece . . . but only a cinephile could uncover the glories, all the more wondrous for being hidden, of minor, even failed work that might be refashioned, if only by force of will, into greatness of another kind, perhaps even a better kind because of the heady exertions its conversion demand[s]" (12). Committed to the recuperation of movies dismissed even by fellow aficionados of paracinema, Franco's fans are perhaps the quintessential cinephiles, eschewing the "easy" amusements of mainstream cinephilia for the more esoteric pleasures of sleaze.

The cinephiliac pleasures of Franco's sixties cinema are in some ways highly specific. They are not always to be found in the director's later work, much less in the "B," trash, or exploitation movies of other filmmakers. If we return to the closing lines of Willemen's landmark meditation on movie love, however, we are reminded that "downright sleaze movies like those of Jesus Franco" are just one possible source of cinephilia at the cultural and cinematic margins. Others await reclamation. And that process of reclamation is already underway, begun by what Thomas Elsaesser calls the "fan cult" branch of contemporary cinephilia, where the love of movies takes "very different and often enough very unconventional forms, embracing the new technologies, such as DVDs and the internet, finding communities and shared experiences" (36). This new cinephilia is "turning the unlimited archive of our media memory, including the unloved bits and pieces, the long forgotten films or programs into potentially desirable and much valued" texts, "confer[ring] a new nobility on what once might have been mere junk" (Elsaesser 41). Employing the same gaze that has rehabilitated Franco's work as an object of cinephilia, cult cinephiles are sifting through a century's worth of cinematic sleaze, now digitized and streaming online, in search of other "unloved bits and pieces" to celebrate.

What cinephiliac pleasures will the films of Terence Fisher yield? Those of Koji Wakamatsu? And those of José Mojica Marins? Obviously, such questions are beyond the scope of this essay, but, like Willemen, I am enough of a cinephile still to wonder about cinephilia.

WORKS CITED

Barnett, Rod. "Lucky, the Inscrutable (1967)." *The Latarnia Forums* ("The Franco Lounge"). 28 Nov. 2010. Web. 12 Sept. 2015.

De Baecque, Antoine, and Thierry Frémaux. "La Cinéphilie ou L'Invention d'une Culture." Trans. Timothy Barnard. *Vingtième Siècle* 46 (Apr.–June 1995): 133–42. Print.

Elsaesser, Thomas. "Cinephilia or the Uses of Disenchantment." *Cinephilia: Movies, Love and Memory.* Ed. Marijke de Valck and Malte Hagener. Amsterdam: Amsterdam UP, 2005. 27–43. Print.

"From *Necronomicon* to *Succubus*—Interview with Director Jess Franco" (supplementary material by David Gregory). *Succubus.* Blue Underground, 2006. DVD.

Gallman, Brett. Rev. of *Succubus* (1968). *Oh, the Horror!* 16 Nov. 2012. Web. 28 Sept. 2015.

Hardy, Phil, ed. *The Aurum Film Encyclopedia: Horror.* Vol. 3. London: Aurum, 1985. Print.

Hawkins, Joan. *Cutting Edge: Art-Horror and the Horrific Avant-Garde.* Minneapolis: U of Minnesota P, 2000. Print.

Hills, Matt. "Para-Paracinema: The *Friday the 13th* Film Series as Other to Trash and Legitimate Fan Cultures." *Sleaze Artists: Cinema at the Margins of Taste, Style, and Politics.* Ed. Jeffrey Sconce. Durham, NC: Duke UP, 2007. 219–39. Print.

Keathley, Christian. *Cinephilia and History, or The Wind in the Trees.* Bloomington: Indiana UP, 2006. Print.

Kyrou, Ado. *Le surréalisme au cinéma.* Paris: Le Terrain Vague, 1963. Print.

Lipinski, Mirek. Rev. of *El secreto del Dr. Orloff* (1964). *Castilian Crimson.* Web. 31 Aug. 2015.

Lucas, Tim. Introduction. *Obsession: The Films of Jess Franco.* Ed. Lucas Balbo and Peter Blumenstock. Berlin: Graf Haufen and Frank Trebbin, 1993. 13–30. Print.

———. "Jess Franco's Declaration of Principles: How to Read the Early Films, 1959–67." *Video Watchdog* 157 (2010): 16–49. Print.

Mendíbil, Álex. "Franconomicon interviews uncle Jess (English version)." *El Franconomicon/I'm in a Jess Franco State of Mind.* 30 Oct. 2009. Web. 21 June 2015.

Monell, Robert. "Favorite Franco Scenes/Moments: Francesco Cesari." *I'm in a Jess Franco State of Mind*. 12 Dec. 2006. Web. 31 Aug. 2015.

———. "Favorite Franco Scenes/Moments: Tim Lucas." *I'm in a Jess Franco State of Mind*. 10 Dec. 2006. Web. 31 Aug. 2015.

Morrison, James. "After the Revolution: On the Fate of Cinephilia." *Cinephilia in the Age of Digital Reproduction: Film, Pleasure and Digital Culture*. Vol. 2. Ed. Scott Balcerzak and Jason Sperb. London: Wallflower, 2012. 11–27. Print.

Mulvey, Laura. "*Le Mépris* (Jean-Luc Godard 1963) and Its Story of Cinema: A 'Fabric of Quotations.'" *Critical Quarterly* 53 (2011): 225–37. Print.

O'Brien, Geoffrey. *The Phantom Empire: Movies in the Mind of the 20th Century*. New York: W. W. Norton & Company, 1993. Print.

Olney, Ian. *Euro Horror: Classic European Horror Cinema in Contemporary American Culture*. Bloomington: Indiana UP, 2013. Print.

———. "Haunted Fascination: Horror, Cinephilia, and Barbara Steele." *Film Studies* 15 (Autumn 2016): 7–29. Print.

Poveratti, Johnny. "Lucky, the Inscrutable (1967)." *The Latarnia Forums* ("The Franco Lounge"). 14 Dec. 2010. Web. 12 Sept. 2015.

Richards, Rashna Wadia. *Cinematic Flashes: Cinephilia and Classical Hollywood*. Bloomington: Indiana UP, 2012. Print.

Sconce, Jeffrey. "'Trashing' the Academy: Taste, Excess, and an Emerging Politics of Cinematic Style." *Screen* 36.4 (Winter 1995): 371–93. Print

Shipka, Danny. *Perverse Titillation: The Exploitation Cinema of Italy, Spain and France, 1960–1980*. Jefferson, NC: McFarland, 2011. Print.

Standridge, Scott (The Vicar of VHS). "*Succubus* (1968): or, I Have Always Lived at the Castle." *Mad Mad Mad Mad Movies*. 4 Aug. 2009. Web. 28 Sept. 2015.

Thrower, Stephen, with Julian Grainger. *Murderous Passions: The Delirious Cinema of Jesús Franco*. London: Strange Attractor, 2015. Print.

Tohill, Cathal, and Pete Tombs. *Immoral Tales: European Sex and Horror Movies, 1956–1984*. New York: St. Martin's Griffin, 1995. Print.

Vernon, Howard. Foreword. *Obsession: The Films of Jess Franco*. Ed. Lucas Balbo and Peter Blumenstock. Berlin: Graf Haufen and Frank Trebbin, 1993. 11. Print.

Willemen, Paul. *Looks and Frictions: Essays in Cultural Studies and Film Theory*. Bloomington: Indiana UP, 1994. Print.

3

"HALLO, HIER SPRICHT JESS FRANCO"

How Franco Recoded the Krimi

Nicholas G. Schlegel

inema radical Jess Franco's lengthy and prodigious career as a film-maker experienced predictable cycles of creative highs and disappointing lows; this is an inevitability when any endeavor is pursued year after year and decade upon decade. Unequivocally, the late 1960s and early 1970s marked one of Franco's artistic, financial, and critical high points. Among Franco's obsessions, his admiration for Sax Rohmer's legendary Fu Manchu and Rialto Studio's *Kriminalfilms* (many based on the works of British crime writer Edgar Wallace) is conspicuous during this period, manifesting itself in numerous Franco productions.

Yet Jess Franco's two *Kriminalfilms* (hereafter "*Krimis*"), *Der Teufel Kam aus Akasawa* (*The Devil Came from Akasava*, 1971) and *Der Todesrächer von Soho* (1972), both West German-Spanish coproductions, have received little to no critical attention or appraisal. Rialto, a Danish studio traditionally thought of as the more proper home for Wallace's *Krimi* series, produced a well-defined film cycle informed by West German perceptions of Wallace's work and fictitious representations of England. The midcentury era of the Edgar Wallace *Krimi* began in 1959 with the back-to-back releases of *Der Frosch mit der Maske* (*Face of the Frog*) and *Der rote Kreis* (*The Crimson Circle*). As Sascha Gerhards notes,

Although both films were made in Denmark, they targeted the German film market and were enormous box-office successes. The production was subsequently relocated to Germany, and the German Rialto was founded as a subdivision of Constantin-Film, which then exclusively distributed the Edgar Wallace films. What followed in the next fifteen years was Germany's longest feature-film series, with thirty-two films produced by Rialto. (134)

Franco's *Krimi*s, however, arrived at the end of the German Wallace phenomenon in the early 1970s and were made by Rialto's competitor, Artur Brauner's industrious CCC (Central Cinema Company). Franco's long-standing marginalization as a filmmaker (even in his native Spain) is also an important factor in explaining the relative obscurity of these two films. Even among Francophiles and *Krimi* devotees, these two titles are not well known or often name-checked as favorites.[1] *The Devil Came from Akasava* has achieved some degree of notoriety simply because of its stunning and tragic star, Soledad Miranda, and *Der Todesrächer von Soho*—which lacks a North American release, further helping to explain its rarity and relative obscurity—is an eccentric, fun, and almost farcical approach to the sub-genre that appropriately showcases Franco's stylistic eccentricities and his noted sense of humor.

This chapter is principally guided by the following questions: How do Franco's films contribute to, detract from, or simply amend the Wallace *Krimi*s? How do they overlap with other *Krimi*s as well as differ in tone and aesthetic? And, more broadly, why are they important to both *Krimi* and Franco studies? Herein, I argue that with these two films, one of cinema's most daring provocateurs added his distinctive touch to an established cycle of filmmaking and stamped it as his own. As Tim Lucas notes, "In many ways, Franco's sprawling filmography exists outside the realm of film proper. It is film *improper*. It holds up a perverse mirror to the world of movie-making, commenting on its myriad genres, deconstructing and mocking its most popular characters and conventions" ("Jess Franco's Declaration" 20). Lucas's notion of "film improper" perfectly captures the relationship between *The Devil Came from Akasava* and *Der Todesrächer von Soho* and the larger *Krimi* cycle. Indeed, the best way to classify them is as Jess Franco films first, *Krimi*s second, products of the Edgar Wallace and Bryan Edgar Wallace cycle third, international coproductions fourth, and so on. *The Devil Came from Akasava* and *Der Todesrächer von Soho* bear the unmistakable hallmarks of their era, genre, and cycle; demonstrate the immutable forces of market, economy, and production; and point to the ideologies that bind all of these variables together. But they are also *Jess Franco* films. The best path forward in contextualizing and discussing these films is with these important factors in mind.

Edgar Wallace and the German Kriminalfilm

Around the same time that film noir gradually disappeared from the American cinematic landscape, England's Hammer Films, which incidentally released several "British noirs" in the early 1950s, was responding to the same societal stimuli that fueled its fading American counterpart. Hammer, however, chose a different genre altogether (horror) through which to channel collective trauma, postwar anxieties, and repressed sexual desires. Indeed, in 1958, Hammer claimed new territory and boldly drove a fresh stake in the ground with the watershed releases of *The Curse of Frankenstein* (1957) and *Dracula* (*Horror of Dracula*, 1958). What is far less known, in both scholarly and mainstream circles, is that a contemporaneous and strikingly parallel film movement was under way in West Germany.

The origin of the *Krimi* is literary, not filmic. *Der Krimi*, "the crime novel" in the German-speaking world, is used as shorthand to describe all varieties of crime literature from the psychological thriller to the police procedural (Hall 3).[2] And while German-language *Krimis* do exist, it was the collective works of the prolific English crime and mystery author Edgar Wallace that initially captured the imagination of German audiences, giving rise to one of the most successful literary series in German history. But its success needs to be seen in the context of Germanic arts and culture in the early twentieth century, and in relation to German cinema in particular. Early German cinema demonstrates a preoccupation with, and a predilection toward, darkness and madness:

Histories of the horror film often pinpoint the cinema of this period as an inventory of tropes and styles from which horror films have been drawing in all their national and thematic variations. This is the heritage of German cinema from the silent film era—films associated with the glory days of the Ufa and the Decla, with the stylistic influence of Expressionism, and with a thematic preoccupation with the darker aspects of the human psyche. (Hantke ix–x)

Indeed, for a brief period Germany hosted and nourished Europe's cinematic womb of dark and disturbing things. Germany was the home of the insane carnival hypnotist Caligari and his somnambulist assassin Cesare in Robert Wiene's *Das Cabinet des Dr. Caligari* (*The Cabinet of Dr. Caligari*, 1920); of vampire Graf Orlok in F. W. Murnau's *Nosferatu* (1922); of Jack the Ripper and the unfortunate Lulu in G. W. Pabst's *Die Büchse der Pandora* (*Pandora's Box*, 1929); of the brilliant Rotwang and his *Maschinenmensch* Maria in Fritz Lang's *Metropolis* (1927); and of the criminal mastermind Dr. Mabuse in Lang's *Dr. Mabuse, der Spieler* (*Dr. Mabuse: The Gambler*, 1922) and *Das Testament des Dr. Mabuse* (*The Testament of Dr. Mabuse*, 1933). Lang's Mabuse movies, along with his brilliant serial killer film *M* (1931), are especially important to note. They, more than any other examples of early German cinema, laid the groundwork for the *Krimi* wave of the 1950s and 1960s.[3]

By the late 1940s, the appetite of German audiences for the dark fantasies of the prewar era had waned. Weimar expressionism had no place in post–World War II occupied Germany. The trauma and guilt with which the nation wrestled in the immediate postwar era was reflected in the seriousness and realism of the so-called rubble films (*Trümmerfilms*). The *Trümmerfilm* was "made under trying conditions, subject to Allied censorship, and executed with a minimum of resources. These films collectively dealt with the ever-present effects of the war and its aftermath in the ruins of Germany's major cities, especially Berlin" (Rasch 2). It was only a decade later, at the end of the 1950s, that viewers were ready for the sheer escapism and titillation offered by a genre whose roots stretched back to the prewar era. The *Krimi*, with its potent mixture of crime, mystery, and thrills, was embraced by German audiences, who were especially keen on films based on the works of British crime novelist Edgar Wallace.

Although little has been written in scholarly or mainstream fora about *Krimis* in general and Edgar Wallace adaptations in particular, pioneering work on the genre was done in the late 1980s and early 1990s, most notably by film historian and *Video Watchdog* editor Tim Lucas and film scholar David Sanjek. Of Wallace's prodigious output, Lucas notes:

> Born in 1875, he [Wallace] didn't discover his true calling until his thirties, when he decided to write fiction suitable to his times. "I am going to give [my readers] crime and blood and three murders to the chapter," he decided, adding, "such is the insanity of the age that I do not doubt for one moment the success of my venture." Within a period of 25 years (1905–1930) Wallace wrote 175 novels, 17 plays, and hundreds of short stories on the subject of bloody murder. (Lucas, "Dial 'W'" 138)

Likewise, in his insightful essay, "Foreign Detection: The West German *Krimi* and the Italian *Giallo*," Sanjek provides valuable historic context for situating the *Krimi* within a larger, intercontinental framework of generic composition and expectations. He writes: "The West German crime narratives draw their name from the line of paperbacks known as *Taschenkrimi*, the paperback form of the *Kriminalroman*, that the society read in prodigious numbers, and of which quite a few were written by British crime specialists Edgar Wallace and his son, Bryan Edgar" (84). Of the cinematic adaptations, Sanjek continues, "The resulting films are, in effect, self-conscious acts of bricolage. Each ransacks established visual and narrative codes and interpolates elements from them, giving each work a distinct intertextual dimension" (84).

While intertextual tropes are unquestionably present in the *Krimi* canon, it is also true that a distinctly German expressionist bloodline flows through the aesthetics of the Wallace *Krimis*:

These works deliberately reanimated visual and narrative tropes of the German Expressionist heyday. . . . That eerie mood [of nightmare and terror] furthermore illustrates the degree to which the *Krimis* carried over from German Expressionism, particularly from the works of the silent period, the practice of *Stimmung* or mood. In the hands of such prominent *Krimi* directors as Alfred Vohrer or Harald Reinl (the best practitioners of the genre), standardized generic tropes help to conjure up a bleak and uncertain universe. (Sanjek 86, 87)

While this pioneering work on the *Krimi* is certainly helpful in situating the genre, the question remains: what exactly is a *Kriminalfilm*? In short, *Krimis* are a species of crime film under the larger genus of thrillers. They are marked by their intense criminal elements but are also given the atmospheric flourishes of the gothic thriller. Common and often standard archetypes populate these stories—for example, the dashing hero, a heroine in distress, a dryly humorous Scotland Yard inspector, a sidekick who serves as comic relief, and a mysterious super criminal (Hanke 114). It is worth noting that this basic story template, with its ready-made situations and characters, resembles that of a number of genres found in other national cinemas—for example, the Mexican *luchador* films featuring masked wrestlers like Santo, the Blue Demon, and Mil Máscaras in pulpy stories with elements of mystery, horror, and science fiction—which perhaps accounts for the lasting popularity of *Krimis* not only in Germany but elsewhere in the world as well.

Given its long-standing popularity, it is unfortunate that the *Krimi* has been so neglected, especially in Anglophone academic scholarship. As Hanke notes, *Krimis* "are insufficiently known and appreciated, even by fans of the stronger *gialli*, and, as a result, have never really gained a foothold in the history of the development of the horror film" (123). Happily, in recent years, scholars have begun to give the *Krimi* the attention it deserves. One of the first to address the academic neglect of the Wallace cycle was Tim Bergfelder, who staged a historiographic intervention with his *International Adventures: German Popular Cinema and European Co-Productions in the 1960s*. Bergfelder provides first-rate economic and industrial analyses of the Wallace *Krimi* cycle, but ultimately characterizes their thematic and aesthetic elements as a "form of progressive nostalgia" that transcends—in fact, deliberately avoids—questions of German national identity. As he puts it: "For German audiences in the 1960s, I would suggest the Wallace series articulated a very particular fantasy about England and London, a fantasy grounded both in established generic expectations (which in some cases reach back to . . . as early as the 1910s), and in the interrelationship with other forms of cultural consumption" (166). In other words, the Wallace *Krimis* were, more or less, stateless comforts (not bound to any particular dominant or residual ideologies) that allowed audiences to safely obsess over the past but simultaneously look forward to postwar peace and prosperity. Bergfelder asserts that this, perhaps more than any other factor, explains the "phenomenal success of these cultural forms" (167). On the other hand, Sascha Gerhards sees the Wallace *Krimi* cycle as germane to German national character and interests, just not manifestly so. In his essay "Ironizing Identity: The German Crime Genre and the Edgar Wallace Production Trend of the 1960s," he suggests that while "Bergfelder's argument concerning escapism through another (imagined) culture is very persuasive, it does not . . . take what scholars have termed the generic life cycle of the Wallace cycle into adequate account" (134). Gerhards ultimately asserts that throughout the 1960s, German identity was articulated in the Wallace films through a pervasive sense of irony and self-reflexivity.

My intent here is not to moderate, intervene in, or attempt to settle this discussion. Indeed, I am in agreement with both scholars' larger claims. In my judgment, although they take a different position regarding the *Krimi*—Bergfelder emphasizes its overt transnationalism, while Gerhards stresses its latent nationalism—both are amply supported by the genre. I believe the best way to contextualize the broader *Krimi* cycle is through a broad-based cultural studies approach that considers these and other points of intervention. In this manner, one can cover the range of cultural, political, social, and industrial factors that shaped this era and genre of filmmaking. The factor that most interests me here is one that Bergfelder describes as the challenge *Krimi* producers faced in "find[ing] narrative formulae that were accepted by different national audiences as being part of an 'indigenous' cultural framework" (127). Rialto's Edgar Wallace cycle proved "that a foreign cultural source could be successfully adapted into a recognisably 'German' film series" (127). But how far could such "foreignness" be stretched? I would argue that a consideration of Jess Franco's *Krimis* helps us answer this question.

It is odd that neither Bergfelder nor Gerhards addresses Jess Franco's back-to-back CCC *Krimi* productions, *The Devil Came from Akasava* and *Der Todesrächer von Soho*, particularly given that Franco was quite talented at directing "stateless" coproductions that had appealed to diverse audiences since 1962, when his first horror film, the internationally successful *Gritos en la noche* (*The Awful Dr. Orlof*), was released. Franco ventured away from Spain during its politically inhospitable 1960s, positioning himself as an ideal director for the series. During this period, he forged transnational connections in the film industry and developed the much-vaunted "Franco charm," which he often employed to solicit financing, actors, locations, equipment, and so on.[4] When Franco did return to Spain to mount productions that were now "officially sanctioned" by the Francoist government, he was saddled with the same obstacles that Rialto and later CCC faced—namely, the production of cinematic content that was currently *en vogue*, with export potential, but that offered no explicit (or implicit) ideological critique of nation or of state apparatuses. Franco's omission from the scholarly discussion around the *Krimi* is thus notable. His inclusion would certainly support Bergfelder's and Gerhards's broader assertions concerning how national character can be expressed or, conversely, attenuated through cultural artifacts like film.

Then again, Franco may have given *Krimi* producers themselves pause in the early 1970s. Although a filmmaker of Franco's caliber seems like a natural fit with the cycle, anyone familiar with his directorial ethos and his catalog of obsessions might have hesitated to hand him the reins of a lucrative and popular cinema franchise. Would he remain faithful to, and preserve continuity with, the *Krimi* canon? The question was not academic but rather a matter of commercial imperative. From 1959 to 1972, over forty West German films were adapted from the works of Edgar Wallace and his son, Bryan Edgar Wallace, the majority of which were "either produced by Rialto Film, a production company run by Horst Wendlandt and Preben Philipsen, or by the Central Cinema Comp. (CCC) headed by the better known Artur Brauner" (Sanjek 84). The genre was a cash cow. Fortunately for Franco, he and Brauner enjoyed a positive working relationship that dated back to the director's successful spy spoof *Lucky el intrépido* (1967). As a result, Franco signed a contract to shoot *The Devil Came from Akasava* over a three-week period beginning in June of 1970.

What is abundantly clear from the start of each of Franco's *Krimis* is that there is no real interest (beyond commercial interest) in preserving continuity with Rialto's mostly monopolistic franchise. In the 1960s and 1970s, the Rialto and CCC Wallace adaptations employed an increasingly fixed collection of conventions that were consistently utilized (and modernized as cultural shifts dictated) throughout the series. These defining features included police-procedural plots, supernatural red herrings, class conflict, revenge, eerie moods, castles, moors, sets clumsily evoking London, and expressionist mise-en-scène and lighting. The late shift to color photography with *Der Bucklige von Soho* (*Hunchback of Soho*, 1966) transformed the genre by stripping it of its most defining characteristic, chiaroscuro lighting, and substituting in its place an eye-popping vividness reminiscent of Britain's Hammer films. But Franco's *Krimis* took it even further afield by prioritizing the director's own favored cinematic tropes, among them sexy cabaret acts, robots, incessant zoom shots, unconventional casting, and confusing plot elements. *Krimi* iconography is given secondary consideration. The sun-drenched, non-U.K. tropical environments of *The Devil Came from Akasava* alone signify a shift in tone and strikingly depart from the established *Krimi* orthodoxy. The following discussion highlights some of the ways in which Franco embraced, rejected, and transformed the Wallace *Krimi*.

THE DEVIL CAME FROM AKASAVA

The tropical locale of Akasava is established during the opening credit sequence of *The Devil Came from Akasava*. An assortment of typically abrupt Jess Franco zooms and pans capturing fishing boats, pelicans, docks, palm trees, and verdant tropical flora lure us into a subterraneous cavern, where a man in a (perilously flimsy) radioactive suit pries free a dense mineral resembling a crystal and proceeds to measure it with his Geiger counter. It reads as highly radioactive. The crystal, it seems, "changes a certain metal to gold under the right circumstances." The unfortunate side effect of the crystal's Midas properties is a widespread catatonia that plagues the island's residents. The island's leading geology authority, Professor Forrester, is kidnapped, and his assistant is murdered. Enter Scotland Yard detective Rex Forrester (Fred Williams), nephew of Professor Forrester, and sexy agent Jane Morgan (Soledad Miranda). Under the aegis of Metropolitan Chief Sir Philip (Siegfried Schürenberg), both are assigned the task of locating the professor, who has suddenly disappeared from the island; however, neither is aware of the other's true identity. In London, these various plot strands come together and, in typical *Krimi* fashion, an "unlikely" criminal mastermind is thwarted in his grandiose bid for world domination.

Like most Franco films, *The Devil Came from Akasava* boasts a plot that feels more than a little schizophrenic. Loosely adapted from three different Wallace short stories—"The Akasava," "The Rising of the Akasava," and "Guns in the Akasava"—it is only nominally a *Krimi* if we judge it based upon its fidelity to its literary sources. Indeed, it is arguably just as much a semi-remake of Robert Aldrich's film noir masterpiece *Kiss Me Deadly* (1955). No doubt this narrative hybridity is one reason why the film has often been overlooked or marginalized in studies of the genre. It is part of what makes *The Devil Came from Akasava* so enjoyable, however. As Robert Monell, *Krimi* fan and creator of the blog *I'm in a Jess Franco State of Mind*, writes: "The film itself will want to make [*sic*] Edgar Wallace purists, pedants and stuffed shirts want to lynch Jess Franco. Include me out of that scenario. I love this film. It's like a giddy ride through a specially appointed

Franco funhouse with all the regulars (Alberto Dalbés, Paul Muller, Howard Vernon, and Franco himself) popping up to conduct us on our merry way." More importantly, the trademark "genre stew" that Franco concocts in *The Devil Came from Akasava* is precisely what makes it a distinctive and significant contribution to the *Krimi* cycle. As Bergfelder comments, genre mixing was a key component of popular European cinema of the late 1960s and early 1970s generally, and Franco was perhaps its foremost practitioner:

> Crime, horror, costume melodrama, and the sex film also rarely defined "pure" genres and were more often used as narrational components in hybrid combinations (one particularly productive exponent of the sex/horror film was the Spanish director Jess Franco). Next to such "straight" hybrids were innumerable genre parodies, drawing on the conventions of all the other major genres in circulation. (66)

Franco's hybrid approach to narrative in *The Devil Came from Akasava* gave it a unique cross-market appeal, demonstrating Brauner's good sense in hiring him to direct the film. Blending together elements from the *Krimi*, the Euro spy film, and his own work, Franco created a *Krimi* that was both inimitably his own and perfectly in tune with the times.

Narrative aside, however, the style of the film is more than enough to merit its inclusion both in the canon of Franco's work and in the *Krimi* cycle. Franco's movies are bound together by many defining factors—foremost among them, their director, followed by their producer, distributor, cinematographer, subject matter/genre, actors, composers, technicians, production era, and so on. *The Devil Came from Akasava* sits quite comfortably within its moment in Franco's career, which was dominated by adult fantasy elements and informed by European art cinema of the late 1960s and early 1970s, as well as pop culture in general (Lucas, "Jess Franco's Declaration" 18). Consider the film's soundtrack. In a manner more reminiscent of a James Bond spy thriller than a Wallace *Krimi*, the movie opens over groovy period music provided by the German duo of Manfred Hübler and Siegfried Schwab. Hübler and Schwab composed a total of three much-admired soundtracks for Franco—the others were for *Vampyros Lesbos* (1971) and *Sie Tötete in Ekstase* (*She Killed in Ecstasy*, 1971). From its opening frames, *The Devil Came from Akasava* sonically positions itself within Franco's body of work and stretches the established boundaries of the *Krimi* cycle.

No formal element of the film is more characteristic of Franco's work during this period or plays a bigger role in reshaping the genre template of the *Krimi* than its casting, particularly where the lead role is concerned. *The Devil Came from Akasava* was the first of a trio of successful Brauner-CCC-Franco productions to center on Soledad Miranda (the others being the aforementioned *Vampyros Lesbos* and *She Killed in Ecstasy*). Franco wastes no time in introducing her as secret agent Jane Morgan in an erotic nightclub scene, and the film contains some of the most recognizable, celebrated, and sensational images captured of Miranda before her tragic death in an automobile accident in 1970. A compelling presence, she completely commands the viewer's gaze in a way that is entirely typical of Franco's films but skews the usual masculinist bias of the *Krimi* genre, which tends to focus on the rivalry between heroic male detectives and villainous male criminals. As cinema historian and Franco biographer Carlos Aguilar suggests, the Franco-Miranda relationship is analogous to other famous collaborations between directors and stars like Josef von Sternberg and Marlene Dietrich, Federico Fellini and Giulietta Masina, Ingmar Bergman and Liv Ullmann, Michelangelo Antonioni and Monica Vitti, and so on. Aguilar concludes that "in the end . . . she impersonates Franco's conception of eroticism better than any other female star of his movies" (*Jess Franco* 89). Ultimately, it is the chemistry between Franco and Miranda that makes *The Devil Came from Akasava* so memorable, both as a Franco film and as a *Krimi*.

In his second *Krimi*, *Der Todesrächer von Soho*, Franco adopted a lighter touch, emphasizing its comedic overtones. Aesthetically, he also exhibited a more sophisticated approach in his handling of the subject matter. But if *The Devil Came from Akasava* represented Franco's tentative exploration

The hypnotizing beauty of Soledad Mirada in Franco's first *Krimi* and, tragically, her last film, *The Devil Came from Akasava*. (Cooperativa Fénix Films and CCC Filmkunst. Courtesy of Photofest.)

of the *Krimi* form, his next effort was an all-out assault on the genre, one that turned it inside out and upside down.

DER TODESRÄCHER VON SOHO

Set in early-1970s London, *Der Todesrächer von Soho* begins in a narrow alley with a close-up of a blind organ grinder named Patakes (Andrea Montchal, as Viktor Feldman), who becomes a recurring character cast in the mold of Tiresias. In the lobby of a nearby hotel, a guest prepares to check out. Upon returning to his hotel room, he finds that his bags have, mysteriously, already been packed. Back in the alley, via a distinctive low-angle, fish-eyed shot, a poised and cocked dagger is revealed, heightening tension. Just as the guest exits the hotel and reaches for a taxi door, the bodiless arm flings the dagger into his back. An extradiegetic exclamation in the form of a "*boing!*" mickey-mouses the action on-screen. As he does in *The Devil Came from Akasava*, Franco marks this *Krimi* as his own in the precredit sequence. An exceedingly eager and gregarious crime scene photographer, Andy Pickwick (Luis Morris), who "likes to keep a finger on London's pulse," arrives at the crime scene and quickly pays Patakes for any tips or useful information he might gather. Scotland Yard's top inspector and most eligible bachelor, Rupert Redford (Fred Williams, essentially reprising his role in *The Devil Came from Akasava*), is assigned the case and teams with the famous crime fiction author Charles Barton (Horst Tappert) to solve the murder, which is apparently the latest in a series of similar slayings. Redford's love interest, a bespectacled and coquettish nurse, Helen Bennett (Elisa Montés), accompanies him for much of the investigation, which involves a number of red herrings and confusing subplots. Eventually, it exposes an international drug manufacturing and trafficking syndicate. The drug in question, Mescadrin, a concentrated form of opium five times stronger than heroin, is being sold out of a London nightclub, The Flamingo, allowing Franco to stage one of his signature sexy nightclub acts.

Summarizing the plot of *Der Todesrächer von Soho* beyond this would be a rather pointless exercise. If there is one undeniable flaw it shares with

The Devil Came from Akasava, it is that they are semi-incomprehensible (at least on the first few viewings). Narrative causality is present in both films, but it is irrefutably anemic. This is common across Franco's entire oeuvre. For Franco, as for Hitchcock, preproduction was a tempest of ebullient creativity in which obsessions and fetishes were stimulated and sated; production was far more mundane, and the tedium of postproduction could often led to ennui. Jack Taylor, one of Franco's regular actors, offers an explanation for the production and postproduction malaise that occasionally mars Franco's films:

> I think that Jess was more enthusiastic about the concept of making a film rather than the discipline of filming and editing, etc. By this I don't imply that he was not creative or enthusiastic while shooting. I was always impressed and amused by his solutions, but his was an active mind, and, as you know, devoting months to repeatedly doing one thing over and over while your imagination is whirling around with other ideas is distracting. He worked best when there was a producer to do exactly that—produce. Brauner or Harry Alan Towers are two good examples.[5]

Der Todesrächer von Soho has an interesting pedigree. It is actually a remake of CCC's earlier *Das Geheimnis der schwarzen Koffer* (*Secret of the Black Trunk*, 1961), and both films are loosely adapted from Bryan Edgar Wallace's novel *Death Packs a Suitcase*. As Bergfelder notes, the relationship that CCC established with the younger Wallace was what enabled it to become a major player in the *Krimi* cycle: "Brauner's strategy to contract Edgar Wallace's son was perhaps the most ingenious in gaining a foothold in the Wallace boom. Brauner secured the film rights of Bryan Edgar Wallace's novels, which were more or less indistinguishable pastiches and imitations of his father's style" (152). In the span of a decade (1962–72), ten Bryan Edgar Wallace films were produced by CCC; stylistically, they attempt to replicate the original Rialto *Krimi* productions, with varying degrees of success. In the case of *Der Todesrächer von Soho*, the film's vaunted connection to Rialto's thrillers was a classic bait and switch. The artwork

The Italian one-panel for *Der Todesrächer von Soho* depicts traditional iconography from the Rialto-era *Krimis*, but does Jess Franco deliver on this promise? (Cooperativa Fénix Films, CCC Filmkunst, and Tele-Cine Film. Courtesy of Ronald V. Borst and Hollywood Movie Posters.)

designed for its promotional campaign—the colorful one-panel created for the Italian market, for example—effectively evokes the iconography and the aura of the Rialto *Krimis*, but the film doesn't quite deliver on this promise. What it does deliver are high doses of Franco's signature film-making that nevertheless yield a suitable finale to the Wallace *Krimi* cycle.

Franco is frequently on point throughout *Der Todesrächer von Soho*, and, as usual, there are several memorable shots and sequences that linger in the mind. One such shot, featuring clever blocking and dynamic composition, occurs early in the film. Three characters—Redford, Pickwick, and Barton—are arranged in front of a mirror, discussing the murders. An eye-catching mahogany and amber color palette drives the mise-en-scène. Shortly thereafter, Pickwick exits and the shot becomes an even more sophisticated two-shot which primes us for his unexpected reentry (captured only in the mirror's reflection) a few moments later. The shot invokes the spirit of one of Franco's idols and collaborators, Orson Welles, who orchestrated similar compositions in *Citizen Kane* (1941) and *The Lady from Shanghai* (1947).

Along these lines, and in keeping with the *Krimi* pedigree, there is a stunning use of expressionistic framing and shadow play throughout the film. Many of the film's most striking moments push it in the direction of the *giallo*—or Italian murder-mystery—genre inspired in part by the Wallace *Krimi* cycle and developed over the 1960s and 1970s by Mario Bava, Dario Argento, Lucio Fulci, and others. Franco's film features stylish, prowling camera work, deep pools of shadow, black gloves, the employment of knives as murder weapons, a revenge motive, repressed sexual tension, misdirection and red herrings, eerie musical leitmotifs (often in the form of transformed nursery rhymes), and strong, angular set design. *Der Todesrächer von Soho* was lensed by the accomplished and prolific cinematographer Manuel Merino, a regular collaborator of Franco's throughout the late 1960s and early 1970s. A fascinating idiosyncrasy of the film is its use (or overuse) of static wide-angle establishing shots, which give way to traditionally framed coverage (medium close-ups, over-the-shoulder shots, and so on). Perhaps this was simply Franco's way of compensating for the lack of his trademark zoom shots, which are conspicuously absent in the film.

Another major asset in *Der Todesrächer von Soho*, one that makes it a distinctive example of *Krimi* cinema, is its constellation of notable European stars. Not unlike Hammer Films, which also developed a well-established company of actors, CCC boasted a stable of performers who regularly appeared in its productions throughout the 1960s and 1970s. Some of the more active (many of whom achieved cult status for their appearances in *Krimi* films) included Eddi Arent, Joachim Fuchsberger, Karin Dor, Klaus Kinski, and Horst Tappert. CCC also had a stable of regular producers such as Horst Wendlandt and Artur Brauner; directors such as Alfred Vohrer, Harold Reinl (Karin Dor's husband), and Franz Josef Gottlieb; and cinematographers such as Ernst W. Kalinke and Richard Angst. For *Der Todesrächer von Soho*, Franco reassembled much of his cast from *The Devil Came from Akasava*. Sadly, Soledad Miranda was not among them. The European film community was collectively mourning her loss: she died tragically from injuries sustained in an automobile accident in August 1970, making *The Devil Came from Akasava* her final film (see chapter 11 of this volume for an in-depth discussion of Miranda's dark stardom).

The entire cast is in fine form in *Der Todesrächer von Soho*, but it is Elisa Montés who truly shines. She shoulders the unenviable responsibility of replacing the inimitable Soledad Miranda, the lead actress in several of Franco's films around that period and the star of *The Devil Came from Akasava*. Her loss affected Franco deeply: "Visibly shaken by the death of his muse, [he], much like James Stewart in Alfred Hitchcock's *Vertigo* (1958), set out to 'revive' Soledad Miranda" (Aguilar, *Jess Franco* 91). He attempted to accomplish this through the casting of several Miranda surrogates.[6] Montés, a veteran of many Spanish productions and coproductions (particularly spaghetti westerns), had previously worked with Franco on *99 mujeres* (*99 Women*, 1969) and *Die Sieben Männer der Sumuru* (*The Girl from Rio*, 1969), and she more than rose to the occasion here, charming her way through the picture. In addition to Montés, German character actor Dan Van Husen is memorable as Kronstel—a potential blackmailer and goon for the Mescadrin syndicate. Van Husen, a veritable workhorse in European coproductions (particularly spaghetti westerns) at that time, recalls how he was "cast" in the role. As a German-Spanish coproduction, *Der Todesrächer von Soho* had to fill a quota of actors from both countries, and he was awarded the part "sight unseen" based upon his professionalism, reputation, and nationality. Van Husen says, "I liked him [Franco] because he was different. Jesús did things you just didn't see working on other films."[7] For example, in the scene where Van Husen's character, Kronstel, lithely jumps over an estate wall (rather than risk a more obvious breaking and entering), Franco improvised an impromptu setup at an unsecured (illegal) location: "Somebody came and we had to leave very quickly—we didn't have permission to do that! Jess got away with a lot of things because he was talented, fun to be around and exciting." The estate Van Husen refers to was in Murcia (the film was shot primarily in Alicante and Murcia, both being long-standing "pet locations" for Franco). Van Husen also remembers that these locations "had a lot to do with the restaurants. Jess loved good food . . . and selected the restaurants, wonderful lunches!"[8] Here, Van Husen captures what made Franco such a fascinating, controversial, and provocative artist. Like Jackson Pollock, Franco engaged in a brand of abstract expressionism via idiosyncratic, spontaneous creation. It is finally this quality in his work that makes *The Devil Came from Akasava* and *Der Todesrächer von Soho* such distinctive and fascinating examples of the *Krimi* cycle.

CONCLUSION

In the final analysis, these films belong to Franco. A prolific auteur, Franco approached filmmaking in the same way a composer approaches theme, variation, and leitmotif. In the process of cinematic orchestration, he would modulate key, play with time signatures, experiment freely, and often work miracles. An inveterate improviser (like many of the jazz musicians he admired), he brought inexhaustible passion and often more than a little magic to his projects. As Jack Taylor remembers,

> Jess was a rebel or, better said, a non-conformist . . . something quite understandable because of the period when he was born. Growing

up under the restrictive Franco regime dominated by bigotry and puritanical censorship was partially responsible for forming his attitude concerning life in general. Jess was successful because he didn't conform during a period when so many did.[9]

This nonconformism frequently manifested as a sort of "cinematic will." When Franco imposed his will on a literary character, franchise, or cycle of films, it was invariably reshaped by his distinctive drives, desires, and obsessions. Consequently, while *The Devil Came from Akasava* and *Der Todesrächer von Soho* fit seamlessly within Franco's body of work, they sit askew within the larger *Krimi* canon, and the Wallace cycle particularly.

When Franco is brought up at all in the conversation around the *Krimi*, the most common complaint leveled at the director is that he "killed off" the genre by pushing it into the realm of parody with his two films. A similar argument is often made about Charles Barton's *Abbott & Costello Meet Frankenstein* (1948) in the context of discussions about classic Universal horror cinema. The film is unfairly accused of "killing off" Universal Studio's golden era of movie monsters. In fact, many factors contributed more directly to the end of this era. The horror genre (at least at Universal) was wobbling on tired legs. Predictable formulas, clichéd thematic treatments, the monster rallies, and, most importantly, studio president William Goetz's decision to abandon the horror franchise, as well as shut down their B-unit, in favor of "quality" and "prestige" pictures had more to do with the demise of classic Universal horror than *Abbott & Costello Meet Frankenstein*, which was the studio's second-biggest moneymaker (and second-cheapest production) in 1948 and remains the template for the successful fusion of comedy and horror. Yet, in volume after volume, Abbott and Costello have borne the lion's share of blame for the genre's burnout. In like manner, by the time Franco made his distinctive contributions to the Wallace *Krimi* cycle, it was already in decline, having exhausted itself after a decade of rampant production. In fact, far from killing off the genre, Franco took it in bold and interesting new directions by imprinting *The Devil Came from Akasava* and *Der Todesrächer von Soho* with his own directorial style and sensibility. Just as filmmaker Stanley Kubrick used Stephen King's novel *The Shining* to realize his own vision of horror, Franco effectively utilized the *Krimi* as a template for self-expression. Remaining committed to his muse while still fulfilling the requirements of the genre, he provided the *Krimi* cycle with a memorable coda.

NOTES

1. Film historians Carlos Aguilar and Tim Lucas have devoted some writing to these titles. Aguilar reviews them in his *Jess Franco: El Sexo del Horror* and his book-length study, *Jesús Franco*. Tim Lucas briefly discusses the films in his article "Horrotica! The Sex Scream of Jess Franco" from his cinephiliac digest, *Video Watchdog*. Stephen Thrower covers them more thoroughly in the recently published volume *Murderous Passions: The Delirious Cinema of Jesús Franco*.
2. For more on the *Krimi*'s literary origins, see Hall's *Crime Fiction in German: Der Krimi*.
3. Two German Edgar Wallace adaptations were actually filmed in the early 1930s: Mac Fric and Karel Lemac's *Der Zinker* (*The Squeaker*, 1931) and E. W. Ema's *Der Doppelganger* (*The Double*, 1933). Propaganda minister Joseph Goebbels, however, saw no room for more of these types of films in Hitler's new Reich.
4. Franco's charm is legendary and well documented. The director is remembered as a gifted raconteur, a connoisseur of art and culture, and, quite simply, a very charismatic man.
5. Jack Taylor, e-mail interview, 15 Mar. 2015.
6. The search for surrogates for Soledad Miranda ended when Franco finally found a new star in Lina Romay (born Rosa María Almirall Martínez), who was his creative collaborator and romantic partner from the early 1970s until her death in 2012.
7. Dan Van Husen, Skype interview, London, 22 Mar. 2015.
8. Ibid.
9. Jack Taylor, e-mail interview, 15 Mar. 2015.

WORKS CITED

Aguilar, Carlos. *Jess Franco: El Sexo del Horror*. Ed. Carlos Aguilar, Stefano Piselli, and Riccardo Morrocchi. Florence: Glittering Images, 1999. Print.

————. *Jesús Franco*. Madrid: Cátedra, 2011. Print.

Bergfelder, Tim. *International Adventures: German Popular Cinema and European Co-Productions in the 1960s*. New York: Berghahn Books, 2005. Print.

Gerhards, Sascha. "Ironizing Identity: The German Crime Genre and the Edgar Wallace Production Trend of the 1960s." *Generic Histories of German Cinema: Genre and Its Deviations*. Ed. Jaimey Fisher. Suffolk: Boydell & Brewer, 2013. 133–56. Print.

Hall, Katharina, ed. *Crime Fiction in German: Der Krimi*. Swansea: U of Wales P, 2016. Print.

Hanke, Ken. "The 'Lost' Horror Film Series: The Edgar Wallace Krimis." *Fear Without Frontiers: Horror Cinema Across the Globe*. Ed. Steven J. Schneider. Godalming: FAB, 2003. 111–23. Print.

Hantke, Steffen. "Postwar German Cinema and the Horror Film: Thoughts on Historical Continuity and Genre Consolidation." *Caligari's Heirs: The German Cinema of Fear after 1945*. Ed. Steffen Hantke. Lanham: Scarecrow, 2006. vii–xxiv. Print.

Lázaro-Reboll, Antonio. *Spanish Horror Film*. Edinburgh: Edinburgh UP, 2012. Print.

Lucas, Tim. "Dial 'W' for WALLACE!: The West German 'Krimis.'" *The Video Watchdog Book*. Cincinnati: Video Watchdog, 1992. 138–61. Print.

————. "Jess Franco's Declaration of Principles: How to Read the Early Films, 1959–1967." *Video Watchdog* 157 (2010): 16–49. Print

Monell, Robert. "The Devil Came from Akasava/The Devil came from Akasava" *Latarnia*. 2003. Web. March 2015.

Rasch, William. "Introduction: Looking Again at the Rubble." *German Postwar Films: Life and Love in the Ruins*. Ed. Wilfried Wilms and William Rasch. New York: Palgrave Macmillan, 2008. 1–5. Print.

Sanjek, David. "Foreign Detection: The West German *Krimi* and the Italian *Giallo*." *Spectator* 14.2 (1994): 82–95. Print.

Thrower, Stephen, with Julian Grainger. *Murderous Passions: The Delirious Cinema of Jesús Franco*. London: Strange Attractor, 2015. Print.

II

HORROR AND
EROTICISM
IN FRANCO

4

LATENT DURABILITY IN JESS FRANCO'S FILMS

His "Horrotica"

Tatjana Pavlović

According to Walter Benjamin, the afterlife of a piece of art can be formulated as its ability to survive. Benjamin called this trait the "translatability" of an artwork, an essential quality of certain works that enables their renewal or, as Benjamin says, "a new flowering" (72). A notable case of Benjamin's principle in twentieth-century Spanish cinema is the opus of Jesús "Jess" Franco. Thanks to their "translatability," Franco's landmark 1960s and 1970s films enjoyed an unexpected revival beginning in the 1990s, stirring new critical appreciation for his work and inspiring what can only be described as a cult following. Admittedly, new forms of film consumption—such as the internet circulation or DVD and Blu-ray releases of his hitherto hard-to-see titles—have aided this revival. But there is more to this phenomenon than mere changes in technology, taste, or fashion. This chapter maintains that there is an indisputable connection between the revival of Franco's films and their latent durability, which escaped early critics who saw his work primarily as profitable trash cinema.

One of Franco's major contributions to European exploitation cinema— and one key to his reception and recuperation—was his development of "horrotica." Tim Lucas rightly claimed that "more so than any other film-maker, Franco was singularly responsible for wedding the thrills of cinematic sex and horror into a third *frisson*, which could be described as 'horrotica.' In Franco's universe, the viewer never encounters joyous sex; there is always some dark element of guilt or pain or emotional dislocation involved, and most of the erotic acts he depicts are dramatized in concert with the specter of Death" (Introduction 13). The term *horrotica* itself—wedding horror and sexuality and denoting cult sensibility, alternative taste, and hipness—has been co-opted by cult movie websites and magazines as well as by DVD and Blu-ray companies to characterize the majority of Franco's oeuvre. Lucas's own *Video Watchdog* publication, as well as other American paracinematic publications such as *European Trash Cinema*, *Psychotronic Video*, and *Sleazoid Express* have intellectualized, cultivated, and marketed Franco's films in this manner.[1] The same is true of psychotronic film distributors such as the Seattle-based Something Weird Video, Sinister Cinema, Image Entertainment, and Mondo Macabro.

"Horrotica" is to be regarded as a politicized term, a strategic category for the questioning of the elitist classifications of the "legitimate" film culture, for the revalorization of "lowbrow" cinema, for the recuperation of "lowbrow" filmmakers, and for the marketing of their work. More than twenty years ago, Jeffrey Sconce mapped out the terrain of cult "paracinema," demonstrating how the shaping of its contours involved "a pitched battle between a guerrilla band of cult film viewers and an elite cadre of would-be cinematic tastemakers" (101). In the case of Jess Franco, most of whose films belong to the category of paracinema, his scorn of "elite" film culture and his subcultural aesthetic sensibility are aligned with those of his fans (and nowadays also with most academics working on Franco's oeuvre). Indeed, as Lázaro-Reboll has maintained, Franco strategized and encouraged his placement on the pedestal of Eurocult exploitation cinema: "Franco himself has actively cultivated his (pulp) auteur status, trafficked in cinephile and popular culture connoisseurship, and prepared the ground for the making of his cult auteur reputation" ("Jess Franco" 167).

The representation of sex in Franco's oeuvre—and its manifestations as horrotica in particular—is grounded in the historical moment of the 1960s and 1970s, when his films evolved in response to the changing cultural context and the greater relaxation of censorship in the countries in which he worked during these years, often in multinational coproductions (with companies in Spain, France, West Germany, and elsewhere). Multinational coproductions and the repackaging of films for different markets, for which Franco was notorious, remained one of the most effective mechanisms for avoiding the censorship of sex scenes. Contemporary paracinematic fan culture has dubbed him the king of European horrotica on the strength of his own uncensored directorial imagination, particularly "his passion for filth and filmmaking" (Wingrove), but the sleaze and sex that have made his films almost instantly recognizable and marketable throughout the decades are as much the result of changing laws in Europe regarding the permissibility of sexually explicit or pornographic material in film.

The purpose of this chapter is to follow the development of Franco's horrotica from *Miss Muerte* (*The Diabolical Dr. Z*, 1966), a Spanish-French coproduction, to that film's remake, *Sie Tötete in Ekstase* (*She Killed in Ecstasy*, 1971), a West German-Spanish coproduction.[2] *She Killed in Ecstasy* will, in turn, be paired up with another West German-Spanish coproduction, *Vampyros Lesbos* (1971). Made within a month of each other, *She Killed in Ecstasy* and *Vampyros Lesbos* are arguably the films in which Franco's horrotica reaches its artistic peak and finds a perfect vehicle in the figure of Franco's beloved star, Soledad Miranda. The last film discussed in the final section of this chapter is *La Comtesse noire* (*Female Vampire*, 1973), a French-Belgian coproduction that can be seen as a "loose" remake of *Vampyros Lesbos*, as well as an attempt by Franco to replace Soledad Miranda with his new muse and soon-to-be wife Lina Romay. All four films display in a consistent manner Franco's transgressive emphasis on sex and eroticism in a relatively straitlaced era and his reimagining of stereotypical gender relations (women in prominent roles such as mad scientists, serial killers, lesbian vampires, and so on). It is in their exceptional horrotica—artistic, poetic, seductive, retro, and jazzy-psychedelic but now also political and institutionalized—that we can locate the durability of Franco's films.

THE DIABOLICAL DR. Z

The Diabolical Dr. Z, a Spanish-French coproduction financed by Michel Safra for Hesperia (Madrid) and Serge Silberman for Speva and Ciné-Alliance (Paris), is a blend of Gothic terror, detective story, and science fiction already explored in Franco's *Gritos en la noche* (*The Awful Dr. Orlof*, 1962). Like its predecessor, the film belongs to the immensely popular horror subgenre of the mad-surgeon movie, while also following the conventions of the French *roman policier* genre. When Dr. Zimmer—whose research centers on annihilating human personality and manipulating brain centers for good and evil—presents his research to the Medical Board, he is ridiculed and succumbs to a heart attack. His daughter Irma (Mabel Karr) swears to avenge her father's death and continue his work. To this end, she kidnaps Nadia (Estella Blain), "the strange, the voluptuous, the mysterious" cabaret artist/performer whose stage name is Miss Muerte. Using her father's invention of mind control, Irma sets Nadia on a revenge spree against the board members she considers responsible for his death: Drs. Vicas, Moroni, and Kallman. The first victim is Vicas (Howard Vernon), killed on the night train by Nadia, who slits his throat with her long, poisoned, razor-sharp nails. After her next victim, Moroni, is found dead (gassed in his car), Inspectors Tanner (Jess Franco) and Green (Daniel White) begin investigating these mysterious murders. Aided by Nadia's boyfriend, Dr. Philip Fraser (Fernando Montés), Tanner solves Miss Muerte's disappearance and stops Irma's murderous revenge.

Considered a third film in Franco's black-and-white Orlof trilogy, *The Diabolical Dr. Z* nevertheless departs from *The Awful Dr. Orlof*, creating a new template that would solidify into Franco's recognizable style soon thereafter. Most importantly, the protagonism is granted to women: a female, revenge-driven mad scientist and her puppet, Miss Muerte. *The Diabolical Dr. Z* is built around the fusion between eroticism and horror and tensions between desire/fear and eroticism/death (as seen in Miss Muerte's nightclub performances and her murders), a combination that would soon thereafter become the signature of Franco's horrotica. As Irma makes clear in the film: "I need a girl of flesh and blood, a beauty to seduce and to destroy those I wish." Attributing the film's power to the emerging centrality of sexuality in Franco's work, Lucas Balbo rightly remarks that it is "much more effective than *The Awful Dr. Orlof*, the story is as captivating as Miss Blain's generous anatomy which is beautifully highlighted by her net body-stocking and a dark cloak" (51). In Miss Muerte's performance number, we can already discern how Franco's pop art sensibility will soon thereafter warp into psychedelic horrotica. Her attire, a fetishistic catsuit with a huge spider woven throughout its length, easily stands up to Jean-Paul Gaultier's impressive futuristic costumes made decades later for Almodóvar's *Kika* (1993) and *La piel que habito* (*The Skin I Live In,* 2011). The stage act itself, involving the seduction and murder of a male mannequin trapped in a spider's web, another of Franco's signatures, points forward to the mannequin scene from *Vampyros Lesbos*, one of the most celebrated sequences of our director's entire cinema.

Nadia (Estella Blain) in costume for her cabaret act as "the strange, the voluptuous, the mysterious" Miss Muerte in *The Diabolical Dr. Z*. (Hesperia Films, S.A., Speva Films, S.A., and Ciné Alliance. Courtesy of Photofest.)

Evocative black-and-white photography and chiaroscuro lighting reinforce the nightmarish atmosphere of this strange tale of surgical revenge. The film emphasizes medical horror, with a mind-control device utilizing long needles and an operating table alive with mechanical arms. This technological gadgetry makes it a classic mad-scientist movie. Through the derangement of Dr. Zimmer and his experiments on humans, the film explores the boundaries and/or fusion of human and animal, male and female, proper and improper, elements further developed in both *She Killed in Ecstasy* and *Vampyros Lesbos*. Legitimate scientific discourse and its symbolic weight are therefore contrasted with the fetishized monstrous excesses of Dr. Zimmer's laboratory, with its futuristic machines and medical paraphernalia. This tale of revenge is set in motion precisely when Dr. Zimmer, a neurologist humiliated by the establishment at the medical congress, loses his symbolic place in it.

The Diabolical Dr. Z, like most of Franco's subsequent films, is also framed by the tension between the patriarchal legal realm (the law enforcement and medical establishments) and feminine sexuality and excess, a contrariety that disturbs and questions the master's discourse. As in classical film noir, the femme fatale is "the other side of knowledge . . . unrestrained female sexuality constitutes a danger. Not only to the male but to the system of signification itself. Woman is 'the ruin of representation'" (Doane 103). This pattern also points to an inevitable interdependency of law, fear, and desire. But an excessive, monstrous feminine is precisely the product of Franco's fusion of horror and eroticism. Nadia's nails, the *ne plus ultra* of her femininity, are also her weapons. Even her boyfriend Philip's fate is uncertain since the film closes with a close-up of Nadia's fingernails on his neck in an ambiguous embrace (giving the ending a menacing and uncertain air). Miss Muerte, the film's femme fatale, is therefore "the figure of a certain discursive unease, a potential epistemological trauma. For her most striking characteristic, perhaps, is the fact that she never really is what she seems to be" (Doane 1).

The narrative of *The Diabolical Dr. Z* is classical, legible, and linear. The editing is similar to that of classical mad-scientist films. By the same token, in *The Diabolical Dr. Z*, Franco's unique signature landscapes of the 1970s have not yet emerged from the classic black-and-white horror Gothic landscapes of the Dr. Orlof series. The bizarreness of music and sound, however, prefigures Franco's future investment in film scores as peculiar and uncanny as his films (an investment that has resonated with fans and connoisseurs of European horror film scores, as the commercial success of the soundtracks for some of these films on CD and vinyl, including the 2011 album *Vampyros Lesbos: Sexadelic Dance Party*, attests.) In *The Diabolical Dr. Z*, incessant animal noises accompany the theme of monstrous scientific experimentation while the impressively edgy jazz scoring for the nightclub scenes, the theater chase, and the killing of a hitchhiker is both modern and emotional. The original music—personal, strange, and experimental—was composed by Daniel White, who frequently collaborated with Franco throughout his career and here appears (uncredited) as Inspector Green. Daniel White's music intensifies Franco's rendition of twisted female sexuality: Irma is one of the first of Franco's beautiful, exotic women with murderous minds.[3]

Toward a Psycho-Sexo-Delic Horrotica

Five years later, the key leitmotifs of "pop art" in *The Diabolical Dr. Z* were rendered in psychedelic color and music and infused with 1970s aesthetics, ushering in one of the most successful and fruitful periods of Franco's career with the "twin productions" *She Killed in Ecstasy* and *Vampyros Lesbos*. Though made just a short time later, these two films are radically different from *The Diabolical Dr. Z*, reflecting rapidly and drastically changing cultural and industrial contexts. Since the production of *The Diabolical Dr. Z*, Franco had worked with British producer Harry Alan Towers (1968–70), producing films that would become a model and blueprint for his 1970s psycho-sexo-delic horrotica phase. Previous to working with Towers, Franco had already tested the European and American sexploitation markets with his highly successful West German production *Necronomicon* (*Succubus*, 1968). However, his work with Towers was more systematic in its attempts to penetrate these markets. As Lázaro-Reboll has pointed out, Towers and Franco tapped into sexploitation circuits in the United States via Commonwealth United Entertainment, American International Pictures (AIP), and Distinction—a subsidiary of AIP that specialized in the distribution of X-rated films ("Daring Cycles" 97).

But even within this Franco-Towers partnership (which yielded a total of nine films between 1968 and 1970), there was a marked passage from the early Fu Manchu cycle—comprising *The Blood of Fu Manchu* (1968) and *The Castle of Fu Manchu* (1969)—to a much more explicit and daring second set of films represented by *99 mujeres* (*99 Women*, 1969), *Justine* (*Marquis de Sade's Justine*, 1969), and *Paroxismus* (*Venus in Furs*, 1969). Danny Shipka has perceptively observed that "there is something slightly off in those films with Towers. They have the look and feel of big-budget traditional Hollywood fare, yet they are so seedy in content you can't really believe you're seeing what is on the screen" (188). In other words, the transition from the early to the later Franco-Towers films signals Franco's move away from pulp to the world of sexploitation. At this point, Franco's horrotica entered the lurid and seedy spaces of New York's Times Square grind houses, becoming a favorite with the Deuce audiences. His appeal as a sleaze artist would be later invoked by grind-house connoisseur Bill Landis in the fanzine *Sleazoid Express* as an early example of the durability of his cinema among emerging paracinematic fan cultures in the 1970s and 1980s.

As the titles of the Franco-Towers collaborations themselves indicate, the international film industry in the late 1960s changed notably. Shifts in consumer taste demanded more explicit sexual material or commodities "which trafficked in sensation and sexuality" (Lázaro-Reboll, "Daring Cycles" 102). The market was ripe for female nudity and sexually spiced "lowbrow" pleasures: sex films, soft porn, and erotic cinema. The trend into which Franco and Towers tapped both preceded and enabled the popularization of hard-core pornography in America by such U.S. films as *Mona* (1970), *Behind the Green Door* (1972), and the infamous *Deep Throat* (1972). They heralded the arrival of the so-called Golden Age of

Porn in America, aided by the 1973 modifications in state and municipal antiobscenity laws and ordinances.[4]

During the Towers years, Franco honed both the rapid production strategies that would become his trademark and his thematic predilections, since Towers and Franco shared a penchant for accelerated output and sexploitation. As Lázaro-Reboll points out, the success of this Franco-Towers softporn cycle had its origins in production and distribution patterns already in place with the Fu Manchu movies. These patterns included "Towers' own presence as screen writer, multinational sources of finance, lucrative pre-sales deals with distribution companies on both sides of Atlantic, and the casting of Hollywood veterans and European genre actors to appeal to various territories and audiences" ("Daring Cycles" 102). It was at this time that Franco's movies, like other Eurocult sexploitation films, became popular fare for American grindhouses, drive-ins, and television stations, three main exhibition venues of European sexploitation in the United States.

Significantly, the U.S. market's hunger for the new and provocative material outlined above was met by both European art cinema and Eurocult. While these two categories of European film appear to lie on completely opposite sides of the spectrum, they nevertheless shared key marketable features, profiting on the one hand from sex, nudity, and violence and on the other by covering subjects not broached in the mainstream cinema, such as incest, necrophilia, sadomasochism, and lesbianism (all staples of Franco's own cinema). Eurocult movies, just like highbrow art films of the European New Wave *cinéastes*, saturated American screens, many outperforming their critically acclaimed counterparts at the box office, a fact that probably delighted the notoriously anti-high-art Franco. Ironically, then, such films as Franco's *Succubus* or *99 Women* rode the same wave of permissiveness as international art films whose function was to legitimize American audience's viewing of sex and violence without making them feel as if they were indulging in illicit pleasures. The two markets in which they operated—American and European—were more than mildly imbricated, especially given that several U.S. companies were major players in the exploitation and genre markets in Europe. This was a network that both spanned Europe and relied on economic and industrial transatlantic connections.

As in the United States, in Europe (especially in the more northerly countries) there were also drastic changes in audience sensibility and market needs. The legalization of pornography in Denmark and Sweden in the late 1960s was a landmark event. In 1973, exhibiting hard-core sex films became legal in France, and in 1974 the same thing occurred in Germany. These legal and industrial changes on both sides of the Atlantic offered exploitation filmmakers, including Franco, an opportunity to take sexuality to cinematic limits not previously seen in their films. Franco, now seasoned by the Towers period, indulged his imagination and pushed even further the limits of his horrotica. From this moment on, most of Franco's films focused on sexuality, aiming at a blend of soft-core porn and horror.

A consideration of the West German market is also central to any discussion of *She Killed in Ecstasy* and *Vampyros Lesbos*, which are both West German-Spanish coproductions. We cannot underestimate the role of Artur Brauner (CCC/Telecine Film), the Berlin-based producer of these features, in Franco's trajectory in the early 1970s. Franco directed three extremely successful films with Soledad Miranda for Brauner, after which she was offered an exclusive, lucrative contract with Central Cinema Company (CCC). (The third film produced by Brauner was *Der Teufel Kam aus Akasawa* [*The Devil Came from Akasava*, 1971].) Franco recounted: "The day before she died, she received the greatest news of her life. I visited her apartment in Lisbon with a German producer, who came to offer her a two-year contract with CCC, which would assure her of at least two starring roles per year in big-budget films. She was going to become a major star in Germany. The next day, as her contract was being drafted, she had the accident. When the hospital called me to break the news . . . I nearly passed out" (qtd. in Lucas, "Black Stare": 196). Had she not died so suddenly in an automobile collision, Soledad Miranda would have become a decidedly lucrative asset for Brauner, who, like other key producers in the German market, ventured into quite profitable coproductions in the early 1960s. Brauner founded CCC in Berlin in 1946. As Tim Bergfelder has pointed out, "Already in the first postwar years, CCC's output was characterized by stylistic and ideological eclecticism" (106). Brauner stood out as a key figure in several postwar German market trends, ranging from films made by Hollywood repatriates coming back from California to the production of over twenty Holocaust movies. However, Brauner's more serious movies (treating the Holocaust, for example) were not as successful as his popular film productions in Germany, which included Karl May westerns, Edgar Wallace adaptations, and secret agent/spy thrillers in the James Bond mold.

The most important factor in the German market during the making of *Vampyros Lesbos* and *She Killed in Ecstasy*, and a partial reason for the films' success, was shifting trends in the German film industry in general and in the sex-films niche in particular. According to Bergfelder, by 1966: "the various spy and exotic-adventure cycles showed early signs of exhaustion . . . and from the late 1960s, the West German B-film sector changed its generic focus from exotic adventure film to the production of soft-porn" (222). We can therefore see how Franco's "evolution" and generic reorientation—from the Fu Manchu exotic adventures series of yore and Franco-Towers soft-porn-horror hybrids to the horrotica of *She Killed in Ecstasy* and *Vampyros Lesbos*—clearly derive from this market logic. Most significant for a Franco always busy at the cutting edge was the fact that the German sex-film market, according to Bergfelder, was dominated by the "reports" (sex films comprising soft-porn episodes and pseudosociological comments by a "reporter"), the sex-education cycles commissioned by the West German Ministry of Health, and the bawdy costume sex comedy.[5] The relatively bland German sex market opened up lucrative working opportunities for transgressive and innovative filmmakers such as our Spaniard. Franco's reception in Germany therefore shows how national cultural horizons of expectation interacted successfully with a transnational imagination and international coproduction formulae.

Besides the racier sexual topics that an already seasoned Franco could provide for the German market, coproductions with Spain also offered major advantages in purely industrial terms, since Spain was one of the lowest-cost film markets in Europe. For example, Wolf C. Hartwig, Brauner's competitor and another key figure in the German film business, called for the production of "the widescreen adventure film in colour, where suspense and exoticism are effectively combined, and where the beauty of foreign countries can be realistically captured in images" (qtd. in Bergfelder: 212). Hartwig added: "These days I can produce much more cheaply in Spain, Bangkok, Rangoon, Hong Kong, or Manila than Germany where the costs have gone through the roof" (qtd. in Bergfelder: 212). Hartwig's comments point to the demand for inexpensive locations with an exotic flair. In the 1960s, Spain had both. Besides heavily marketing its exoticism in the form of sunny beaches, bullfights, and flamenco, the Spain of the economic miracle (or so-called *desarrollismo* of the 1960s) also provided tax loopholes and financially favorable working contracts for foreign producers. Other international corporations had already flooded Spain in the early 1960s, with a profound impact on the production of exploitation cinema (first "spaghetti" westerns and later horror films). The Spanish film industry, despite the country's politically restrictive dictatorship (or, one could argue, precisely because of it), offered some of the best economic and political conditions in Europe for foreign film investment. Hollywood productions such as Samuel Bronston's *King of Kings* (1960), *El Cid* (1961), *55 Days in Peking* (1963), and *Dr. Zhivago* (1965) influenced the new coproduction laws and the new tax system, which might include beneficial subsidies or write-offs for production costs, or both. Moreover, this internationalizing trend brought a new professionalism to Spain and thereby lowered the costs of "native" productions by providing them with access to foreign-built film studios, more sophisticated technical equipment, and better trained film crews.

Like Spain at this time (and not unlike today), most other national European film industries faced precarious financial conditions, such that trans-European and transatlantic coproductions were some of the most cost-effective production strategies. This was so since the financing and risks could be shared across two or three countries, with significant state subsidies from each of them. European coproductions, especially those focusing on "lowbrow" entertainment cinema, proved extremely profitable. The unique production template began with financing from a different number of producers and distributors in varying countries, which gave them rights over the release in their respective territories. For that reason, as the difficulty of trying to "piece together" the various cuts of Franco's films illustrates, any one version of a Eurocult film rarely stands as a complete work. For example, one version could emphasize sex over violence while another might emphasize actresses or themes popular in a particular country, depending on the audience expectations in that territory. Extra footage (mostly pornographic inserts) would be shot by directors having nothing to do with the original production in order to make films more profitable. But this production template had a serious downside. The pressure of ever-tighter shooting schedules favored speedy and skilled directors such as Franco, but as often as not lowered the overall quality of the films. The need for various versions to satisfy territory-specific demands also impacted the economies of sound quality of that period, since actors working side by side were frequently speaking lines in different languages that were later dubbed in the target language. Furthermore, the coproduction method of financing, directing, producing, and marketing by its very nature undermined the concept of "national" cinema, distorting the nationalities of "final" products in terms of stars, language, crews, and directors. For these reasons, coproductions were not without risks or problems. This is reflected in Jess Franco's steady pattern of seeking new producers, indicating both his restless personality and industry-linked difficulties in coordinating divergent production practices, conventions, and audience expectations.

Because of the competitiveness of transnational coproductions in general and the aggressive expansion of the sexploitation market in particular, the industry was forced to lower its already trifling production costs. Franco's providential meeting with Artur Brauner regarding plans for *She Killed in Ecstasy* and *Vampyros Lesbos* was telling in this respect. It was arranged by Karl-Heinz Mannchen, and according to a revealing (if perhaps apocryphal) anecdote: "[Franco and Karl-Heinz Mannchen] showed

Brauner an eight-page script. Brauner was a very charming gentleman and a shrewd businessman. He invited them to dinner and worked out costs on his napkin. No matter how low their budget was, he'd always try to beat them down" (Tohill and Tombs 101). Hard to discourage and accepting the budget drawn on Brauner's napkin, Jess Franco set about making his twin psychedelic masterpieces, the films that still rank as the director's best and most celebrated works of horrotica.

SHE KILLED IN ECSTASY

She Killed in Ecstasy, as the "ecstasy" in the title indicates, is an erotically charged remake of *The Diabolical Dr. Z*, with the earlier movie's film noir aspect shifted into a more sadomasochistic and psychedelic mode. Franco used the same basic story line, but this time the vengeful daughter from *The Diabolical Dr. Z* is cast as a vengeful wife. Like *Vampyros Lesbos*—its more complex twin film—it features a vividly psychedelic mise-en-scène, an outstanding score, and violent sex murders.

Soledad Miranda stars as Mrs. Johnson, a woman intent on avenging the death of her husband, a doctor who committed suicide after his experiments on human embryos were condemned by the medical establishment. She sets out to kill those responsible for his suicide, seducing, torturing, and murdering them one by one. The four scientists are played by Franco regulars: Howard Vernon, Paul Muller, Ewa Strömberg, and Franco himself. Dr. Walker (Howard Vernon) is stabbed to death after being inveigled into sadomasochistic sexual intercourse in Mrs. Johnson's hotel room. The second victim, played by Ewa Strömberg, is suffocated with a see-through pillow, also after sexual intercourse. The same fate awaits the third doctor, but this time he is stabbed with scissors. The film culminates in a typical "Hitchcock-style" gesture, where Franco—who could never resist being on camera in his own films—is terribly tortured by his muse (Soledad Miranda). All four victim-lovers, as the title foretells, are therefore killed by her in ecstasy. Peter Blumenstock has remarked that "the resulting film strikes a bizarre balance between a disturbing tale of dark romanticism and a simple, rather illogically structured pulp-novel in the German thriller tradition" (79).

Most of the screen time is built around Soledad Miranda, the star of the film. Following standard strategies of the sexploitation market, in the more explicit versions of her films made for Germany, Miranda was billed under the pseudonym Susann Korda. Franco, who always had great talent for picking his leading actresses, paired Soledad Miranda up with Swedish actress Ewa Strömberg in both *Vampyros Lesbos* and *She Killed in Ecstasy*. The two stunning actresses are a perfect match for these stories of soft-core sex, nudity, violence, and lesbianism. It becomes clear that one of the key motifs in Franco's horrotica is lesbian sex, the degree of explicitness depending on the country of release. Here, the lesbian seduction and murder scene is staggeringly kitschy, but also arousing. It begins with a campy discussion of Mrs. Johnson's paintings, piled as they are around the living room. Strömberg's female scientist remarks: "I think your style is very masculine," while at the same time making advances on Miranda's Mrs. Johnson. Mrs. Johnson responds: "I wouldn't call it masculine, but personal." The other woman continues: "The shapes are so hard." Mrs. Johnson again demurs: "The painting is my mirror. It seems to be hard, but it's soft and warm." This game of foreplay, filled with double entendre, is embedded in the decor itself by virtue of the paintings. The marriage of story line and visual background is underlined further by the two women's remarkable outfits; one is dressed in a 1970s pantsuit in beige and the other in red. As they make love on the shaggy white carpet, they seemingly become part of this mid-twentieth-century decor. The sensual seduction scene ends with the victim's grotesque black-and-white see-through pillow murder. We get a close-up of Strömberg's agony-ridden face, tongue protruding, staring at the spectator through the pillow's plastic strips before she dies at the end of the sequence. Notably, and in keeping with Franco's idiosyncratically fashion-conscious love for detail, the black-and-white pillow itself replicates patterns in the oversized modernist black-and-white painting on the bedroom wall.

Franco's signature psychedelic landscapes (which supplanted the earlier Gothic settings) date from this period of his career. The director lovingly filmed on the Mediterranean beaches of early 1970s Europe, in Portugal, Spain, and Turkey. His camera fractures and fragments such spaces into an abstract landscape. Emptied of any habitual associations, Franco's Mediterranean beaches (with their undifferentiated high-rise resorts or empty stretches of seashore) become what the anthropologist Marc Augé has termed "non-places" or what Deleuze has described as "any-space-whatever" (*espace quelconque*) (109). This trait is one that contributes to the eerie feeling of repetition in Franco's films. Mrs. Johnson's pagoda-like mansion, the beach house, and different hotel rooms (in which she kills two of the victims) are the three principal places featured in the film. But they become a labyrinthine space around which Franco's camera floats hypnotically, adding to the dreamy, psychedelic narrative elements of the movie. *She Killed in Ecstasy* is built around a contrast between abstract, detached coastal landscapes and its mod interior sets and avant-garde decors. A wacky ship-like bar at the beach hotel, the venue for one of the film's seduction scenes, is a case in point. Moreover, the fashion touches and costumography complement the avant-garde feel of the whole. For example, an early sequence in the film shows Soledad Miranda wearing nothing but a stunning metal "bra-necklace" combo suspended from her neck. Throughout the rest of the film, she wears a purple velvety cape, sometimes draped over her tight black dress and fishnet stockings and sometimes covering only her nude body, obviously one of the main draws of Franco's horrotica from this era.

She Killed in Ecstasy is an ultimate showcase for the most compelling of Franco's period touches: psychedelic color, slow-motion effects, love as obsession, inventive sex, sadomasochism, and jazzy psychedelic scores. The movie's phantasmagoric, poetic admixture is supported by Manuel Merino's unusually picturesque photography and the able psychedelic score by Manfred Hübler and Siegfried Schwab, which has come to sonically embody Franco's horrotica. In fact, their soundtrack had been used previously in *Vampyros Lesbos*, as we shall see in the next section. Based on all of these elements, the film has been categorized and marketed as a psychedelic soft-core or "sexadelic" horror classic. The categorization itself, which aptly ties in with what we have previously said under the heading of "horrotica," points up Franco's own contemporary fashionableness and well illustrates our director's constant desire to remain in vogue by injecting trendy aesthetics (mise-en-scène and cinematography) into established cinematic traditions (pulp and horror), pushing the envelope of sex and eroticism, and exploiting the allure of his horrotica muse Soledad Miranda.

VAMPYROS LESBOS

Vampyros Lesbos was made only a couple of months before *She Killed in Ecstasy*, between April 27 and May 30, 1970.[6] Soledad Miranda, once again credited as Susann Korda, stars in the film. The story line is abstract and more convoluted than the one in *She Killed in Ecstasy*, thanks to the dream sequences, a technique already successfully explored in *Succubus*. In Franco's vampire fantasy, conventional consciousness is supplanted by oneiric surrealism. The film's frequent non-narrativity and nonlinearity account for its poetic freedom, which sometimes comes close to the experimental filmmaking of Dušan Makavejev, Kenneth Anger, Paul Morrissey, and others in the 1970s.

Linda Westinghouse (Ewa Strömberg), an Anglophone lawyer in Istanbul, is tormented by strange and orgasmic dreams about a mysterious and voluptuous brunette vampire who seems to be calling for her. One day she goes to a nightclub with her boyfriend Omar and excitedly recognizes one of the performers as the woman from her dream. Shortly thereafter, she is sent by her office, Simpson & Sons, to an Anatolian island to untangle Countess Nadine Carody's inheritance (in the movie, this scene is actually filmed in Büyükada, one of the Princes' Islands close to Istanbul). Upon arriving, Linda discovers that the woman haunting her dreams is none other than Countess Nadine Carody (Soledad Miranda) herself. Linda's meetings with the countess, a vampire in the line of Dracula, take on a decidedly sensual subtext. Falling under the countess's spell, Linda experiences sexual passion as well as terror in her embrace (each encounter ends with a sensual, but painful and bloody bite on Linda's neck). Meanwhile, Doctor Seward (Dennis Price), a psychiatrist and vampirologist running a private practice, tries to help Linda out in his clinic. Franco shows up in a minor role as Memmet, who turned into a psychopathic killer after losing his wife to the charms of the countess (she is locked away as a mental patient in Doctor Seward's clinic). The story ends with Linda stabbing the countess to death. As Linda (accompanied by Omar) departs the accursed island, she wonders if she dreamt it all up.

The film again brings together Ewa Strömberg and Soledad Miranda, both perfect vehicles for the lesbian vampire motif. Melancholy, enigmatic, and darkly erotic, Miranda plays perfectly against the blonde, naïve, and carnal Strömberg. Franco would exploit this contrast many times in the future, but he never came close to the perfection of his first lesbian vampire and blonde lover matchup. Unlike Franco's earlier *Count Dracula* (1970), *Vampyros Lesbos* turns the archaic and well-worn vampire formula on its head by having a female vampire seek out female victims for sex and life-giving blood. Countess Carody longingly and seductively calls Linda's name throughout the film. Her disembodied voice, a phenomenon that Michel Chion has aptly termed the *acousmêtre*, sutures the seduction sequences (9). Countess Carody, like her voice without any body to anchor it, inhabits what Žižek has described as "the place 'between two deaths,' the forbidden domain of the Thing" (25). The film's eroticism is therefore firmly inscribed within a frame of horror.

Ignoring both the original Dracula myth and the rules and conventions of the vampire movie (embodied by the British Hammer films he so much disliked), Franco alters the formal structures of classic horror cinema by turning his film into a melancholic and poetic musing on existence, peppered by sexually explicit material. Significantly, in *Vampyros Lesbos*, to quote Žižek again: "the 'undead' are not portrayed as embodiments of pure evil, of a simple drive to kill or revenge, but as sufferers, pursuing their victims with an awkward persistence, colored by a kind of infinite sadness (as in Werner Herzog's *Nosferatu*, in which the vampire is not a simple

The melancholy, enigmatic, and darkly erotic Soledad Miranda as the vampire Countess Nadine Carody in *Vampyros Lesbos*. (Fénix Film, CCC Filmkunst, and Tele-Cine Film-und Fernsehproduktion. Courtesy of Photofest.)

machinery of evil with a cynical smile on his lips, but a melancholic sufferer longing for salvation)" (22–23).[7] There is a similar air of tragic inevitability in *Vampyros Lesbos*, and one could even argue that Franco successfully captures the moodiness of F. W. Murnau's original 1922 masterpiece, *Nosferatu*. The fatality stems from the morbid yet mortal sexuality of Franco's female vampire.

Vampyros Lesbos was shot in Turkey (Istanbul and Büyükada), in Spain (Alicante and Barcelona), and in Germany (Berlin) in the spring of 1970. Most of the film is set on the busy Oriental streets of Istanbul, the romantic shores of the Bosphorus, and a sunny Büyükada island, rather than in the wintry snow-covered mountains of the original Dracula story. However, the romantic, bright, and airy Istanbul is juxtaposed with the labyrinthine retro interiors of Countess Carody's beach house, as well as the dark interiors of her castle (Franco used the same footage for the interiors of *She*

Killed in Ecstasy; for example, the mod living room of the lesbian seduction scene). The outside spaces are decidedly campy. When Linda Westinghouse meets Countess Carody for the first time, the latter is tanned and attired in a white bikini, her eyes shielded by huge sunglasses—a paradoxical sunbathing vampire. This sets up a tension with the strangeness that pervades the interiors. This oddity of settings is produced by the *point de capiton* effect (Lacan) "where the perfectly 'natural' and 'familiar' situation . . . becomes 'uncanny,' loaded with horror and threatening possibilities, as soon as we add to it a small supplementary feature, a detail that 'does not belong'" (Žižek 88). Besides the many thematic and spatial incongruities, much of the narratively crucial material is also organized around the menacing motifs of fog, spiral staircases, misty seas, labyrinths, or castles (as is the case in all four films under discussion). One of Franco's techniques in creating his films' uncanny spaces is imbuing his interiors (that is, his stories' fantasy spaces) with a "surplus of inside" (Žižek 12–16).

The nightclub where the melancholic but bloodthirsty countess performs her erotic striptease routines is another menacing yet alluring space. The stage, enveloped in gloom, is set as a baroque chamber with mirrors, velvet curtains, and a candelabra. The countess removes her clothing piece by piece, using it to garb a wooden mannequin. But the mannequin unexpectedly shows signs of life, revealing that instead of wood there is warm flesh beneath its scant clothing. Seductive lesbian sex between the two follows—both concealed (their bodies are veiled by either a silky red scarf or a sheer black dress) and revealed (by explicit, lascivious gestures). As Doane has pointed out: "In the cinema, the magnification of the erotic becomes simultaneous with the activation of objects, veils, nets, streamers, etc., which intercepts the space between the camera and the woman, forming a *second screen*" (49). Franco is a classical Freudian fetishist: the gaze finds itself consistently displaced onto another object to avoid the horror of the void (castration): "The props and stereotypes of the striptease are all there but its product—the completely nude body—is not" (Doane 104). Performance art, therefore, just like in *The Diabolical Dr. Z*, structures the narrative and punctuates the film.

The meditative, moody, and atmospheric feel of the movie is enhanced again by the psychedelic music score of Hübler and Schwab. The music (used in both *Vampyros Lesbos* and *She Killed in Ecstasy*) originates from the album *Psychedelic Dance Party* (released in 1969) and the later *Sexadelic* album by The Vampires' Sound Incorporation. The Vampires' Sound Incorporation was an obscure German 1960s psychedelic band led by Hübler and Schwab. The soundtrack functions as "the elementary 'frame of reference' enabling us to orient ourselves in the diegetic space . . . taking over the function of the establishing shot" (Žižek 40). It is an organ-heavy, loungy psychedelic score. The sound is a truly unique blend of smooth beats, ebullient horns, weird vocal effects (like the repeatedly whispered word "ecstasy"), supplementary brass, fuzz guitar, funky keyboards, and twangy Indian sitar strings. The use of Oriental instruments adds an alienating tone and an Eastern touch that impeccably matches the film's exotic setting in Istanbul. The music—sensuous, playful, and upbeat—can energize the spectator. However, it is also imbued with more ominous, dark, and delirious undercurrents that bewitch us in a different way. In sum, the soundtrack is indispensable to the film because of its mesmerizing dimension, but also because it "gives us the basic perspective, the 'map' of the situation, and guarantees its continuity, while the images are reduced to isolated fragments that float freely in the universal medium of the sound aquarium" (Žižek 40).

Significantly, the most sublimely isolated fragment of the film is Soledad Miranda herself, both in a diegetic sense (in the film, as such), as well as outside the film (in the shape of our actress's cult following). Slavoj Žižek has pointed out that, "The sublime object is precisely 'an object elevated to the dignity of the Thing,' an ordinary, everyday object that undergoes a kind of transubstantiation and starts to function, in the symbolic economy of the subject, as an embodiment of the impossible Thing, i.e., as materialized Nothingness. . . . As soon as we try to . . . reveal the substance, the object itself dissolves; all that remains is the dross of the common object" (83, 4). The spectator's gaze is directed at Soledad Miranda via Franco's persistent close-ups. The film's ethereal and immaterial quality is embedded in Franco's fascination with appearances—an emphasis on surfaces over deeper meaning and aesthetic thrills over narrative logic. Franco's sensual, affect-driven camera lingers on his muse for most of the film.

Overall, the movie is horrotica at its purest—a brilliant mixture of art, melancholy, camp, and trash, all of which Franco was skilled in rendering. Together with *She Killed in Ecstasy*, *Vampyros Lesbos* marked a new era for Franco films: weird, unusual, avant-garde, and extremely creative, within their commercial boundaries. The hallucinogenic sets, intoxicating atmosphere, psychedelic music, and fashion—great reminders of 1970s chic—all add an element of excess and strangeness to the two movies. As Thompson has argued, the excess renews "the perpetual freshness of the work" (consonant with Benjamin's "new flowering" mentioned at the outset) and "suggests a different way of watching and listening to a film" (qtd. in Sconce: 116). Franco's cinema is eccentric, excessive, and bizarre. Its excess is a product of the inimitable camera movement, mise-en-scène, acting, voice, and music that mark his films and form the basis of their latent durability. As Jeffrey Sconce has written in regard to the politics of excess: "The 'surface' diegesis becomes precisely that, the thin and final veil that is the indexical mark of a more interesting drama, that of the film's construction and socio-historical context" (116).

FEMALE VAMPIRE AND THE DECLINE OF FRANCO'S HORROTICA

Soledad Miranda's accidental death shortly after finishing *She Killed in Ecstasy* sent Franco in search of a new star. Bereft emotionally by the bitter blow and thrown off balance artistically, Franco turned to Lina Romay (who subsequently became his longtime partner), and his output began to suffer in quality. *Female Vampire*,[8] a French-Belgian coproduction financed by Marius Lesoeur for Eurociné (Paris), Les Films Marc (Paris), and Brux International Pictures (Brussels), is the fourth film to merit discussion in this chapter. Directed by Franco under the pseudonym James P. Johnson, it was both an attempt to remake *Vampyros Lesbos* and a desperate effort to replace Soledad Miranda. Lina Romay unfortunately did not deliver the edge to Franco's horrotica that Miranda had. Despite a certain physical similarity, the more prosaic Romay never managed to recapture Miranda's star quality, although Franco claimed to the contrary: "[Miranda] left behind an incredible legacy. All of the women who acted in my films after her were deeply affected by her legend. Lina Romay, for example, has had moments in which she was completely possessed by Soledad. She *became* Soledad Miranda! My actors, my crew, and myself as well—we all had tremendous feelings for her. She still exists for us" (qtd. in Lucas, "Black Stare": 196).

Nevertheless, meeting Lina Romay in 1972 was pivotal for Franco's career: "Willing to do almost anything for the pleasure of Franco's zoom lens, Lina Romay would dominate his films for the next 15 years—over 100 films!" (Lucas, Introduction 24). While Franco's famous fascination with zoom shots dates from an earlier period (attested to by a notorious shot taken on the set of *Vampyros Lesbos* where the kneeling Franco points his camera between Miranda's spread legs), they became ubiquitous in his films with Romay.[9] And the zooms in on his actresses' genitals—"the first place my eye looks," Franco is quoted as saying (qtd. in Tohill and Tombs: 113)—became cruder and cruder. Once this overused feature was paired with inexpensive makeup, unconvincing special effects, and starker film sets, Franco's movies started to look cheap, grainy, and elementary. However, this was not simply because Lina Romay could not live up to Soledad Miranda's legend. Franco's tiresome genital zooming illustrated the major changes in the industry that the couple was facing at the time, especially the move toward hard-core pornography, which Eurociné, the main production company behind *Female Vampire*, had embraced.

Slavoj Žižek has emphasized that, "As it is ordinarily understood, *pornography* is the genre supposed to 'reveal all there is to reveal,' to hide nothing, to register 'all' and offer it to our view. It is nevertheless precisely in pornographic cinema that the 'substance' of 'enjoyment' perceived by the view from aside is *radically lost*—why? . . . The unattainable/forbidden object approached but never reached by the 'normal' love story—the sexual act—exists only as concealed, indicated, 'faked.' As soon as we 'show it,' its charm is dispelled, we have 'gone too far.' Instead of the sublime Thing, we are stuck with vulgar, groaning fornication" (109, 110). One would be tempted to claim that the stellar success of Franco's "psychedelic Soledad Miranda" phase came from his ability "to preserve this impossible harmony, the balance between narration and explicit depiction of the sexual act" (Žižek 110). Interestingly enough, and in the same vein as Žižek's argument, Franco himself has remarked: "Not that I think I am D. W. Griffith or something . . . but I know my job and I am capable of shooting a scene that in principle goes too far [however] in a way that the result is not too much" (Gregory).[10] For Carlos Aguilar, Franco's approach was dictated by his simultaneous attraction to "romanticism and perversion" (157).

The circulation of *Female Vampire* in numerous versions is very telling as an illustration of the above-mentioned changes during this period. Among others, there was (1) a horror version known as *Erotikill*, (2) a soft-core version trimmed of some hard-core fellatio scenes known as *Female Vampire*, and (3) a hard-core version known as *Les Avaleuses* in which Countess Irina Karlstein feeds on her victims at the moment of their sexual climax (via explicit scenes of fellatio and cunnilingus).[11] Lina Romay and Franco continued working on ultra-low budgets with very little participation from major production companies. This led to a decline in the quality of Franco's output to the point where his films became little better than adroit home movies. Lucas accurately sums the situation up: "The late 1970s were the creative *nadir* of Franco's career. After breaking off with Dietrich in 1977, Franco and Lina Romay (now a couple) returned to Paris, where they could apparently no longer work under their own names. As 'Clifford Brown' and 'Candy Coster,' they made only a few unimaginative hardcore films in 1978. Franco's least productive year since the mid-60s" (Introduction 27). While *Female Vampire* remains one of Franco's most popular films—one to which fans and critics persistently return—and therefore exhibits some durability, it also signals for many commentators the beginning of a steep decline in the quality of Franco's productions due to a set of circumstances, among them the irreplaceability of Soledad Miranda, the crude representation of sex as mere (hard-core) pornography, and the meager budgets at Franco's disposal.

Wherein, then, lies the latent durability of *Female Vampire*, and, by extension, the other examples of Franco's horrotica discussed in this chapter? For some, it rests with the mysterious, dark, and sensual presence of Soledad Miranda; for others, it owes to viewers' persistent and obsessive search for the various versions of these movies. But the "new flowerings" of Franco's horrotica, to return to Benjamin's notion, have also been enabled by the unique proliferation and obsessive repetition of themes, characters, settings, tropes, and musical motifs embedded in his complex film-puzzles—to which fans return time and again in their attempts to grasp the "totality" of his work, an impossible task in his case. In addition, we must consider the unceasing circulation of these films, which continue to be imported and exported, transferred, translated, adopted, and reinterpreted. In the end, the latent durability of Franco's horrotica can perhaps be located at the intersection of these factors and others; as I have suggested in this chapter, it may finally lie precisely in the transnationality, the translatability, and the transmutability of his unique brand of erotic horror cinema.

Notes

1. European paracinematic publication equivalents include *Mad Movies* in France, *Eyeball* and *Flesh and Blood* in the United Kingdom, and *2000maníacos* in Spain. See Lázaro-Reboll's "Jess Franco: From Pulp Auteur to Cult Auteur" (168).
2. *The Diabolical Dr. Z* was also released as *Dans les griffes du maniaque* in France, as *Dr. Z and Miss Death* (or *Miss Death and Dr. Z*) in Great Britain, and as *Das Geheimnis des Doktor Z* in West Germany.
3. Cathal Tohill and Pete Tombs remark that: "White is one of the unsung geniuses of soundtrack music. Nobody turns out tunes with the same sleepy, lascivious qualities that he does. Over the years he's become a staple ingredient in the Franco canon, and as Franco moved deeper into uncharted erotic waters, White's music followed, endlessly echoing his lingering sensibilities" (88).
4. The U.S. Supreme Court's 1973 decision in Miller v. California redefined the definition of obscenity.

5. See Tim Bergfelder's *International Adventures*, 223–25.
6. Here I follow the dates given in Aguilar's *Jess Franco: El Sexo del Horror*, 89.
7. Žižek refers to George Romero's *Night of the Living Dead* (1968).
8. An alternative title used for the horror version of the film released on video in the U.S. is *Erotikill*. In Great Britain it was released as *The Bare Breasted Countess* and in Italy as *Un caldo corpo di femmina*. It was retitled *Erotikiller* for the Italian video market. In Spain it is known as *El ataque de las vampiras*, and the French pornographic version was titled *Les Avaleuses*. There are several other versions and titles. For more details, see *IMDb*.
9. See the image on page 188 in Balbo, Blumenstock, and Kessler's *Obsession: The Films of Jess Franco*.
10. Franco was interviewed in French. I have here transcribed the pertinent English subtitles as the basis for the quotation.
11. Redemption has released both the horror (*Erotikill*; 70 minutes) and extended erotic (*Female Vampire*; 100 minutes) versions on Blu-ray.

Works Cited

Augé, Marc. *Non-Places: Introduction to an Anthropology of Supermodernity*. Trans. John Howe. New York: Verso, 1995. Print.

Aguilar, Carlos. *Jess Franco: El Sexo del Horror*. Ed. Carlos Aguilar, Stefano Piselli, and Riccardo Morrocchi. Florence: Glittering Images, 1999. Print.

Balbo, Lucas. "*Miss Muerte* (Sp) / *Dans les Griffes du Maniaque* (Fr)." *Obsession: The Films of Jess Franco*. Ed. Lucas Balbo and Peter Blumenstock. Berlin: Graf Haufen and Frank Trebbin, 1993. 51–52. Print.

Balbo, Lucas, and Stéphane Derdérian. "Interview—Monica Swinn." *Obsession: The Films of Jess Franco*. Ed. Lucas Balbo and Peter Blumenstock. Berlin: Graf Haufen and Frank Trebbin, 1993. 223–26. Print.

Benjamin, Walter. "The Task of the Translator." *Illuminations*. Trans. Harry Zohn. Ed. Hannah Arendt. London: Fontana, 1973. 71–72. Print.

Bergfelder, Tim. *International Adventures: German Popular Cinema and European Co-Productions in the 1960s*. New York: Berghahn Books, 2005. Print.

Blumenstock, Peter. "*Sie Tötete in Ekstase*." *Obsession: The Films of Jess Franco*. Ed. Lucas Balbo and Peter Blumenstock. Berlin: Graf Haufen and Frank Trebbin, 1993. 79. Print.

Chion, Michel. *The Voice in Cinema*. Trans. and ed. Claudia Gorbman. New York: Columbia UP, 1999. Print.

Deleuze, Gilles. *Cinema 1: The Movement-Image*. Trans. Hugh Tomlinson and Barbara Habberjam. Minneapolis: U of Minnesota P, 1986. Print.

Doane, Mary Ann. *Femmes Fatales: Feminism, Film, Theory, Psychoanalysis*. New York: Routledge, 1991. Print.

Gregory, David. "Jess Women: Interview with Jess Franco." *99 Women* Blue Underground, 2005. DVD.

Lázaro-Reboll, Antonio. "Daring Cycles: The Towers-Franco Collaboration, 1968–1970." *New Review of Film and Television Studies*. 11.1 (2013): 92–110. Print.

———. "Jess Franco: From Pulp Auteur to Cult Auteur." *A Companion to Spanish Cinema*. Ed. Jo Labanyi and Tatjana Pavlović. Oxford: Wiley-Blackwell, 2013. 167–71. Print.

Lucas, Tim. "The Black Stare of Soledad Miranda." *Obsession: The Films of Jess Franco*. Ed. Lucas Balbo and Peter Blumenstock. Berlin: Graf Haufen and Frank Trebbin, 1993. 183–96. Print.

———. Introduction. *Obsession: The Films of Jess Franco*. Ed. Lucas Balbo and Peter Blumenstock. Berlin: Graf Haufen and Frank Trebbin, 1993. 13–30. Print.

Sconce, Jeffrey. "'Trashing' the Academy: Taste, Excess and an Emerging Politics of Cinematic Style." *The Cult Film Reader*. Ed. Ernest Mathijs and Xavier Mendik. New York: Open UP, 2008. Print.

Shipka, Danny. *Perverse Titillation: The Exploitation Cinema of Italy, Spain and France, 1960–1980*. Jefferson, NC: McFarland, 2011. Print.

Tohill, Cathal, and Pete Tombs. *Immoral Tales: European Sex and Horror Movies, 1956–1984*. New York: St. Martin's Griffin, 1995. Print.

Wingrove, Nigel. *The Diabolical Mr. Franco*. Dir. Andy Starke and Pete Tombs. Boum Productions, 1999. DVD.

Žižek, Slavoj. *Looking Awry: An Introduction to Jacques Lacan through Popular Culture*. Cambridge: MIT P, 1991. Print.

5

TRANSGRESSIVE OR MALADJUSTED?

Nymphomania, Frigidity, and Lesbianism in Franco's Gothic Sexology

Glenn Ward

t is tempting to argue that Franco's better-known erotic dramas and Gothic sexploitation films of the late 1960s to mid-1970s echo the general liberalization of sexuality and eroticism of their era. Often featuring characters in obsessive pursuit of sexual gratification, they undoubtedly capitalized on relaxed censorship codes in some European markets and adjusted to the rise of hard-core pornography, particularly (at least in their "hot" versions) in their representations of nudity. Readings of Franco's films of the period, especially his loose Sade adaptations, often frame them as arguments for and expressions of erotic anarchy. As Sadeian narratives are thought to deterritorialize desire by displacing genitals from the center of erotic interest, so many of Franco's films are often prized for their subversive capacity to "upset notions of order and hierarchy" (Pavlović 118). Evidence for this potential may be found in Franco's gallery of lethal, desiring, and lethally desiring women characters. Films such as *Justine* (*Marquis de Sade's Justine*, 1969), *Sie Tötete in Ekstase* (*She Killed in Ecstasy*, 1971), *Le Journal intime d'une nymphomane* (*Sinner: The Secret Diary of a Nymphomaniac*, 1973), *Des Frissons sur la peau* (*Tender and Perverse Emanuelle*, 1979), *Eugenie* (*Eugenie de Sade*, 1974), *Die Marquise von Sade* (1977), and *Shining Sex* (1977) focus on the (mis)adventures of Sadeian women who act alternately or sometimes simultaneously as agents and objects of desire, led by either curiosity, erotomania, or compulsion into outré sexual escapades and predicaments.

Some viewers may on this basis regard even Franco's more slowly paced and morose films of the 1970s as fairly Dionysian. Yet this cinematic orgy does not extend an open invitation. For instance, although fantasies about lesbian and bisexual women are ubiquitous, gay male characters are limited to a few risible stereotypes. And while certain oral and genital pleasures are well accounted for, anal eroticism is, with notable but fleeting exceptions, scarce in Franco's universe. Finally, whereas Georges Bataille conceived of eroticism as expenditure diverted from genital finality, Franco's framing of pleasures is predictably zoned: although the films vary in explicitness, female genitalia are at the epicenter of what I will call Franco's sexology. As a cinematic attraction playing a key role in what Linda Williams terms the "auditory and visual imagination of sex" (*Screening Sex* 5), the vulva is often the target of Franco's lens, the locus of extended shots to be trimmed or inserted by editors according to the censorship codes and market demands of different countries. It may invoke an uncanny mixture of eroticism and death; it may be the font of inordinate lust; it can be a dangerously seductive object of curiosity, not just for Franco's errant camera but for his hapless male characters; it can be the focus of cunnilingual rather than phallic gazes, or of gynecological investigation as much as of captivating mystification. It may also be subjected to violence: in *Exorcismes et Messes noires* (*Exorcism*, 1975), a staged "black mass" culminates in the (fake) knifing of a cabaret performer's crotch; the heroine of *Eugenie de Sade* is stabbed between the legs with a pair of scissors, offscreen, by her suicidal stepfather; a doctor announces that the vampire in *La Comtesse noire* (*Female Vampire*, 1973) has "pierced the clitoris" of her dead victim. To highlight the relatively narrow range of erotic obsessions Franco pursues in his 1970s Gothic exploitation films is not to say that the films in question are conventional. It is simply to point out that we should not take their transgressiveness for granted.

While a historically situated but ideologically knotty economy of fascination with genital, gender, and sexual difference is apparent in many aspects of Franco's films, my focus here will be on their approach to female orgasms (or, more precisely, notions of the female orgasm), representations of which can be read productively against a matrix of interconnected contemporary discourses around sexual and libidinal politics. Although any number of Franco's psychosexual scenarios may in Freudian terms be informed by infantile fantasies of castration and phallic "lack," I propose that the more culturally salient differences addressed by Franco are those between types or species of orgasm. The following account therefore sketches just some of the ways in which the Gothic films Franco made in the 1970s play out heteronormative masculinity's attempts to come to terms with the female orgasm as understood, disputed, and politicized at their historical juncture. Franco's hastily assembled and often ramshackle attempts to capitalize on the cinematic opportunities offered by sexual modernity do not amount to a systematic exploration of issues, let alone a cogent position on the politics of desire. Nonetheless, many of his scenarios of gothicized sexploitation negotiate multiple notions of women's pleasures and desires as debated in his films' turbulent cultural moment.

By "sexual modernity," I refer to notions of permissiveness, sexual revolution, and emancipation as dispersed through and fought over in much of Western culture during the period. For both its libertarian adherents and its conservative detractors, the radicalism of sexual modernity lay largely in its uncoupling of sex—including and perhaps especially women's sexual pleasure—from reproduction, and in its confrontation with definitions of normality as inscribed in traditional structures of marriage and family life. Irrespective of how we might assess its causes and effects, the discourse of sexual modernity challenged conventional forms of monogamous sexuality and attempted to change attitudes to non-normative gender roles and nonprocreative sexual activities. Although the impact of factors such as the contraceptive pill or feminism were not equally felt internationally, and although idealistic claims about free love, permissiveness, or libidinal revolution did not always correspond to lived social reality, controversies about female sexual experience and entitlement to pleasure were exemplary of sexual modernity across the discursive intertextual spaces of popular, "low," and elite culture. Media and genres as diverse as avant-garde art, radical philosophy, marital guides, pornographic magazines, sexological studies, and sexploitation cinema alike could be found dipping into the rhetorical pool of libidinal revolution. For example, as Linda Williams points out, pornography and sexploitation, through their depiction of women's pleasures, had the potential to participate actively in contemporary sexual dissent rather than merely co-opting, trivializing, or reifying its rhetoric.

Thus Franco's representations of the "tender and perverse" are staged within an intertextual economy of sexual representation that extends far beyond cinema's immediate institutional borders. In the time frame under discussion here, many of sex cinema's character types, psychosexual theories, and narrative conventions (in particular the case history and the "confessional" narrative) cross-fertilized with those of sexological, psychoanalytical, and psychiatric literature. Meanwhile, sexological studies drew eclectically on medical, zoological, ethnographic, psychoanalytic, and other research in ostensibly authentic case histories that had more than a passing resemblance to erotic fiction. Many of Franco's narratives resemble the kind of case histories (dramatized or otherwise) presented in studies such as Havelock Ellis's *Studies in the Psychology of Sex* (1897), W. F. Robie's *The Art of Love* (1921), or Victoria Morhaim's *Casebook: Nymphomania* (1964). At the same time, Franco films like *Sinner*, *Paroxismus* (*Venus in Furs*, 1969), and *Female Vampire* are narrated by voice-overs in a "confessional" or "analysand" address familiar from sexological and psychoanalytic texts as well as from contemporary erotic fiction; the therapist figure in *Plaisir à trois* (*How to Seduce a Virgin*, 1974) describes his client as a "fascinating subject," while the heroine's psychotherapist plays an important role in *Vampyros Lesbos* (1971). Although Jimmy (James Darren) in *Venus in Furs* is never seen upon a psychiatrist's couch, the film is more comprehensible if the viewer imagines it. In all instances, desire is a complex that causes nothing but trouble.

Exemplifying these cross-genre and cross-media overlaps, mail-order companies of the period advertised miscellaneous sex manuals, reprints of literary "erotic classics," exposés of the "permissive society," and mass editions of more reputable works like Richard von Krafft-Ebing's *Psycopathia Sexualis* (1886) in the back of adult magazines. Likewise, features in those magazines often—like some genres of exploitation cinema—employed an investigative mode of narration that blurred distinctions between fact and fiction, education and titillation. Reportage on the activities of the sexual underground was frequently printed alongside "candid" interviews with subjects about their sexual preferences, reviews of the latest "blue movies," features on current scientific sex research, and articles by eminent sex therapists. In all of these forums, the particularities of female orgasms were repeatedly scrutinized and debated, while male orgasms appeared too commonsensical, readily obtained, and nuance-free to merit detailed discussion or debate. Hence, the proliferating discourses of sexual modernity feeding into Franco's films were preoccupied with what women want, how they might get it, what it feels like when they do, what contribution—if any—men might make to it, and what its consequences for male prowess might be. In this context, it is no coincidence that the hyperbolic terms with which enthusiasts are prone to describe Franco's work—a quasi-surrealist lexicon of transgression, delirium, excess, and convulsiveness—recall the terminology often used by the discourses of sexual modernity to describe female pleasures and orgasms.

Many of Franco's films concern unruly women characters who appear to emblematize liberatory and feminist conceptions of the right to experience orgasms outside marriage and procreation. While male homosexuality is conspicuous by its near absence, the action tends to center on lesbians, female prostitutes and striptease artistes, unwed *haute bourgeois* orgiasts, and perverted loners—figures, that is, who in different ways transgress the bounds of sexual normativity. When married couples are represented, they tend to be socially elite, dissipated sexual epicureans who exploit tender flesh in search of fresh thrills. In Franco's several versions of Sade's *Philosophy in the Bedroom* (1795), for instance, upper-class couples enslave virginal debutantes as playthings for frequently fatal games. In *How to Seduce a Virgin*, Alice Arno purrs that her husband's kinky plan for abusing the childlike Lina Romay "turns [her] on." *La Comtesse perverse* (*Countess Perverse*, 1973) similarly concerns the taste of a pair of wealthy voluptuaries (Alice Arno and Howard Vernon) for hunting, torturing, and cannibalizing ingenues. Recognizing that continually seeking what Vernon calls "the pleasures of the flesh" spirals into ever greater depths of depravity, their associate (Robert Woods) acts as the film's avatar of morality and proclaims disgust at their "vile orgies." As Pavlović points out, such gendered transgressivity potentially subverted the conservatism of General Francisco Franco's Fascist regime and the Catholic Church in the Spain of the 1960s and early 1970s (118). Yet the terms in which transgressivity is signified often involve more reactionary impulses, bearing out Peter Hutchings's remark that Gothic cinema is simultaneously appalled and enthralled by its own projections of female sexuality (90). For example, as I argue below, Franco's representations of female pleasure—or rather, women's orgasms and quest for them—mobilize sexological stereotypes of nymphomania, frigidity, and lesbianism in ways that oscillate between excitement and discomfort about the impact of sexual modernity on marriage and heterosexual monogamy.

In this cultural moment, filmic representations of sex—French, German, Italian, and Scandinavian adult films were especially praised for articulating the contemporary sexual zeitgeist—were often promoted through what Michel Foucault would later call the repressive hypothesis. Erotic films were championed in some quarters as possible vehicles for knowledge, freedom, and tolerance, and as foils to the hypocrisy and obfuscation of previous generations. As one soft-core men's magazine narcissistically remarked in the 1970s, thanks to the combined forces of recent sex research, oral contraception, and relaxations of censorship, repression had finally given way to a "joyous feeling of complete freedom to experiment" (Steiner 64). Foucault's critique of the repressive hypothesis may be too pessimistic; for example, whatever its shortcomings, the field of sexology arguably made previously excluded sexualities visible while implicitly destabilizing the concept of a universal sexual norm. Nevertheless, Foucault usefully cautions against assuming that the "incitement to discourse" about sex unproblematically frees desire from institutionalized power. According to Foucault, the modern imperative to "speak about sex" or disclose your "sex life" continually threatens not to emancipate subjects but to entwine them in taxonomies of "bodies and pleasures" that produce ever-expanding categories of sexual practice and identity. The proliferation of sexual discourse since the mid–nineteenth century spawned a heterogeneous "dispersion of sexualities . . . [an] implantation of 'perversions'" (37) that, while often promoting tolerance, also propagated multiple strategies for organizing people and their pleasures into measurable, commodifiable, and regulatable objects of knowledge.

If exploitation cinema can be seen as an instance of this discursive multiplication, examples of the sexual "types" populating Franco's output include the prostitute, the nymphomaniac, the frigid wife, and the impotent husband. Foucault identifies the central figures produced by disciplinary sex discourse as the masturbating child, the responsible married couple (Foucault calls them the Malthusian couple), the sexual deviant whose behavior is "annexed to mental illness" (including "the impotent, sadistic, perverse husband"), and the "hysterical woman" (a category that can include "the nervous woman, the frigid wife, the indifferent mother . . . or neurasthenic girl" [105]) whose body is "thoroughly saturated with sexuality" (104). These discursive constructions abound in Franco's work, and I will have more to say about perverts, impotent men, and nervous women later. The "masturbating child" motif, meanwhile, is primarily manifested in Franco's numerous, sometimes ephebophilic, images of autoerotic young women. At a time when female orgasm was something of a cultural preoccupation, this motif was replete with tropes ranging from the piquancy of youthful female sexual "innocence" (and its loss) for the patriarchal imaginary to the frighteningly "oversexed" woman; in any case, scenes of female masturbation appealed to male curiosity about how women pleasure themselves in the absence of men and about anatomical and affective differences with regard to sexual stimulation and orgasm.

Foucault does not write about films, but the staging and framing of bodies in adult cinema of the period participated, as Linda Williams demonstrates, in the ideological complexities of putting sex into discourse. On the one hand, arguably by the very nature of fantasy, it challenges censorship and transgresses prohibitions; on the other hand, it classifies and measures bodies through a visual apparatus that claims to record and observe libidinal truths, especially "visual 'knowledge' of women's pleasure" (Williams, *Hardcore* x). As Seymour Fisher concluded in his *Understanding the Female Orgasm*, "our understanding of female sexuality remains at an elementary stage. Many more studies will have to be carried out before we accumulate a wide range of dependable knowledge concerning the nature of the female sexual experience" (212). Gothic fantasy, hard-core pornography, sexploitation, and hard-to-categorize Franco films alike offer their own take on such studies, their entangled investments in "knowledge," pleasure, and spectacle partaking of cultural interest in the old "question" of "where to locate and how to portray a woman's pleasure" (Williams, *Screening Sex* 156). Perhaps partly because signs of female engorgement and climax tend to be deemed less obviously eye-catching than those of the virile male, and partly because the female orgasm seems (at least for the benefit of sexually illiterate men) easy to simulate, female pleasure remained during Franco's most productive years a fascinating and lucrative enigma. In both sexological and cinematic discourse, women seemed to feel more: compulsive or monotonous close-ups on the agitated bodies and faces of women characters in the throes of orgasm and/or pain seem transfixed by the idea that women experience a level of sexual intensity unavailable to men. We might speculate on this basis that Franco's "hysterized," beautifully convulsive female bodies are projections of dominant masculinity's own desired (but emasculating, feminizing, and therefore unacceptably queer) "sexual saturation."

Female Vampire, for example, ruminates at leisure on the attractions and risks of female desire for patriarchy, and devotes much screen time to the camera's lingering around, roving over, and fixing on the crotch of the vampire Countess Irina Karlstein (Lina Romay). Combining the demand for sexploitation spectacle with the theme of the living dead's corporeal/spectral liminality, Franco's camera zooms in and out of the vampire's pubic area, which fills the screen prior to each "kill." In the film's credit sequence, Romay, naked except for an open cloak, thigh-high boots and a wide leather belt, walks toward the camera through a mist-shrouded forest, moving in and out of focus as the camera drifts between tight close-ups and full-length shots of her body. The camera halts, moves forward then withdraws as Romay advances, before zooming slowly into her darkly shadowed groin. The game of push and pull between Franco's camera and Romay's body visualizes the theme of seduction and desire: clarity and indistinctness, distance and proximity, approaching and receding, corporeality and otherworldliness, revelation and concealment play off against each other. Popular Freudianism is, of course, worn on the lace sleeve of a film that barely sublimates inquisitiveness about what lies between a woman's legs. Seeking knowledge of women's secret and solitary pleasures, later scenes replace the first hazy images of Romay emerging from the mist, and of the tenebrous region below her belt, with the more explicitly inquisitive "staring" and "peering" of Franco's camera at the vampire interminably masturbating.

According to Foucault, the strategies of midcentury sex discourse included a "psychiatrization of perverse pleasure" and a "responsibilization" of sex that constructed a standard of normality from which to define some libidinal conduct as irregular (105). Kinsey's *Sexual Behavior in the Human Female* of 1953, for instance, claimed to "contribute to an ultimate adjustment" between human sexuality and "the needs of the total social organization" (10), and from a Foucauldian perspective this notion of adjustment serves to model a sexuality "that is economically useful and politically conservative" (Foucault 37). On this basis, Foucault argues that the repressive hypothesis sustains distinctions between "normality" and "deviance"; nonprocreative and "fruitless pleasures" (36) such as masturbation, fetishism, homosexuality, and nongenital sex were defined as objects of inquiry that departed from normal sexual development. Since, as Ken Gelder puts it in his analysis of the filmic vampire, we can therefore "only comprehend 'deviancy' through the discourses of 'normal[ity]'" (58), the transgressive activities of characters like Irina may be read as an "implantation of perversions" in Foucault's sense. The "difference" of women's sexuality—as implanted in the 1960s and '70s through such tropes as female insatiability, the multiplicity of women's erogenous zones, and the apparently momentous "discovery" (or new elevation) of the clitoris—is projected as transgressive to the extent that it diverges from heteronormative masculinity's notional discipline and containment.

Female Vampire's first lethal encounter shows Irina apparently fellating her anonymous victim (Roger Germanes) to death. Why this blow would be lethal is less than clear: the action is shot from behind the victim's back, and no blood appears to be spilled. One of the physicians in the film, Dr. Roberts (a cameo by Franco), barely solves the mystery by later explaining that Irina's victim "was bitten, in the middle of an orgasm, and the vampire sucked his semen and his life away." On one level, the image of orgasmic death in the female vampire's clutches mythologizes the period of postejaculation fatigue in which most men are unable to achieve another erection; as many pre-nineteenth-century antimasturbation tracts proposed, this discharge of liquid "energies" temporarily "feminized" the male by making him docile and immobile. The scene also, of course, chimes with archetypal "fantasies of castration and devoration" stirred when patriarchy attempts to comprehend women's sexual "difference" (Fredric Jameson, qtd. in Gelder: 42), and reflects the "deep-seated Victorian unease about womanhood" that Robin Wood finds in most contemporary adaptations of *Dracula* (366). Elaine Showalter has argued along similar lines that fin-de-siècle and early twentieth-century representations of vamps, vampires, and femmes fatales represented patriarchy's shudder at the "sexual anarchy" threatened by feminist intellectuals and unmarried New Women, and many vampire films of the 1960s and '70s followed suit by understanding women's sexual agency as debilitating for men. In this respect, *Female Vampire* highlights the strangeness of female desire—and of lesbianism in particular—for the heteronormative imagination.

Franco's literal approach to the deep-rooted symbolic connection between sexual desire and vampirism may have gained an extra frisson of transgressivity from the fact that, although oral sex was becoming popularized in hard-core pornography, it was still a somewhat exotic "kink." That it continued to be regarded suspiciously as a tempting but basically aberrant diversion is illustrated by the fact that Paul Ableman's 1969 book

The Mouth—billed as "the first comprehensive survey of orality"—was the subject of (unsuccessful) obscenity trials in Britain and America. Oral-genital stimulation had rarely been entirely taboo, but it had been a marginalized proclivity, not least because of the problem of hygiene. Earlier in the century, the sexologist Theodore Hendrik van de Velde had cautiously advocated this sort of intimacy as part of the "Holy Ground" of "ideal marriage"; cunnilingus was a delectable remedy for "lack of local secretion" in "inexperienced women," but indulging in it without progressing to intravaginal climax could open the "Hell-gate of the Realm of Sexual Perversion" because it was an affront to biological destiny and lacked the deep emotional connection that took place during penetrative sex in responsible, loving marriages (Van de Velde 127–29). Fellatio was even riskier. Because its lewdness compromised "woman's instinctive modesty," it could only be welcomed into the connubial bed on the proviso that one's wife retained her "dignity and sweetness" in the process (Van de Velde is vague, but it seems she must not bring the man to orgasm) (129). Read against this discursive context, Irina's far from dignified or modest draining of her victim's life, and his irresponsible succumbing to it, encapsulates the characteristic ambivalence of Gothic sexploitation's implantation of perversions: while the spectacle of vampiric fellatio might be said to subvert the enduring puritanism still lingering subconsciously around some erotic activities (while accommodating post–*Deep Throat* [1972] pornographic tropes), it also articulates puritan dread by demonizing sexualities outside the approved trajectory of courtship, marriage, and procreative sex.

Thus, antiquated beliefs about the degenerate effects of "self-pollution" contaminate Franco's depictions of "the pleasures of the flesh." The fantasy of fatal fellatio has some roots in the mystification of the life-giving nature of semen and the attendant vilification of onanism (defined as any, not only masturbatory, "waste" of sperm) as sinful. Dijkstra notes that the femmes fatales of fin-de-siècle fiction gorged themselves on the male "brain, that 'great clot of genital fluid'" (212), and Klaus Theweleit describes the male nightmare that "the sexualized woman would become an erotomaniacal monster who was out to suck the marrow from men's bones" (349), a superstition iterated when Dr. Roberts declares that Irina feeds herself on male "hormones." The eighteenth-century antimasturbation campaigner Samuel-August Tissot proposed that bodies functioned through a hierarchy of humors, with semen at the pinnacle and blood a close second (Stengers and Van Neck 68). In light of such beliefs about onanism, the Freudian psychoanalyst Ernest Jones's theory that in vampire fictions blood and semen are analogous, and his deduction that the vampire's erotic yet frightening bedtime visits represent adolescent male concerns about wet dreams, makes sense (Twitchell 58). But whether the associated substance is bone marrow, blood, or a more metaphysical force, *Female Vampire*'s equation between the enervating oral extraction of semen and the extinction of life is shot through with archaic superstitions about man's exclusively vital "essence." Seminal continence was crucial to the preservation of male fortitude; as Theweleit argues in an echo of Kristevan theories of abjection, fantasies about female lubricity help men to guard themselves against "the 'streaming' of their own desire" (xvi), thereby assuring dominant masculinity of its own robustness. Yet defenses against nonprocreative spillage were inevitably ambiguous. While medico-religious discourses presented surplus and improper discharge as catastrophic for masculine vigor, fantasy figures like the bewitching bloodsucker intensified the appeal of transgressing the interdiction.

Female Vampire's interest in generative and nongenerative liquids continues when, accompanied on the soundtrack by sinister, warped bird sounds reminiscent of those used in Hitchcock's *The Birds* (1963), Irina pays a nocturnal visit to the journalist Anna (Anna Watican). At first terrified by the sight of Irina licking her lips and masturbating at the end of her bed, Anna suddenly relents, and the scene proceeds in a flurry of close-ups of teeth on nipples. Before we have a chance to dwell on how vampiric sucking and biting seems a queering of breast-feeding (Gelder 51), cunnilingus takes center stage while throbbing "porn" music takes over the score. The music stops when Anna, like the film's first male victim, appears to die in orgasm. Without entering into a discussion of the relationship between Eros and Thanatos or the surrealist mystification of *jouissance*, paroxysms of orgasmic death are common in Franco's films (the mesmerizing/monotonous, vagina-centric *Shining Sex* is, for example, practically a paean to the theme). Irina's slurps and sighs are noisily audible as she continues lapping urgently between the inert journalist's thighs; a far cry from the hedonistic, pornotopian image of emancipatory orgasms-for-all, this lugubrious scene imagines sex as deadly masturbation. Although oft-reproduced publicity shots for the film show blood dripping from Irina's mouth, we, in fact, see vaginal fluid around her lips and chin; the chain of associations between this "fruitless" secretion, cunnilingus, clitoral orgasm, lesbianism, and death offers a heady brew of heteronormative fantasies. Lest Irina's uncanny unquenchability and the fluid around her mouth suggest fabulous abundance, the scene's necrophiliac implications remind us that lesbianism and orgasms without men are pitifully barren exercises.

To invoke another figure typically deployed in the contemporary medical and psychiatric discourse of "perversion," the female vampire is a nymphomaniac. In his *Sexual Deviations in the Female* (1957), Louis S. London recounted the case of an "oversexed" woman whose "compulsion" led her to fellate dozens of men per year, and whose oral fixation was so extreme that she would bite men on the shoulders and neck until they bled. London names her condition "vampirism" (Ellis and Sagarin 88). It is unnecessary here to unravel the contradictory definitions of the term "nymphomania" and its sometimes confusing links to discursive constructions of the "oversexed," the "promiscuous," the "hypersexual," the "maladjusted," the "nonorgasmic," and the "frigid" woman. Suffice to say that, however its symptoms or etiology were understood, nymphomania was defined as an uncontrolled, morbid sexual compulsion that caused women to debase themselves by repeatedly engaging in degrading intercourse with any number of sexual conquests. In his introduction to Victoria Morhaim's *Casebook: Nymphomania* (1964), Albert Ellis reminds the reader that only a few nymphomaniacs had an inherited "hormonal or brain disorder": most of their suffering was based on low self-esteem, which led them to seek validation through sex (qtd. in Morhaim: 8–9). In their 1968 tome

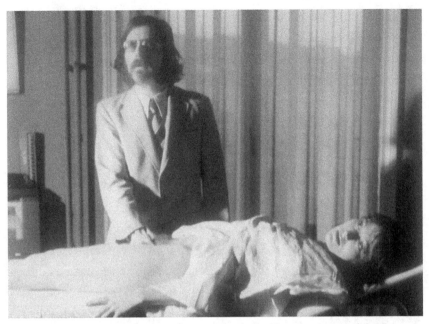

Dr. Orloff (Jean-Pierre Bouyxou) examines the half-nude corpse of the Princess de Rochefort (Monica Swinn), one of a number of women killed midorgasm by the title character in *Female Vampire*. (Eurociné and Général Films. Courtesy of Photofest.)

Nymphomania: A Study of the Oversexed Female, Ellis and Edward Sagarin elaborate on how these pathetic, self-loathing souls are compelled by "irrational ideas such as the dire need to be loved and the need to conquer other human beings" (137), but—much as Irina slurps unquenchably at what might as well be a corpse (the journalist has merely been vampirized)—the nymphomaniac's quest for orgasm is doomed or leads to suffering. Evidently incredulous toward the possibility that women might have better orgasms when men got out of the way, many sex therapists insisted that these hypersexual but maladjusted and unwed women "rarely or never receive orgasmic release" and were "inclined toward lesbianism" (Ellis, qtd. in Morhaim: 8–9). Lacking the true "release" possible in monogamous relations, nymphomania was a miserable affair—hence Franco's protracted shots of the tragic Irina masturbating in gloomy isolation to the strains of

Daniel White's doleful score. In *Vampyros Lesbos*, Agra (Heidrun Kussin) is similarly "oversexed" yet starved of orgasm; hysterized and sexually "saturated," Agra is incarcerated in an asylum after having been seduced but not "completed" by that film's lesbian vampire. Unable to attain or consummate vampiric transformation—which would in any case leave her an unsated parasite—Agra is left thrashing in her cell in frenzied frustration.

Clitoral pleasures had, like oral sex, long posed a problem for patriarchy's definitions of femininity. For instance, many moralists of the seventeenth century regarded the clitoris as the "seat of sin," knowledge of which could only lead to lamentable overindulgence. Clitoral orgasm was scandalous for two related reasons: it seemed recreational rather than procreative, and the phallus was at best peripheral to it. Despite Foucault's skepticism about sexology, the science and pseudoscience of sex evidenced what women had probably known, but patriarchy had suppressed, all along: that their orgasms could only very rarely be reached through the friction of penetrative intercourse alone. Kinsey's studies demonstrated that while men's peccadilloes were intriguing, neither their sexual equipment nor their orgasms were as complicated or, therefore, as worthy of research as those of women. Kinsey established not only that women (purportedly unlike most men) use a wide variety of masturbation techniques but that since the interior walls of most vaginas are bereft of nerve endings, those solo pleasures overwhelmingly focused not on vaginal insertion but on the clitoris and the labia minora (192), therefore proving that the "importance of male genitalia in coitus" was nothing more than a male "conceit" (162). Following Kinsey's lead, William Masters and Virginia Johnson's *Human Sexual Response* (1966) documented differences between the sexual responses (and responsiveness) of male and female subjects and confirmed Kinsey's "discoveries" about vaginal orgasms being based on direct or indirect stimulation of the clitoral area. Given the anatomical redundancy of penetration where arousal and climax were concerned, the consequences of the female orgasm for men and women's sexual behavior were, by the mid-1960s, debated in countless publications. Liberal-minded mass-market tracts and manuals, such as Inge and Sten Hegeler's *An ABZ of Love* (1963) and Mette Ejlersen's *I Accuse!* (1969) agreed that vaginal orgasm was a phallocentric fiction, and feminist critics like Barbara Seaman, Anne Koedt, and Mary Jane Sherfey celebrated women's uniquely "prolonged plateau of orgasmic experiences" (Escoffier 68).

Patriarchy had for some time been, as Williams puts it, "perplexed to find the female seat of pleasure so disconnected from the organs of reproduction" (*Screening Sex* 156). Being the only organ with the sole function of providing enjoyment, and being largely independent of men's penile exertions, the clitoris threatened to distract women from the propriety and gentleness demanded by marriage and motherhood. Among other neurotic patriarchal reactions to this threat, the organ was either shrouded behind stereotypes of feminine mystery and mildness or demonized as a site of women's many and varied sexual pathologies—a suppression perpetuated when Freudians condoned the clitoris as an instrument of foreplay but demoted it to a mere way station on the road to coital satisfaction. Since clitoral stimulation was regarded only as an entree to penetration, loitering in that department constituted for both partners an adolescent, perverse delay, as extraneous to mature sexuality as were masturbation, frottage, and the use of dildos, all of which were widely thought to estrange rather than enhance conjugal relations. Thus, patriarchy did not so much rule out female sexual gratification as try to adapt it to the supposed needs of the Malthusian couple by encouraging a degree of erotic experimentation as an aid to marital harmony. In his 1903 book *Sex and Character*, Otto Weininger warned men that, since "sexual excitement" was "the supreme moment" of a woman's life, their spouses were likely to be voluptuously preoccupied with intercourse. According to Weininger, the sex drives of husbands and wives differed from each other in as much as the former, but not the latter, needed to occupy themselves with useful work or intellectually stimulating interests other than sex ("Sex and Character" 25). Unlike women, and unlike the victims of vampiric seduction, healthy men can fairly quickly regain mental strength after their efficient ejaculation and moment of post-coital *tristesse*, and move on to other, less time-wasting, activities. Hence men can and should perform their marital duties purposefully but with a minimum of fuss or useless expenditure because while "man possesses sexual organs . . . woman's sexual organs possess her" (qtd. in Bland: 13). In these circumstances, if only to protect their marriage, sexually "saturated" women had to be steadied by the purposeful hand of their husband or therapist.

Vampyros Lesbos embodies the contradictions in heteronormativity's fascination with its own constructions of women's sensuality. The film declares its modernity in many ways. The "groovy" Hammond organ and sitar-drenched soundtrack; angular montage sequences; sets consisting of minimalist decor in modernist homes; updating of Stoker's Dracula tale (including the central gender reversal and moving of the story to the modern-day Mediterranean); use of a sans-serif, non-Gothic font for the credits; seventies fashion (particularly Linda's lilac trouser-suit and Nadine's sunglasses and bikini): these and other features proclaim the film's contemporaneity. Moreover, the film's central couple, the betrothed Linda Westinghouse (Ewa Strömberg) and Omar (Andrea Montchal, billed as Viktor Feldmann), appear to be aspiring members of the swinging society and thus of an expanded conception of "normal" relationships. They have premarital sex and watch gothico-erotic, lesbian-themed nightclub acts together, and Linda visits a psychotherapist to discuss her sexual problems. But for all their seemingly burgeoning advancedness, Linda and Omar are, and *Vampyros Lesbos* itself is, a battleground between new sexual ideals and residual ideologies of pleasure. Indeed, the surface modernity of *Vampyros Lesbos* locates the film's fantastic subject matter within then-topical concerns over what were still often seen as the "social problems" of permissiveness/licentiousness and female freedom/promiscuity.

With marriage, monogamy, and motherhood (and, therefore, social stability) apparently at stake, contemporary popular culture often dealt with the challenges of premarital sex, divorce, swinging, and open relationships by investigating their effects on attractive, professional young couples like Linda and Omar. The crux of the issue was, of course, the dangerous effects of women's pleasures and demands on male stature. In his reactionary 1966 book *Maladjusted Female*, Dr. A. Joseph Bursteln claimed that having "won equality with men . . . the modern female is now out to capture the male's most cherished bastion: the prerogative to pursue the sex partner. . . . The male's traditional role in lovemaking is changing—much to his disadvantage" (120). In 1969, the ironically titled *New Man* magazine reported that gynecologists and psychiatrists at the American Medical Association convention in New York City had agreed that as a result of the introduction of the contraceptive pill, "hot-blooded" women had become "aggressive partners in marital relations," with the result that man was "no longer master of his house," a situation that had worsened rather than alleviated his sexual frustrations and left him struggling to understand and satisfy the "forces which her new-found sexual freedom has unleashed" in his wife (Boulton 18–19). Such texts were typical of a hegemonic masculinity that saw itself as besieged by sexual modernity and found in women's "unleashed" desires the threat of emasculation.

Marriage could, however, be saved. A typically "concerned" feature in one British magazine of 1969 reassured readers that although some fashionable "'permissives'" initially find conventional matrimony outmoded, most ultimately keep "love, moral values, religion" alive by getting married (Cooper 13). *Vampyros Lesbos* in some ways follows a similar path. In many respects, the film adheres to the convention of projecting "other" desires as a menace to the status quo. Some sense of otherness is, of course, inherent to any presentation of entrancing exoticism, disgusting monstrosity, or, in the case of Gothic sexology, both. Hence Linda is a sexually curious career woman disconcerted by her attraction to the enticing vampire/erotic dancer Countess Nadine Carody (Soledad Miranda). Echoing the narrative trope of the psychoanalytic and sexological case history, as well as what Foucault names the "obligation to confess" (60), she nervously informs Dr. Steiner (Paul Muller) that she has been having "strange," arousing dreams about Nadine, and admits that "more than once I've reached orgasm" independently of her fiancé's presumably lackluster attentions.

According to the mainstream of mid-twentieth-century sex therapy, the key to successful monogamous relationships was, as Weininger and Van de Velde had argued decades earlier, to absorb sexual modernity into tradition, with simultaneous orgasm bridging what Foucault termed the "responsibilization" of sex and the "new ideal of eroticised marriage" (Robb 103). While many therapists continued to stress the hitherto inattentive husband's role in directing his restive wife to "correct" intercourse—a part Omar seems unable to play—mutual climax became the standard to which all must aspire. Eustace Chesser's *Love without Fear* (1941), for example, assured readers that attaining it would help keep alienating, unhealthy temptations (such as, we might add, lesbian-themed vampire nightclub acts) out of relationships. It has been argued that presenting mutual—and seemingly compulsory—orgasm as a condition of conjugal health increased the performance anxiety of sexual subjects, who now felt compelled to measure their pleasures against a supposedly universal orgasmic ideal (McLaren 62). For its part, *Vampyros Lesbos* suggests that, while the situation was frustrating for women, men like Omar—apparently facing permissive woman's dethroning of the phallus—were hardest hit by the fear of inadequacy, at least in the short term. As several critics (Dyer, Creed, Zimmerman, Auerbach) have pointed out, female/lesbian vampire narratives iterate heteronormative men's dread of women being stolen away from them, but they also play to phallocentric confusion over the titillating prospect that women might willfully act on desires no phallus can satisfy. Whether we are to read Omar as impotent, phallocentric, uneducated about the clitoris, or simply lazy is as perhaps as moot a point as whether Linda should be read as the "frigid wife" type or as an autonomous sexual adventurer. Whatever the case, Linda's disclosure reverberates with the sexual disquiet of the period.

More than a trace of such anxious gender mythology is worked into Franco's sometimes reflexive representations of "disadvantaged," diminished, and bewildered male characters, many of whom self-consciously ponder, or in some cases clinically investigate, maladjusted/liberated female sexuality. Hence in *Vampyros Lesbos* the chagrined Omar casts suspicious sideways glances in Linda's direction as she enjoys the spectacle of an onstage vampire-lesbian striptease (her eyes widen and she bites her moist bottom lip as she watches the show). In the same film, the vampire's impassive male servant, Morpho (José Martínez Blanco), mutely observes his mistress's antics from a distance. Nina Auerbach has noted the tendency of filmic female vampires to "spring to life only under men's eyes" (53); thus *Vampyros Lesbos*'s cutaways to Morpho's dispassionate stare or to Omar's anxious, envious regard are part of the film's attempts to contain or restrain the "excessive," delirious pleasures that it has imagined as women's unique domain. Yet these defense mechanisms are neither complete nor wholly successful attempts to restore masculinity to its heteronormative throne. Morpho, Omar, and other intradiegetic male onlookers are distanced from the very unattainable desires about which they fantasize. Like sexologists of the period, they find female pleasures and orgasms perplexing, but are equally unable to coherently answer the question: What do men want?

If feminist critics and some progressive marriage counselors demanded that hetero-patriarchy discard its stereotypes about women's sexual appetites, not all of those stereotypes were easy to dislodge. Although they came at it, so to speak, from different angles, therapists, feminist critics, and sexploitation filmmakers often concurred in presenting clitoral orgasm as an inordinate, delirious energy that upset dominant gender codes. While some thinkers, notably Wilhelm Reich and Herbert Marcuse, feted the countercultural, liberating possibilities of nonproductive orgasms, many feminist critics of the 1960s specifically reclaimed the sexually saturated or "possessed" female body from heteronormative sexological discourse by elevating the clitoris as a totem of self-sufficient female agency. Encouraged by the potential of the pill and permissiveness, but risking an anatomical reductivism that enshrined some pleasures at the expense of others, many feminists celebrated the fact that, in Sherfey's words, a woman could "go on having orgasms indefinitely if physical exhaustion did not intervene" (91). As David Ley puts it, the notion of "insatiability" can be used in "awe, fear, celebration, and condemnation of female sexual capacity" (47). Unsatisfiable demands can be imagined through fantasies of constant availability or of male inadequacy, but Franco's Gothic sexology repeatedly demonstrates that just as fears and desires are often inextricably entwined in the psyche, the notion of women's endlessly orgasmic capacity is readily appropriated by reactionary as well as radical agendas, and back again. For example, Sherfey's reference to physical fatigue as the only hindrance to limitless "plateaus" not only foreshadowed scenes of death-by-clitoral-orgasm in films like *Shining Sex* and *Female Vampire* but also unintentionally echoed the sexologist Richard von Krafft-Ebing, who related the awful fate of a nymphomaniac who, upon being "seized with an unlimited desire for sexual gratification," suffered "death from exhaustion within a few days" (Ellis and Sagarin 74).

Unlike Omar, Steiner seems to have moved with the times. Perhaps because he, or rather Franco, is losing faith in clinical orthodoxy (the film comically suggests as much when we see Steiner doodling distractedly in his notepad while Linda relates her woes), he does not advise Linda to consult sex manuals or to work with Omar on a solution to the problem in preparation for marriage. His wise counsel instead comes in the wake of Reich, Masters and Johnson, Sherfey, and Ejlersen: "You mustn't think your problem is unique. Many women are sexually frustrated. Let me tell you the best cure. Find yourself a lover . . . a better lover." That better lover is, of course, the vampire countess. A complex (and rather self-contradictory) combination of Steiner's advice, her own adventurousness, her innate sexuality, her sexual dissatisfaction, and the countess's uncanny lure leads Linda into the vampire's arms. The agency of desire is often uncertain in Franco's films: many characters act on the sexual bidding of others, sometimes through the medium of mind control, sometimes through simple coercion; nymphomaniacs and "sex-crazed" women may appear autonomous, but desperation often leads them to compliance. Meanwhile, women like Linda may "roam" thanks to the inadequacy of their male partners or their seduction by lesbianism, feminism, and new-fangled erotic experimentation. Relationships between the emotions and the body, desire and free will, are undecided. Yet, depending on one's perspective, and despite the ineptitude of all the male characters in the film, *Vampyros Lesbos* surreptitiously reinserts the phallus as the norm against which the lesbian turns (McClintock 8). Krafft-Ebing, for example, observed in 1886 that lesbians often have perverted or "impotent husbands who can only sexually excite, but not satisfy" their "constitutional hypersexuality" or "cure" their frigidity (46). Thus when *Vampyros Lesbos* suggests that Linda's desire for, and willing seduction by, a more satisfying female partner is driven by disappointment with Omar, it adheres to the belief that most lesbians are thwarted or confused heterosexuals, likely suffering from "nymphomania" and/or "frigidity."

The signified of the term "frigidity" has always been elusive. In some instances, the "frigid," "unresponsive," "inhibited," or "anorgasmic" woman was one who failed to climax with men. In other cases, frigidity referred to a woman's inability to relax enough for vaginal penetration to take place. In others still, it was said to occur when either fear of or a misguided faith in vaginal penetration and orgasm led women to refuse clitoral manipulation. Regardless of the definition, the supposed condition was usually thought symptomatic of psychological flaws or "maladjustment," although for the feminist critic Anne Koedt a diagnosis of frigidity simply meant that the client was not "stimulated sufficiently" by the sexual positions prescribed by die-hard phallocrats (100–101). Either way, files from the sexologist's nymphomania casebook invariably told titillating yet moralizing tales of young women whose sexual neediness put them in harm's way and plunged them into moral ruin. Concerns about the debasement of this fallen woman were almost always classed. The nymphomaniac usually had a bourgeois family background. Bursteln warns of the "well-bred girl, carefully dressed, clean and immaculate," who cannot resist "intercourse with some dirty vagrant" (31), while Krafft-Ebing describes tragic cases of "modest and decent" women who descend into a succession of self-destructive sexual encounters (qtd. in Ellis and Sagarin: 74). In different ways, shades of this narrative trope cross-hatch films like *Vampyros Lesbos*, with Linda as the smartly dressed middle-class young woman too easily tempted into treacherous sexual waters.

Exemplifying Franco's recycling of this well-worn theme, *Sinner: The Secret Diary of a Nymphomaniac* traces the tragic sexual history of Linda Vargas (Montserrat Prous), a young woman described by her exploitative older lover, the Countess Anna de Monterey (Anne Libert), as being of "refined breeding." After the fashion of many a "sexual awakening" narrative, the countess explains in voice-over that, having never "responded . . . each time a man entered her" (in classic psychotherapeutic style this unresponsiveness is traced in flashback to a traumatic early sexual encounter), the "naive," childlike Linda learns the "pleasures of physical love" under her tutelage and blossoms into a promiscuous and therefore predatory bisexual woman, using discos and jazz clubs as her hunting ground. *Sinner* is organized around a series of increasingly dissolute sexual encounters that inevitably spiral into Linda's drug addiction and, finally, suicide. Like a page ripped from any paperback "study of the oversexed female," Linda's actions are driven by her "maladjusted" self-disgust: she confesses in her diary that she uses sex as a weapon against men and that this is her only escape from the fact that "everything else is meaningless and dead."

In *Vampyros Lesbos*, Linda Westinghouse not dissimilarly leaves "normality" behind and embarks (to borrow the subtitle of another of Franco's films) on a "journey into perversion." As the effete Dr. Seward (Dennis Price) remarks, Linda very nearly crosses the threshold to "their world." Dramatic tension comes from the ineffectual Omar's attempts to rescue Linda, and from Linda's struggles with her own conflicted desires. In the lesbian vampire subgenre of the period, men typically resolve to kill the fanged seductress, thereby suppressing the egregious forces she has unleashed and reinstating normative equilibrium; in *Vampyros Lesbos*, several rather unconvincing representatives of patriarchal law struggle to understand, contain, and suppress her "strange desires." But it is Linda herself who overcomes those mysterious yearnings and destroys Nadine. Despite its signifiers of closure, the denouement encapsulates the film's ambivalence. Perhaps regretting his faltering attempts to be a sexual modernist (attending the lesbian vampire show was probably Linda's idea), the cuckolded Omar arrives typically late to the scene, but has presumably learned his lesson about the perils of woman's "new-found sexual freedom." He is relieved by Linda's victory over Nadine, but Linda seems less than elated by it, or by her reunion with Omar.

Linda (Ewa Strömberg) is tempted to leave "normality" behind and embark on a "journey into perversion" with the alluring Countess Nadine Carody (Soledad Miranda) in *Vampyros Lesbos*. (Fénix Film, CCC Filmkunst, and Tele-Cine Film- und Fernsehproduktion. Courtesy of Photofest.)

In one version of the film, *Vampyros Lesbos* highlights its ludic approach to the staples of vampire fiction by showing Nadine and Linda throwing off their bikinis and sunbathing by, and skinny dipping in, the Black Sea. Briefly reminiscent of naturist images of wholesome nakedness, this scene is quite unusual for a Franco film, in that it also provides a euphoric image of liberated desire that not only appears to envision feminist and lesbian emancipation but buys into sexual modernity's repressive hypothesis. The sun shines, the score is up-tempo, the camera is mobile, and the characters' joyful gamboling suggests that independence from men and marriage is both natural and a route to contentment. Given that she has been released from her everyday sexual discontent, Linda's remark to Nadine, "it's a long time since I sunbathed," suggests pleasures beyond tanning: the carefree scene seems evocative of nonphallic bliss. The fact that this scene does

Transgressive or Maladjusted? **163**

not exist in the gloomier Spanish version of the film, *Las vampiras*—cut presumably because Linda's apparent embrace of homosexuality was unacceptable to the Spanish censor—perhaps underlines the possibility that the scene's bright and breezy eroticism allegorizes escape from phallocracy. Female orgasm may be Franco's chief signifier of delirium and excess, yet his (or the subgenre's) ambivalence with regard to transgressive desire and to contemporary "permissiveness" is such that these moments can only be short-lived. Hence the beach scene may momentarily associate Sapphic love with nature, health, and happiness, but the film finds it necessary to include many reminders of the sinister aspects of lesbian seduction. Recalling the account of nymphomaniacs as women who confuse love with conquest, the film is peppered with foreboding visual metaphors for predation and entrapment, among them butterflies caught in nets and crash zooms into scorpions' tails, which both remind us that this is a cautionary tale and suggest that Linda is after all led astray rather than "naturally" prone to what Krafft-Ebing would call congenital sexual inversion.

In the often fatalistic world of Franco's Gothic sexploitation, desire is frequently a matter of enslavement rather than release, and even his images of orgasm seldom dispel the films' enervated, disconsolate ambience. So it is that, in common with the majority of Franco's pessimistic, even porno-dystopian, sex dramas of the period, Linda's temporary escape from Malthusian coupledom to Sherfey's endless plateaus of useless orgasmic expenditure merely leads her into another snare. Tensions like these clearly accord with both the psychosexual complexes of Gothic fantasy and the generally erratic texture of Franco's work at this prolific point in his career, but I have tried to argue that they are also consonant with the cultural tensions present in the intertextual discourses of sexual modernity. By, among many other maneuvers, presenting protagonists like Linda Westinghouse and Linda Vargas simultaneously as modern, permissive women and as maladjusted victims of nymphomania, Franco's figuring of notional female delirium and excess often approaches the fraught discourse of sexual modernity through archaic mythologies. Mediating aspects of the nominal sexual revolution and its radical hedonism as they disseminate into the 1970s, many of Franco's films constitute topically inconsistent responses to debates about women's sexual agency and their orgasmic difference from men. Whatever potentially reactionary or subversive readings may be gleaned from Franco's apparently transgressive Gothic sexology, it undoubtedly resonates with the sexual perturbations of its time.

WORKS CITED

Ableman, Paul. *The Mouth*. London: Sphere, 1972. Print.

Auerbach, Nina. *Our Vampires, Ourselves*. Chicago: U of Chicago P, 1995. Print.

Bland, Lucy, and Laura Doan, eds. *Sexology Uncensored: The Documents of Sexual Science*. Cambridge: Polity, 1998. Print.

Boulton, T. L. "How to Master Today's Sex-Starved Woman." *New Man* 7.6 (1969): 18–19, 70. Print.

Bursteln, A. Joseph. *Maladjusted Female*. New York: Midwood Enterprises, 1966. Print.

Chesser, Eustace. *Love without Fear: A Plain Guide to Sex Technique for Every Married Adult*. London: Rich & Cowan Ltd., 1941. Print.

Cooper, R. T. "Is Marriage Divorced from Reality?" *Parade* Feb. 1969: 12–13. Print.

Creed, Barbara. *The Monstrous-Feminine: Film, Feminism and Psychoanalysis*. London: Routledge, 1993. Print.

Dijkstra, Bram. *Evil Sisters: The Threat of Female Sexuality in Twentieth Century Culture*. New York: Henry Holt, 1996. Print.

Dyer, Richard. "It's in His Kiss: Vampirism as Homosexuality, Homosexuality as Vampirism." *The Culture of Queers*. London and New York: Routledge, 2002. 70–89. Print.

Ejlersen, Mette. *I Accuse!* London: Tandem, 1969. Print.

Ellis, Albert. Introduction. *Casebook: Nymphomania*. Ed. Victoria Morhaim. London: Mayflower-Dell, 1964. 7–9. Print.

Ellis, Albert, and Edward Sagarin. *Nymphomania: A Study of the Oversexed Female*. St. Albans: Granada, 1968. Print.

Ellis, Havelock. "Congenital Sexual Inversion in Women." *Sexology Uncensored: The Documents of Sexual Science*. Ed. Lucy Bland and Laura Doan. Cambridge: Polity, 1998. 45–47. Print.

———. *Studies in the Psychology of Sex*. Vol. 1. London: Watford UP, 1897. Print.

Escoffier, Jeffrey, ed. *Sexual Revolution*. New York: Thunders Mouth, 2003. Print.

Fisher, Seymour. *Understanding the Female Orgasm*. Harmondsworth: Pelican, 1973. Print.

Foucault, Michel. *The History of Sexuality, Volume 1: An Introduction*. Trans. Robert Hurley. New York: Vintage, 1980. Print.

Gelder, Ken. *Reading the Vampire*. London: Routledge, 1994. Print.

Hegeler, Inge, and Sten. *An ABZ of Love*. London: NEL/Neville Spearman, 1963. Print.

Hutchings, Peter. "Masculinity and the Horror Film." *You Tarzan: Masculinity, Movies and Men*. Ed. Pat Kirkham and Janet Thumim. London: Lawrence and Wishart, 1993. 84–93. Print.

Kinsey, Alfred C., et al. *Sexual Behavior in the Human Female*. New York: W.B. Saunders/Pocket Books, 1953. Print.

Koedt, Anne. "The Myth of the Vaginal Orgasm." *Sexual Revolution*. Ed. Jeffrey Escoffier. New York: Thunders Mouth, 2003. 100–109. Print.

Krafft-Ebing, Richard von. "Congenital Sexual Inversion in Women." *Sexology Uncensored: The Documents of Sexual Science*. Ed. Lucy Bland and Laura Doan. Cambridge: Polity, 1998. 45–48. Print.

Ley, David J. *Insatiable Wives: Women Who Stray and the Men Who Love Them*. Lanham, MD: Rowan and Littlefield, 2009. Print.

London, Louis S. *Sexual Deviations in the Female: Case Histories of Frustrated Women*. New York: Julian Press, 1957. Print.

Masters, William, and Virginia E. Johnson. *Human Sexual Response*. Boston: Little, Brown & Co., 1966. Print.

McClintock, Anne. "The Return of Female Fetishism and the Fiction of the Phallus." *New Formations* 19 (1993): 1–22. Print.

McLaren, Angus. *Twentieth Century Sexuality: A History*. Oxford: Blackwell, 1999. Print.

Morhaim, Victoria. *Casebook: Nymphomania*. London: Mayflower-Dell, 1964. Print.

Pavlović, Tatjana. *Despotic Bodies and Transgressive Bodies: Spanish Culture from Francisco Franco to Jesús Franco*. Albany: State U of New York P, 2003. Print.

Reich, Willhelm. *The Sexual Revolution*. London: Vision, 1951. Print.

Robb, George. "Marriage and Reproduction." *The Modern History of Sexuality*. Ed. H. G. Cocks and Matt Houlbrook. Basingstoke and New York: Palgrave Macmillan, 2006. 87–108. Print.

Robie, W. F. *The Art of Love*. New York: Paperback Library, Inc., 1921. Print.

Sherfey, Mary Jane. "A Theory of Female Sexuality." *Sexual Revolution*. Ed. Jeffrey Escoffier. New York: Thunders Mouth, 2003. 91–99. Print.

Showalter, Elaine. *Sexual Anarchy: Gender and Culture at the Fin de Siècle*. London: Virago, 1992. Print.

Steiner, Karl. "Normal is a Dirty Word." *Men Only* 41.6 (1976): 64–70. Print.

Stengers, Jean, and Anne Van Neck. *Masturbation: The History of a Great Terror.* Basingstoke: Palgrave, 2001. Print.

Theweleit, Klaus. *Male Fantasies.* Minnesota: U of Minnesota P, 1987. Print.

Twitchell, James B. *Dreadful Pleasures: An Anatomy of Modern Horror.* New York: Oxford UP, 1985. Print.

Van de Velde, Theodore Hendrik. "Ideal Marriage." *Sexology Uncensored: The Documents of Sexual Science.* Ed. Lucy Bland and Laura Doan. Cambridge: Polity, 1998. 125–29. Print.

Weininger, Otto. *Sex and Character* [*Geschlecht und Charakter*]. Vienna: Wilhelm Braumüller, 1903. Print.

———. "Sex and Character." *Sexology: Uncensored: The Documents of Sexual Science.* Ed. Lucy Bland and Laura Doan. Cambridge: Polity, 1998. 25–28. Print.

Williams, Linda. *Hardcore: Power, Pleasure and the "Frenzy of the Visible."* London: Pandora, 1990. Print.

———. *Screening Sex.* Durham: Duke UP, 2008. Print.

Wood, Robin. "Burying the Undead: The Use and Obsolescence of Count Dracula." *The Dread of Difference: Gender and the Horror Film.* Ed. Barry Keith Grant. Austin: U of Texas P, 1996. 364–78. Print.

Zimmerman, Bonnie. "*Daughters of Darkness*: The Lesbian Vampire on Film." *The Dread of Difference: Gender and the Horror Film.* Ed. Barry Keith Grant. Austin: U of Texas P, 1996. 379–87. Print.

6

VAMPIRES, SEX, AND TRANSGRESSION

Jess Franco's and Jean Rollin's "Countercinema"
Aurore Spiers

win figures of "trash" cinema in Europe, Jess Franco and Jean Rollin were among the most prolific directors of the second half of the twentieth century, with filmographies boasting hundreds of movies ranging from horror to hard-core pornography. Their films share many of the same features, including taboo subject matter (incest, cannibalism, non-heteronormative sexualities), graphic depictions of sex and violence, campy sets and costumes, low production values, and overall "bad taste." They have often alienated mainstream audiences and critics alike. The debut of Rollin's first (finished) feature, *Le Viol du vampire* (*The Rape of the Vampire*, 1968), supposedly caused a scandal in Paris, where it left the audience "hissing, roaring that they were being made a fool of," and "throwing things at the screen" (Rollin).[1] A critic from the daily newspaper *Le Figaro* described the film as a "joke" that "bored amateurs without talent shot after a picnic in the park" (Mazars 30, my translation). In general, Rollin's and Franco's films were met with contempt, shock, or indifference upon their release throughout the world, and until recently they have been excluded from most scholarly histories of French, Spanish, and European cinemas. Indeed, with the exception of the international community of (s)exploitation film fans who revel in the excesses of these two Eurotrash masters, most viewers have been unable to see past the shocks their movies purvey, or the "joke" of their often campy aesthetic.

This chapter addresses, however, whether the sex, blood, and violence of Rollin's and Franco's cinema may also be seen as a form of transgression that challenges established representations of gender and sexuality, forging a European "countercinema" out of so-called trash.

In his seminal article "'Trashing' the Academy: Taste, Excess, and an Emerging Politics of Cinematic Style," Jeffrey Sconce claims that exploitation cinema, which he calls "paracinema," is less a genre than a "reading protocol, a counter-aesthetic turned subcultural sensibility devoted to all manner of cultural detritus" (101). As he focuses on discourses about "paracinema," Sconce considers how "paracinematic" audiences transform these films' trash aesthetic into a countercinematic strategy a posteriori. He writes that, "while the academy prizes conscious transgression of conventions by a filmmaker looking to critique the medium aesthetically and/ or politically, paracinematic viewers value a stylistic and thematic deviance born, more often than not, from the systematic failure of a film aspiring to *obey* dominant codes of cinematic representation" (111). In the case of Jess Franco and Jean Rollin, however, their idiosyncratic styles and provocative narratives do not result from fortuitous circumstances, lack of talent, low budgets, and technical mishaps only. While the unique circumstances of these films' production must not be ignored, one needs to consider the countercinematic qualities of Franco's and Rollin's movies independently of their reception. In doing so, this chapter relocates transgression from the audience back to the texts themselves.

In particular, Jess Franco's and Jean Rollin's lesbian vampire films are compelling examples of the directors' subversion of generic conventions, of traditional conceptions of femininity, and of what Barbara Creed has named the "monstrous-feminine" in the horror text. In her review of Harry Kümel's landmark lesbian vampire film *Les Lèvres rouges* (*Daughters of Darkness*, 1971), Bonnie Zimmerman argues that the function of the lesbian vampire is usually to present lesbianism as vampirism, to associate it with sexual violence, and ultimately to reject it as an alternative to heterosexuality within patriarchy. But for Zimmerman, *Daughters of Darkness* depicts heterosexuality and lesbianism ambiguously, revealing that "the myth of the lesbian vampire . . . carries in it the potentiality for a feminist revision of meaning" (23). This is also the case in Franco's *Vampyros Lesbos* (1971) and *La Comtesse noire* (*Female Vampire*, 1973), and Rollin's *The Rape of the Vampire* and *Le Frisson des vampires* (*The Shiver of the Vampires*, 1970).[2] I argue that despite their problematic images of women, their representation of alternative sexualities and female independence allows for a feminist interpretation of the lesbian vampire. Against standard readings of female representation in horror cinema and pornography, my analyses show that these films are not merely cinematic reflections of juvenile lesbian fantasies demeaning to women. Their transgressiveness goes beyond eroticism, while relying on it in order to depict women as powerful figures and sexual subjects and, in the end, to offer another form for the political articulation of gender on-screen.

Scholars like Tatjana Pavlović and Antonio Lázaro-Reboll have shown that, in the 1960s and 1970s especially, Jess Franco was an "anomaly" (Pavlović, *Despotic Bodies* 109) who emerged in the interstices between Spanish popular cinema (comedies, melodramas, *españoladas*), the New Spanish Cinema in Madrid, and the Barcelona School in Catalonia. Pavlović has argued that, in contrast with the conservatism of both Spain's "official" cinema and new Spanish filmmakers, Jess Franco's feminist enterprise created a "radically different women's space from the films of the times that were saturated by an idealized picture of woman/mother within the nuclear family and the nation (fascist model)" (*Despotic Bodies* 109). At around the same time in France, Rollin's filmmaking also represented something of an "anomaly" compared to the commercial and auteur cinemas, whose conservative depiction of women usually reaffirmed the director's male gaze and, in Geneviève Sellier's words, "male domination by way of fiction" (16). Through the study of the narrative and formal distortions in Franco's and Rollin's films, this chapter further illustrates the ways in which the Eurotrash paradigm may constitute a "third space" outside the official tradition of quality and modernist new waves—a space where sex, blood, and violence have the power to challenge social, cultural, and political norms.

Instead of considering Franco and Rollin purely as anomalies in their respective countries, however, I discuss them in the pages that follow as creating "alternative" examples of the European countercinema of the 1960s and 1970s. This framework emphasizes Franco's and Rollin's strong connections to the contemporaneous film landscape, relations that the notion of their anomalousness risks undermining by setting their films too far apart from both the official and the dissident cinemas of the time. Emulating and subverting these more widely accepted cinemas, with which they interacted repeatedly, and reflecting on similar social, political, and cultural changes, Franco's and Rollin's paracinema forms another, more provocative countercinema whose narrative and formal transgression is born of vampires, sex, and trash.

Vampyros Lesbos and *Female Vampire*

Produced and released during the "Spanish Horror Boom" (1968–75), Jess Franco's lesbian vampire films *Vampyros Lesbos* and *Female Vampire* were key contributions to Spanish horror cinema and to transnational horror culture during an era when Hollywood horror cinema was being supplemented by European companies like Hammer Films in England and Eurociné in France. Following *Daughters of Darkness*, European lesbian vampire films typically draw on the Hungarian myth of Countess Elizabeth Báthory and Joseph Sheridan Le Fanu's *Carmilla* (1871), about the Countess Millarca Karnstein, a vampire who survives through the centuries by preying on young girls. Extremely popular during the 1960s and 1970s, when the second-wave feminist movement was spreading throughout the United States and Europe, these films express male fears about women's independence by making the vampire a woman and often a lesbian. While they showcase images of powerful women seducing, rejecting, and killing weak and socially inadequate men, most lesbian vampire films of the time spoil their feminist potential through conservative endings, where the vampire is destroyed for the good of the patriarchy.

In *Vampyros Lesbos* and *Female Vampire*, women also fall prey to attractive lesbian vampires, who are seemingly portrayed as man-haters, bloodthirsty monsters, and, more generally, the signifiers of a chaotic world in need of order. Men are then challenged to save these women, themselves, and the patriarchy with the assistance of (male) doctors and detectives who help to defend the rational male order against irrational female disorder. Like Elizabeth Báthory and Millarca Karnstein, Franco's protagonists, Countess Nadine Carody (Soledad Miranda) in *Vampyros Lesbos* and Countess Irina Karlstein (Lina Romay) in *Female Vampire*, use their wild, "deviant" sexuality in order to attract women and men, who then meet their death in the course of the sexual act.[3] In *Female Vampire*, which takes place in Madeira, Countess Irina Karlstein's family curse causes her to kill her male (and female) partners when she performs oral sex on them. Fellatio (and cunnilingus) therefore replaces the vampire's biting of her victims' necks, allowing for teasing sex scenes and a more explicit connection between female sexuality and violence against men. When Irina meets and falls in love with a poet (Jack Taylor), she finds in him a potential savior, someone who wishes to cure her of her vampirism, which is coded as sexual frustration. In *Vampyros Lesbos*, Linda Westinghouse (Ewa Strömberg), an expatriate working for a legal firm in Istanbul, is seduced by Countess Nadine Carody in a dream and must be saved by her boyfriend, Omar (Andrea Montchal), who helps her battle the temptation of an alternative sexual identity.[4]

Male viewers are repeatedly invited to identify with the male characters in these films and to project their fantasies and anxieties about women onto the female vampires. In *Female Vampire*, Irina constantly yearns for sex (and semen), while her inability to speak and her nudity throughout the film reinforce her status as a blank canvas. Near the end, the poet with whom Irina falls in love appears as the most obvious surrogate for the male audience, as he is drawn to her and then (accidentally) killed when the two finally consummate their love. *Vampyros Lesbos* makes its complicity with the audience even more explicit in its opening scene at the nightclub, during which Nadine, like the eponymous character in Franco's *Miss Muerte* (*The Diabolical Dr. Z*, 1966), undresses onstage in front of an audience. *Vampyros Lesbos* exposes the voyeurism of its protagonists and spectators alike, as we are all watching Nadine present her body to us as a mesmerizing spectacle. The dangers of vampirism also become apparent through this display, with the nude female body designated as both intoxicating and vulnerable to the male gaze.

At the end of *Female Vampire*, another scene of voyeurism comments on the power of the male gaze. Dr. Roberts, played by Franco himself, enters Irina's house without an invitation and then watches her bathe in blood. When her manservant tries to prevent him from violating the vampire's privacy, Roberts kills him and then resumes his position behind the door, from where he observes Irina for the remainder of the scene. Although she never acknowledges his presence, which makes this scene a true voyeuristic episode, her lascivious body movements in and out of the blood create an alluring dance for her own pleasure and for the pleasure of her admirer and the film's audience. The filmmaker's character functions as a surrogate for the assumed male spectator sharing his fascination with the female body and his perversion in the act of voyeurism. As the camera fetishizes Irina's body, zooming in on her sex, breasts, and thighs, in and out of focus, it also relays the male gaze objectifying the female character. Whether or not Irina is aware of this gaze, it briefly neutralizes the danger she represents by transforming her blood bath into a sexual spectacle. She is thus designated in this scene as an ambiguous figure, both threatening and vulnerable.

Yet beyond the images of monstrous, victimized, and objectified women in *Vampyros Lesbos* and *Female Vampire* lies a feminist potential. It resides in the depiction of Nadine and Irina as desirous and rebellious women and men as despicable, violent, weak, and unable to cure Irina and Linda. It also resides in the depiction of the male gaze as ultimately impotent in the face of the lesbian vampire's power. All of this cuts against the grain of the more traditional constructions of femininity and masculinity found in classical horror cinema. In *Vampyros Lesbos*, when Nadine is alone with her manservant Morpho, she explicitly expresses her revulsion for men: "Men still disgust me, I hate them all!" But Nadine is not exactly a stereotypical, man-hating lesbian. Her sentiment comes from a childhood trauma, when a soldier raped her before Count Dracula arrived to save her and then turned her into a vampire. As she retells these events lying down on a sofa, fully dressed and immobile, in long shots and close-ups, Nadine insists on the brutality of both the soldier and Dracula, and she refers to heterosexuality as threatening insofar as it establishes men's domination over women. Morpho stands near her, and through her interactions with him here and throughout, Nadine constantly exerts her authority over him. Morpho is a mute character who has already appeared in Franco's *Gritos en la noche* (*The Awful Dr. Orlof*, 1962), and as his name—from the Latin *forma*, for "mold" or "form"—suggests, his silence makes him supple and easily manipulated, the perfect executor of Nadine's orders and the most docile victim of her tyranny. By contrast, in *Female Vampire*, Irina's speechlessness is a subterfuge intended to trick men and women into seeing her as the blank canvas onto which they may project their fantasies. Once they are within her reach, Irina reclaims her power by taking their lives. For example, after the danger she represents has apparently been neutralized by the scene in which Dr. Roberts (and we) voyeuristically watch her bathe, Irina is filmed on the hunt in the forest, walking through the fog toward us, her body entirely covered. This scene resembles the opening sequence, where Irina appears half naked in the forest, the camera lingering on her breasts and her sex, but asserts her control and the power of her gaze in a reversal of gender relations and a subversion of genre conventions.

In *Vampyros Lesbos*, the opening scene at the nightclub where the vampire performs a striptease with a female partner also modifies the gender dynamics of that voyeuristic moment. After the camera focuses on the erotic spectacle of lesbian desire onstage, it shows Linda, in close-up, fascinated by the spectacle of the two nude, female bodies and by Nadine's eroticism in particular. Omar, who sits next to her, does not seem to respond to the performance with the same intensity, despite what one might expect from a heterosexual male spectator. Against Laura Mulvey's argument about the male gaze in cinema, this scene shifts the power from the male viewer signified by Omar to the female spectator represented by Linda. At that moment, Linda acquires power and yields it to Nadine, who exerts her control over the audience through her undressing and dressing of the other woman, who remains as still as a mannequin or a doll onstage, a substitute for Linda in this show within the show. In the rest of the film, Linda obeys Nadine exactly as the vampire's previous female victim, now a patient in a psychiatric clinic, likely did before her. A charming manipulator and seductress, the vampire calls Linda's name, attracts her to her isolated house, and separates her from her boyfriend in an attempt to destroy their heterosexual union. In addition to Linda's rapture at the nightclub, Nadine's lust for Linda places lesbian desire at the center of the narrative.[5]

The appeal of *Vampyros Lesbos* actually relies on the distribution of power between Nadine and Linda, the victim/hero, which makes the apparently antifeminist conclusion, when Nadine is killed, ambiguous. Although Nadine first seduces Linda, the vampire later confesses her own fascination with the young woman: "I'm under her spell." This sentiment triggers Nadine's need to "initiate [Linda] into [her] circle" of vampires, a need she is ultimately unable to satisfy. Despite Linda's apparent desire for

Linda (Ewa Strömberg), in close-up, fascinated by the erotic spectacle of the lesbian vampire's striptease onstage in *Vampyros Lesbos*. (Fénix Film, CCC Filmkunst, and Tele-Cine Film-und Fernsehproduktion. Screen capture.)

Nadine and her weakness when it comes to resisting Nadine's power, she eventually seeks a doctor's help in order to save herself from the "Spirits of the Night." Linda is frightened by this possessive woman who desires to recreate her in her image and rob her of her identity. The last time the two women share a moment of intimacy together, Linda even admits: "No, I don't want to belong to you." Later, after the doctor explains to Linda that her survival "depends on the desire to live and free [herself]," the heroine reclaims her power and kills Nadine, eliminating the temptation of an alternative sexuality.

Yet her liberation is not from the lesbian vampire only, as Linda must also escape the grasp of a frightening man (played by Franco), who admits to having killed many women after his wife, the woman kept at the clinic, disappeared. In the end, although she returns to Omar and therefore chooses the safety of heterosexuality, Linda successfully defies two recurring figures of horror cinema, the female vampire and the misogynistic killer, liberating herself from two forms of oppression. On the boat returning them home, Omar wishes to erase any memory of Linda's perilous escapade and perhaps to annihilate any desire the woman might have to leave him again in the future: "It was a bad dream, Linda." Empowered by her recent emancipation, however, the young woman contradicts Omar's denial and prevents him from taking back his power. She declares: "No, it wasn't a dream." Like *Female Vampire*, *Vampyros Lesbos* honors female independence and emphasizes images of strong, empowered femininity that act as a counterweight to male phallocentrism.

THE RAPE OF THE VAMPIRE AND THE SHIVER OF THE VAMPIRES

Like the two Jess Franco films just discussed, Jean Rollin's early lesbian vampire films both repeat and revise genre conventions popularized by Hollywood and European horror cinema. In *The Rape of the Vampire*, Thomas (Bernard Letrou), Marc (Marquis Polho), and Brigitte (Catherine Deville) travel to a castle where Thomas, a psychoanalyst, plans to study four sisters whom the people in a nearby village consider vampires. As in other films of the subgenre, the lesbian vampires challenge Marc and Brigitte's heterosexuality as well as Thomas's scientific beliefs. The protagonists of *The Rape of the Vampire* vacillate between seeing vampirism as the mad châtelain's fantasy and believing in the existence of the supernatural creatures. In the second part of the film, we are introduced to the "Queen of the Vampires" (Jacqueline Sieger), who, like a black Venus, emerges half nude from the sea, and completely commands the castle owner's devotion. Her arrival presents us with a scientific explanation for vampirism, which lies in an experiment performed by the queen. This blurs the boundary between the rational and the supernatural, subverting the standard depiction of the lesbian vampire as an avatar of occult evil. Rollin's film also designates the queen as the madman's master, thus reversing the typical power dynamic between men and women in horror cinema, at least until the queen dies at the end.

Set at a Gothic castle in another distant village, *The Shiver of the Vampires* also stages the downfall of a lesbian vampire, Isolde, as the men under her

The Queen of the Vampires (Jacqueline Sieger) in Rollin's *The Rape of the Vampire*, a figure who challenges the depictions of sex and gender typically associated with horror cinema. (Les Films ABC. Screen capture.)

control reclaim their power when they rape her. Isolde first appears after two newlyweds, Isle (Sandra Julien) and Antoine (Jean-Marie Durand), arrive at the castle on their honeymoon. At first, Isle remains in her wedding dress and embodies the archetype of the bride and wife. The camera shows Isle and Antoine next to each other, looking straight at us, and this mock wedding portrait suggests both their recent union and the threat their arrival at the castle might represent to it. Indeed, when they go up to their bedroom, Isle refuses to consummate their marriage. She is then seduced by Isolde, who emerges from the castle's grandfather clock as it strikes midnight. Isle willingly follows the vampire to a nearby cemetery, where Isolde undresses and kisses her in front of two other female vampires in a Sapphic ceremony. Later, when Isle and Antoine find themselves alone in their bedroom for the second time, she tells him, referencing their unconsummated marriage: "You aren't truly my husband yet." Throughout the film, the female vampires work to keep Isle and Antoine apart, challenging the institution of marriage and the normative sexuality of the protagonists. When Isolde is raped, the camera briefly adopts her point of view before it moves away from the characters to focus on the wall, which is covered in blood. As the rape occurs offscreen, the film designates the men's sexual assault as reprehensible and not as a potential source of pleasure for male viewers. But by turning the figure of the dominatrix into a victim of male sexuality and Isle into a victim of lesbianism/vampirism, *The Shiver of the Vampires* depicts women as monsters, threats, and the objects of male desire and violence, and, more generally, of the male gaze. Even if the female characters embrace their sexual desire for one another, *The Shiver of the Vampires* and *The Rape of the Vampire* are partly symptomatic of the phallocentric order and its oppression.

Yet Rollin's films oppose the institution of marriage as a form of male domination by challenging the traditional structure of the horror film, which Welch Everman has identified as inherently reactionary:

Virtually all horror films are basically conservative. Think for a moment of how the horror film works. In the beginning, things are okay. Then something unusual turns up . . . and everything is a mess. But someone figures out how to solve the problem, and in the end, things are pretty much as they were in the beginning. This basic horror-film formula assumes that the way things are is the way things ought to be, and so the goal of the movie is to get everything back the way it was, back to normal. This is a fundamentally conservative view of the world. (215)

In *The Rape of the Vampire* and *The Shiver of the Vampires*, the initial "normal" order is never restored. While they display many features of the horror movie, such as vampires, old castles, the murder of innocent victims for their blood, and the heroes' attempts to "solve the problem" represented by the monster, Rollin's lesbian vampire films defy the narrative structure typical of the genre by disrupting the status quo without ever restoring it.

In *The Rape of the Vampire*, the group of young people who come to study the four sisters is disbanded when Thomas is turned into a vampire and Brigitte is killed by Marc himself when he tries to save her at the hospital. In a way, the film celebrates the new vampire couple, Thomas and one of the sisters, over the heterosexual couple, although the two vampires are also doomed to die after they lock themselves in a house from which they will never emerge. Likewise, the ending of *The Shiver of the Vampires* goes against the "basic horror-film formula" described by Everman. After Isolde is destroyed, her two former servants approach her cave and, realizing they are now free, kiss tenderly and run away. The film's celebration of alternative sexuality goes even further when Isle refuses to return to her husband during the final sequence on the beach. Instead, she joins the two male vampires and the trio begins to engage in rapturous sex. Although they die moments later when the sun rises, Isle is given the choice between freedom and marriage, a choice that is usually denied to women in horror. Meanwhile, the female vampires in *The Shiver of the Vampires* and *The Rape of the Vampire* define themselves outside the phallocentric order and seek to attract other women away from the male-dominated society and its various forms of oppression. The two films deviate from the conservative world-view usually adopted by horror films, since the heteronormative status quo is disrupted and finally demolished in favor of alternative identities and sexualities.

From Narrative to Formal Distortion

At the level of narrative, traditional images of women as victims or monsters threatening to patriarchal social structures are "distorted" to the breaking point in the lesbian vampire films of Jess Franco and Jean Rollin, who instead put forward alternative identities and sexualities via the figure of the female vampire. But the narrative distortions of *Vampyros Lesbos*, *Female Vampire*, *The Rape of the Vampire*, and *The Shiver of the Vampires* are matched—and intensified—by distortions at the level of film form. Considering strategies of formal transgression in conversation with those of narrative transgression is crucial to our understanding of Franco's and Rollin's films as countercinematic paracinema in and of itself, apart from extrafilmic considerations like the audience's reception. In these texts, distortion occurs at every level, offering an alternative both to Hollywood horror and to the official and dissident European cinemas of their era.

In addition to their nonstandard representations of sex and violence, Franco's and Rollin's films feature the unconventional use of mise-en-scène, editing, and sound, rejecting the classical ideals of continuity and unity in favor of disruption and excess. Like Jean-Luc Godard's *Vent d'Est* (1972), which Peter Wollen has credited with replacing the "seven deadly sins" of the dominant cinema with the "seven cardinal virtues" of countercinema, *The Rape of the Vampire* privileges fragmentation over narrative transitivity and "foregrounding" over "transparency." Its unusual two-part structure, its confusing in medias res opening with the villagers' hunt for the vampire sisters, and its deceptive flashbacks, which are later identified as the sisters' fabricated memories, certainly complicate one's understanding of the narrative. At many points, the film also uses jump cuts and inverted shots in order to make "the mechanics of the film/text visible and explicit" (501) in the way Wollen describes. When Brigitte dies in the field at the end of the first part, she is shown walking from four different angles (from behind and the front, then from the left and right) and falling four times from the same angles as before (behind, front, right, left). At the end of the second part of the film, as Thomas and the vampire sister wait for their death in the abandoned house, they are shown kissing one last time in a series of five shots, three right side up and two upside down. Opening in black and white with what one later understands to be the funeral of the two cousins, *The Shiver of the Vampires* also experiments with the image by shifting to color when the two servants visit two male prisoners in a red-lit dungeon before they return to the cemetery and Isolde awakes from the dead. The significance of these initial events and the identity of the two imprisoned men are never explained in the film. In Franco's *Vampyros Lesbos*, the opening sequence disrupts narrative continuity by first presenting the scene at the nightclub and then images from Linda's dreams, although she first saw Nadine in her dreams and then onstage. Throughout the film, unmotivated shots of a scorpion, a kite, and blood dripping on a window endow certain sequences with a surrealism that similarly troubles one's understanding of the plot.

Along with such unconventional visual strategies, the soundtracks of the films often work as an unsettling counterpoint to their images. Three years after the release of their October 1965 album, *Free Jazz*, a watershed moment for the burgeoning free jazz community in Paris, pianist and composer François Tusques and his band, which included Barney Wilen, Jean-François Jenny-Clark, Beb Guérin, and Eddie Gaumont, improvised much of the soundtrack for *The Rape of the Vampire* without using the footage as a point of reference.[6] Discussing music in the context of the events of May '68 in France, Eric Drott writes that "a subterranean connection existed between the spontaneous character of the protest movement and improvisatory practices of avant-garde jazz" (111), which participated in the modernist movement alongside the *Nouveau Roman* and the *Nouvelle Vague*. Together with other countercinematic stylistic devices, the use of free jazz brings *The Rape of the Vampire* closer to the experimentations of French auteur cinema and to the revolutionary zeitgeist of the late 1960s in France.

The opening sequence in *The Shiver of the Vampires* also features experimental music—performed by the rock band Acanthus—that contrasts
with the Gothic mise-en-scène while contributing to the eerie atmosphere.
Cathal Tohill and Pete Tombs have emphasized the importance of the
soundtrack in this film, which was mostly improvised during the recording
session, describing the music as a "sort of free-form progressive rock, replete
with crashing guitar chords and odd, lyrical snatches of flute and organ"
(145). In an interview with Peter Blumenstock in *Video Watchdog*, Rollin
elaborates on the hippie movement's influence on the music in *The Shiver
of the Vampires*, establishing an explicit connection between his film and the
counterculture movement of the time. To a certain extent, *Female Vampire*
appears quite conservative in comparison with the other films' "distortion"
of formal conventions. One noticeable feature remains, however: the recurrent sound of a bat flapping its wings used to signify Irina's duality as both
human and animal, although no actual bat is ever seen in the sky. Through
this unsettling use of sound, the film further demonstrates Franco's virtuos-
ity in offering his spectators a rich audiovisual experience that goes beyond
the contemplation of naked female bodies on-screen.

CONCLUSION

My final remarks about formal disruption in Franco's and Rollin's lesbian
vampire films fail to exhaust the ways in which they constitute another,
more provocative countercinema in their treatment of sex and gender.
These films illustrate a number of ways in which paracinema can represent
an "alternative vision of cinematic 'art,' aggressively attacking the established canon of 'quality' cinema and questioning the legitimacy of reigning
aesthete discourses on movie art" (Sconce 102). For Sconce, paracinema is
only read as countercinematic because of its "technical ineptitude" (112),
whereas the avant-garde's opposition to mainstream practices constitutes
an actual "strategic intervention" (111). In the case of *Vampyros Lesbos*,
Female Vampire, *The Rape of the Vampire*, and *The Shiver of the Vampires*,
however, low production values do not exclude the deliberate use of

countercinematic strategies. Consciously pushing at the limits of classical style and heteronormative modes of representation, Franco and Rollin create an alternative countercinema rooted in vampires, sex, and trash.

As my analysis of these four films has shown, their countercinematic potential lies in their transgressive depiction of women as powerful figures and sexual subjects at the level of both narrative and form. In Jess Franco's and Jean Rollin's lesbian vampire films, the representation of women differs from that in more traditional horror films, where the monstrous-feminine, misogyny, and female victimization buttress the oppressive phallocentric order. Franco's and Rollin's female vampires and victims often reject the norms of heterosexuality and marriage, embracing liberation through "deviant" sexual identities such as lesbianism or bisexuality instead. In showing how these films convert "paracinema" into "countercinema," I hope to spark further exploration of the ways in which Eurotrash might have constituted a "third space" for the resistance to cinematic and cultural norms outside the official cinema and the modernist new waves of the 1960s and 1970s.

Acknowledgments

I wish to thank Rob King for introducing me to the cinema of exploitation and helping me formulate these ideas early on. I am also indebted to Carolyn Jacobs and Kate Saccone for their advice on early drafts, and Ian Olney and Antonio Lázaro-Reboll for their patience and thoughtful editorial suggestions.

Notes

1. Before this, Jean Rollin made at least two short films: *Les Amours jaunes* (1957), inspired by the work of the French poet Tristan Corbière, and *Ciel de cuivre* (1961). After working as an assistant director on various projects, Rollin was later given the opportunity to direct his first feature film, *L'Itinéraire marin*, written by himself and starring Gaston Modot, in 1963. Because of financial issues, however, this film remained unfinished. Rollin's first finished feature, *The Rape of the Vampire*, was initially commissioned

by a distributor who asked him to direct a short film to play before the American "B" movie *Dead Men Walk* (Sam Newfield, 1943), released as *Le Vampire, créature du diable* in France. This short constitutes the first part of the feature *The Rape of the Vampire*, whose second part, titled "Les Femmes Vampires" ("The Female Vampires"), was added later.

2. Different versions of these films have circulated since their release, with different run times and various titles. In this chapter, I am using the version of *Vampyros Lesbos* released on DVD by Synapse Films in 1999, and the versions of *Female Vampire*, *The Rape of the Vampire*, and *The Shiver of the Vampires* released by Redemption Films/Kino Lorber in 2012, 2001, and 2012, respectively.

3. *Vampyros Lesbos* and *Female Vampire* feature Jess Franco's two favorite actresses, Soledad Miranda (1943–70) and Lina Romay (1954–2012). Before her untimely death in 1970, Miranda starred in eight of Franco's films, while Romay, Franco's longtime partner and wife, appeared in more than one hundred of his films prior to her death in 2012, starting with *A filha de Drácula* (*Daughter of Dracula*, 1972). His showcasing of them in these films is part of what lends their characters their appeal.

4. In Sheridan Le Fanu's *Carmilla*, the vampire, Carmilla/Millarca Karnstein, also appears to her young victim, Laura, in a dream, before the two meet years later. Like Linda in *Vampyros Lesbos*, Laura is both terrified by and inexplicably attracted to the female vampire.

5. In her essay on "Gender and Spanish Horror Film," Tatjana Pavlović notes that Franco's films have a "significant female [and lesbian] following" (140). This is not surprising, given the privileging of lesbian desire in movies like *Vampyros Lesbos*.

6. Tusques is interviewed about the score in a special feature included on the Encore DVD edition of *The Rape of the Vampire*. Some of the musicians appear as extras in the film, playing their instruments in the scene at the Théâtre du Grand Guignol, where the queen of the vampires stages an initiation before she is defeated.

Works Cited

Blumenstock, Peter. "Jean Rollin Has Risen From the Grave!" *Video Watchdog* 31 (1996): 36–57. Print.

Creed, Barbara. "Horror and the Monstrous-Feminine: An Imaginary Abjection." *The Dread of Difference Gender and the Horror Film*. Ed. Barry Keith Grant. Austin: U of Texas P, 1996. 35–65. Print.

Drott, Eric. *Music and the Elusive Revolution: Cultural Politics and Political Culture in France, 1968–1981*. Berkeley: U of California P, 2011. Print.

Everman, Welch. "What Is a Cult Horror Film?" *The Cult Film Reader*. Ed. Ernest Mathijs and Xavier Mendik. New York: Open UP, 2008. 212–15. Print.

"Interview with François Tusques." *The Rape of the Vampire, The Collector's Edition*. Encore Filmed Entertainment, 2007. DVD.

Lázaro-Reboll, Antonio. *Spanish Horror Film*. Edinburgh: Edinburgh UP, 2012. Print.

Mazars, Pierre. "Les Femmes vampires." *Le Figaro* 14 June 1968: 30. Print.

Mulvey, Laura. "Visual Pleasure and Narrative Cinema." *Screen* 16.3 (Fall 1975): 6–18. Print.

Pavlović, Tatjana. *Despotic Bodies and Transgressive Bodies: Spanish Culture from Francisco Franco to Jesus Franco*. Albany: State U of New York P, 2003. Print.

———. "Gender and Spanish Horror Film." *Gender and Spanish Cinema*. Ed. Steven Marsh and Parvati Nair. Oxford and New York: Berg, 2004. 135–50. Print.

Rollin, Jean. Liner notes. *The Rape of the Vampire*. DVD. Encore Filmed Entertainment, 2007.

Sconce, Jeffrey. "'Trashing' the Academy: Taste, Excess and an Emerging Politics of Cinematic Style." *The Cult Film Reader*. Ed. Ernest Mathijs and Xavier Mendik. New York: Open UP, 2008. 100–118. Print.

Sellier, Geneviève. *Masculine Singular: French New Wave Cinema*. Durham: Duke UP, 2008. Print.

Sheridan Le Fanu, Joseph. *Carmilla*. Kansas City, MO: Valancourt Books, 2009. Print.

Smith, Clarissa. *One for the Girls! The Pleasures and Practices of Reading Women's Porn*. Bristol: Intellect LTD., 2007. Print.

Tohill, Cathal, and Pete Tombs. *Immoral Tales: Sex and Horror Cinema in Europe, 1956–1984*. London: Primitive, 1994. Print.

Wollen, Peter. "Godard and Counter-Cinema: Vent d'Est." *Film Theory and Criticism: Introductory Readings*. 5th ed. Ed. Leo Braudy and Marshall Cohen. Oxford: Oxford UP, 1999. 499–507. Print.

Zimmerman, Bonnie. "Lesbian Vampires." *Jump Cut* 24/25 (March 1981): 23–24. Print.

7

ELECTIVE AFFINITIES

Another Sade of Jess Franco

Alberto Brodesco

Among the main sources for Jess Franco's cinema are the literary works of the Marquis de Sade, of whom the director declared himself a "devoted reader" (qtd. in Aguilar, *Jess Franco*: 150).[1] The Sadeian universe is for Franco a fantasy space open to elaboration, an arena that offers him the opportunity to experiment with his two favorite pairings: love and death, and sex and fear. As Franco put it: "The work of Sade is melodrama. . . . I always thought that a melodrama, to be interesting, needs to be both romantic and perverse" (qtd. in Aguilar, *Jess Franco*: 150). But Franco's Sadeian cinema is much more than a tribute to an author by a book lover.[2] We see in it a remarkable superimposition of intentions, impulses, and styles. Jess Franco's "adaptations" (we will see that quotation marks are necessary) borrow and transform a number of Sadeian figures and topics—the innocent female victim of evil and misfortune (from *Justine*); the vampish mistress of her own destiny (from *Juliette*); incest (from "Eugénie de Franval"); the sexual initiation, education, or corruption of a virgin (from *Philosophy in the Bedroom*); lesbian love (from "Augustine de Villeblanche")—bringing Sade's work to the screen in a unique fashion.

Considered together, these films represent a kind of Sadeian puzzle. Fragments from Sade's novels (circumstances, names, plotlines) combine to form a visual collage of narrative clues. They reveal a contradictory or at best enigmatic approach to Sade: stories from different sources are tangled up, forming modular, contingent, nonsequential compositions. The director keeps coming back to the same topics and characters, creating cinematic mash-ups that involve repetition, variation, and wholesale invention. Sade's opus is for Franco a palimpsest to be written, erased, and rewritten. He adapts Sade's texts without a real interest in being faithful to them. What truly intrigues Franco is the space of possibility offered by the Sadeian corpus. Blending elements of different books, Franco veers between naive symbolism and sophisticated surrealism, trivial illustration and heightened lyricism, banal readings and illuminating interpretations that rework or amplify Sade's themes, scenes, and styles. It is indeed what we expect from good intertextual works: a relationship with the original text that extends (or even distorts) its meaning. "Adaptations"—especially when they are in quotation marks—say in a different way things that the source has already said, but can also open up the unsaid, revealing things that were not in the original text. As Albrecht-Crane and Cutchins suggest, it is in this "space of disjunction" (20) that lies the real interest of intertextual relations.

A self-referential moment in the opening credits of *Eugenie de Sade* uniting Jess Franco and the Marquis de Sade in the glow of the movie projector's beam. (Prodif Ets. and Eurociné. Screen capture.)

A Sadeian Palimpsest

We can differentiate three categories in Franco's Sadeian filmography. The first includes films where the link with Sade is clear and explicit: *Justine* (*Marquis de Sade's Justine*, 1969), *Eugenie . . . the Story of Her Journey into Perversion* (1970), *Eugenie* (*Eugenie de Sade*, 1974), *Plaisir à trois* (*How to Seduce a Virgin*, 1974), *Cocktail spécial* (1978), *Sinfonía erótica* (1980), *Eugenie* (*Historia de una perversión*) (*Wicked Memoirs of Eugenie*, 1981), and *Gemidos de placer* (1983). A second group of films including *Juliette 69* (1976) and *Historia sexual de O* (*The Sexual Story of O*, 1983) has a fainter relation with Sade. In *Helter Skelter* (2000) and *Flores de perversión* (2005), Sade is just used as a "voice-over." A third group of films makes only a generic reference to sadism.[3] Sade's name is used as a catchphrase (sometimes only for a specific national market), as in the cases of *La mano de un hombre muerto* (*The Sadistic Baron Von Klaus*, 1964), *Die Marquise von Sade* (1977), *El sádico de Notre-Dame* (*The Sadist of Notre Dame*, 1981), and *Sadomania—Hölle der Lust* (*Sadomania*, 1981).

Because all of these films are built on a patchwork of references to Sade, the sources for each are not always easy to determine. The bases for *Marquis de Sade's Justine*, *Eugenie . . . the Story of her Journey into Perversion*, and *Eugenie de Sade* are, starting from the titles, quite obvious, even if we have to deal with two different "Eugénies" (one, Eugénie de Mistival, the main character of *Philosophy in the Bedroom*, and the other, Eugénie de Franval, whose tale is told in the eponymous short story). Other productions are more complicated. *Cocktail spécial* essentially takes its core concept from *Philosophy in the Bedroom*, as does *How to Seduce a Virgin* and *Wicked Memoirs of Eugenie*, but the latter two add references to the story of the Bressac family as told in *Justine*. *Sinfonía erótica* and *Gemidos de placer* are founded instead mainly on the episode of the uxoricide arranged by Bressac in *Justine* and do not involve the corruption of a virgin.

In the end, it is perhaps most accurate to say that Franco adapts Sade in part, not in whole. He is less interested in bringing the author's complete works to the screen than he is in sampling and remixing certain of their narrative motifs. We can identify five tropes that are especially important to Franco's Sadeian cinema: (1) the trope "Justine": a girl pays for the unfortunate consequences of her innocence (*Marquis de Sade's Justine*); (2) the trope "Eugenie": the tale of incest between a father and his daughter (*Eugenie de Sade*); (3) the trope "Philosophy in the Bedroom": the story of the initiation of a girl into perversion (*Eugenie . . . the Story of her Journey into Perversion* and *Cocktail spécial*); (4) the trope "Bressac": in an isolated house, a man conspires to murder his wife or his sister (*Sinfonía erótica* and *Gemidos de placer*); and (5) the trope "Philosophy in the Bedroom with Bressac": a combination of the two previous tropes (*How to Seduce a Virgin* and *Wicked Memoirs of Eugenie*). It is from these blocks that Franco's Sade adaptations are built.

Beyond the individual film (more or less accomplished and more or less faithful to its Sadeian source), it is interesting to consider the affinity between Sade's approach as a writer and Franco's approach as a filmmaker. Of Sade's writing, Pier Paolo Pasolini notes:

> De Sade was not a writer of pages, his pages are pretty bad, except for a few phrases that you can privilege and that are very beautiful . . . , but there is one every now and then; he has not the page, he just did not have the quality of the writer of a page [*non ha la pagina, non aveva proprio la qualità dello scrittore della pagina*], there was no chance he could be. . . . He was a writer of structure, and this structure was sometimes quite elegant, firm, well defined, such as in *The 120 Days*, where there is a quite accurate structure's design; other times there were instead infinitely open structures, like an accordion, poorly delineated, without boundaries. (3024)

Likewise, Franco may be called a "structural" director who focuses on the concatenation of events and characters rather than psychological or narrative unity. It is the same irrepressible desire to communicate that compels Sade and Franco to write in one go, valuing rapidity and accumulation more than precision and synthesis. The page, the single film, can certainly be "ugly," but the open, unbound construction of the composition can offer the greatest "structural" beauty.

In essence, the mechanisms of Franco's cinema and Sade's literature are quite similar. The latter works fundamentally on four operations, identified by Marcel Hénaff: planning, execution, variation, and saturation (32). In the first, *planning*, Sade's libertines discuss the terms of their actions and fix their performances. The second, *execution*, sanctions the passage to the act. What follows are *variations*, the play of changes that keep the libertines' desire busy. Each small difference "grounds the singularity of the resulting figure" (33), establishing a new unit and allowing the total sum of variations to increase. In *The 120 Days of Sodom*, especially, the subtle nuances of "passions" allow for the delineation of an original passion and illustrate the mechanics of permutation. Sade's writing strives to find new words to describe identical actions. Gestures that appear flat, monotonous, and reiterative are made fresh and vivid through the search for new descriptions that serve to differentiate the qualities of the sexual acts. The fourth and last operation, essential for the Sadeian combinatory logic, is described by Hénaff as *saturation*. It manifests itself in two subspecies: the first is the saturation of the scene through the addition of a large number of characters involved in the sexual action (with an artistic sensibility that is very close to the principles of an exalted and pansexual Baroque—see Boutoute); the second is the saturation of the body, which must be kept occupied in all of its parts.[4] The Sadeian strategy requires the saturation of space through a mass of bodies based on the saturation of each body involved in that space. What results is a body-mass, an enjoyment machine.

Planning, execution, variation, and saturation. To adapt this scheme to Franco's method, planning can be seen as the general intention to work on a subject—signaled, for example, by an appropriation of certain Sadeian themes. Just as significant, however, is the execution, which, because Franco embraced a production process driven by spontaneous ideas and unplanned moments, takes his work in unforeseen directions. Variation is a central mechanism in Franco's cinema: the same few obsessions (lesbianism, incest, the link between violence and sexuality) are exploited and elaborated over many films and across multiple sequences within the same film, producing "a cinema that never changes in order to always be different, where the compulsion to repeat becomes the means by which to stage a vision of the world that shifts from time to time" (Curti 24). Saturation, in Franco's films, is connected with excessive representation. His work is distinguished by the "frenzy of the visible" (Williams, *Hard Core* 50), especially where representation of the female body—and particularly female genitalia—is concerned. In this respect it is similar to pornography. But pornography has its own grammar, and Franco is not capable of operating like an "average" porn director: he flouts the "rules" of pornography (meat shots, money shots), improvising and following his instinct when photographing the female form. Rather than filming a "proper" pornographic shot, he sets out, in a much more ambitious way, to capture the hidden secret of sexual desire. Franco goes searching for its "very origin"[5] in the most obvious place, saturating the screen with close-ups of female genitalia. The fourth Sadeian operation is fulfilled. But when Franco gets too close, he seems to realize that representing desire is an impossible task. He consequently zooms out, just to be pulled back again, producing the typical movement of Franco's cinema, the zoom-in/zoom-out loop.

Franco uses the Sadeian palimpsest as an unconventional catalyst for "body genre" cinema (Williams, "Film Bodies") featuring ejaculation, blood, and tears. This "lowbrow" treatment of his literary source is productive on many different levels, permitting the director to add his own valuable insights to the discussion surrounding the writer's work, despite the fact that they remain unconsidered, underestimated, or even discredited by Sadeian scholars who have investigated the relationship between Sade and the image (see, for example, Pauvert and Beuchot, and Delon). In the pages that follow, I will try to underline the "elective affinities" between Sade and Franco, investigating a number of artistic and personal obsessions shared by the writer and the director—the pairing of sadism and masochism, the role of philosophy and ideology, certain kinds of spaces (islands, stages), and an interest in incest and voyeurism. The peculiar intertextual relationship between the director's films and their literary sources reveals that Franco does not always treat these subjects the same way Sade does. At some points, Franco's Sadeian palimpsest coincides with the writing that inspired it; at others, it rewrites Sade. Moreover, as a low-budget exploitation filmmaker, Franco was not always artistically or financially equal to the task of adapting Sade. In some cases, he powerfully captures the essence of the French author's work; in others, he demonstrates an unwillingness or inability to match its terrible and virtuosic qualities. In every instance, however, his engagement with Sade is complex, passionate, and fully deserving of further study.

SADOMASOCHISM, THE GAZE, AND SPACE

As they do in Sade's writing, sadism and masochism occupy a pivotal place in Franco's cinema. It is important to expose, as Gilles Deleuze does in *Masochism: Coldness and Cruelty*, the common fallacy that sadism and masochism are simply opposite sides of the same coin. They are not complementary passions. The sadist and the masochist do not share the same stage; indeed, they play in two different theatres. Every "pervert" has to be situated within his or her own "perversion": "Each subject in the perversion only needs the 'element' of the same perversion and not a subject of the other perversion" (Deleuze 46). In sadistic interplay, the victim has to be just and properly a *victim*: "The victim cannot be masochistic, not merely because the libertine would be irked if she were to experience pleasure, but because the victim of the sadist belongs entirely in the world of sadism and is an integral part of the sadistic situation" (Deleuze 41).

That said, Franco's Sadeian palimpsest frequently treats sadism and masochism as intertwined. Staging the parables of Justine and her sister Juliette, for example, Franco sets the trope of the misfortune of a virtuous girl against the trope of the prosperity of a woman who abandons herself to vice. In *Marquis de Sade's Justine*, masochism takes the center stage—and not simply in narrative terms. On the artistic value of the film, opinions are generally negative. Stéphane Du Mesnildot speaks of a carnivalization of the Sadeian novel (30), Ferrán Herranz of a "decaffeinated" Sade (53). The parodic and partly iconoclastic manner in which Franco reads his favorite author is deliberate, however. He declared in some interviews that he was forced to "change the whole story and turn it into a kind of Walt Disney" (qtd. in Aguilar, *Jesús Franco*: 143) by a series of production circumstances—particularly the imposition of the lead actress Romina Power, almost unanimously considered miscast by Franco fans and critics.

One could argue, though, that the Italian actress's flat interpretation of the role perfectly suits the material. In Sade's fiction, the obstinacy with which Justine goes looking for troubles renders her an unbearable character. Unable to evaluate with a modicum of reason the consequences of her actions and the intentions of her neighbors, the innocent maiden remains throughout the story at the mercy of her own stupidity, which leads her to repeat again and again the same mistakes. As Angela Carter writes, Justine's virtue is as self-centered as the libertines' vice, a symmetrical tragedy produced by bourgeois individualism (77). Romina Power's childish, naive, and "annoying" interpretation of the role captures this spirit. Her deficiency as an actor is in paradoxical harmony with the Sadeian character. Her youth (Power was seventeen at the time of shooting) and (at least apparent) innocence, violated in a film with sadistic-erotic components, is perfectly in tune with Justine's errors of assessment. Deciding to appear in a Jess Franco film, Romina Power goes searching for her own misfortune—a mistake *à la Justine*. In this sense, she does not act as a masochist in a scenario where masochism and sadism are compatible, but as a victim in a sadistic context. Her presence in a film directed by Jess Franco and inspired by Sade is physically awkward. She becomes the target of the sadism not only of her fictional tormenters but also of a director who considers her unfit to play the part and of Franco's viewers, critics, and fans. Thanks to Romina Power, Justine's victimization is complete.

We must acknowledge that Jess Franco is much more attracted by *active* female models, by Juliette more than Justine. In Franco's cinema, women realize their happy autonomy from men thanks to the violence of which they are capable (as in *Gemidos de placer*). They perfectly correspond to the model of cruel heroines of Sade's novels, where woman are able to ejaculate or are provided with "erectile clits." Angela Carter's description of the

Sadeian woman captures with amazing accuracy the "vampire lesbians" and their kin in Franco's cinema:

> The virility of these demonic whores . . . suggests male appetites; but, since the avidity of the male appetite is a social fiction, their very insatiability is a mark of their femininity. Clairwil, the man-hater, can exhaust the combined pricks of all the inhabitants of the monastery of the Carmelites, since this insatiability has in itself a castratory function. Male sexuality exhausts itself in its exertion; Clairwil unmans men by fucking them and then retires to the inexhaustible arms of her female lovers. For these women, the living prick and the manufactured dildo are interchangeable. Both are simply sources of pleasure; the body itself, to which the prick is or has been attached, is no more than a machine for the production of sensation. (104)

We witness the presence of the same kind of castrating and/or murderous women in *Shining Sex* (1977) and *Die Marquise von Sade*, where their sexual lure is an uncontrollable and dangerous force. In *Shining Sex*, Lina Romay's vagina hides a poison or a virus killing those who mate with her. In *Die Marquise von Sade*, Romay plays Doriana Grey, another sexual vampire who murders her male and female victims by bringing them to orgasm. Sucking life from the genitals of her victims is apparently what allows her to maintain her youth and beauty. Sex, in a very Sadeian way, keeps her alive at the expense of others. As Sade puts it: "the heaviest dose of agony in others ought, assuredly, to be as naught to us, and the faintest quickening of pleasure, registered in us, does touch us; therefore, we should, at whatever the price, prefer this most minor excitation which enchants us, to the immense sum of others' miseries, which cannot affect us" (*Philosophy* 1975).

In Franco's cinema, the dangers associated with the female body demand a special gaze. For all of their allure, female genitalia evoke the castrating Medusa described by Freud. To survive the sight of them, Franco suggests, one needs to see without being seen, to see and not see at the same time, to watch through mirrors, masks, reflections, or barriers. To avoid being drawn into a ritualistic dance of death, the viewer must become a voyeur, must stare from a distance. Like Perseus before Medusa, one must defend oneself with a shield. Only the ability to accurately measure the space between the eye and the object will protect one from the perils of the "shining sex" while still allowing one to enjoy its gleam. But this is an impossible task. The voyeur and the director are stuck in a double bind. Zooming in and out in search of the "right distance" from the object of their desire is just a futile attempt to break the impasse.

In Sade, watching (at the level of the enunciate) and the internal focus on a character who is watching (at the level of enunciation) are sine qua non conditions for the execution of a passion. The gaze of the libertines is constantly staged: "the pleasure of seeing and, in return, [being] seen, the will to track down the most beautiful victims, to monitor them and contemplate their sufferings are definite proofs of the ocular omnipotence of the libertines" (Sauvage 205). The eyes of Sadeian heroes are described as "penetrating and lascivious" (226), capable of "eye rapes": they devour, burn, kill, paralyze, fascinate. The eye "turns into an instrument of touch, extension or replacement of the 'sex-weapon'" (205).

For Franco, voyeurism works in a similar way. In *How to Seduce a Virgin*, Charles Bressac shows his wife Martine a slide show of their next victim, Cécile, the twenty-year-old daughter of a diplomat. Her entry into their field of vision is the prerequisite for her entry into a space of violence. Scopic drive and sadistic action overlap. Charles announces that he has rented a flat in front of the diplomat's house with an "impressive view of the room of this young woman," from which he took the photos of her. At the end of the sequence, the projector beam shines directly into the camera, dazzling the viewer. The energy produced by the lure of voyeurism blinds the audience watching the film, indulging in the same passion that excites the Bressacs. The couple eventually moves into the apartment in front of the diplomat's house. Like true voyeurs, they are equipped with binoculars. Their voyeurism seems to find a match in the exhibitionism of Cécile, who masturbates in front of her open window. Inflamed by the sight, exchanging the binoculars several times, the Bressacs start caressing each other. Inside the room, their mute servant Adèle watches them watching, a diegetic presence that once more echoes the position of the film viewer.

In *Wicked Memoirs of Eugenie*, the voyeuristic gaze is again linked with the use of binoculars, which frequently play a key role in films devoted to the theme of voyeurism, such as Alfred Hitchcock's *Rear Window* (1954) and Pasolini's *Salò o le 120 giornate di Sodoma* (*Salò or the 120 days of Sodom*, 1975). Eugenie walks down the beach as Alberto observes her from his apartment while Alba stimulates him sexually. Alba then undresses and takes possession of the binoculars, interposing herself between her husband and the object of his gaze. After a moment, she gives the binoculars back to Alberto and, still positioned between him and Alba, offers herself as a fleshly medium for his voyeuristic fantasies.

Peeping Toms, voyeuristic killers, libertines who like to look . . . In a sort of confirmation or rearticulation of Christian Metz's theory that voyeurism is always (in part) sadistic—Metz states that "there is none which is not so at all" (62)—Franco includes in this rogues' gallery the film viewer, who has to confront the fact that his or her gaze coincides with theirs. In light of the link in Franco's films between voyeurism and violence, the viewer is forced to acknowledge the fact that sadism is inherent in the very act of looking. The notion that a mutually beneficial relationship unites voyeur and exhibitionist (I like to see your naked body / I like my naked body to be seen) is exposed as false. In *Wicked Memoirs of Eugenie*, Eugenie is certainly an exhibitionist and Alberto a voyeur. But the sadistic acts he conceives create a rupture in the allegedly "perfect" voyeur-exhibitionist relationship. The "innocent" voyeuristic game leads to tragic consequences. After killing the voyeur who threatened to kill her, Eugenie ends up wandering in the sands, on the run from herself and her previous role.

What *Wicked Memoirs of Eugenie* then underlines is the falseness of the complementarity not only between voyeur and exhibitionist but also between sadist and masochist.[6] If the masochist Eugenie rushes voluntarily into the arms of a sadist, she will not be able to interact with sadism appearing in its "real," Sadeian form, set against every idea of contract and despising every request from the partner, who is nothing more than a victim. Jess Franco's filmography aligns with the interpretation of Sade and Sacher-Masoch expressed by Deleuze: in their purest elaboration, sadism and masochism are not complementary passions. If watching is the prodrome of killing, the safety of the pact that would establish a mutually gratifying relationship between voyeur and exhibitionist is totally undermined, even in its cinematographic configuration. The exhibitionism embodied with playfulness and unashamed grace by Lina Romay in more than a hundred Franco films is, as a consequence, deeply troubling.

The interplay in Franco's cinema between sadism and masochism, voyeurism and exhibitionism, requires a special space. Franco often sets his Sadeian films on the coast of the Mediterranean Sea, in sunny, even touristic places (like villas with swimming pools and private beaches). These spots might seem a poor match for the dark, somber stories told in Sade's novels. Eschewing traditional Gothic iconography, Franco stages the relationship between Eros and Thanatos not in the shadows but in full sunlight. But there is a deeper affinity connecting the use of space in Sade and Franco: isolation. In the films that find inspiration in *Philosophy in the Bedroom*, we regularly witness travel to an isolated location—sometimes an island—that allows the libertines to perform their rites undisturbed.

Indeed, the sovereignty of the libertine is predicated on isolation. Architectural or natural spaces characterized by remoteness and inaccessibility are a prerequisite for Sadeian ritual. Theorizing this concept, Sade defines it with a neologism: *isolisme*. This condition is ontological, it represents a "philosophical thesis," the "stoic motto of the libertines," a "promise of enjoyment," the "core of Sadeian impoliticness," and "negative anthropology" (Roger 88). Isolation enables the more authentic existential situation of the sovereign man—the "whole man," the One (Bataille 165)—who needs privacy to bring his enjoyment to the maximum degree of intensity. Franco supports this logic, although he does not emphasize the ideology and element of autarchy it implies.[7]

For Franco, *isolisme* is also a way to integrate architecture and character. *Gemidos de placer* features only five people throughout the whole film, but the isolated villa where the action takes place itself becomes an additional character. This sunny but scary "holiday space"—in association with a filming technique based on long shots and very few cuts—acts like a black hole, immobilizing time, freezing the characters in front a future that is in fact their past, as the whole film is a long flashback begun in the first scene, where we see the dead body of the main character, Antonio. This fits very well with Sade's treatment of temporality: in his writings the isolated castle is also a place where time folds back on itself "like a Möbius strip" (Airaksinen 2). Among the countless types of perversions hosted in the Sadeian space, there is also the perversion of Chronos.

Performance, Masks, and Taboo

Another central condition of Franco's Sadeian cinema is performance, in which role-playing and the donning of masks makes possible the exploration of sexual taboos like incest. For instance, in the last sequence of *Cocktail spécial*, we see an orgiastic masquerade during which the guests mate with masked people they do not recognize. Eugenie's father, who is visiting the house, is convinced to join the group and is pushed into the arms of his daughter, who practices fellatio on him. When one participant orders everyone to take off their masks, mutual recognition occurs. Without any embarrassment, however, father and daughter continue the sexual act until the final cum shot.

What is interesting in this scene is the use of the mask, or the *passage* through it. The father and daughter's phantasm—for Lacan, "the form on which depends the subject's desire" (99)—appears only if it is disguised. It is thanks to the fact that father and daughter are wearing masks that they might take them off. In the film, we observe in fact three levels of relationship between Eugenie and her father: in the first, they are unmasked in their home, in the course of their normal daily life; in the second, they wear masks during the orgy; in the third, they still participate in the orgy, but unmasked. The unmasking that allows father and daughter to recognize each other does not bring them back to the first level: the fall of the mask, like a guillotine, sanctions the abandonment of moral and social conventions. The point at which they meet is no longer that of departure. The first and third levels show different unmasked faces. The disguise is necessary to enable their relationship to leap into the space of the phantasm. The *real* mask is the one worn in the first moment of their relationship, when they are forced by social norms to assume a fictional role. As Slavoj Žižek writes:

> Our social identity, the person we assume to be in our intersubjective exchanges, is already a "mask," it already involves the repression of our inadmissible impulses, and it is precisely in the conditions of "just gaming," when the rules regulating our "real-life" exchanges are temporarily suspended, that we can permit ourselves to display these repressed attitudes. Think of the stereotypical computer nerd who, while playing an interactive game, adopts the screen identity of a sadistic murderer and irresistible seducer. It is all too simple to say that this identity is just an imaginary supplement, a temporary escape from real-life impotence. The point is rather that, since he knows that the interactive game is "just a game," he can "show his true self," do things he would never have done in real-life interactions. In the guise of a fiction, the truth about himself is articulated. (74–75)

Masks also afford the opportunity to play with shifting sexual identities, to switch with the utmost indifference from male to female and vice versa. This "queer motif" in Sade is certainly an additional reason for Franco's attraction to the author. As Edmiston writes, Juliette, in particular, embodies "Sade's queer character par excellence. . . . Anatomically female, she nonetheless reveals a male sexual psyche and speaks of having erections. She crosses gender boundaries throughout her story" (266). Masks also have a central role in Sade's short story "Augustine de Villeblanche," where a young man, disguised as a woman, succeeds in seducing a lesbian. The theme of lesbianism is of obvious interest for Jess Franco, who, in a late production from 2005, *Flores de perversión*, reads in voice-over extracts from this tale. The film is essentially a pornographic *kammerspiel* where the words from Sade accompany the sexual coupling of two female managers, who are continuously interrupted in their intercourse by business phone calls—a grotesque scene that shows how *isolisme* is unachievable in a contemporary overconnected and hypercapitalist society.

As we have seen, the universal taboo of incest is a personal obsession for both Sade and Franco. Sade insists on pursuing the subject in almost all of his books. His fixation is motivated in part by his view that incest is a disruptive act capable of destroying the whole structure of society, preventing any constitution of social life or passage from nature to culture. Franco does not share Sade's radical nihilism, but is nonetheless very interested in incest as an impulse that undercuts social norms with sexual desire. This impulse manifests itself across Franco's oeuvre. In *Gritos en la noche* (*The Awful Dr. Orlof*, 1962), for example, incestuous desire drives Orlof's obsession with giving a new face to his disfigured daughter. The protective glass under which the girl is placed—an almost transparent border not to be trespassed—defines the incestuous frame of the film (Du Mesnildot 40).

Incestuous desire operates most powerfully in the director's Sadeian cinema, however. In *Eugenie de Sade* (from Sade's short story "Eugénie de Franval"), the moral threshold holding taboo desire at bay is represented by the door of Eugenie's childhood room, which is filled with dolls and teddy bears. But this boundary is fragile. At first, we see Eugenie's father, Albert De Franval, peeping through the open door at the provocatively naked body of his daughter, who is lying on her bed. We witness his hesitation between the social duty not to look and the voyeuristic temptation to look. Father glances at daughter and then departs, slamming the door. His self-discipline does not last for long. And in this morbid family context, his desire for his daughter is answered by her desire for him, which leads not only to incest but also to murder, as they enhance the thrill of their taboo sexual relationship with the random slaying of unwary victims.

The first homicide committed by father and daughter is particularly revealing of the process of overcoming social norms. The couple stand among the audience in a Parisian cabaret called Taboo, but the De Franvals soon leave the show, change their clothes, and take a plane to Brussels, where they kill a model who earns a living by posing naked for amateur photographers. Afterward, Albert and Eugenie change their clothes again and return to the cabaret, where the show is still going on. Entry into Taboo (the taboo of incest) enables them to sadistically kill an anonymous woman. In the second murder, which is shown in detail, the victim is a hippie hitchhiker. The De Franvals, who present themselves as a newlywed couple, introduce her into their residence. After dinner, they ask her to play an erotic game. Eugenie stages a striptease, while the hitchhiker is required to lie on a sofa, pretending to be dead. It is in this moment that Albert kills her by suffocation. In both murders, the mise-en-scène constitutes a fundamental step in the deadly play. As it is for Sade's tableaux—the fixed, frozen, but living compositions, often of orgiastic groups, that are of the utmost importance to the libertines' pleasure (Kozul 44, 193–94)— the spectacle must be enjoyed not just via projection but via intrusion (Barthes 155): the reader/viewer must not simply "identify" with the actors; he or she has to desire joining the actors onstage.

The first murder depends on the following variables: access to the show; wearing a mask; murder; then return to the show. The circularity of the process is complicated by the fact that the model's death takes place in a spectacular context, a photography studio. The frame of the Taboo theater that encloses the murder (and works as an alibi for the couple) contains, en abyme, another spectacular setting. The model in Brussels falls into the deadly trap when asked to pose for sadistic photographs: she grabs some chains and simulates a few wounds on her body with red paint. This self-produced entry into Albert and Eugenie's fantasy condemns her. The second murder is built on a similar sequence: mask (or disguise, as the De Franvals pretend to be a married couple); show (the little erotic game staged in the living room); murder. It is again the naive hitchhiker's performative entry into the territory of Sadeian fantasy—her willingness to "play dead"— that ultimately ensures her demise. The homicide is followed by a series of excited, orgasmic cries from Eugenie, who can now run into her father's arms. Murderous ecstasy produces the first real incestuous intercourse

Donning disguises, the incestuous De Franvals, Eugenie (Soledad Miranda) and Albert (Paul Muller), prepare to commit their first murder in *Eugenie de Sade*. (Prodif Ets. and Eurociné. Screen capture.)

between them. As in *Cocktail spécial*, it is the mask, the passage through the mask, that liberates their true selves.

CONCLUSION

For all of their affinities, Franco's films do not agree with Sade's writing on every point. Take, for example, their differing attitudes toward philosophy and sex. In Sade, sex in itself is not dangerous, while philosophy is. In Franco, conversely, sex inevitably leads to violence. To escape the second, one has to give up to the first. In the stories inspired by the *Justine* episode of Bressac, sex is twice as dangerous: it harms—as her doctor insists—the mental health of the wife, and it hurts because of its sadistic character. In *How to Seduce a Virgin*, Martine Bressac is released from the psychiatric institution where she has been hospitalized. Her doctor prescribes her calm, moderation, continence, and chastity ("like censorship," is the ironic and metacinematic comment made by her husband). At home, a maidservant and a "simple-minded" hunchbacked gardener wait for her return. The servants (retarded, blind, deformed) take on the role of Augustin in *Philosophy in the Bedroom*. The gardener, as presented by Sade, is "as frank as he is fresh," "precious," and "charming" (*Complete Justine* 1606–17), with an incredible sexual power. When it comes to the discussion of philosophy, just before the reading of the pamphlet, *Yet Another Effort, Frenchmen, If You Would Become Republicans*, Dolmancé orders Augustin to leave: "Out with you, Augustin; this is not for you; but don't go too far; we'll ring when we want you back" (2242). In Sade, innocence of spirit is not incompatible with the participation in sexual acts. Augustin can maintain his virtuousness while taking part in the orgies. What really corrupts is the philosophy from which he is excluded. In contrast, Franco's pseudo-Augustins remain innocent only if they do not take part in the orgiastic sex (with a few exceptions, as in *Cocktail spécial*). To save oneself from evil, one must avoid participating in the erotic act, which almost always turns into sadism and murder. Sexuality generates violence as a consequence.

The philosophical layers of Sade's oeuvre, on the other hand, are very difficult for the Spanish director to manage: Franco describes *Philosophy in the Bedroom* as "a terrible story, written with a 'Sadeian' mentality, so to speak, too explicit to be filmed in the way it is written" (qtd. in Herranz: 87). In the films he draws from the book, Franco tries to rival Sade with his own trademark combination of sex and violence (or "horrotica"); it is the ideological component that he eschews. Franco does not give space to Sade's dissertations, fundamental in a literary work conceived as seven dialogues and occupied for about a quarter of its length by the aforementioned revolutionary manifesto, *Yet Another Effort, Frenchmen, If You Would Become Republicans*. If in the novel it is the philosophy that convinces Eugénie to abandon any moral objection to taking part in the orgy, in a film like *Eugenie . . . the Story of her Journey into Perversion* ideology is replaced by drugs, the only possible means of surmounting the barrier of Eugenie's moral education. During the orgies, Eugenie appears dazed, intellectually absent. What is lost is the perlocutory property that Sade attributes to the written word, the procedure at the basis of Sade's work: as Eugénie is seduced by her guests' philosophy, so will the reader be convinced by Sade's. In the absence of this component of the novel, Eugénie de Mistival (who in the novel, with a gesture that is probably iconic of the whole Sadeian opus, ends up sewing her mother's vagina shut) is just a "nouvelle Justine," a victim of her own innocence. Not being touched by philosophy, Eugenie, naked and still innocent, can wander among the sand dunes of the island at the end of the film. Franco surrenders to the unrepresentability of *Philosophy in the Bedroom*, recognizing that the problem lies in Sade's "mentality," not just in the violent or pornographic content. Franco's relentless focus on the body is precisely the product of this awareness.

Indeed, differences aside, the Sadeian palimpsest offered Franco the ideal opportunity to work on the pleasures and wounds of the body. Franco focused on Sade's "body language," choosing to leave aside the dimension of the mind that is at the core of Sade's writing, where philosophy is the product of the same combination of materialism and unruly imagination that fuels the sexual acts it chronicles. In Franco's cinema, the entrance of a body into the frame is the essential, continually reinvented action that allows the director to produce an infinite set of figurative possibilities. As is the case in jazz improvisation, "unruly" expressive freedom is nonetheless rooted in precise harmonic modulation. For his jam sessions, Franco therefore goes searching for "modes," for "standards"—such as the ones offered by Sade—to rehearse and play, offering his own variations.

The strange affinity between Sade's literature and Franco's cinema certainly depends on the Spanish director's passion for the French writer, but runs deeper than that. It is ultimately rooted in their shared desire for proximity to the reader/spectator, their wish to make him or her feel the breathing presence of the author/director. The characteristic movement in Franco's filming—the incessant zooming in and out—reflects the same theoretical-practical purpose that animates Sade's writing: the stylistic hunt for a haptic and perlocutory form capable of conveying to the reader, through language, the ecstatic and sovereign perspectives of the characters in the novels. In Franco, the ambition to overcome the distance between the film and its viewer translates into the constant attempt to get closer, to look better, to charge the image with a synesthetic intensity, to effect its saturation.

Bridging the divide between text and audience is not an easy task in literature or in film. For Sade, representation involves imitation, repetition, *mises en abyme* of one scene into another (Sauvage 73). Semantically, the word *abyme*, abyss, evokes the ideas of depth, infinity, vertigo, and fall (see Dällenbach). A frustration with the limits of writing—"as if the form of the texts were being devoured by their object" (Hénaff 4)—pervades the Sadeian oeuvre, this immense dream of power and domination written in prison by a man in chains. A similar frustration suffuses Franco's films. Finding the right place from which to stare (at sex) is impossible, since the voyeur has to avoid both being too close and being too far from the object of the gaze. What we are left with is a trembling uncertainty, a perpetual hesitation, before the power of desire. In the end, this profound ambivalence, which Franco compels the viewer to share, is perhaps the defining characteristic of his Sadeian cinema.

NOTES

1. All translations from French, Italian, and Spanish are mine.
2. For a general survey and definition of Sadeian cinema, see Brodesco.
3. Sadism is defined by Roland Barthes as "only the coarse (vulgar) contents of the Sadian text" (170).
4. One example from *The 120 Days of Sodom*: "He employs eight men at a time: one in his mouth, one in his ass, one beneath his left testicle, one beneath his right; he frigs two others, each with one hand, he lodges a seventh between his thighs and the eighth frigs himself upon his face" (7048). And one from *Juliette*: "Sandwiched between the two of them, I sometimes had both their tools wedged in my cunt, or, at other times, I simultaneously entrapped one prick in my anus and the other in my vulva. . . . Noirceuil, reluctant to see a single one of my orifices vacant, stabbed his member into my mouth and there let fly with his final discharge while my cunt and bowels were washed by the two little pederasts' exhalations" (3611).
5. Gustave Courbet's painting *The Origin of the World* is a common reference in critical discourses on Jess Franco's cinema. See, for example, Rauger (5) or Cesari (28–33).

6. The true voyeur likes to peek in secret, without being recognized as a subject who looks. Voyeurs are not particularly eager to watch someone who strips for their benefit, and exhibitionists take pleasure in baring themselves to a person who is not an accomplice: "Between voyeurism and exhibitionism there are all forms of transition; given that the desire of the partner must however be forced, it is understood that the voyeur does not look for an exhibitionist partner and, in the same way, the exhibitionist does not seek a voyeur" (Valas 187).
7. As Roland Barthes writes of the isolated castle in Sade, "Once shut in, the libertines, their assistants, and their subjects form a total society, endowed with an economy, a morality, a language, and a time articulated into schedules, labors, and celebrations" (17).

WORKS CITED

Aguilar, Carlos. *Jess Franco: El Sexo del Horror*. Ed. Carlos Aguilar, Stefano Piselli, and Riccardo Morrocchi. Florence: Glittering Images, 1999. Print.

———. *Jesús Franco*. Madrid: Cátedra, 2011. Print.

Airaksinen, Timo. *The Philosophy of the Marquis De Sade*. London: Routledge, 1995. Print.

Albrecht-Crane, Christa, and Dennis Cutchins. "Introduction: New Beginnings for Adaptation Studies." *Adaptation Studies: New Approaches*. Ed. Christa Albrecht-Crane and Dennis Cutchins. Madison, NJ: Fairleigh Dickinson UP, 2010. 11–24. Print.

Balbo, Lucas, Peter Blumenstock, and Christian Kessler. *Obsession: The Films of Jess Franco*. Ed. Lucas Balbo and Peter Blumenstock. Berlin: Graf Haufen and Frank Trebbin, 1993. Print.

Barthes, Roland. *Sade, Fourier, Loyola*. Trans. Richard Miller. Berkeley: U of California P, 1989. Print.

Bataille, Georges. *Erotism: Death and Sensuality*. Trans. Mary Dalwood. San Francisco: City Light Books, 1986. Print.

Boutoute, Eric. *Sade et les figures du baroque*. Paris: L'Harmattan, 1999. Print.

Brodesco, Alberto. *Sguardo, corpo, violenza: Sade e il cinema*. Milan: Mimesis, 2014. Print.

Carter, Angela. *The Sadeian Woman: An Exercise in Cultural History*. London: Virago, 1979. Print.

Cesari, Francesco. "L'origine du monde." *Nocturno (Dossier "Succubus. Guida al cinema di Jess Franco")* 60 (2007): 28–33. Print.

Curti, Roberto. "Il diabolico dottor Satana contro le donne dal seno nudo: Jess Franco e il Belpaese." *Il caso Jesús Franco*. Ed. Francesco Cesari. Venezia: Granviale Editori, 2010. 21–33. Print.

Dällenbach, Lucien. *Le récit spéculaire: essai sur la mise en abyme.* Paris: Seuil, 1977. Print.

Deleuze, Gilles. *Masochism: Coldness and Cruelty.* Trans. Jean McNeil. New York: Zone Books, 1991. Print.

Delon, Michel. *Vies de Sade: Sade en son temps. Sade après Sade.* Paris: Textuel, 2007. Print.

Du Mesnildot, Stéphane. *Jess Franco: Énergies du fantasme.* Paris: Rouge Profond, 2004. Print.

Edmiston, William F. *Sade: Queer Theorist.* Oxford: Voltaire Foundation, 2013. Print.

Hénaff, Marcel. *Sade: The Invention of the Libertine Body.* Minneapolis: U of Minnesota P, 1999. Print.

Herranz, Ferrán. "Cómo convertir la literatura en autofagia: ejemplos de adaptación y autoadaptación en el cine de Jesús Franco." *Il caso Jesús Franco.* Ed. Francesco Cesari. Venezia: Granviale Editori, 2010. 45–94. Print.

Kozul, Mladen. *Le Corps dans le monde: Récits et espaces sadiens.* Louvain: Peeters, 2005. Print.

Lacan, Jacques. *The Ethics of Psychoanalysis: 1959–1960. The Seminar of Jacques Lacan. Book VII.* Trans. Dennis Porter. Ed. Jacques-Alain Miller. New York: Routledge, 1992. Print.

Metz, Christian. *The Imaginary Signifier: Psychoanalysis and the Cinema.* Trans. Celia Britton and Annwyl Williams. Bloomington: Indiana UP, 1986. Print.

Pasolini, Pier Paolo. *Per il cinema.* Vol. 2. Milan: I Meridiani, Mondadori, 2001. Print.

Pauvert, Jean-Jacques, and Pierre Beuchot. *Sade en procès.* Paris: Mille et une nuits / Arte Editions, 1999. Print.

Rauger, Jean François. "Jess Franco: Fragments d'une filmographie impossible." *Dossier de presse Jess Franco.* La Cinémathèque Française, 2008. Web. 3 Jan. 2014. http://www.cinematheque.fr/cycle/jess-franco-248.html.

Roger, Philippe. "A Political Minimalist." *Sade and the Narrative of Transgression.* Ed. David B. Allison, Mark S. Roberts, and Allen S. Weiss. Cambridge: Cambridge UP, 1995. 76–99. Print.

Sade, Donatien Alphonse François. *The Complete Justine, Philosophy in the Bedroom, and Other Writings.* Trans. Richard Seaver and Austryn Wainhouse. New York: Grove, 1965. Kindle Edition.

———. *Juliette.* Trans. Austryn Wainhouse. New York: Grove, 2007. Kindle Edition.

———. *The 120 Days of Sodom and Other Writings.* Trans. Richard Seaver and Austryn Wainhouse. New York: Grove, 2002. Kindle Edition.

———. *Philosophy in the Bedroom.* Trans. Joachim Neugroschel. London: Penguin, 2007. Kindle Edition.

Sauvage, Emmanuelle. *L'oeil de Sade: Lectures des tableaux dans* Les Cent Vingt Journées de Sodome *et les trois* Justine. Paris: Champion, 2007. Print.

Valas, Patrick. "De la perversion." *Le sexes de l'homme.* Ed. Geneviève Delaisi de Parseval. Paris: Seuil, 1985. 171–94. Print.

Williams, Linda. "Film Bodies: Gender, Genre, and Excess." *Film Quarterly* 44.4 (1991): 2–13. Print.

———. *Hard Core: Power, Pleasure and the "Frenzy of the Visible."* Berkeley: U of California P, 1999. Print

Žižek, Slavoj. *The Fright of Real Tears: Krzysztof Kiéslowski between Theory and Post-Theory.* London: British Film Institute, 2001. Print.

III

The Cult Reception of Franco

SCREAM QUEENS AND QUEER DREAMS

The Politics of Monotony and Zoning Out in Franco's Direct-to-Video Productions

Finley Freibert

The late 1990s marked the reinvigoration of Jess Franco's prolific output. From the mid-1960s to the mid-1980s, there was seldom a year in which fewer than two Franco films were released, but the late 1980s and early 1990s saw few new releases from the director. However, the distribution of his films on video through niche mail-order catalogs and the proliferation of cult fanzines had by then secured him a relatively strong transnational fan base.[1] Moreover, video was becoming a viable option for commercial filmmaking after a long history of development in television and the avant-garde (Antin 57–72). And the video rental and retail boom in the United States had created a direct-to-video market that provided an opportunity for the production and distribution of independent shot-on-video horror films such as *Boardinghouse* (1984), *Blood Cult* (1985), and *The Burning Moon* (1995). These circumstances proved advantageous for the affordable turnaround and distribution of Franco's work on video and DVD from the late 1990s to around 2005.

At roughly the same time that Franco was enjoying a late-career renaissance, a lively academic conversation began around his earlier films. Much of this scholarship has appraised Franco's work in relation to dominant ideologies around gender, often in national contexts of production or reception.[2] Additionally, there has been emphasis on the spectatorship and reception of Franco's films by female and queer audiences.[3] Consideration of Franco's work after 1980 has remained limited, however, aside from unfavorable comparisons to his earlier cinema. For scholars like Tatjana Pavlović, his films "became less interesting technically and visually as a result of financial constraints that called for faster and faster production, the overuse of zoom, and mediocre actors" ("Gender and Spanish Horror Film" 140). This chapter takes his later works seriously for their potential as sites of queer cultural production that facilitate non-normative viewing positions. Financial and aesthetic constraints do not necessarily limit avenues for queer reception; indeed, I demonstrate that such constraints, in conjunction with certain subcultural signifiers, can encourage queer viewing practices.

While the term "queer" is occasionally used as an umbrella term for LGBTQ+ identities, in this chapter it is most often used to foreground the coalitions among socially marginalized constituencies that involve LGBTQ+ practices or desires but are irreducible to a specific sexual identity. This chapter engages queer studies in order to tie scholarly debates in that field to the overlooked queer production and reception of cult cinema.[4] Late in his career, Franco made direct-to-video films that open avenues for queer spectatorship while simultaneously frustrating a heteronormative male gaze. The queer sensibility of these films can be linked with the larger tradition of camp in horror cinema and beyond.[5] My intent in using the term "queer" is twofold. First, the term acknowledges the continued relevance and genealogy of lesbian and gay film studies to which this and other Franco film scholarship is indebted. Second, while "queer" has its pitfalls, it captures how the films I discuss represent sexuality in ways that outstrip identity categorization.[6] The term is used here to affirm viewing positions and readings that are bisexual, gay, lesbian, or otherwise, while also acknowledging the possibility of non-normative perspectives that are irreducible to these or other identity categories. Thus at stake in this chapter is a reflection on how Franco's less-acknowledged later work is open to a multiplicity of viewing positions.

In the pages that follow, I examine the queerness of Franco's transnational coproductions with One Shot Productions in the late 1990s. The first section examines the interface between Franco's status as an auteur in European cult fan circles and One Shot's scream queen casting as reflective of American shot-on-video "Z"-grade horror practices. While subcultural scream queen media of the 1980s and 1990s employed marketing techniques and production strategies aimed at heterosexual men, there is a queer following for these films, and some of them exhibit queer labor through their camp sensibility.[7] Queer labor comprises forms of exertion that actively oppose or covertly encode opposition to the intended meaning of a product—for instance, a distinctly queer sensibility asserted within a film otherwise targeting a heterosexual market.[8] While Franco's later films were often marketed as "straight" soft-core, in this chapter I argue that the combined labor of scream queen performance and Franco's direction coalesced in these films as a form of queer dissent that challenges the heteronormative gaze. The first section concludes by describing the effect of this dissent on the films' popular reception, which has frequently been characterized by misogyny and ageism. Building on these discussions, the next two sections then explore the techniques of queer dissent employed by two of Franco's late-1990s productions: *Mari-Cookie and the Killer Tarantula* (1998) and *Lust for Frankenstein* (1998).

HISTORICAL CONTEXTS: FRANCO'S TRANSNATIONAL VIDEO COPRODUCTIONS AND THEIR RECEPTION

Franco's foray into video was facilitated by a transnational collaboration with the U.S.-based media company One Shot Productions. During the production of *Killer Barbys* (1996), Franco and his longtime partner, Lina Romay, were introduced to One Shot's Kevin Collins; Collins was interviewing Romay for a British book, *The Lina Romay File: The Intimate Confessions of an Exhibitionist*, coauthored with Tim Greaves ("First Taste" 24–26). Franco's extended collaboration with One Shot spanned twelve films, culminating with *Snakewoman* (2005). One Shot's first feature with Franco, *Tender Flesh* (1997), drew from a diverse pool of collaborators, among them Euro horror fans. Producers of the film included Hugh

Gallagher, notable to fans of American shot-on-video horror and scream queen subculture for his early 1990s *Gore* trilogy and scream queen fan magazine *Draculina*; and Christian Kessler, a German film critic who co-authored *Obsession: The Films of Jess Franco* with Peter Blumenstock and Lucas Balbo.

Franco's initial three productions for One Shot, *Tender Flesh*, *Mari-Cookie and the Killer Tarantula*, and *Lust for Frankenstein*, were each shot on Super 16mm, whereas the other films he directed for the company in the late 1990s, *Dr. Wong's Virtual Hell* (1998) and *Vampire Blues* (1999), were shot on video.[9] All the films were processed through video postproduction, allowing for the implementation of the effects that contribute to the remediated video aesthetic of these works, such as ultrasaturated colors, chroma key overlay, and superimposed images. After *Tender Flesh*, a number of collaborators returned for further work with Franco and One Shot Productions. Gallagher continued in the producer role for four more films, also making a cameo in *Mari-Cookie*. Amber Newman starred in the next two One Shot films, *Lust for Frankenstein* and *Mari-Cookie*. Of course, Romay continued to star in Franco's subsequent films even after his association with One Shot ended; and Analía Ivars returned for five more of the One Shot films. What this production history indicates is the increasing propensity for transnational collaboration that informed these films' mode of production.

While seeking to engage both American and European cult-horror markets, *Lust for Frankenstein* and *Mari-Cookie*—and Franco's later political thriller *Blind Target* (2000)—heavily courted American 1980s and 1990s "B" horror audiences through the casting of Michelle Bauer and Linnea Quigley in starring and supporting roles. In the mid- to late 1980s, Bauer and Quigley had achieved subcultural star status as scream queens through their appearance in a number of low-budget horror films and their presence in horror magazines and at horror conventions. In popular horror vernacular, the expression "scream queen," popularized in part by Calvin Beck's 1978 book *Scream Queens: Heroines of the Horrors*, typically denotes any female star who has made a career playing women who survive extreme trauma or peril—a character type Carol Clover has dubbed the "final girl" (35–64). For example, in early- to mid-1980s pop culture publications, Jamie Lee Curtis was often described as a scream queen for her appearances in slasher films (Knoedelseder). During the period under discussion here, it was also more specifically employed as a marketing term to denote a specific horror subgenre and kind of subcultural star. Although initially promoted to a heterosexual male audience, the scream queen films starring Bauer and Quigley developed a queer fandom, and David DeCoteau, one of the frequent directors of these movies, is openly gay. My usage of "scream queen" is therefore meant to evoke the term's relation to the queer space of late 1980s and early 1990s American "B" horror cinema.

The cult usage of "scream queen" is distinct from its general usage as a synonym for an actress playing a final girl. Unlike the asexual final girl, the cult scream queen is diegetically endowed with both sexual and physical prowess. In keeping with the horror-comedy genre hybridity of their films, cult scream queens usually exude a sardonic wit reminiscent of Cassandra Peterson's Elvira. At the same time, they share qualities with "B-movie bombshells"—actresses in "B" horror movies who are attractive by the normative standards of American femininity. Within the cult-horror nexus of the late 1980s, the specificity that scream queendom acquired was largely due to the emergence of a trio of stars: Linnea Quigley, Michelle Bauer, and Brinke Stevens. Indeed, the renewed popularity of the term "scream queen" was in no small part due to the success of a set of horror-themed sex-comedies in which the three starred. Scream queen cult subculture thrived into the early 1990s with the proliferation of various media: comics, trading cards, and magazines (*Femme Fatales*, *Draculina*, and *Scream Queens Illustrated*) featuring photo spreads and interviews. This fan subculture even became visible, perhaps briefly, to more mainstream horror fans in *Fangoria*'s May 1991 issue featuring Brinke Stevens on the cover and a special section titled "Scream Queens Complete A-to-Z Guide" tying the subcultural phenomenon of the scream queen to the more general presence of women in horror films, the topic of that issue.[10] This history provides an important context for *Mari-Cookie* and *Lust for Frankenstein* because the cult celebrity of Quigley and Bauer informed not only the casting of those films but also their marketing campaigns.

In 1998, ten years after first costarring in David DeCoteau and Fred Olen Ray's camp horror classics, Bauer's and Quigley's last major appearances had been in movies released in 1995: Bauer in Ray's *Witch Academy* (1995) and Donald Farmer's *Red Lips* (1995), and Quigley in *Jack-O* (1995). Thus there was considerable fan anticipation for Bauer and Quigley's comeback with the release of *Mari-Cookie* and *Lust for Frankenstein*. There was also excitement among Francophiles over his productions for One Shot. Scream queen cult fandom and Franco fandom are not necessarily congruent, but there was overlap between the two in this case. Between 1997 and 1999, Hugh Gallagher's *Draculina* remediated *Tender Flesh*, *Mari-Cookie*, and *Lust for Frankenstein* as photo-comics that comprised stills from the productions, cropped into panels and overlaid with speech bubbles in a linear comic book format (a form evoking Italian *fumetti* and Spanish *fotonovelas*). Regular issues of the magazine also featured production coverage and photo spreads, such as Amber Newman's interview in issue 29, on-set field notes for *Tender Flesh* in issue 29, and a feature on *Lust for Frankenstein* in issue 32. Brook Edwards Video handled the initial VHS distribution in the United States for One Shot Productions' first releases: *Tender Flesh* in 1997, as a box set including a making-of documentary, and *Mari-Cookie* and *Lust for Frankenstein* in 1998.[11]

After a few more years of anticipation, the early One Shot productions received widespread retail distribution in the United States through the companies E. I. Independent and Sub Rosa Studios.[12] This was at the historical moment of DVD's ascent and VHS's slow fall into obsolescence, so E. I. Independent and Sub Rosa initially released the films on both VHS and DVD, the DVDs usually including a number of special features. *Tender Flesh* was the first to be released, in June 2000, by Seduction Cinema, and *Lust for Frankenstein* soon followed in May 2001 under the Shock-O-Rama label. Both are subsidiaries of E. I. Independent: Seduction Cinema specializes in cult soft-core and Shock-O-Rama in cult horror. There is evidence that Sub Rosa released *Mari-Cookie*, *Vampire Blues*, and *Blind*

Target all on VHS in 2001 and waited to release DVDs beginning in late 2002 and into 2003. The rest of the One Shot titles were only released on DVD, by Sub Rosa—first on individual discs between 2003 and 2006, and then in multi-packs between 2008 and 2011.[13]

The cover designs for the releases of *Lust for Frankenstein* and *Mari-Cookie* prominently promote their connection to the scream queen sub-culture described above.[14] Michael Raso's cover art for the VHS and DVD releases of *Lust for Frankenstein* displays Michelle Bauer's name in the largest font size used for the three actresses listed. Bauer's image is featured twice on the cover, and in the back-cover blurb she is the only player described in terms of her star legibility, as "legendary Scream Queen Michelle Bauer" (Faoro). Similarly, the VHS release of *Mari-Cookie* lists Bauer and Quigley first, and although Quigley has only a supporting role in the film, she hosts the DVD's tongue-in-cheek "nude" commentary.

The marketing of these Franco films as "scream queen movies" is worth noting because it links them not only to the historical context of their emergence but also to the queer production and reception practices discussed later in this chapter. The queerness of the scream queen is a function of at least three factors: the formal qualities of the films that privilege camp as a form of queer irony, the cult celebrity of scream queens as diva-like female stars exceeding male heterosexual consumption, and the queer reception of scream queen media. First, while generally marketed to a heterosexual male audience, many cult scream queen films privilege campy elements over enactments of soft-core spectacle. Second, following soft-core scholar David Andrews's observation that cult scream queendom evokes the classical Hollywood star system (240), one could connect the queer iconicity of scream queens with that of Hollywood divas such as Bette Davis, Joan Crawford, and Marlene Dietrich. Finally, there is an avid queer audience for scream queen cinema, especially the early scream queen films directed by gay filmmaker David DeCoteau.[15] The key point is that the queerness of many scream queen movies and their viewers challenges the historicization of soft-core and its audience as invariably heterosexual.[16]

This becomes clear from analyzing audience data on popular websites featuring reviews of *Mari-Cookie* and *Lust for Frankenstein*, which provide us with a sense of their mainstream reception. As Andrews points out, it is difficult to track public discourse about soft-core due to the silence around it, which is engendered both by the design of distributors and by the stigma surrounding consumption of the genre (184–89). While Franco's cult films arguably exceed the category of soft-core, at least two of the early One Shot films were marketed as such. One exception to the silence around soft-core, Andrews notes, is the online cult network, which is dominated by vocal, overwhelmingly male viewers who often review titles on niche fan sites as well as on mainstream retail sites. Although there have been some reviews of *Mari-Cookie* and *Lust for Frankenstein* on fan sites, reviews of both films appear on these sites only intermittently. Additionally, while reviewers on fan sites occasionally comment on their subjective experience of viewing a film, they tend to restrict themselves to plot synopses and evaluations of the "quality" of the releases specific to the medium of distribution. For these reasons, I focus here on reviews from mainstream retail and rental sites.

Andrews's project traces the industrial emergence, distribution, and reception of soft-core films post-1980. Examining reception of these films on *Amazon* and *IMDb*, Andrews notes three categorical trends with regard to the balance reviews strike between an attention to narrative and an attention to sexual spectacle (197–98). These trends include: reviews that disavow the sexual spectacle as a deficiency that disrupts the film, reviews that acknowledge the dichotomous form of soft-core yet evaluate it negatively due to budget, and reviews that "understand" the generic status of soft-core, but ultimately disdain it, often due to its perceived distance from "Real Cinema" (Andrews 199). Andrews thus concludes that the valuation of soft-core is universally negative: "this is not a game softcore can 'win.'" (198). An examination of the reception of *Mari-Cookie* and *Lust for Frankenstein* reveals another important negative trend, one that is specific to these two films. Sampling the reviews on *Amazon*, *IMDb*, and *Netflix*, one notices an overwhelming misogyny expressed through an evaluation of women's bodies in the films. This tendency intersects with reviewers' ageist inclination to judge the actresses' attractiveness in comparison to how they appeared in earlier films.[17] Reviewers' misogyny is expressed at different rates with respect to the two films, however. On *Amazon*, there are currently six reviews of *Mari-Cookie*, while there are ten for *Lust for Frankenstein*; one-sixth of the former and half of the latter display this trend. On *IMDb*, there are currently only three reviews of *Mari-Cookie*, two of which display the trend, and seventeen reviews of *Lust for Frankenstein*, nine of which display the trend. *Netflix* reviews do not include usernames, which permits members to review films with a greater confidence of anonymity. It currently features around fifteen reviews for each film, and reviews commenting negatively on the actresses' bodies similarly skew toward *Lust for Frankenstein* (in this case, nine of fifteen, compared to *Mari-Cookie*'s five of fourteen). *Lust for Frankenstein*'s overall accumulation of more misogynistic comments might be due to its overt misandry. As Andrews says of soft-core: "male viewers might denigrate such vehicles because they feel attacked by them" (199).

Yet because the comments are not just negative toward the films but toward the female cast members' bodies, I would argue they are also a symptom of something else. In part, they point to the fact that the sexual objectification of women has persisted in scream queen fandom despite the growing number of scream queen media producers and consumers operating outside a heterosexist economy.[18] That *Lust for Frankenstein* has accumulated more reviews on all sites and appears to have a larger proportion of misogynistic responses is also likely due to the different marketing strategies deployed by Shock-O-Rama and Sub Rosa. Shock-O-Rama's cover design for *Lust for Frankenstein* employs soft-core codes through the framing, placement, and display of Newman's and Bauer's bodies. At least four reviewers explicitly claim that the cover deceptively features women not actually present in the film ("EEEEWWWWWWWWW!!!!!!!!!!!!!!!!!!"; Bottom; Mesmerise; "Terrible . . ."). Misogynistic reviews mentioning the cover include the following comments: "the hot chicks on the cover are nowhere to be seen, the nude scenes will make you wretch [sic]" (Bottom), and "unlike the cover, most of the girls in this film are ugly" ("Terrible . . .").[19] On the other hand, Sub Rosa, known more as a horror label, seldom marketed their films as soft-core; their cover for *Mari-Cookie* more resembles that of a cult film featuring an ensemble cast, with the ten lead actors, tinted monochromatically, encircling the film's title. Rather than engaging in titillation, this marketing stresses the film's tongue-in-cheek comedy and wacky comic book intrigue.

But I argue that the key reason for the misogynist reception of *Lust for Frankenstein* and *Mari-Cookie* online is the queerness of these films. While there does not appear to be substantial online documentation of their queer reception, I will show that they are geared toward queer perspectives. These movies expand on the queerness of earlier cult scream queen media both by privileging the diva-like agency of their scream queens and by combining narrative and soft-core elements into a queer admixture that frustrates the heteronormative gaze typically invited by soft-core. To a large degree, the aversion to *Mari-Cookie* and *Lust for Frankenstein* evident in their reception can be directly attributed to this queer quality and its disruptive power. In the sections that follow, I will engage with and build on the literature on Franco spectatorship by articulating how *Mari-Cookie* and *Lust for Frankenstein* invite a queer gaze through their subversion of normative forms of narrative, spectacle, and reception. Ultimately, I aim to establish that while they have been dismissed and denigrated by fans and scholars alike, Franco's direct-to-video productions are unique in their insistence on the pleasures of abandoning both linear narrative and heteronormativity.

MARI-COOKIE AND QUEER ZONING OUT

Whereas *Lust for Frankenstein*'s narrative follows a kind of melancholy love story, *Mari-Cookie and the Killer Tarantula* plays out as an exuberant post-punk spoof of pulp crime cinema packed with vibrant colors and a multiplicity of characters intermingling in unpredictable ways. *Mari-Cookie*'s loosely woven narrative revolves around an "avant-garde punk rock star" named Tarantula van Spielberg (Lina Romay), who can transform into a tarantula with a human face. Romay also plays the second character of the title, Mari-Cookie, a mild-mannered, upper-middle-class platinum blonde whose connection to Tarantula is ambiguous within the narrative (near the conclusion it is implied that they are the same person). During and after her burlesque performances, Tarantula seduces and subsequently kidnaps her audience members. An initial kidnapping victim, Chuck Morrison (Pedro Temboury), is already hanging in her web in an early scene when she brings Leona Tarantino (Mavi Tienda) to her lair. As a result of these kidnappings and a complicated rivalry between Tarantula and another burlesque performer, Queen Vicious (Analía Ivars), the plot finally coalesces around the supporting characters' attempt to infiltrate Tarantula's lair en masse.

Mari-Cookie continually delays construction of a clear protagonist, instead distributing possibilities for spectatorial identification among a broad number of characters, including Mari-Cookie/Tarantula, Marga (Michelle Bauer), Tere (Linnea Quigley), Amy (Amber Newman), Queen Vicious, and Leona. The resulting spectatorial negotiations recall those prompted by earlier Franco films discussed by Joan Hawkins and Ian Olney. Hawkins analyzes the way in which the formal techniques employed in *Gritos en la noche* (*The Awful Dr. Orlof*, 1962) shift viewers away from the heterosexual male gaze and challenge "police hegemony and control through the measured use of a female's point of view" (207). *Mari-Cookie* also employs a police procedural subtext, yet within its tenuous narrative web, the majority of characters with narrative agency are gendered female. In dialogue with Hawkins, Olney has placed some of Franco's earlier films within a genealogy of Euro horror that encourages viewers "not only to adopt a variety of viewing positions and to experiment with different subjectivities in a potentially transgressive way, but also to define themselves on a personal and social level while challenging cinematic and social norms" (*Euro Horror* 99). *Mari-Cookie* prompts such spectatorial play through its large ensemble cast, and I argue that this play additionally engages strategies of queer dissent by inviting the spectator to partake in the kind of queer promiscuity associated with the camp sensibility (Babuscio 121).

Take, for example, the sequence following Tarantula's kidnapping of Leona in which Tere and Mari are sunbathing by a pool. Narratively, the sequence functions to introduce Sheriff Marga (the law enforcement officer investigating the kidnappings) and her suspicion that Mari is Tarantula. The presence of Tere and Amy in this sequence frustrates the fulfillment of this function, however, and instead the sequence acts extradiegetically to suture the cast into a scream queen ensemble whose performed personalities become its focus. Rather than maintaining Mari as the central figure, the sequence begins by privileging Tere's perspective, then oscillates among others in a circular fashion via the ensemble's interaction. A long shot frames Tere's approach from behind Mari, who sits on a reclining chair in the foreground. The camera actively privileges Tere during a monologue about her inept and adulterous husband. Through a variation on shot–reverse-shot editing, Tere's point of view is maintained as follows. When she speaks, there is a zoom to a close-up from over Mari's shoulder, then a cut to a full shot of both women reclining, and a subsequent repetition of the over-the-shoulder zoom. The back-and-forth between zoom and full shot is repeated three times with a variation that zooms into a plate of peanuts. The effect of this technique is an emphasis on Tere's perspective. Another shift occurs with the arrival of Sheriff Marga. As Marga approaches, the camera follows her movement with a long pan. Tere exits the scene, and the framing and editing now favor Marga, who begins to interrogate Mari. Prior to this moment, Mari has been portrayed as the protagonist, but the viewer's identification slips toward Marga as Mari becomes aligned with the scheming and murderous Tarantula. In a final refusal of singular perspective, Amy, Tere's bubbly daughter, interrupts the interrogation by handspringing into the scene to ask where her mother has gone. In all, this sequence introduces four characters and, like other scenes in the film, opens up a range of possibilities for spectatorial identification by employing variations on standard cinematic techniques. Unusual over-the-shoulder shots, pans, zooms, and shot-reverse-shot editing all work to frame and accentuate multiple individuals and their agencies. The film practices a technique of queer dissent in its prohibition of individualized forms of identification. In their place, it offers a multiplication of viewpoints evoking a queer collective sensibility.

Additionally, this sequence becomes queer through its formal enactment of camp via exaggerated performance and gaudy costume design. For example, the confrontation between Marga and Mari described previously serves more to foreground the queer pleasures of immersion in the stilted back-and-forth exchanges between the actresses and Bauer's tongue-in-cheek take on her pulpy detective role than to accomplish a narrative function. The campiness of Bauer's performance is enhanced by her costuming, which generically encodes her as part noir detective and part Western sheriff: she wears a black fedora, matching jacket, hip holster, and boots. The diva-like acting and the kitschy wardrobe work to queer the figure of the scream queen. They also contribute to the film's queer perspectival play by enabling a range of camp scream queen characterizations as opposed to the limited woman-in-peril role emphasized in more traditional scream queen films. As the film progresses, these shifting viewpoints foster a queer collectivity in which unitary identifications are replaced by what I call queer zoning out: an embrace of camp solidarity and revolt against the convergence of narrativity and heteronormativity.

In its efforts to queer "the act of spectatorship itself, by destabilizing the heteronormative male gaze and introducing ways of seeing that run counter to it" (Olney, *Euro Horror* 173), *Mari-Cookie* is similar to earlier Franco films. Yet there are important differences to note as well. Rather than filming "obliquely—in reflections in mirrors with segmented glass, pulling in and out of focus—making it difficult for the viewer to see exactly what is going on" (Olney, *Euro Horror* 174), Franco instead disrupts the heteronormative male gaze with a barrage of camp and trash iconography, from pulp crime drug syndicates to slow motion psychedelic burlesque to feminist post-punk performances in neon and tinsel fright wigs to queer giant tarantula kidnappings. While the film thus undoubtedly opens a "queer zone"—Doty's term, applied by Olney (168) to Franco's earlier films—I would argue that it does so by encouraging a queer zoning out, a negotiation between the spectator and its heterogeneous affective economies and possibly meaningless digressions into queer monotony.

Such negotiation portends a feeling that distinctively breaks from the ennui previously observed in Franco's films by Tim Lucas, who describes an "oneiric detachment" ("How To Read" 26) and "projection of existential boredom" (27) resulting from the spectator's identification with a male protagonist's leisurely traversal of the distinctive architecture and barren landscapes of the Spanish coast. Here, ennui indicates the spectator's melancholic idleness, which is motivated by the narrative as it presents a lull preceding moments of more sensational spectacle; in Lucas's words, it is "the state of mind wherein (it could be argued) all aberrant behavior begins" (26). Queer zoning out is connected not with notions of bourgeois leisure and idleness but instead with a queer collectivity evoked through shifting characterizations and viewing positions that unravel the narrative and spectatorial conventions of soft-core. Rather than advancing the narrative, this kind of zoning out knocks it askew, and perhaps reverses it. Camp and trash signifiers gesture toward ways of encoding and perceiving linked to a mode of reception historically associated with queer audiences: the feeling that one "is trying to enter a hole backwards, trying to go back in time, through the looking glass, to find a phantom" (Koestenbaum 53).[20] The queer pleasures of Franco's scream queen films depend on a backward or against-the-grain reading of media typically understood as privileging a heterosexual viewing position. The queer spectator's backward traversals into "zoned out" disorientation are made possible not only by the films' spatial and temporal disarticulation but also by their rejection of perspectival singularity and suturing of the viewer into the queer collective represented on-screen. Ultimately, queer zoning out leaves the viewer "in a state of confusion about the intention of the film, unsure whether to align themselves with the gaze of the camera or not" (Krzywinska 205). It is precisely because they actively work against heterosexist spectacle in this manner—leading to their violent rejection by some mainstream viewers, as we have seen—that Franco films like *Mari-Cookie* represent a fruitful site for the revaluation of scream queen media.

In *Mari-Cookie*, queer zoning out reaches its greatest intensity in the final scene, in which the entire cast descends upon Tarantula's lair as she is seducing Amy. This sequence resists linearity, disrupts the heterosexist gaze, and stages a final act of misandry that disciplines the sadistic voyeur (Martin) while cementing a queer kinship. After Amy is brought into the lair (located on "Jess Franco Street"), Tarantula begins embracing her and then pushes her onto a mattress. As the seduction unfolds, the camera zooms in on the couple, who occupy the midground amid three spiderweb ropes running parallel to the back wall and spanning the set's pillars. One web partly obscures the camera's view, while the others evoke the depth of the space the zoom traverses. This zoom, accompanied by a reverberating, oscillating drone on the soundtrack, initially codes the moment voyeuristically, implying that a scene of sexual spectacle is about to occur. However, this coding is immediately undercut as Amy sees Leona and Chuck trapped in Tarantula's web. Amy says, "They look like human beings," and the camera swiftly zooms out, negating the previously implied voyeuristic scenario. The miniature human-spider form of Tarantula begins to taunt Chuck with a pair of scissors positioned at his groin; she demands, "Sing for me, stupid," and then, "Sing for me or I'll cut your thing off." While humming a song, the miniature spider dangles down the web, with fishing line visibly articulating her movements. Finally, anchored on a table beside glass goblets and a skull, Tarantula recites a brief poem with the lines, "I'm the spider. Oh yes. I'm the killer. Oh yes. I'm the tarantula. Oh yes." During the sequence, the backward drift of queer zoning out is facilitated first by the literal zoom-out, which disrupts a voyeuristic gaze, and then by the close-ups of Romay's face superimposed on the tiny spider as she recites the poem, a detour from the narrative that places us within the spider's microrealm. The digressive presentation of the spider's performative misandry—an absurdist spectacle that could be read either as a diegetic interlude or as Amy's hallucination—creates a phantasmic post-punk camp aesthetic that readily lends itself to a queer reading.

A scream queen collective framed in depth between neon webs. Queen Vicious (Analía Ivars), Marga (Michelle Bauer), Tarantula (Lina Romay), Tere (Linnea Quigley), and Amy (Amber Newman) in *Mari-Cookie and the Killer Tarantula*. (One Shot Productions and Sub Rosa Studios. Screen capture.)

In this brief yet complex interlude of camp animal agency, there is a repositioning of human characters onto a spectrum of queer human-animal seduction and spectacle. The viewer becomes caught in the web of identificatory trajectories that materializes on-screen. Franco visualizes it via the colorful spiderweb that the actors gaze through in slow motion, looking both at the sexual spectacle unfolding and back at the disoriented spectator in shot-reverse-shot. Although a crude version of cross-species intermingling, the queerness of the tarantula-human and her oppositional relationship with Marga, Tere, and Amy gestures toward Jack Halberstam's concept of "creative anthropocentrism" (51), which "imagines oppositional groups in terms of real or fantasized beasts" (51) to "invent the models of resistance we need and lack in reference to other lifeworlds, animal and monstrous" (51).[21] It is worth noting that this queer collective has extradiegetic significance. As first-wave cult scream queens, Quigley and Bauer's presence in protectoral roles (parent and sheriff) in relation to characters like Amy (played by a second-wave cult scream queen) can be read as an ironic comment on the ebb and flow of stars in the industry. Additionally,

Romay's role as the nexus of this sardonically misandrist constellation of scream queens reflects her extradiegetic status as a Eurocult icon retroactively added to the scream queen canon by magazines and online forums (Alexander 19). But this queer collective is primarily meant to denote a refusal of identificatory singularity. In the crucial final moments of the film, Tarantula, Sheriff Marga, Tere, Amy, and Queen Vicious, along with Chuck and Leona, who are still dangling from Tarantula's web, bring the narrative of pulp infiltration and intrigue to a grinding halt by forming an oppositional alliance of queer kinship. Chuck croons "we are a happy family" as he dangles naked and hungry from the web. Then the sole figure of paternal authority, Mari's husband Martin, is killed off by Tarantula's microphone, which doubles as sex organ and lethal stinger. After his incapacitation, the remaining characters make collective plans for a life outside anthropocentric patriarchy. The spectator's ability to "take sides" or identify with any one character is compromised by queer kinship—both the literal entanglement of bodies on-screen and the spectatorial zoning out they enable.

LUST FOR FRANKENSTEIN AND QUEER MONOTONY

In the previous section, I described queer zoning out as a type of spectatorial distanciation that operates through a backward consideration of *Mari-Cookie*'s form and content. In this section, I consider the related feeling of monotony that can accompany enactments of queer zoning out. Monotony's queerness has been discussed by Lee Edelman as backward turns and mechanistic repetitions that negate meaning: "'monotonous repetition' evokes the machine-like, desubjectivizing aspect of the *sinthom*osexual's jouissance—the antipathy to natural meaning intrinsic . . . to nature itself" (178).[22] Repetition as an aesthetic strategy is not unique to Franco's films or to exploitation cinema in general.[23] Yet, unlike other movies, where recurrences might serve to convey a character's internal struggles, Franco's later films employ repetition as an explicit rejection of linear productions of meaning. Repeated dream sequences and motifs inhibit narrative progression and do not contribute to characterization. Instead, these recurrences, in conjunction with the nonstandard use of framing, blocking, and editing, create a queer monotony. They demonstrate that, as Winnubst writes, "to be queer . . . is to be involved in acts or pleasures that offer no clear or useful meaning. To be queer is not to respond to the law of desire: it is to have no idea who or what you are, or where you're going" (91). In this section, I examine how disorientations and estrangements from meaning work in *Lust for Frankenstein*, specifically through its engagement with camp iconography.

Lust for Frankenstein's narrative loosely revolves around the efforts of Moira (Lina Romay) to decipher messages from the ghost of her father, Dr. Frankenstein (Carlos Subterfuge). Via these messages, which are often intercepted by her stepmother Abigail (Analía Ivars), Moira finds her father's reanimated creation, Goddess (Michelle Bauer), a patchwork Frankenstein monster with both male and female genitalia. The film evolves into a love story between Moira and Goddess in which the two work to sustain Goddess's (living dead) existence by providing her nourishment through the transference of vital energies from human bodies. This love story consumes much of the film, making it a unique example of a queer scream queen romance, made all the more fabulously camp by Bauer's stiff gait and monotone voice in the role of Goddess and Romay's high-strung performance as an outcast from the house of Frankenstein.

Beyond these broad strokes, the story is difficult to reconstruct due to the film's repetitive retreats into unexplained flashbacks and refusal to clarify what its antiheroines (Moira and Goddess) are ultimately attempting to accomplish, if anything. Since the movie begins in medias res with Moira waking up from a dream—a sequence in which the opening credits play over psychedelically tinted, slow-motion images of events that occur later in the film—all background information is conveyed through the narration of Dr. Frankenstein, whose voice is altered by pitch conversion and tonally saturated choral effects. This device is consistently employed in conjunction with others that engender and reflect the concentric monotony of the viewing experience. Examples include a repeated "record" motif (discussed below), shots of characters asleep, lengthy soft-core sex sequences filmed in slow motion and accompanied by an acid-rock soundtrack, flashbacks employing overexposed lighting, and images of characters or animals stylized via telescopic or kaleidoscopic effects. The repeated use of these devices is occasionally linked with the disjointed story, but generally resists any subordination to narrative function and frustrates the delivery of typical soft-core spectacle.

All but ignoring the narrative focus of its literary source, *Lust for Frankenstein* instead unfolds as a series of narratively repetitive yet stylistically distinct sequences involving Moira and Goddess's campy romance and their attempts to find Goddess sustenance. At the level of production and reception, the film may appear dangerously close to what Caryl Flinn calls "body camp" (54), a form of camp encoded (and received) via specific material and performative codes of embodiment. As Flinn argues, one problematic version of "body camp" (54) holds aging female stars up for ridicule by coding their bodies in terms of death and decay. *Lust for Frankenstein* does feature actresses who were once (and arguably still remain) stars within a specific subculture; however, it does not devolve into a derisive "necro romp" (Flinn 55), but rather figures living death as catalyzing queer forms of being and fulfillment. Decay is still present, but not embodied as femininity, subject to misogynistic ridicule; instead, the film transfers decomposition and delegitimation, by way of a queer, camp-infused misandry, to the bloody apparition of Dr. Frankenstein. The ageist-misogynistic tendencies rampant in consumer readings of the film, I would argue, are the reaction of an audience demographic frustrated by the fact that the film does not deliver the anticipated heteronormative spectacle. The posturing of these viewers can be read as an attempt to shore up hetero-masculinity as the "proper" soft-core viewing position.[24] Furthermore, it communicates—often with lame attempts at witticism—which "proper" signifiers of femininity are valued from such positions, and who the ideal consumer of those codes is.[25] This posturing can be seen as a version of what Bruce LaBruce has dubbed "bad straight camp": a reactionary appropriation of camp that is marked by a "complete normalization and de-contextualization away from subversive or transgressive impulses in the service of capitalist exploitation." *Lust for Frankenstein* deploys queer countermeasures that work against such bad straight camp normalization.

Dr. Frankenstein is initially situated as the driving force of the narrative, appearing to Moira with directions and clues so that she might decipher his untimely death. The implication is that he was murdered by Moira's stepmother, Abigail. Yet as the story progresses, the male-driven, linear narrative of clues followed by revelations is short-circuited by queer monotony and subsumed by Moira and Goddess's living-dead relationship. Like the queer zoning out described previously, this process recalls Koestenbaum's discussion of record collecting as temporal reversal: "to collect is to go backward in time: you don't amass objects unless you believe, on some level, that you'll never die, or unless you want to defy death" (63). In fact, in one early scene, the ghost of Dr. Frankenstein, blood streaming down his face and nose pressed against a glass door, appears to Moira, urging her to "find my records." Moira and the viewer finally realize that he is referring to vinyl grunge records, which she locates and places on the turntable. These "records" provide a campy visual and aural refrain connoting a melancholic resistance to death and are juxtaposed with other gaudy artifacts, including Goddess's gold platform boots, multiple shots of a seemingly random dog (once shown in a giant cage), a porcelain rendition of three wise angels (kitsch Westernization of the three wise monkeys), and matador and flamenco dolls. On a basic level, this kitsch effects the "perverse democratization" (Flinn 63) of the objects' materiality in a classic camp sense where "surface, feel, and texture bring their campiness to life" (Flinn 77), but it also has implications for spectatorial positioning. The gratuitous presentation of these artifacts, insignificant to the narrative, upsets normative avenues of spectatorship—in this case, masculinist connoisseurship both of "high" art and of "low" trash culture. What this collection of kitsch without "clear or useful meaning" (Winnubst 91) ultimately produces instead is the spectatorial experience of queer monotony.

Such monotony also suffuses the many scenes revolving around sensual encounters between the human, the partly human, and the nonhuman.

In one psychedelic dream sequence, Moira voyeuristically gazes through a screen that she caresses for an extended period of time. The appearance of Dr. Frankenstein's ghost mentioned earlier involves his close encounter with a glass window. In another scene, Moira finds Goddess in the midst of a sexual encounter with a palm tree and joins in as Franco deploys his signature swoop zooms, periodically cutting away to track across the shirtless chest of a man cutting wood. This extended sequence thus sutures the non-human (tree, axe), the partly human (living-dead Goddess), and the ostensibly human (Moira, woodcutter) into a visual entanglement of queer desire defined largely by its bewildering, unhurried quality.

The monotony of this last sequence queerly enacts what Patricia MacCormack calls "necro folding and unfolding" (351), a synthesis of activity and passivity that "de-parts bodies and sexual acts iterated through perception as reification" (351). In other words, relational reflections that work to constitute the self as a distinct entity are disallowed as bodies are staged and interact or fall out of contact. The fact that absolute sameness or difference (which might be evoked via purely dyadic concepts like hetero/homo, human/nonhuman, etc.) is not permitted facilitates a monotony

Queer arboreal intimacy. Goddess (Michelle Bauer) and Moira (Lina Romay) in *Lust for Frankenstein*. (One Shot Productions and E. I. Independent Cinema. Screen capture.)

that challenges normative viewing positions. Attempts to adopt a voyeuristically objective or diegetically aligned gaze are all but impossible, and spectatorship is queered by the viewer's immersion in Franco's campy take on scream queen sensuality, effected partly through the director's discordant use of sound and mise-en-scène. The soundtrack initially consists of a single bowed instrument, which is soon joined by an alluring saxophone; both clash, however, with diegetic sounds, including the ultrareverberated moans of Goddess, the incessant thuds of the woodcutter's chopping, and the clatter of palm leaves. Such contrapuntal aural arrangements complement the off-kilter cutting between Moira and Goddess and the woodcutter. The sequence does not serve a teleological end and "contrasts with an investigative purpose of the audience setting-up of specific questions that must be answered" (MacCormack 360). Instead, the intimacy between Moira and Goddess engenders a queer form of monotony. Serious to the point of impassivity, their faces connote exhaustion as they are compositionally embedded within their sensuous tropical surrounding. The spectator is pulled through a series of affective registers, leaving his or her perception divided among them. By all but negating this sequence's relevance to the narrative and by scrambling the perspectival focus, Franco accentuates the queer camp pleasures to be taken in the scream queen performances, the unconventional aural-visual rhythms, and the peculiar tropical-pulp imagery.[26]

The sequence finally ends with a zooming shot of Goddess sleeping on a leather couch, snoring and still wearing her fabulous golden platform boots. Since most of the multicolored hallucinations of *Lust for Frankenstein* are implied to be dream flashbacks, there are a number of sleeping sequences in it. In a sense, the film falls asleep on the viewer. It deflects the critique that it puts viewers to sleep by being the first to arrive at that state, highlighting the monotony of staying awake in the presence of another's slumber. The final sequence returns to this notion by downplaying what could have been a crucial narrative reveal for an attentive spectator—a dream sequence suggesting that Moira was complicit in her father's murder—and instead lingering on a shot of Moira and Goddess embracing while asleep. Dr. Frankenstein's ghost rambles on about not being able to visit her again, but as she and Goddess sleep, Moira's voice-over counters with a dismissal as the close-up of her fades to a fragmented, kaleidoscopic visualization of Frankenstein's face. She states, "I hope I never dream of stupid things again." Thus, in its final frames, the film effectively communicates a disregard for the spectator's desire for narrative meaning in favor of queer monotony. This queer monotony is congruent with Eve Sedgwick's reparative impulse that "wants to assemble and confer plenitude on an object that will then have resources to offer to an inchoate self" (149). By refusing to homogenize or foreclose viewing positions, the film encourages the spectator to remain open to the vagaries of camp reception and queer pleasure. At its conclusion, the dream sequences and narrative threads to which the viewer has attended are rendered insignificant in an ultimate camp trick played on the audience. What matters, in the end, is its profound disregard for narrative meaning, its delight in the camp pleasures of scream queen performance, and its queerly collective challenge to the singular normative viewing position.

CONCLUSION

Franco's later 16mm and video work has often been denigrated by mainstream viewers and cult fans alike as boring, pointless, shoddy, and, in misogynistic terms, as "grotesque" or "ugly." Furthermore, academic consideration of this work has been scant and generally negative. Ironically, it was created at the very moment when Franco's earlier films were being rediscovered, celebrated, and remediated for the digital marketplace. In comparison to his earlier films, Franco's later productions are admittedly minimalist and often baffling, marked by their repeated use of the same locations, a grainy video aesthetic, low-quality sound, and highly elliptical narratives. Yet I would argue that their amateurish quality and repetitive character lend them a political edge. While Franco's decision to film on 16mm and video was no doubt economical, the resistance of these media to cinematic norms of image resolution and sound quality matches the resistance of the films themselves to normative meanings and values. The present chapter has aimed to take his later works seriously both as important historical artifacts and as films with the capacity to facilitate spectatorship open to the pleasures of queer monotony and zoning out.

Whereas both fans and scholars have recuperated Franco's earlier films by highlighting their ties to "legitimate" cinema—their art house associations (Hawkins 87–116) or Franco's connections to Orson Welles (Hawkins 88) and other renowned auteurs—his direct-to-video films are not as easily canonized. Consequently, even Franco's most ardent fans tend to dismiss them or consider them deficient.[27] In my view, the value of the director's late 16mm and video work lies in the way it addresses queer audiences. His direct-to-video productions encourage and support queer dreams in ways that his earlier, more renowned films do not. As I have shown in this essay, a key source of their queer sensibility is the subcultural figure of the scream queen. Indeed, it is difficult to imagine them having the same impact absent their cult stars. At the same time, we should also recognize Franco's role in revitalizing scream queen culture. While cult scream queendom developed in the late 1980s as an American subcultural phenomenon that forged a distinctive camp sensibility and a queer following, Franco's late films helped to extend that legacy into the twenty-first century. Moreover, as they were among the first transnational coproductions starring Linnea Quigley and Michelle Bauer, they helped market scream queen stardom to audiences outside North America. They also added a new star to the pantheon of cult scream queens: in 2006, Franco's partner and frequent star, Lina Romay, was celebrated by the Canadian horror magazine *Rue Morgue* as not only "Europe's most famous and fearless exhibitionist" (Alexander 19) but also a "sexploitation scream queen" (19). Ultimately, then, Franco's intervention in the scream queen subgenre both infused his cinema with new forms of queer dissent and recoded the scream queen phenomenon for audiences around the world.

Notes

1. See Antonio Lázaro-Reboll's *Spanish Horror Film* (156–97) for a discussion of horror fan cultures in Spain with reference to the circulation of discourse on Franco's later work. Also, see Joan Hawkins's *Cutting Edge* (3–32) for a discussion of cultural taste and Euro horror's circulation in the United States.

2. An early example is Hawkins's reading of the transgressive aspects of *Gritos en la noche* (*The Awful Dr. Orlof*, 1962) that disrupt a male gaze (102–3). Others have considered Franco's representation of gender in a national context—as, for example, challenging the "representation of women in (Spanish) subgeneric cinema as inferior" (Lázaro-Reboll 63). Recently, queerness in Franco's work has been decoded through close visual-textual analysis by Ian Olney in both *Euro Horror* (142–81) and "Unmanning *The Exorcist*" (561–71).

3. Tatjana Pavlović has emphasized the pleasures of Jess Franco's films for female spectators (*Despotic Bodies* 119) and also discussed their lesbian and gay reception: "The lesbian following centres on Franco's lesbian vampires and WIP ('women in prison') genres . . . that especially appeal to the gay audience, with their campy legacy of sadistic wardresses, (female) dictators with strong sexual appetites, innocent young women corrupted in jail, cruel lesbian guards, and so on" ("Gender and Spanish Horror Film" 141).

4. Queer studies is a scholarly field that emerged in the late 1980s out of gay and lesbian studies and was inspired by AIDS activists' reclaiming of the derogatory term "queer" for anti-assimilationist purposes. For a discussion of this emergence, see David Halperin (339–40).

5. Camp was historically a method of communication and world-making within gay and bisexual male subcultures predating twentieth-century liberation movements. Over the years, horror cinema has often provided a home for camp and queerness more generally. For instance, Bonnie Zimmerman (23–24) and Andrea Weiss (84–108) appraise lesbian representations in films like *Les Lèvres rouges* (*Daughters of Darkness*, 1971), and Jack Babuscio discusses gay camp's relation to film, particularly the horror genre (121–22). See Fabio Cleto's introduction to *Camp* (1–42) for genealogies of camp's discursive and cultural legibility.

6. I am wary of the pitfalls and blind spots that queer studies has created, such as the erasure of bisexuality (Richter 273–74). This is why I invoke the coalitionary version of its usage, rather than the deconstructive version that often results in such erasures.

7. The explicit marketing of scream queen films to heterosexual men is evinced by the tactic of prominently featuring scantily clad women in advertising materials. This tactic is evident in the marketing of such canonical scream queen films as *Hollywood Chainsaw Hookers* (1988), *Nightmare Sisters* (1988), and *Sorority Babes in the Slimeball Bowl-O-Rama* (1988). Production strategies such as the abundancy of female nudity also point to the intention to appeal to straight men. But the marketing and production of these films was not uniformly heteronormative. In the audio commentary on the DVD for *Nightmare Sisters*, gay director David DeCoteau discusses his resistance to the inclusion of full-frontal female nudity in the film, explaining that he regarded it as being at odds with the camp sensibility he intended.

8. For a discussion and theorization of queer labor in film industries, see Matthew Tinkcom's *Working Like a Homosexual*. Tinkcom describes how queer men, as well as other marginalized groups, have engaged in distinct forms of labor (such as camp) to negotiate ambivalences and oppositions in film production (9–11).

9. This has been verified on Franco fan platforms by actor and filmmaker Pedro Temboury; see the comments thread on a blog post from 2009 (Mendíbil). Temboury appeared in four of Franco's One Shot features and directed a recent documentary on Franco, *La última película de Jess Franco* (2013), for the French company Eurociné (a French coproducer and distributor for many of Franco's earlier films).

10. The term "scream queen" crossed back over into mainstream horror vernacular with the slasher renaissance of the late 1990s, which was spearheaded by the *Scream* (1996–2011) and *I Know What You Did Last Summer* (1997–2006) franchises. And it still has mainstream cachet today, thanks in part to the popular television series *Scream Queens* (2015–16), in which Jamie Lee Curtis plays a major role.

11. For the purposes of this chapter, I focus on the American releases and reception of these films.

12. Tim Lucas's article "Catching up with Jess Franco" appeared in 2001 and functioned as a report to American Euro horror and genre fans on the wildness of the One Shot productions, stoking cult anticipation of their commercial release.

13. To briefly comment on the difference in distribution: while I recall the two films from E. I. Independent being available widely in the Midwestern United States through the Musicland and Trans World retail chains, I recall observing the early Sub Rosa DVD releases only at Best Buy. The former recollection is confirmed by the wide distribution advertised on E. I.'s website at the time ("Retail"). The latter is confirmed by the still prominent

quote on One Shot's website: "All Jess Franco titles are also in stock at Best Buy and many JC Penney stores" (*One Shot*). Their stated availability at JC Penney, a department store, is somewhat surprising.

14. *Lust for Frankenstein*'s cover art was designed by Michael Raso, with photography by Ward Boult. *Mari-Cookie*'s DVD package design is credited to the distributor, Sub Rosa Studios, LLC.

15. For both an interview with DeCoteau and an example of the gay reception of his early films, see CampBlood.org (Juergens). Queer camp content and reception have become even more prominent in contemporary scream queen media and fan subculture. For example, DeCoteau's *1313* franchise (2011–12) and *3 Scream Queens* (2014) openly revel in homoerotic depictions of scantily clad men.

16. In his innovative book *Soft in the Middle*, David Andrews traces the genealogy of American soft-core film. While I agree with Andrews that soft-core's history is not analogous to that of hard-core, his argument that "softcore is more uniformly heterosexual" (13) than hard-core ignores the queer dimensions of soft-core we see in cult scream queen cinema.

17. For example, one Amazon reviewer states: "I have one other Jesus Franco film with Lina Romay . . . and in it she is young and beautiful" (Kane). The reviewer then goes on to describe Romay in *Lust for Frankenstein*: "I don't believe anybody who buys Franco films is hoping to see a woman in her mid-50s at youngest, complete with liverspots and vericose veins, expose herself and have love scenes" (Kane).

18. Again, as noted previously, the production and reception of DeCoteau's recent scream queen beefcake films offer a powerful testament to the queer pleasures offered by the subgenre. The fact that Stevens, Bauer, and Quigley star in some of these movies serves to underscore their centrality to the scream queen canon.

19. Other reviewers were frustrated by the presence of Romay (not pictured on the cover artwork) in the film. This frustration is expressed with varying degrees of objectifying judgment ranging from "not sexy" (Mesmerise) to "an OLD dumppy [*sic*] lil seahag" ("EEEEWWWWWWWWW!!!!!!!!!!!!!!!!!"). That the actresses from the cover, Newman and Bauer, actually do appear in the film may reinforce the reading that Franco did not intend to deliver sexual spectacle via codes legible to a soft-core audience.

20. Koestenbaum is specifically speaking about a material aspect of the collection and appreciation of opera records by gay male fans. His articulation of a backward acclimatization resonates, from my perspective, with Richter's view (273–80) that queer optics are not exhausted by codification within

a monosexual dichotomy. For instance, I would argue that Koestenbaum's backward mode of reception is open to queer people who are bisexual.

21. Halberstam's concept stems from his study of animated enactments of collective anthropomorphic revolt, specifically in Pixar films (27–52). However, he indicates its applicability to exploitation horror films such as *Invasion of the Bee Girls* (1973), which focuses on the nonreproductive queerness of apian women (52).

22. In Edelman's discussion, monotonous depictions of "suspended animation" (55) and arachnid narcissism (56) allegorically correlate with queerness, which is positioned as abject in the context of reproductive futurist politics. However, as Edelman argues, abjection can be used to facilitate queer opposition to such politics (1–31).

23. For discussions of repetition as a structuring tenet of European horror and American soft-core, respectively, see Olney's *Euro Horror* (23–45) and Andrews's *Soft in the Middle* (1–22).

24. See Hollows (35–53) and Read (54–70) for histories of the exclusion of women and the celebration of masculinity within both academic and subcultural discourses. Several online reviews of the Franco films discussed in this chapter imply, through their complaints, the reviewers' exclusionary view of the films' proper viewers—men with normative heterosexual ideals of feminine beauty. Recall the reviewer who writes in response to *Lust for Frankenstein*, "I don't believe anybody who buys Franco films is hoping to see a woman in her mid-50s at youngest" (Kane).

25. For example, an anonymous reviewer of *Lust for Frankenstein* on Netflix is obviously making an attempt at humor when he or she writes: "The skin in this skin flick is really wrapped around some ugly women—when you can see it" ("First Let Me Say . . .").

26. The queer camp sensibility has been linked to the multiplication of and play with perspectives in various media, as well as to the pleasure in encountering the sensuous and material aspects of the objects or images represented (Babuscio 121).

27. For instance, in an excellent survey of the first half of Franco's career, Stephen Thrower describes the "drawbacks" (45) of Franco's cinematic freedom in his later films, such as the necessity of shooting on video in his own home.

Works Cited

Alexander, Chris. "Spotlight Eurotic Horror: Sexploitation Scream Queen." *Rue Morgue.* Apr. 2006: 19. Print.

Andrews, David. *Soft in the Middle: The Contemporary Softcore Feature in Its Contexts*. Columbus: Ohio State UP, 2006. Print.

Antin, David. "Video: The Distinctive Features of the Medium." *Video Art: Institute of Contemporary Art, University of Pennsylvania, Philadelphia, Pennsylvania, January 17 to February 28, 1975*. Philadelphia: The Institute, 1975. 57–72. Print.

Babuscio, Jack. "The Cinema of Camp (AKA Camp and the Gay Sensibility)." *Camp: Queer Aesthetics and the Performing Subject: A Reader*. Ed. Fabio Cleto. Ann Arbor: U of Michigan P, 1999. 117–35. Print.

Beck, Calvin T. *Scream Queens: Heroines of the Horrors*. New York: Macmillan, 1978. Print.

Bottom, J. "A 1 Star Rating is Too Kind." Rev. of *Lust for Frankenstein*. *Amazon*. 22 Sept. 2002. Web. 31 May 2017.

Cleto, Fabio. *Camp: Queer Aesthetics and the Performing Subject: A Reader*. Ann Arbor: U of Michigan P, 1999. Print.

Clover, Carol J. *Men, Women, and Chain Saws: Gender in the Modern Horror Film*. Princeton: Princeton UP, 1992. Print.

DeCoteau, David, and John Schouweiler. Director and Producer Commentary Track. *Nightmare Sisters*. Dir. David DeCoteau. Perf. Linnea Quigley, Brinke Stevens, and Michelle Bauer. Chatsworth: Image Entertainment, 2003. DVD.

Doty, Alexander. *Flaming Classics: Queering the Film Canon*. New York: Routledge, 2000. Print.

Edelman, Lee. *No Future: Queer Theory and the Death Drive*. Durham: Duke UP, 2004. Print.

"EEEEWWWWWWWW!!!!!!!!!!!!!!!!!" Rev. of *Lust for Frankenstein*. *Amazon*. 30 Sept. 2001. Web. 31 May 2017.

Faoro, Jeffrey. Cover Synopsis and Copy. *Lust for Frankenstein* DVD. Dir. Jesús Franco. Glenwood: E. I. Independent Cinema, 2001. Print.

"First Let Me Say . . ." Rev. of *Lust for Frankenstein*. *Netflix*. Web. 31 May 2017.

"First Taste of *Tender Flesh* or How to Produce a Movie Without Really Trying." *Draculina*. February 1997: 24–26. Print.

Flinn, Caryl. "The Deaths of Camp." *Camera Obscura* 35.35 (1995): 52–84. Print.

"From Scream Queen to Box-Office Dream: the Daughter of Tony Curtis and Janet Leigh Stoops to Conquer." *Esquire* Jul. 1985: 66. Print.

Halberstam, Jack. *The Queer Art of Failure*. Durham: Duke UP, 2011. Print.

Halperin, David. "The Normalization of Queer Theory." *Journal of Homosexuality* 45.2–4 (2003): 339–43. Print.

Hawkins, Joan. *Cutting Edge: Art-Horror and the Horrific Avant-Garde*. Minneapolis: U of Minnesota P, 2000. Print.

Hollows, Joanne. "The Masculinity of Cult." *Defining Cult Movies: The Cultural Politics of Oppositional Taste*. Ed. Mark Jancovich, Antonio Lázaro-Reboll,

Julian Stringer, and Andy Willis. Manchester: Manchester UP, 2003. 35–53. Print.

Juergens, Brian. "Interview with Voluntary Canadian Dave DeCoteau." *Camp Blood: Queer Eye for the Straight-Jacket.* 17 Jan. 2005. Web. 31 May 2017.

Kane, J. "Romay Should Keep Her Clothes On." Rev. of *Lust for Frankenstein. Amazon.* 12 May 2002. Web. 31 May 2017.

Knoedelseder, William K. Jr. "Jamie Lee Curtis: A Scream Queen Attracts Attention." *Los Angeles Times* 16 Nov. 1980: Q4. Print.

Koestenbaum, Wayne. *The Queen's Throat: Opera, Homosexuality, and the Mystery of Desire.* New York: Poseidon, 1993. Print.

Krzywinska, Tanya. *Sex and the Cinema.* London: Wallflower, 2006. Print.

LaBruce, Bruce. "Notes on Camp and Anti-Camp." *The Gay & Lesbian Review Worldwide* 21.2 (2014): 9–13. *ProQuest.* Web. 31 May 2017.

Lázaro-Reboll, Antonio. *Spanish Horror Film.* Edinburgh: Edinburgh UP, 2012. Print.

Lucas, Tim. "Catching Up With Jess Franco." *Video Watchdog* 68 (2001): 4–10. Print.

———. "How to Read a Franco Film." *Video Watchdog* 1 (1990): 18–34. Print.

MacCormack, Patricia. "Necrosexuality." *Queering the Non/human.* Ed. Noreen Giffney and Myra J. Hird. Hampshire: Ashgate, 2008. 339–62. Print.

Mendíbil, Álex. "Dr. Wong's Virtual Hell." *El Franconomicon / I'm in a Jess Franco State of Mind.* 7 May 2009. Web. 31 May 2017.

Mesmerise, S. "Lust for Frankenstein." Rev. of *Lust for Frankenstein. Amazon.* 19 Sept. 2011. Web. 31 May 2017.

Olney, Ian. *Euro Horror: Classic European Horror Cinema in Contemporary American Culture.* Bloomington: Indiana UP, 2013. Print.

———. "Unmanning *The Exorcist*: Sex, Gender and Excess in the 1970s Euro-Horror Possession Film." *Quarterly Review of Film and Video* 31.6 (2014): 561–71. Print.

One Shot Productions. Website. 31 May 2017.

Pavlović, Tatjana. *Despotic Bodies and Transgressive Bodies: Spanish Culture from Francisco Franco to Jesús Franco.* Albany: State U of New York P, 2003. Print.

———. "Gender and Spanish Horror Film." *Gender and Spanish Cinema.* Ed. Steven Marsh and Parvati Nair. Oxford: Berg, 2004. 135–50. Print.

Read, Jacinda. "The Cult of Masculinity: From Fan-boys to Academic Bad-boys." *Defining Cult Movies: The Cultural Politics of Oppositional Taste.* Ed. Mark Jancovich, Antonio Lázaro-Reboll, Julian Stringer, and Andy Willis. Manchester: Manchester UP, 2003. 54–70. Print.

"Retail, Etail, Wholesale and Internet Customers." *E. I. Independent Cinema.* Internet Archive Wayback Machine. 16 Oct. 2002. Web. 31 May 2017.

Richter, Nicole. "Bisexual Erasure in 'Lesbian Vampire' Film Theory." *Journal of Bisexuality*. 13.2 (2013): 273–80. Print.

Sedgwick, Eve. *Touching Feeling: Affect, Pedagogy, Performativity*. Durham: Duke UP, 2003. Print.

"Terrible . . ." Rev. of *Lust for Frankenstein. Netflix*. Web. 31 May 2017.

Thrower, Stephen, with Julian Grainger. *Murderous Passions: The Delirious Cinema of Jesús Franco*. London: Strange Attractor, 2015. Print.

Tinkcom, Matthew. *Working Like a Homosexual: Camp, Capital, and Cinema*. Durham, NC: Duke UP, 2002. Print.

Weiss, Andrea. *Vampires & Violets: Lesbians in Films*. New York: Penguin Books, 1993. Print.

Winnubst, Shannon. "Bataille's Queer Pleasures: The Universe as Spider or Spit." *Reading Bataille Now*. Bloomington: Indiana UP, 2007. 75–93. Print.

Zimmerman, Bonnie. "Daughters of Darkness: Lesbian Vampires." *Jump Cut: A Review of Contemporary Media* 24–25 (1981): 23–24. Print.

9

ENDLESS RE-VIEW

Jess Franco in Video Watchdog *and* Eyeball

Antonio Lázaro-Reboll

n his evocation of horror film viewing in the grind houses of New York's Forty-Second Street, cultural historian and poet Geoffrey O'Brien recalls being "adrift in a world of European exploitation movies, unstable mixtures of poetry and gothic melodrama and outright pornography— Belgian vampires, Italian cannibals, Spanish sex murderers, hooded inquisitors from Portugal," and observes that once enthralled by such rich cinematic fare, "there was no easy way out" (182). A particular Jess Franco film stuck with O'Brien: *Paroxismus* (*Venus in Furs*, 1969) "interwove random components—of jazz combos, sadomasochistic orgies, stock shots of the Rio carnival and the Blue Mosque in Istanbul, Klaus Kinski wearing a djellaba, and a nude body washed up on a beach—to yield an endlessly unresolved dream" (182). Were one to attempt to fathom the director's "ultimate intentions" in this—or any other notoriously "unresolved"— Franco film, O'Brien ventures, "Franco could well reply that 'The cinema is not my livelihood but my life. . . . In movies I look for movies. They don't interest me as a means but as an end'" (183). Jess Franco had already made a staggering 150 movies when O'Brien's *The Phantom Empire: Movies in the Mind of the 20th Century* was published in 1993, "so many . . . that an entire subculture [has been] required simply to keep track of his activities" (183); "serious students" of Franco set themselves the task of tracking down with something akin to "devotion" the "multilingual variants and alternate titles and repackagings" (184) of his work. If I have quoted at length from O'Brien's words on Franco, it is because they serve here as a point of departure to delineate Franco's trajectory from the demimonde of Times Square in the late 1960s and early 1970s to his central role in the horror film fanzine subculture that emerged in the late 1980s and early 1990s on both sides of the Atlantic following the advent of video. They also frame my discussion of writings on Franco as a transnational exploitation and cult auteur in Anglo-American contexts of reception and consumption since the late 1980s in relation to changing viewing and reviewing practices (that is, from grind house to VHS and DVD), fetishist fixations and cinephile obsessions, and specialized discourses of connoisseurship and collectorship.

This chapter examines the two most prominent publications of the subculture devoted to a cult appreciation and connoisseurship of Franco. Arguably, the writings of Tim Lucas and Stephen Thrower, who have returned repeatedly and compulsively to his films for almost three decades, have carved out a niche on the study of Franco that deserves critical attention. In parallel yet distinctive ways, these like-minded European lowbrow genre connoisseurs have contributed to the unearthing of information about his work in a detailed and sustained manner, the transvaluation of his films for VHS and DVD consumption, the assembling of a catalog for potential film collectors, and the discursive constructions of Franco that have made critics, fans, and scholars alike think differently about his cinema. Sifting zealously through Franco's work, Lucas and Thrower have enabled access to his cinema by documenting imports, bootleg videotapes, and special editions; identifying retitlings, running times, and cut or uncut versions; comparing film transfers; and guiding consumers, fans, and scholars through the tangled histories of the production, distribution, exhibition, and consumption of his films. Initially from the pages of *Fangoria* and its sister publication *Gorezone* in the late 1980s, and then painstakingly from the pages of his very own self-published magazine *Video Watchdog: The Perfectionist's Guide to Fantastic Video* (1990–2016), Lucas led the way in tracking down Franco's films for American (and global) fans. His first article on the director was the often-cited "How to Read a Franco Film" (1990), which was most recently revised in "Jess Franco's Declaration of Principles: How to Read the Early Films, 1959–67" (2010); in between there have been many other iterations, such as his introduction to *Obsession: The Films of Jess Franco* (1993), an updated version of his 1990 piece, and his copious reviews of individual Franco releases over the years, whether on VHS, laser disc, DVD, or Blu-ray format. No doubt, more are to come. Similarly, Stephen Thrower, editor of the British fanzine *Eyeball: The European Sex & Horror Review* (1989–98), has offered a discerning reading of many a Franco film. (*The Eyeball Compendium* [2003] collated all of the Franco reviews published in the fanzine.) His fixation on the films of Franco has been poured into his recent *Murderous Passions: The Delirious Cinema of Jesús Franco* (2015), which covers the director's output between 1958 and 1974, the first of two volumes to provide a completist approach to Franco's filmography. Collaborations and interactions between *Video Watchdog* and *Eyeball* point to a collective work-in-progress between fanzine editors, reviewers, and readers involving the mapping of the circulation, consumption, and reception of Franco films in contemporary American and British horror cultures; Lucas, for example, credited regular *Eyeball* contributor Mark Ashworth with the "UK videography notes, and . . . Craig Ledbetter [*European Trash Cinema*] and Michael Secula [*Demonique*] for additional listings" in his original "Jess Franco Selective Videography" (35).

Underlying their respective critical projects is the attempt to come to grips with a body of work that has been repeatedly described as tangled and impossible to manage, a notion aptly captured by the title of the Franco retrospective organized by the Cinémathèque Française in 2008, "Fragments d'une filmographie impossible." Both Lucas and Thrower have come up with imaginative maxims in their attempts to explain the films of Franco. While the former proclaimed that, "*You can't see one until you've seen them all. A degree of immersion is essential*" ("How to Read a Franco Film" 23), the latter has provided a not dissimilar reflection on how Franco's films do not stand alone but are to be regarded as "[a] rippling borderless continuum, with individual films less important than the wider trends and currents passing through [them]" ("Jesús 'Jess' Franco" 19). While the main aim of this chapter is to consider their archival, critical, and, I would argue, curatorial work, my interest also lies in examining what brings Lucas and Thrower back to Franco time and again. In other words, what made the films of Franco a major exemplar of the (re)viewing practices of *Video Watchdog* and *Eyeball*? Particular attention, therefore, is paid to their critical practices and sensibilities, which are located against the background of the contexts and ideologies from which their writings emerge, namely American and British horror film cultures and their interactions.

To be sure, there is a broader network of cultural intermediaries and traders who have played a crucial role in the circulation and dissemination of Franco films over the last three decades, from genre magazines to fanzines, mail-order video catalogs to DVD distributor companies, and blogs to online forums. The "entire subculture" to which O'Brien refers, and, to a certain extent, prefigures, went into overdrive when *Video Watchdog* and *Eyeball* came out in the early 1990s as part of a momentous shift in the availability and coverage of genre fare on video. Lucas's ties to the contemporary emerging horror film fanzine scene, for example, can be traced in the pages of Craig Ledbetter's *European Trash Cinema* (1988–98). The 1990s witnessed the proliferation of publications on Franco. Franco's transnational reach within the world of fanzines devoted to horror and exploitation films extended to the United States, the United Kingdom, France, Spain, and Australia. Among the contemporary fanzines including coverage of available Franco material, as well as interviews with the director, are (to name a few): *European Trash Cinema*, the British *Shock Xpress* (edited by Stefan Jaworzyn, 1985–89), the French *The Manacoa Files* (Alain Petit, 1994–95), the Spanish *2000maniacos* (edited by Manuel Valencia, 1989–present), and the Australian *Fatal Visions* (edited by Michael Helms, 1988–98).[1] The first volumes produced by Franco fans also correspond to this period: *Obsession: The Films of Jess Franco* (Balbo, Blumenstock, and Kessler, 1993), to which Lucas himself contributed the introduction, and *Jess Franco: El Sexo del Horror* (Aguilar, 1999). More recent manifestations such as Robert Monell's blog *I'm in a Jess Franco State of Mind*, "dedicated to the archaeology of Franco's films," and *El Franconomicón*, a blog alliance between Álex Mendíbil and Monell, are indicative of the consuming passions of fans and the enduring appeal of Francophilia in the digital age.[2]

ON THE FRANCO CASE: TIM LUCAS'S *VIDEO WATCHDOG*

As Lucas unreservedly acknowledges in his editorial tribute to Franco after the filmmaker's death in April 2013, "[Franco] was in many ways the foundation block upon which this magazine [*Video Watchdog*] rests" ("The Watchdog Barks" 174:3). The Spanish director had been the subject of the first article featured in the "VW Directrospective" section, and for Lucas, "the many marks worn by the variations of his work defined the very problems of identification that made this magazine essential in the first place" (3).[3] Of course, the implication that Franco was at the center of the creation and development of *Video Watchdog* is inextricable from its larger context. A director whose filmography had exceeded 100 titles by 1990 and whose movies circulated on videotape in multilingual variations and versions, he provided the ultimate illustrative example of the "problems of identification" to which Lucas refers. (Certainly, the choice of Franco as a cornerstone of *Video Watchdog* has been validated further since the advent of DVD in the mid-1990s; as Lucas observes, Franco holds "the remarkable distinction of being the film director most widely represented on DVD" ["The Watchdog Barks" 119:3], with around 80 different titles available in 2005 and 130 by 2010.) Let us now contextualize *Video Watchdog*'s philosophy and drive as a publication, as well as Lucas's approach to film (video) reviewing vis-à-vis its historical and cultural moment, namely as part of a new way of conceiving criticism and as part of the wider golden age of horror film fanzines, in order to understand the way in which Lucas wrote about Franco.

At a time when there was a surge of newsletter-sized publications and review-zines competing for the attention of different readerships attracted to lowbrow genre filmmaking, and in particular horror and related genres, Lucas had to carve out his own publication niche. The films of Franco helped him in this process, for the director met the commercial and cultural criteria upon which the publication was founded. Like most contemporary alternative publications that declared their opposition to mainstream and commercial American horror products, Lucas had already asserted his oppositional stance as a critical gesture in his coverage of Franco in *Fangoria*. Writing in 1988, he declared: "Two years ago, I was unable to see past the hasty surface of Franco's work and hated it. Today, in a climate of insultingly mild horror product tailored to fit the MPAA straightjacket, I can't get enough of it" ("The Agony and the Ecstasy of Jess Franco" 15). Lucas's position-taking carried over into *Video Watchdog* and extended to his coverage of foreign horror film in general. But, unlike other lowbrow connoisseurs of that period and kindred-spirit publications that documented and mapped the circulation of exploitation films available on home video, *Video Watchdog* presented itself as "a consumer-oriented guide to horror, science fiction, and fantasy films on video tapes and discs" ("The Watchdog Barks" 1:3). In his first editorial, Lucas advises his potential readers that *Video Watchdog* "will not publish video reviews, at least not in the traditional sense . . . ; instead, we will critique what really counts: the way a film has been *presented* on video" (4). Prior to *Video Watchdog*, Lucas had been developing his "Video Watchdog" concept and honing his video reviewing skills in a column for the Chicago-based magazine *Video Times*, where he soon grasped that there was "a new way of writing about home video" (*The Video Watchdog Book* xx) and that videotapes needed to be reviewed differently. When *Video Times* folded, he moved the column to *Gorezone*, narrowing his scope to cover horror, science fiction, fantasy, and cult films. Indeed, Franco's prolific work across a myriad of genres and his idiosyncratic blending of genre iconography afforded Lucas a fertile terrain to explore. Similar to the work of such horror film directors as Mario Bava and Dario Argento, Franco's work had been subjected to institutional and commercial forces from censorship to distribution or, as Lucas puts it, "to the slings and arrows of outrageous editorial meddling" ("The Watchdog

Barks" 1:3), across a number of film territories. The numerous iterations of Franco's film on home video—recut or uncut, official or bootlegged, soft-core or hard-core—catered to the desires and sensibility of the video collectors to whom *Video Watchdog* was addressed. And horror was at the time arguably the most collectible genre in home video.

Lucas's grounding in genre cinema was driven by a desire to make "the writing devoted to the *genre* . . . more enlightened. Enlighten*ing*" (1:3) and "to usher in 1990 . . . the beginning of a New Decade of Information" (1:4). *Video Watchdog*'s raison d'être was ingrained in the ethos of democratic access to material and of media consumption: "[u]se us," urges Lucas in his earliest editorial, "[W]e're here to inform you, to warn you, and to enrich your appreciation of those films and filmmakers we cover" (1:4). As Lucas Hilderbrand eloquently puts it, "[t]he politics of video have, from the beginning, been a politics of access" (214). As for its reach, *Video Watchdog* did not circumscribe itself to an Anglo-American readership: in Lucas's words, it was a "global bulletin board for devotees of fantastic films on video" ("The Watchdog Barks" 22:3). It is in this context that a new generation of critics pioneered a new type of review that fed into existing and bourgeoning traditions of horror film criticism. Writings on Franco, therefore, went hand in hand with the creation and development of a new form of review(ing), facilitated and accelerated by the development of home video technologies and desktop publishing and mediated through video reviewing as a distinct genre of film criticism.

"The vanguard consumer calls the shots, asserts oppositional taste as a connoisseur of trash," writes Greg Taylor in *Artists in the Audience: Cults, Camp, and American Film Criticism* (1999), a fascinating study of cult and camp as new models of film appreciation and spectatorship beginning in the 1940s and developing across the next two decades. Notwithstanding the differences between Lucas's *Video Watchdog* and Taylor's object of analysis, the critics Manny Farber and Parker Tyler, whose writings are directly associated with the history of vanguard film criticism, there are some parallels to be drawn between the aesthetic and critical sensibilities displayed by Lucas and the new sensibilities surfacing in traditions of

American film criticism, in particular the cult criticism forged by Farber on American genre cinema. An oppositional stance, the appreciation and (re)appraisal of marginal genres and texts, is at the heart of *Video Watchdog*. Taylor argues that Farber "[set] the terms of cultist connoisseurship for a generation of film enthusiasts" (17) and "pioneered new standards of connoisseurship in order to carve out a marginal niche" (32). To a certain extent, Lucas's writings on Franco bear the marks of Farber's appreciation for the intricacies and pleasures of popular genres and the celebration of "the power of spectators to define their own culture in opposition to prevailing standards" (33). But Lucas's distinctive approach to film criticism belongs to a specific technological time and cultural climate that can best be described as videophilic cult connoisseurship.

Elsewhere in this volume, Ian Olney (see chapter 2) discusses how Franco's 1960s cinema invites cinephiliac pleasures and a special kind of cinephiliac gaze. Within the context of my discussion of *Video Watchdog* as a publication dynamically participating in the reconfiguration of cultures of cinephilia, connoisseurship, and film collecting in the early 1990s, the terms "videophilia," "videophile," "video film connoisseurship," and "video film collecting" seem more appropriate for the historicizing of the appreciation, evaluation, and endless re-viewing of Franco's films. "It's a great time for a vidéaste to be alive," Lucas writes gleefully in one of his editorials ("The Watchdog Barks" 3:3). Lucas's publication was instrumental in cataloging and curating individual Franco films (and their multiple variants) on home video, providing an invaluable resource for historiographical research on the director's videography. It was also instrumental in linking Franco's films to larger cycles, trends, genres, and discursive practices. This can be illustrated, firstly, through a discussion of how one particular Franco film was cataloged in *Video Watchdog* as new releases became available across time as a result of the work of mail-order video catalogs and video-trading circles connected to the magazine; and, secondly, through a comparison of Lucas's two major periodizations of Franco's films, written twenty years apart, "How to Read a Franco Film" (1990) and "Jess Franco's Declaration of Principles: How to Read the Early Films, 1959–67" (2010).[4]

The front cover for *Video Watchdog* issue 157 (Jul./Aug. 2010), in which Tim Lucas revisits his pioneering essay "How to Read a Franco Film" after twenty years in "Jess Franco's Declaration of Principles: How to Read the Early Films, 1959–67." (Courtesy of Tim Lucas and Donna Lucas.)

La Nuit de l'etoiles filantes (*A Virgin among the Living Dead*, 1981) is representative of the slings and arrows of Franco's cinematic fortunes. First mentioned in the opening issue of *Video Watchdog* in Craig Ledbetter's contribution "Venezuelan Video Safari—Miami Style," *A Virgin among the Living Dead* is described as a "Spanish-language tape . . . which got our hopes up because the US version on Wizard Video [released in the mid-1980s] is such a butchered mess. Unfortunately, it was the same thing, with all of the violence and unity missing" (16). Lucas returned to the Wizard Video version three years later to bring *Video Watchdog* readers up-to-date with the alternate versions. "Originally released by Wizard Video in a heavily censored (87m 57s) TV print," observes Lucas, the film is now available in a "restored version" ("Jess is More" 7) by Video Search of Miami, "a patchwork reconstruction . . . composed of footage taken from the Spanish video release *Testamento Diabolico* [*sic*] ('Diabolic Oath'), the Italian *Una vergine frai I morti viventi*, and the French variants *Holocauste de Zombi* ('Zombie Holocaust') and *Christina, Princesse de l'Erotisme* ('Christina, Princess of Eroticism'). It makes for very odd viewing . . . but it's *remarkable* odd viewing" (7). Ever the zealous perfectionist, Lucas nevertheless identifies irregularities in the translation from film to video in the "restored" version pursued by videophiles and collectors: although Video Search of Miami "claims that 35m of deleted material has been reinserted into VIRGIN, their 103m 16s restoration is 15m 19s longer than the Wizard tape" (7); however, "the fact remains that this version collects everything that was ever included in this production" (7)—the potentially perfect copy for any Francophile for whom the uncut version is the (unattainable) fetish text. Writing on the paradoxes of video collecting as a video collector and a former employee of the Criterion Collection, Charles Tashiro observes: "The faith in the potentially perfect copy persists, expressed in the exploitation of ever-newer technologies, striving always to get closer to the film original, but never quite arriving" (16). A further discussion of *A Virgin among the Living Dead* appeared in a later piece devoted to the French production and distribution company Eurociné (Lucas, "Eurociné" 24–37) when their back catalog of obscure titles was exploited by VHS and DVD company

Image Entertainment in the United States in the early part of the first decade of the twenty-first century as part of their "Euroshock Collection." Here, the film is recontextualized for U.S. audiences in relation to the larger production and distribution strategies of Eurociné in the late 1960s and throughout the 1970s.[5]

Such revisionist constructions, crucial to the critical practice of *Video Watchdog*, were reliant not just upon the repeated viewings facilitated by VCRs (and later on by DVD players) but also upon the repeated reviewing and reconfiguring of Franco throughout the years. "How to Read a Franco Film" was Lucas's first attempt at periodizing the films of Franco, offering "a neat arrangement of periods" (19), albeit, as he admitted, in a "primitive stage of development" (19) and subject to changes as other releases were acquired. "Without fail . . . ," Lucas celebrates in the piece, "each new tape made available information I should have had before making those earlier acquaintances but hadn't" (19). The crudeness of the first taxonomy is reflected in the headings that Lucas opted for: (1) "The First Period (1959–61)," (2) "The Second Period (1965–67)," (3) "The Harry Alan Towers Period (1968–70)," (4) "The Peak Years (1970–78)," (5) "The Porno Holocaust Years (1976–81)," and (6) "The Homecoming Years (1981–Present [1990])." The conventional chronological structure allowed Lucas to redress "the haphazard and meaningless overview one perceives from the unevenly balanced list of [video] titles available in America" (19). Looking back at a thirty-year career, Lucas traces Franco's formative years ("[a] filmmaker who knew how to work economically and well . . . and approached his films with the care of a man overjoyed to be realizing his dreams" [20]), indicates his career highs ("his most vibrant work" [21] is to be found from *Cartas boca arriba* [1966] to *Necronomicon* [*Succubus*, 1968], "which capture [the sixties'] fleeting cultural explosion on film" [20]) and lows (his "output [in the eighties] is unquestionably more mechanical and workmanlike with few gems to speak of" [23]), and maps the notable cinematic trajectory of an itinerant filmmaker who initially worked in Spain before coproducing in West Germany and Switzerland, "drifting through Portugal and Istanbul" (21), and finally returning to Spain. But it is Lucas's proposed method rather than the retrospective format that has remained an influential *modus legendi* in subsequent approaches to the study of Franco. To reiterate, "with Franco's films . . . a degree of immersion is essential" (23). *Video Watchdog's* immersion in and obsession with the films of Franco continued in the form of print reviews, DVD and Blu-ray liner notes and audio commentaries, and tributes. Lucas, however, would not revisit his original "How to Read a Franco Film" in *Video Watchdog* until 2010, when the availability of the director's work, thanks to the advent of new digital formats, brought him closer to "seeing them all" ("Jess Franco's Declaration of Principles" 17). "Now that we are more than 100 titles nearer to that goal," declares Lucas in this updated account of Franco's films, "it seems a reasonable time to ask ourselves what, if anything, this ongoing process is bringing into focus" (17). From the title, "Jess Franco's Declaration of Principles: How to Read the Early Films, 1959–67," it is evident that Lucas has narrowed his focus by zooming into a specific time period so as to manage Franco's vast corpus of work. But what are the main changes proposed by Lucas? Firstly, shifts in chronological demarcations; secondly, a rejection of previous labels (for example, "The Classical Years" are "anything but traditional or classical in content" [17] and the early films are "radical statements" [18] in the context of contemporary Spanish cinema); and, thirdly, an alignment of labels with industrial and generic categories that group and describe Franco's films in relation to the zeitgeists of the time ("The Adult Fantasy Years (1967–73)," "The Hard Erotica Years (1974–79)," and "The Genre Concentrate Years (1979–87)," which replace the first period, second period, and peak years, respectively).[6] (In order to acknowledge and incorporate Franco's post-1990 production in the intervening years between the two periodizations, Lucas covers the films under "The Comeback Years (1987–96)" and "The Digital Years (1998–Present [2010]).") Lucas also gives a different inflection to his earlier maxim: "the more one sees, the more important becomes the totality of Franco's filmography—not its particulars. . . . How they stand on their own is not as important as how they serve to illuminate other films or groups of films. It's not about the end product with Franco, it's about the process—that's what makes him unique" (19).

Building on the earlier "VW Directrospective" devoted to Franco, Lucas used "How to Read a Franco Film" to lay out a protocol for analyzing and appreciating Franco's works, as he was not constrained by the need to treat individual titles and could write reviews that were shorter, more technical, and to the point in their aim to inform and orient the prospective consumer. His appreciation of Franco notwithstanding, he does not shy away in the piece from noting the "lameness and sameness" of some of Franco's films (19); after all, the double-edged titles for his articles in *Fangoria* had already alluded to the contradictory affective dimension of the director's work: "The Agony and The Ecstasy of Jess Franco" and "The Torture Chamber of Jess Franco." But there are, he insists, pleasures to be found in this work, such as when "Franco's jaded insistence toward destylization, the roughing-away of the gloss, adjusts the confrontational aspects of the horror cinema back to basics" ("Jess Franco's Declaration of Principles" 25). When Lucas had originally noted that *"You can't see one Franco film until you've seen them all"* ("How to Read a Franco Film," 19), he qualified his maxim by saying, "their maker's language at some indistinct moment begins to sink in, after one has seen a certain number of them, and this soft, percussive language coalesces in some films more tangibly, more audibly, more obsessively, than in others" (19). This "soft, percussive language" is closer to a state of mind, an aesthetic, and videophilic experience. As for the critical language he mobilized to read Franco films, Lucas foregrounded recurrent thematic concerns and stylistic devices, namely marginality, destylization, ennui, time and continuity, music, anarchy and identity, nationality, and voice (25–33). These terms tell as much about Franco as they do about Lucas and his *Video Watchdog*: Franco's marginality was echoed in the publication's own "dissatisfaction with mainstream cinema" (25) and interest in aspects "marginal to the mainstream of experience" of film (25); the ennui elicited by Franco's films, a mode of spectatorship, which, like *Video Watchdog*'s mode of reading, requires a certain fascination and "state of mind" (26); or, the international dimension of his films, which, "despite their implicit national vocabulary . . . are at the same time nation-less" (33), the very market and readership to which *Video Watchdog* aspired.

Who Would You Rather See, Jesús Franco or Robert Englund?

This is Thrower's proposition in the closing lines of *Eyeball*'s first editorial in 1989; "If you are the sort of person who would rather see Jesús Franco slicing his way through the leading role in THE SADIST OF NOTRE DAME than witness Robert Englund vainly attempting to join the greats of the genre by portraying THE PHANTOM OF THE OPERA," he writes, "then *Eyeball* is worth your time and money" ("Dead Eyes Open!" 2). Again, Franco features largely as part of the identity and aspirations of an alternative publication aiming to contribute to and to intervene in contemporary horror film cultures. Thrower uses Franco to establish his opposition to other horror film communities via statements of oppositional taste and cultural distinction. In fact, the Franco reference is the culmination of an abrasive dismissal of other horror genre publications in which Thrower draws the battle lines between different horror film cultures, dismissing the "increasingly maligned FANGORIA, and its slightly less abysmal sister-mag GOREZONE . . . , [as well as] the ridiculous . . . SAMHAIN" (2), and vehemently rejecting "Jason, Freddy, Troma and Michael bloody Myers" (2). Like Lucas, Thrower pledges to "take the genre seriously" (2) and to "cast some light on Europe's lost, forgotten or reviled horror output" (2). But, unlike *Video Watchdog*, whose main remit was to inform and guide consumers in the video marketplace, *Eyeball* provided "detailed, extensive, and hopefully informative reviews" (2) to supplement "the appalling scarcity" of these films outside the "bootleg networks scattered around the country" (2). *Eyeball* and *Video Watchdog* trod similar cinematic territory beyond the films of Franco. But whereas *Video Watchdog* had a global dimension, Thrower's publication initially opted for an emphasis on European cinema as "a way of giving *EYEBALL* an inevitable distinct identity" (2); issues 4 and 5, however, went global when the magazine was renamed *Eyeball: Sex & Horror in World Cinema*. Moreover, Lucas and *European Trash Cinema*'s Ledbetter were among the contributors. As part of the growing horror film fanzine scene surfacing on both sides of the Atlantic, *Eyeball* was shaped by the impact of horror films available on video and the changes this wrought in horror film cultures in the late 1980s and the first half of the 1990s. The 1996 editorial captures the frenzy of this "heightened activity": "More film festivals, more Euro-horror and sleaze available on video, more quality publications to choose from . . . even the CD soundtrack market has taken sustenance from Euro-exploitation" ("Editorial" 2).

In his first editorial, Thrower also sets out the horror sensibilities at work in *Eyeball*, sensibilities that would characterize his own individual style and the editorial line of the magazine during its lifespan: "all who write for *EYEBALL* prefer to be disturbed and provoked by a horror film" ("Dead Eyes Open" 2).[7] With this in mind, *Eyeball* contributors yielded reviews shot through with "personal" resonance and relevance ("Dead Eyes Open" 2) and were not averse to a style where close textual analysis thrived alongside enthusiasts' commentaries ("Editorial" 2) and where art and sleaze came eclectically together. In comparison to Lucas, who published numerous reviews of Franco's films, Thrower produced only a handful between 1989 and 1998: *La maldición de Frankenstein* (*The Erotic Rites of Frankenstein*, 1973) in the opening issue, *Venus in Furs* in issue 2 (1990), and *Succubus* in issue 3 (1992), all of which were reprinted in *The Eyeball Compendium* in 2003. (The other Franco films reviewed, *Lorna . . . l'exorciste* [*Lorna the Exorcist*, 1974] and *El sádico de Notre-Dame* [*The Sadist of Notre Dame*, 1981], were written by regular contributors David Kerekes and David Prothero respectively).[8] They read like short essays and, at times, like a compendium of emotional ruminations. In contrast to the methodical and technical language of Lucas's reviews (concerning letter-boxing, transfer quality, cropping, and so on), Thrower's own viewing habits and style were, by his own admission in the introduction to the magazine compilation, influenced by "self-prescribed cartloads of amphetamines and

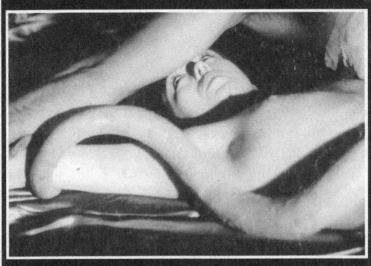

EYEBALL

THE EUROPEAN SEX AND HORROR REVIEW
ISSUE No. 3.3 RECURRING - SUMMER 1992 - £3.50

IN THIS ISSUE:
CANADIAN VIRUS vs. **EYEBALL** IMMUNE SYSTEM:
CRONENBERG'S NAKED LUNCH
SEVENTIES **GIALLI** SLASHED TO BITS
DIRECTOR PROFILE/FILMOGRAPHY - **ANDRZEJ ZULAWSKI**
KIM NEWMAN AT THE ROME FANTAFEST
THROUGH A BROKEN MIRROR - **ARGENTO**'S CAREER AND **MAITLAND**
McDONAGH'S BOOK APPRAISED
PLUS REVIEWS OF:
TRAS EL CRISTAL - FREAK ORLANDO - MATADOR - NECRONOMICON
PIERROT LE FOU - THE SADIST OF NOTRE DAME - SPIDER LABYRINTH
DELICATESSEN - BABY BLOOD - THE NAKED CONCIERGE
SHORT NIGHT OF THE GLASS DOLLS - MONDO WEIRDO
LES MINETS SAUVAGES - WILD BEASTS

In his reviews of European sex and horror films for *Eyeball*, Stephen Thrower regularly included the films of Jess Franco. Reviews of *Succubus* and *The Sadist of Notre Dame* appeared in the issue pictured, no. 3.3 recurring (Summer 1992). (Courtesy of Stephen Thrower.)

LSD . . . and self-programmed marathon all-nighters" (*The Eyeball Compendium* 6), which led to an "ecstatically deranged state" (6). Franco fans would have to wait until 2015 to read Thrower's *Murderous Passions: The Delirious Cinema of Jesús Franco*, a hefty tome where he engages in detail with the director's 1959 to 1974 period.[9]

But let us return to Thrower's reviews in the publication and the period that concerns this chapter. What does Thrower, then, have to say about Franco? And what type of review does he produce? The reader's encounter with Thrower's review of *The Erotic Rites of Frankenstein* is framed by questions around readability and the conventions of film reviewing. He opens with the statement: "The films of Jess Franco defy simple comment" (Rev. of *The Erotic Rites of Frankenstein* 13); "[d]espite their general preoccupation with aberrant sex and violence," he adds, "the range of mood and visual style is greater than one might have expected" (13) from a director as prolific as Franco. In this first review Thrower comes to the conclusion that Franco films require a critical engagement on their own terms because his "work is consistently idiosyncratic" (13). For Thrower, "describing the plot of the movie is almost pointless" (13). Similar views structure his readings of *Venus in Furs* and *Succubus*: the former "is a film in which one could say that 'looking for a narrative' actually becomes the narrative" (Rev. of *Venus in Furs* 25); the latter is "'about' little that is tangible at all" (Rev. of *Necronomicon* 16). Stylistically, *Venus in Furs* "is a deadly, seductive dream-world [in which] photography, music, editing and art design repeatedly coalesce into breath-taking sequences of glacial beauty" (Rev. of *Venus in Furs* 25); in *Succubus* Franco skillfully evokes an "atmosphere of dreamlike morbidity" (Rev. of *Necronomicon* 16). The language of music also provides points of entry to the world of Franco. As a musician in the electronic industrial band Coil at the time, Thrower was attuned to Franco's musical sensibilities. For him, *The Erotic Rites of Frankenstein* "combines disturbingly off-kilter jazz with hellish electronic spasms reminiscent of the seminal Kraut-rock group Faust" (Rev. of *The Erotic Rites of Frankenstein* 13). As for *Venus in Furs*, Thrower writes, "linear narrative is gone [and] is replaced by a series of cycles and variations" (Rev. of *Venus in Furs* 13).

The correspondence between genre films and art films is a common trope in Thrower's discussion of horror cinema. The cultural leveling of distinctions between art and exploitation, which Joan Hawkins explores in the case of video mail-order catalogs such as Video Search of Miami and European Trash Cinema that catered to the world of horror film fanzines (3–32), can be seen in *Eyeball*, which circulated in the same milieus of consumption and of reception. Clearly, this deliberate mingling of art and exploitation worked as a critical gesture whereby Thrower broadened his publication's critical scope, and, at the same time, distinguished *Eyeball* from other contemporary publications in order to create, borrowing from David Sanjek's notes on the horror film fanzine, his own "alternative brand of criticism . . . with its own set of values and virtues" (316). The associations and connections that Thrower draws between Franco's works and art film traditions reconfigure existing views of Franco, even as he discriminates between one Franco production and another. "Anyone who has seen his appalling CANNIBALS or waded through the sludge of the intermittently amusing BLOODY MOON," claims Thrower, "is going to be astonished when confronted by . . . *The Erotic Rites of Frankenstein*" (Rev. of *The Erotic Rites of Frankenstein* 13): the film "operates in a bizarre overlap between Art, Exploitation and Random Lunacy" (13). Pronouncements like these align Franco's movies with similar films and modes of spectatorship. Like Leigh McCloskey's protagonist in Dario Argento's *Inferno* (1980), James Darren's character in *Venus in Furs* is in "a constant state of confusion" and presented "with the same ultimate horror at the centre of their cinematic maze—death" (Rev. of *Venus in Furs* 25). But Thrower also draws a parallel with Luis Buñuel's *Un chien andalou* (1929) and other European art films that invoke surrealist dreamworlds. *Succubus* "is awash with cinematic references" (Rev. of *Necronomicon* 16) from Cocteau's *Orphée* (*Orpheus*, 1950) to Fellini's *La dolce vita* (1960) to Resnais's *L'année dernière à Marienbad* (*Last Year at Marienbad*, 1961). Pulp, art, and craziness meet in a sequence where the character of "Jack Taylor quizzes Reynaud about her identity (in the style of a Mickey Spillane novel) with an unmistakeable air of Godardian irony" (Rev. of

Necronomicon 16). For Thrower, this scene as well as other segments in the film can be read as a "sardonic parody of sixties cinema 'search for meaning,' as exemplified by directors like Godard and Fellini" (16). While the dense "network of namechecks and cultural signposts" in Franco's cinema does not always work out for the viewer, its function and motivation "does afford scope for endless speculation" (16).

"THERE ARE NO ENDINGS . . ."

This chapter has considered the ways in which two formative players in the remediation and legitimation of Franco read and embrace his films, with particular focus on the first half of the 1990s, when Franco came into view at a time of significant technological change, namely, the advent of home video, and in a cultural moment when such genre film publications as *Eyeball* and *Video Watchdog* began to thrive. In other words, the chapter has examined the Franco experience as it unfurled in contemporary genre publications that evaluated Franco films based on video copies. More recent iterations of Lucas's and Thrower's writings on Franco have also been considered so that their respective critical projects are contextualized within a larger work-in-progress narrative shaped by further shifts in technology and in horror film culture. Indeed, the possibilities of the Franco experience afforded by digital technologies have broadened the reach of Francophilia. For example, in October 2005, Lucas launched his *Video WatchBlog*, where he has been posting regularly on all things Franco. (Regrettably, Lucas stopped publishing new print editions of *Video Watchdog* in October 2016 after twenty-seven years.) Bringing their devoted pursuit and study of Franco's work up-to-date, Lucas has returned to the director's 1959–67 period, while Thrower has zoomed in to the years 1959 to 1974. This revisiting of Franco's early productions is less a search for a final (first) meaning than an endless sift and re-view of his catalog. Thrower's closing words in one of his *Eyeball* editorials ("Dead Eyes Open" 2) seem apposite: "There are no endings, only continuation. . . ." The archaeology of a forty-year period remains to be researched. As a critic put it in a review of Thrower's *Murderous Passions*, the book "represents the successful ascension of a quarter-century of pro-Franco proselytizing, begun in the U.S. by Tim Lucas and others in the pages of *Fangoria* and *Video Watchdog* and peaking here, in this mammoth, lavishly illustrated labour of love" (Strub). Labor of love it is. Whether the term "proselytizing" encompasses the various endeavors and ventures of Lucas and Thrower is a moot point. Both have had a central role in the ongoing constructions of Franco—commercial, journalistic, and scholarly. In the pages of *Video Watchdog* and *Eyeball*, they contributed to the building of communities of viewing and reviewing, as well as of video collecting. The curatorial significance of their cataloging and research is undeniable; their connoisseurship of Franco is unparalleled; and their function as cultural intermediaries of the Franco filmography can be traced in genre publications and books, liner notes, and online forums. Above all, their writings together act as interpretations and archives of the director's films, serving as testimony to the allure of an ever-elusive "Franco."

Notes

1. See "Making Zines: *European Trash Cinema* (1988–1998)" (Lázaro-Reboll 2016).
2. Both have a track record of critical engagement with Franco as part of the fanzine scene of the early 1990s, Monell contributing to *European Trash Cinema* and Mendíbil to *2000maniacos*.
3. A regular section of the magazine, the "VW Directrospective" devoted to Franco was followed by pieces on directors as varied as Pupi Avati (issue 3, Jan./Feb. 1991), Mario Bava (issue 5, May/June 1991), and Aleksandr L. Ptushko (issue 8, Nov./Dec. 1991).
4. I am focusing here on the periodizations published in *Video Watchdog* and leaving out of the discussion the introduction to *Obsession: The Films of Jess Franco*, where Lucas makes some minimal adjustments to the organization of the director's work proposed in 1990, revising them as: (1) The Classical Years (1959–65), (2) The Pop Art Years (1965–67), (3) The Harry Alan Towers Years (1968–70), (4) The Peak Years (1970–73), (5) The Porno Holocaust Years (1973–79), (6) The Homecoming Years (1980–87), and (7) The Autumn Years (1987–Today [1993]) (Introduction 13–30).
5. Similar points are made about the various "reconstructions" of *La Comtesse noire* (*Female Vampire*, 1973), which would be duly revisited when the films received Blu-ray treatment "from Kino Lorber and Redemption Films that

offer improvements over their previous [VHS] and DVD incarnations from . . . Image Entertainment" ("Female Vampire / Erotikill" 47).

6. In this revised periodization, "The Harry Alan Towers Years" are subsumed under "The Adult Fantasy Years."

7. *Eyeball* was published irregularly. It lasted only five issues and there were significant gaps between the publication of some of them (the gap between issues 3.3 and 4 was four years).

8. Interestingly, given its temporal and geographic connection to the video nasties phenomenon in the United Kingdom in the previous decade, *Eyeball* did not cover the Franco films that had been listed in the Director of Public Prosecutions records in 1982 and entered in the final 39-title list (known as the DPP39s), namely *Die Säge Des Todes* (*Bloody Moon*, 1981), *El Canibal* (*The Devil Hunter*, 1980), and *Diamants pour l'enfer* (*Women Behind Bars*, 1975).

9. Thrower is also the author of two other exhaustive tomes: *Beyond Terror: The Films of Lucio Fulci* (1999) and *Nightmare USA: The Untold Story of the Exploitation Independents* (2007).

WORKS CITED

Aguilar, Carlos. *Jess Franco: El Sexo del Horror.* Ed. Carlos Aguilar, Stefano Piselli, and Riccardo Morrocchi. Florence: Glittering Images, 1999. Print.

Balbo, Lucas. "Jesus Speaks." *Shock Xpress* 3.1 (Summer 1989): 6–8. Print.

Balbo, Lucas, Peter Blumenstock, and Christian Kessler. *Obsession: The Films of Jess Franco.* Ed. Lucas Balbo and Peter Blumenstock. Berlin: Graf Haufen and Frank Trebbin, 1993. Print.

Collins, Kevin. "Interview with Jess Franco." *European Trash Cinema* 1 (1996): 6–29. Print.

Hawkins, Joan. *Cutting Edge: Art-Horror and the Horrific Avant-Garde.* Minneapolis: U of Minnesota P, 2000. Print.

Hilderbrand, Lucas. "Cinematic Promiscuity: Cinephilia After Videophilia." *Framework* 50. 1 & 2 (2009): 214–17. Print.

Klinger, Barbara. *Beyond the Multiplex: Cinema, New Technologies and the Home.* Berkeley: U of California P, 2006. Print.

Landis, Bill, and Michelle Clifford. *Sleazoid Express.* New York: Fireside, 2002. Print.

Lázaro-Reboll, Antonio. "Making Zines: *European Trash Cinema* (1988–1998)." *Film Studies* 15.2 (2016): 30–53. Print.

Ledbetter, Craig. "Venezuelan Video Safari—Miami Style!" *Video Watchdog* 1 (1990): 14–17. Print.

Lucas, Tim. "The Agony and the Ecstasy of Jess Franco." *Fangoria* 78 (Oct. 1988): 14–18. Print.

————. "Eurociné: The Best Little Horror House in France." *Video Watchdog* 63 (Sept. 2000): 24–37. Print.

————. Rev. of "*Female Vampire/Erotikill.*" *Video Watchdog* 174 (May/June 2013): 47–49. Print.

————. "How to Read a Franco Film." *Video Watchdog* 1 (1990): 18–35. Print.

————. Introduction. *Obsession: The Films of Jess Franco*. Ed. Lucas Balbo and Peter Blumenstock. Berlin: Graf Haufen and Frank Trebbin, 1993. 13–30. Print.

————. "Jess Franco's Declaration of Principles: How to Read the Early Films, 1959–67." *Video Watchdog* 157 (2010): 16–49. Print.

————. "Jess Franco Selective Videography." *Video Watchdog* 1 (1990): 35–38. Print.

————. "Jess is More." *Video Watchdog* 17 (May/June 1993): 7–8. Print.

————. "The Torture Chamber of Jess Franco." *Fangoria* 90 (Feb. 1990): 14–18. Print.

————. *The Video Watchdog Book*. Cincinnati: Video Watchdog. 1992. Print.

————. "The Watchdog Barks." Editorial. *Video Watchdog* 1 (1990): 3–4. Print.

————. "The Watchdog Barks." Editorial. *Video Watchdog* 3 (Jan./Feb. 1991): 3. Print.

————. "The Watchdog Barks." Editorial. *Video Watchdog* 22 (Mar./Apr. 1994): 3. Print.

————. "The Watchdog Barks." Editorial. *Video Watchdog* 119 (May 2005): 3. Print.

————. "The Watchdog Barks." Editorial. *Video Watchdog* 174 (May/June 2013): 3. Print.

Mendíbil, Álex. *El Franconomicon*. Web. 21 Jun. 2015.

Monell, Robert. *I'm in a Jess Franco State of Mind*. Web. 21 June 2015.

O'Brien, Geoffrey. *The Phantom Empire: Movies in the Mind of the 20th Century*. New York: Norton, 1993. Print.

Sanjek, David. "Fans' Notes: The Horror Film Fanzine." *The Horror Reader*. Ed. Ken Gelder. New York: Routledge, 2000. 314–23. Print.

Strub, Whitney. "Francomania Exposed! *Murderous Passions: The Delirious Cinema of Jesús Franco.*" *Senses of Cinema* 80 (Sept. 2016): n. pag. Web. 17 Oct. 2016.

Szpunar, John. "Tim Lucas: The Watchdog Barks!" *Xerox Ferox: The Wild World of the Horror Film Fanzine*. London: Headpress, 2013. 585–605. Print.

Tashiro, Charles. "The Contradictions of Video Collecting." *Film Quarterly* 50.2 (Winter 1996–97): 11–18. Print.

Taylor, Greg. *Artists in the Audience: Cults, Camp, and American Film Criticism*. Princeton: Princeton UP, 1999. Print.

Thrower, Stephen. *Beyond Terror: The Films of Lucio Fulci*. Godalming, Surrey: FAB, 1999. Print.

————. "Dead Eyes Open!" Editorial. *Eyeball* 2 (Summer 1990): 2. Print.

————. "Editorial" *Eyeball* 4 (Winter 1996): 2. Print.

————. Rev. of *The Erotic Rites of Frankenstein. Eyeball* 1 (Autumn 1989): 13. Print.

————. *The Eyeball Compendium*. London: FAB, 2003. Print.

————. "Jesús 'Jess' Franco (1930–2013)." *Sight & Sound* 23.6 (June 2013): 19. Print.

————, with Julian Grainger. *Murderous Passions: The Delirious Cinema of Jesús Franco*. London: Strange Attractor, 2015. Print.

————. Rev. of *Necronomicon. Eyeball* 3 (Summer 1992): 15–16. Print.

————. *Nightmare USA: The Untold Story of the Exploitation Independents*. Godalming, Surrey: FAB, 2007. Print.

————. Rev. of *Venus in Furs. Eyeball* 2 (Summer 1990): 25–26. Print.

10

(RE)BORN AGAIN

When Jess Franco Met the Indies

Vicente Rodríguez Ortega and Rubén Romero Santos

I have returned to counter cinema—Z cinema, or however you want to call it—
with more heart and soul than ever. With very little help from producers—more
than actual producers, they are fans of my films—I can do what the industry never let me do, try things out, taking advantage of new audiovisual devices, making
films, as I have always done, for multiracial, healthy and pure audiences, open to
new horizons.

—Jess Franco

ess Franco makes this statement on the last page of *Memorias del
tío Jess* (2004), his autobiography (all translations from Spanish in
this chapter are our own). He pledges to keep making films, adopting the fast-developing technology of video with a clear goal: to renew
his unbreakable commitment to reach uncharted territories, pushing his
devoted audiences further and further into his idiosyncratic universe. He
also points out that his producers are no longer industry players with specific financial concerns and priorities but his own fans. Franco thus recognizes that he has become a model and source of inspiration for the younger
generation in his own country and vows to honor such a role, banking on
the creative possibilities that his new status allows him to explore.

This chapter examines the reconfiguration of Jess Franco in the late
1980s and early 1990s as both a cult figure and an active agent in the
changing coordinates of the Spanish cultural scene. For this purpose,
we use a wide spectrum of primary sources and a series of interviews
with some key players in Franco's revival—namely, music entrepreneur

and fanzine publisher Carlos Galán, film producer Tomás Cimadevilla, Jess Franco historian Álex Mendíbil, and comic author and curator Borja Crespo. Through our analysis, we define the contours of cult filmmaking, more generally, and cult auteurism, more specifically, within the political, social, and cultural contexts of Spain at the time. We also scrutinize how fan-made Spanish publications circulating in alternative circuits, such as *Subterfuge* (1989–2000) or *Spiral* (1993–96), became pivotal in the redefinition of the Spanish cult film canon. We compare these publications to official documents such as Filmoteca Española's 1993 Franco retrospective brochure—curated by Carlos Aguilar—and mainstream press articles from daily national newspapers such as *La Vanguardia* or *El País*. In addition, we trace a series of connections between the late 1980s and early to mid-1990s Spanish underground and indie scenes and Jess Franco, giving special attention to the intimate relationship that developed between alternative music artists and the director. We focus in particular on Franco's music video for the Los Planetas rock band and the significant contribution made by the music label and publishing house Subterfuge to the production of his film *Killer Barbys* (1996), framing the concept of cult filmmaking as a cross-media phenomenon wherein diverse players from different disciplines intersect. Finally, the chapter explores how Franco's subcultural production has filtered into the Spanish cinematic mainstream through the work of filmmakers such as Álex de la Iglesia, Santiago Segura, and Pablo Berger. As our contribution to this volume demonstrates, Jess Franco became a valuable mentor and reference point for a new generation of artists and creatives who challenged the status quo within the Spanish cultural scene beginning in the late 1980s.

SURVIVING THE 1980S: THE INDIE GENERATION COMES TO THE FORE

In 1983, at the Madrid Imagfic Festival, Jess Franco's *El hundimiento de la casa Usher* (*Revenge in the House of Usher*, 1988) was booed vociferously.

That same year, the so-called Miró Law was passed, effectively pushing genre filmmaking to the side while privileging auteur films that were supposed to epitomize "quality cinema." The new film legislation favored public subsidies—modeled on the French *avances sur recettes* system—for those producers and recognized (auteur) directors who made costume dramas and big-budget literary adaptations. These films were designed to play in both the national and international markets (Ansola Gónzalez 2; Riambau 421) and to promote a cinema that could represent the new democratic Spain at home and abroad (Triana-Toribio 113). One of the main goals of the Miró Law was, therefore, to eliminate improper lowbrow filmic products such as those of Jess Franco and to foster the creation of prestige films (Buse et al. 37).[1] What these film policies triggered was the emergence of a new generation of "official" auteurs epitomized by the director Mario Camus, whose adaptations of Nobel Prize winner Camilo José Cela's *La colmena* (*The Beehive*, 1982) and of Miguel Delibes's *Los santos inocentes* (*The Holy Innocents*, 1984) became paradigmatic of the "quality cinema" fostered by the law. Franco would blame the law repeatedly for his lack of activity during the 1980s: it was a "law welcomed by the rest of the industry, though not all of it. [To be sure] it has closed all paths for my cinema" (qtd. in Freixas and Bassa: 51). Widely overlooked by the film industry, Franco considered himself a total outsider. He watched from the sidelines as cultural industries boomed with the events leading up to the Barcelona Olympic Games, Seville World Expo, and Madrid Cultural Capital of Europe celebrations in 1992, and as formerly subversive cultural movements such as La Movida were co-opted by official policies and institutions, becoming the social and cultural mainstream.[2] Luckily for his career, he was not the only one who did not fit within these hegemonic trends in the Spanish cultural landscape. Just as La Movida had filled the need for new forms of consumption and ideological and artistic expression in the early democratic period, a new movement was attempting to become the voice of a younger generation of Spaniards in an epoch of growing disillusionment with the political and economic institutions that had led the country into a downward spiral of rampant corruption, soaring unemployment, and social and economic inequality during the last years of the socialist government in power in the early to mid-1990s.[3] Soon, commentators from mainstream press outlets like *El País*, cultural supplements like *Vang* (from the Barcelona-based *La Vanguardia*), music magazines like *Rockdelux*, and fanzines like *Subterfuge* labeled these new cultural agents "indies," a term that matched their organizational economics, since they were not part of the process of multinational concentration within Spanish media during this period. This term also captured their feeling of being outsiders in relation to the commercial trends fostered by multinational companies.

The Spanish indie scene was bound by four main characteristics, which it shared with Jess Franco, the ultimate outsider: firstly, the partial (or total) rejection of previously youth-oriented manifestations of art, such as La Movida, and the resulting search for other modes of cultural expression; secondly, the utilization of amateur modes of production and exchange as launch pads for their intervention, displaying a distinct commitment to a do-it-yourself (DIY) ethos; thirdly, the partnership with increasingly relevant but still marginal media players such as RNE3 (Radio Nacional de España 3)[4] in reshaping the Spanish cultural imaginary; and, fourthly, the embrace of a multidisciplinary and voracious approach to cultural production and consumption that operated within a number of fields of expression that became increasingly intertwined. Even though it is perhaps too neat to identify such a wide range of activities under the umbrella of a single phrase, this cultural phenomenon is what we would like to call the "indie scene"—a series of connected and yet diverse practices of cultural production and consumption bound together by their rejection of dominant approaches to the creation, distribution, and circulation of media artifacts. As in other contexts such as England or the United States, these new social actors proclaimed that their means of expression and their channels of communication were more relevant to the youth who produced and consumed them than any other cultural manifestations and practices co-opted by the mainstream. Simultaneously, they attempted to establish "new relationships between creativity and commerce" (Hesmondhalgh 35) that championed the work of those who did not depend on any kind of corporate investment or interest. In other words, they vehemently announced their *independent* mode of production, establishing a connection between this independence and their aesthetic and ideological approach to the processes of cultural creation. The increasing affordability of music and video devices for both the production and the distribution of cultural artifacts also facilitated their agency within the social field, even if, at first, it was limited to small circuits of exchange.

Fanzines would prove particularly important in the articulation of fandom as a subcultural phenomenon generally, and in relation to Jess Franco more specifically. Fanzines are often nonprofessional publications, thriving on a cut-and-paste aesthetic that typically juxtaposes a series of nonmainstream cultural artifacts, and establishing alternative distribution networks in which personal, direct contact is customary (Gelder 145).[5] At the end of the 1980s and the beginning of the 1990s, fanzines worked in concert with another predigital medium, VHS, in rescuing Jess Franco from oblivion. In fact, we need to contextualize the celebration of Franco in the 1990s within a broader trend of Euro horror revivalism created by "new and voracious niche markets for home distribution" (Heffernan 159). Like Mario Bava or Antonio Margheriti, Jess Franco was the focus of a new generation of critics, who, according to Heffernan, modeled their work after the seminal essays of *Cahiers du Cinéma* in the 1960s and ransacked VHS stores, searching for novel auteurs.[6] At the same time, these new critical voices started appearing in magazines such as *Photon, Cinéfantastique*, and, later, *Video Watchdog* (Heffernan 159). Hence, the first critical studies of Franco's work were made outside Spain, in fanzines such as Craig Ledbetter's *European Trash Cinema* and Tim Lucas's *Video Watchdog* (see chapter 9 of this volume). In Spain, this task was mostly in the hands of Carlos Aguilar.

In January 1980, Aguilar published what was arguably the first Spanish fanzine devoted to horror and fantasy cinema: *Morpho*. Highly influenced by foreign fanzines, especially French publications like *Mad Movies* and *The Bat*, its title was a direct tribute to Jess Franco. As

Aguilar has explained, "*Morpho* is the name that he [Jess Franco] usually assigned to monstrous servant characters. But nobody understood this reference, everyone wondered why that title was so weird" ("Morpho Index"). At that moment, Aguilar was farsighted enough to understand the appeal of a figure like Jess Franco for the new generations of fans and how significant his films would become within the local—as well as the international—fanzine world: "In a way, my concept of fanzines was very similar to Jesús Franco's concept of cinema. He did Spanish films thinking about foreign markets, and I did the same, but replacing films with *Morpho*" ("Morpho Index"). *Morpho* would prove pivotal for Aguilar's career, eventually leading to a job as the programmer at Imagfic, the film festival where *Revenge in the House of Usher* was blasted by the audience during its screening, as noted earlier. Despite the film's negative reception, Aguilar was adamantly convinced of Franco's value as a director and, in collaboration with other scholars like Joan Bassa and Ramón Freixas, penned the first two comprehensive studies on Franco in the film magazines *Archivos de la Filmoteca* (1990/1991) and *DeZine* (1991), the former associated with the Valencian Film Institute, the latter linked to the San Sebastián Horror and Film Festival. Soon thereafter, Spanish fanzines would celebrate Jess Franco as a visionary, groundbreaking, and unfairly forgotten filmmaker. These publications, among them *Subterfuge*, *2000maniacos*, and *Serie-B*, conceptualized the Spanish director as a genius and a relentless provocateur with both an encyclopedic knowledge of cinema and music and an inalienable drive to try out new things while navigating the thorny field of international genre coproductions. His canonization in these publications offers another example of what David Sanjek calls "the devotion to uniqueness of vision [that] has led the fanzines to value most works which bear the mark of an uninhibited visionary sensibility, one which pushes the boundaries of social, sexual, and aesthetic assumptions" (423). Put simply, fanzines tend to privilege those directors whose works have a recognizable set of characteristics—an auteurist stamp—and, at the same time, reject social and ideological conformity for the sake of alternative ideological and aesthetic models. In order to "discover" Franco's auteurism, one needed to carry out an archeological effort succinctly summarized by an often-cited line from Lucas: *"You can't see one until you've seen them all"* (23). As supreme Francophile Álex Mendíbil—the Franco historian, fanzine contributor, and creator of the Facebook page Franconomicon—explains in relation to the role of Franco in the home video market boom: "Jess Franco films were a cheap solution for distributors to complete their catalog, especially in the '72 hours section.' Video stores were one of the easiest ways to get into Franco's world, almost by chance" (qtd. in Romero Santos and Rodríguez Ortega: "Mendíbil"). Jess Franco was an auteur whose films were devoured by avid fans frantically searching video stores with the hope of finding a forgotten masterpiece. And, as these Francophile communities grew, so did their modes of exchange.

Jess Franco—who was rechristened "el tío Jess" (Uncle Jess)—was chiefly recuperated in Spain by scores of fans who inhabited the alternative circuits of cultural production during this period. As Lázaro-Reboll remarks, "the resurgence of the fanzine as a cultural form in the early 1990s—alongside a boom in gore shorts—proved to be a determining factor in the celebration and revival of his work for new generations of fans in Spain and the ongoing construction, promotion and perpetuation of his cult reputation" (186).[7] In this context, Franco became one of the key referents through which film and music buffs, aficionados and amateurs, interacted. These cultural agents functioned through a "sense of solidarity amongst themselves, built around their specific interests and practices" (Gelder 144), which is one of the fundamental characteristics of fandom as both a collective enterprise and a (potentially) socially transformative phenomenon. No company represents this form of solidarity better than Subterfuge.

Subterfuge: From Fanzines to Music, Comic Books, and Movies

Do you know Jess Franco? blurted out Johnny Ramone at the gym of the Palacio de los Deportes in Barcelona. *Do you mean the filmmaker?* I answered with caution. *Yes of course! I'm a big fan of his work! I collect all his movies in video.* One can imagine "The Ramones" sitting in a sofa in their New York City home watching *The Texas Chainsaw Massacre* but . . . Jess Franco films!!!!?

—Marc Mateu

This exchange between a *Rockdelux* journalist and one of the members of the mythical punk rock band The Ramones exemplifies quite well Jess Franco's status in the early 1990s: while he was a cult underground figure abroad, he was an "unknown, or badly known, battered, and trashed without reason" filmmaker in Spain (Aguilar et al 91). Yet this was about to change. A new generation of artists and cultural agents would rediscover Franco's work.

Carlos Subterfuge (real name Carlos Galán) was a young film student in 1989. Eager to make his voice heard in the contemporary cultural sphere, he published the fanzine *Subterfuge*, devoted to the things he liked, namely "comics, 'cine fantástico' and pre gore terror" (Subterfuge, 1:2). In its third issue, the fanzine expanded into the music world, releasing four songs by the bands Wipe Out Skaters, Corn Flakes, Cerebros Exprimidos, and La Perrera, paving the way for Subterfuge's involvement in other artistic fields. This ambition went hand in hand with his political rejection of the institutional system at that time, which had been so accommodating with La Movida. As he states in the editorial of the second issue of *Subterfuge*: "The day we want to become rich, we will close this stall to become politicians" (Subterfuge, 2:2). This rejection manifests itself in all of the fanzine's editorials. For example, in issue 10: "We raise our 'No Art' flag against all the shit that surrounds us in whatever realm, no matter if it is music, cinema, or literature. We hate apathy, and conventionalism, the lack of ideas and inaction. We are more than prepared to write our own history and we want to do it now. Enough with waiting for subsidies and licking butts: we are going to show our teeth, we are going to annoy people and you also have a lot to say and do about it" (Subterfuge 10:2). As a fanzine, *Subterfuge* reflected a youthful resentment toward the previous generation in all artistic fields, the institutional status quo, and mainstream networks of cultural exchange. Particularly violent were the fanzine's film reviews. It is worth noting that film was one of the few disciplines not noticeably revolutionized by La Movida, apart from specific cases such as the work of Pedro Almodóvar or Iván Zulueta. Thus it is not surprising that Galán wrote articles like "20 Trash-Sexy Films Celtibéricos" (Subterfuge, 75) or that Borja Crespo, in a report called "The Dark Side of Celluloid" (Crespo 76–77), praises genre movies, launching a ferocious attack against contemporary Spanish commercial cinema: "Paul Naschy cinema, *Acción mutante* by Álex de la Iglesia and the short films of Santiago Segura are against the existentialist dramas set during the Civil War and the insipid comedies and traumatized characters in search of the love of their lives that have been so frequent in this country" (77).

Crespo also offers a good example of how the indie scene came into existence. He started writing in the fanzine *2000maniacos* after offering his services to the editor Manuel Valencia and later moved from his Basque hometown in Getxo to Madrid to direct Subterfuge's new project: the comics publication *Subterfuge Comix* (1995–2003) and its namesake publishing house, which has been supporting Spanish underground artists for the last two decades. *Subterfuge Comix* championed an aesthetic approach that went hand in hand with the short films that Santiago Segura and Pablo Berger were making at that time.[8] In its ninth issue, devoted to comics, contributors Borja Crespo, Enrique Ladrón, and Enrique Lorenzana published a manifesto called "La línea tremenda" (a take on "La línea clara / ligne clare" of the French and Belgium schools). "We stood for humor black as coal," Crespo writes, "the unchained anatomy on the blank page, colorful gore, cheesy porn, swine terror, nonsense. . . . Gruesome jokes were axed more than drawn, influenced by Robert Crumb, Bruguera publishing house and the trash culture of those times" (Crespo, "Prólogo" 4). The Spanish Bruguera cartoons reflected the struggle of the post–Civil War period with dark humor; Crumb, for his part, mocked the American way of life through his countercultural comics. Both influences were mixed in "La línea tremenda," along with the bizarre and gory allure of contemporary comic artists such as Daniel Clowes (*Eightball*) or Charles Burns (*Black Hole*).

1993 was a defining year for a new group of aspiring artists that, like those who wrote in *Subterfuge*, shared a passion for "B" and "Z" films. In January, Canal+'s *Piezas*, a show devoted to short films, broadcast a special titled "Generación Mercromina," which included the works of those close to the San Sebastián Horror and Film Festival—namely, Álex de la Iglesia, Santiago Segura, and Pablo Berger.[9] These shorts perfectly matched *Subterfuge*'s "La línea tremenda" editorial line. According to producer and filmmaker Tomás Cimadevilla, who became Jess Franco's assistant on *Killer Barbys*, Javier Bonilla, the director of *Piezas*, was a key figure in this context since he started to champion a new type of Spanish cinema (Romero Santos and Rodríguez Ortega, "Cimadevilla"). Crespo, who was producing films with comic writer and illustrator Miguel Ángel Martín and film director Koldo Serra, also regards the broadcasting of "Generación Mercromina" as crucial: "It was the first time that we could see that our hobby had a relevant role on television. *Acción mutante* confirmed that feeling. It was different because it showed that things should not necessarily be pretty, that ugliness could also be cinematic. In a way, 'Generación Mercromina' was the film version of 'La línea tremenda'" (Romero Santos and Rodríguez Ortega, "Crespo"). All of a sudden, it became apparent that there was a new generation of producers and consumers; the cultural industries were ready to monetize them. In October, *El País*, the largest newspaper in Spain, joined the fray: it started printing the cultural magazine *El País de las Tentaciones* in an attempt to attract younger readers. This publication became a sort of trendsetter within the hip Spanish cultural sphere.

Franco Reborn: From the Filmoteca Retrospective to Indie Music

If Álex de la Iglesia was, to a certain extent, the up-and-coming figure among young Spanish genre filmmakers, Jess Franco would soon become their cult icon. Filmoteca Española at last commissioned Carlos Aguilar to program the first extensive retrospective of Franco's films in Spain in 1993 (although it had been originally planned for 1991). After decades of undaunted labor and hundreds of films, the director had finally achieved institutional recognition. The official 1993 Filmoteca brochure points out the breadth of Franco's output—over 150 films at that point—and its lack of exhibition in Spain, since most of his films had been distributed only on video. It also brings to the fore his multifarious roles within the cinematic world beyond directing—actor, executive producer, composer—and his illustrious, self-mythologizing collaborations with a roster of renowned filmmakers, from León Klimovksy to Fernando Fernán Gómez to Orson Welles. The text, written by Aguilar, also highlights Franco's unequivocal auteur status: "In his works, there is an uncommon coherence compared to the other European filmmakers of his generation, who willingly or not, operated within the narrow, ungrateful and never sufficiently valued meanders of the B series" (Aguilar). For him, the retrospective provides a comprehensive overview of Franco's films in order to finally provide "the opportunity to ascribe a moderately fair and consistent valorization of the position he deserves in the history of Spanish cinema" (Aguilar). In other words, Aguilar argues for the need to study Franco's large body of work in detail to appreciate him as an auteur and, consequently, reclaim his importance. Aguilar presents himself as a privileged connoisseur of Franco's cinema; he is the facilitator of this unprecedented opportunity to showcase Franco's films in Spain. However, many of the attendees at the Filmoteca Española retrospective were recuperating Franco's work in a very different fashion: whereas Aguilar conceptualized Franco within a traditional auteurist framework, many of the younger Franco fans were searching for new representational models after which to mold their own cultural interventions. If Aguilar aimed to situate Franco within traditional film historiographies, many of these young spectators were simply riveted by the transgressive quality of his films and his status as an outsider. As Ward argues, "Franco's career demonstrates how exploitation films can accrue forms of cultural capital and prestige unavailable to them during their original theatrical runs" (204). The cultification of Franco in Spain in the early 1990s "implies the mobility of value and meaning . . . as a multiply-determined, fluid site of operations rather than a generic essence" (Ward 204).

Carlos Galán and Tomás Cimadevilla attended the Filmoteca retrospective and came away deeply impressed. Galán says, "I remember sold out sessions. I met a lot of former and current film students. It was a rather mixed crowd: actors, genre fans but also architects and painters, seduced by the arty allure of Jess Franco's French period. Certainly, there was more than the so-called 'freaks' who cheer during screenings" (Romero Santos and Rodríguez Ortega, "Galán"). For Cimadevilla, it was a turning point in his relationship with cinema: "I went there with Enrique López Lavigne. We both worked at 'Canal Satélite Digital' and were eager to make a splash in the film industry. Jess attended some screenings, and after the retrospective, we heard that he wanted to make a film and we thought that we should help him. That would be the genesis of *Killer Barbys*" (Romero Santos and Rodríguez Ortega, "Cimadevilla"). While Aguilar had conceived and curated the retrospective from a traditional auteurist perspective, the event turned into a hub that brought together young fanzine writers, music entrepreneurs, cinephiles, and soon-to-become film producers who would go on to reshape the contemporary Spanish cultural scene.

At the beginning of 1994, two other events reinforced the growing power of the new generation within the Spanish cultural landscape: Santiago Segura won the Goya Award for Best Short Film with *Perturbado* (1993), which tells the story of a sexually obsessed man who starts killing the objects of his obsession. It was the first step in the transformation of Segura into one of the most recognizable actors of his generation and, ultimately, into the successful director of *Torrente, el brazo tonto de la ley*

(*Torrente, The Dumb Arm of the Law*, 1998), the highest-grossing Spanish film of the 1990s. Two weeks earlier, the powerful publishing house Planeta had shortlisted *Historias del Kronen* by José Ángel Mañas for the prestigious Nadal Award. Labeled as "the Spanish Generation X novel," it focuses on a youngster disenchanted with Spanish society who fucks, takes drugs, listens to Fugazi, and, in the end, accidentally kills one of his friends while the 1992 Olympic Games constantly play on TV. Soon, Mañas's novel would also become a film, *Stories of the Kronen* (Montxo Armendáriz, 1994). Bruno Galindo, a journalist at *El País de las Tentaciones*, designed the soundtrack. The main theme would be "Chup chup," by Subterfuge's band Australian Blonde.

The final catalyst for the growth of the indie scene and its ultimate mainstreaming would be the music festival fever all around Spain in the early to mid-1990s. The first major event was Actual in Logroño in 1991 (La Rioja). In 1994, Festimad started in Madrid; the same year, Sónar Festival and Primavera Sound began in Barcelona; a year later, members of the Madrid fanzine scene, the Morán brothers, who had close ties to Subterfuge, would launch the FIB (Festival Internacional de Benicàssim) near Castellón. Soon thereafter, festivals started spreading all over the country. They were not only music events but also occasions to share fanzines, VHS tapes, vinyl records, or T-shirts. Through music festivals, the indies built an alternative circuit that championed diverse representational approaches to the processes of artistic creation and consumption. Like film festivals, music festivals were far from individualistic events, favoring interaction, exchange, and the constant circulation of original and recorded artifacts that were not widely available. The goal was to leave behind the exhausted and institutionally hegemonic practices of the youth of the 1980s and offer an alternative understanding of both cultural production and consumption. In this context, as Fran Fernández, singer and guitarist of Australian Blonde, remarks, the emerging indie music scene and the underground circuits were totally interconnected, feeding off each other in their attempt to find new and often radical forms of expression, trying to leave their mark on the Spanish social and cultural scene (Holguera).[10]

Artists collaborated, expanding their fields of intervention: for example, Javier Aramburu, member of the band Family, became the cover artist for the band Los Planetas; Álex de la Iglesia directed the video *Acción mutante* for the band Def con Dos in 1993; Miguel Ángel Martín, who would later design the poster for *Killer Barbys*, did the cover for Sexy Sadie's 1994 album *Draining Your Brain*; and, Jess Franco would direct a landmark video for Los Planetas's "Himno generacional #83" in 1996, which would situate him as a cult figure among new musicians and their fans ahead of the release of *Killer Barbys*.

JESS FRANCO, LOS PLANETAS, AND *KILLER BARBYS*

The collaboration between Los Planetas, an up-and-coming indie band, and the old trash cinema master allows us to define several key characteristics of the mid-1990s indie scene in Spain. Los Planetas is a Granada band that made a splash in the Spanish music scene upon winning the prestigious radio program "Disco Grande" contest on RNE3 in 1992 with the song "Mi hermana pequeña," rereleased in 1993 on in the seven-inch *Medusa* EP by the independent label Elefant. As Jota, singer and guitarist of the band, states, groups like Los Planetas sprang from the fanzine culture and little by little started gaining recognition in other media, although, at least initially, they did not enter the "radio-formula" cycle (qtd. in Muelas: 16). The band's first LP, *Super 8*, however, was released by RCA-BMG—that is, a multinational label.[11] Upon the release of *Super 8*, Los Planetas became immediately successful. RNE3's support of the specific type of music this band epitomized—pop and rock with strong U.S. and British influences—as opposed to other genres was pivotal in this respect.[12] In preparation for the release of their second album, *Pop* (1996), the band issued three singles, all of them released by BMG Spain/RCA in CD format and Subterfuge on seven-inch vinyl—an instance of an independent and corporate partnership. The first single was "Himno generacional #83," for which the band hired Jess Franco to make the music video. The idea to hire Franco, as lead singer Jota claimed, was "rather simple: we love Jesús Franco's films and B movies. We thought it was a good idea that he directed the video. It is a tribute to a type of cinema that we are fond of" (qtd. in Muelas: 16). Before discussing the music video's aesthetics, it is important to highlight that the project was shot at the El Sol disco in Madrid, one of the key venues associated with La Movida. The recording of the video in this location entails a symbolic transfer from the outmoded Movida to the new generation of indie creators, who were appropriating the very spaces of the 1980s Spanish cultural scene for novel ideological and aesthetic reasons. This new wave of artists would gain growing notoriety in the mid-1990s and ultimately enter—like some of the best-known names of La Movida, such as Alaska, Radio Futura, and Almodóvar—the Spanish cultural canon.

Franco's video starts with Los Planetas stepping onto the smoke-filled stage of El Sol as a series of stills flash on the screen—an image of El Santo, a skull, a cannibal eating what appear to be intestines. The spectator thus immediately enters a generic universe that has exploitation and horror imagery as one of its pivotal referents. Immediately following these opening images, the band starts playing. A silent crowd of unmoved children comes near the stage and observes the performance, as though they are studying the musicians. Soon after, the children raise automatic guns, aim at the band, and fire repeatedly, "executing" the musicians while they continue playing. From then on, the clothing and faces of Los Planetas become progressively bloodier. Erotic and violent imagery appears on screen again: a group of skeletons reaching for the naked leg of a woman from below, an image from *Ercole e la regina di Lidia* (*Hercules Unchained*, 1959), a cannibal with a deranged gaze, a still from Russ Meyer's *Faster, Pussycat! Kill! Kill!* (1965) featuring the voluptuous breasts of one of the film's stars. As the children keep shooting, red becomes the dominant color onstage. The video finishes with one of Franco's signature shots (along with the zoom): a quick rack-focus that leads to a close-up of the first child who entered El Sol. From his face, the image fades to red. The end.

What are the aesthetic implications of this music video, then? Franco chose to shoot it on film, as opposed to using the emerging technology of video, thus making a statement about the continuity between his previous works and his engagement with the younger generation. As Crespo states, the "Himno generacional #83" music video "reclaims the romanticism of celluloid and, at the same time, it's cheap, impactful, politically incorrect and captures the very philosophy of its time" (Romero Santos and Rodríguez Ortega, "Crespo"). Furthermore, there are two dominant aesthetic regimes working in juxtaposition: indie—the music itself in compositional terms, along with the internationally resonant, minimalist performative style of Los Planetas—and the imagery of exploitation cinema.[13] This association points to the interconnectedness of the emerging indie aesthetics and DIY, amateur-driven, trash film fandom. Above all, imperfection and appropriation are center stage in the music video's approach: the exploitation stills, which seem to come from magazine cutouts or posters, folded, used, and recycled for the music video, point to an aesthetic of recycling that involves the reutilization of previously existing artifacts bearing the mark of their previous circulation among fan communities that celebrated them as stylistic ideals. Appropriately enough, this aesthetic recalls the DIY ethos at the core of fanzine culture and production; fanzines were precisely the type of publication that had vindicated Franco in the early 1990s.

The music video for "Himno generacional #83" did not escape controversy. No TV network (except for the Catalan regional channel TV3) broadcast it, harming the commercial interests of RCA. Even though Jota shied away from using the term "censorship" to describe its reception and preferred instead to point out that the video was not "commercial enough" for mainstream audiences (qtd. in Muelas: 16), it is hard to deny that this is exactly what occurred. Once again, one of Jess Franco's audiovisual works had been blocked from widespread circulation in his native country. Nonetheless, this controversy would bind the indie band and Jess Franco even more tightly together. As Jota recalled on the occasion of the director's death: "filming a video clip with Jess Franco was very important for us. We admired his work, and when the possibility arose, we were delighted. The experience was very enriching, especially because it gave us the opportunity to talk with him: we learned about his vision of cinema, his life and everything in general. He was a wise man and, above all, an independent person, always free no matter what they say" (qtd. in García). As Tomás Cimadevilla recalls, Los Planetas's video "meant a lot to recuperate Jess' figure, who was almost forgotten and had sought refuge in the porn industry [in the 1980s]. Afterward, he became an icon for the hip people" (Romero Santos and Rodríguez Ortega, "Cimadevilla").

In fact, Cimadevilla sees "Himno generacional #83" as part of a much bigger campaign to rescue Jess Franco from oblivion. *Killer Barbys* would be a second step in this direction. For Crespo, "the nymphomaniac cult of Jess Franco started with *Killer Barbys*. . . . It took advantage of the cool allure of the fanzine crowd and the indie music scene" (Romero Santos and Rodríguez Ortega, "Crespo"). Even though Franco was indeed a cult figure for many aspiring filmmakers, he was still fairly unknown within the wider indie scene. Galán points out that "Jess Franco was given the cold shoulder by the 'cine fantástico' fans. Guerrilla, 'fantástico' and erotic cinema were basically the realm of Paul Naschy and Carlos Aured" (Romero Santos and Rodríguez Ortega, "Galán"). Cimadevilla wanted to change this state of play: "We knew what kind of audience a Jess Franco movie would have. We were not filming *Star Wars*. We just wanted to make a movie as an act of plain and simple mythomania. . . . At this point, almost nobody knew who Jess was" (Romero Santos and Rodríguez Ortega, "Cimadevilla").

The production of *Killer Barbys* would turn into a gathering of young talents, all firmly (so to speak) under Jess Franco's command. (The title of the film was changed from "*Killer Barbies*" to "*Killer Barbys*" to avoid legal problems with the Mattel company.) Cimadevilla and Galán knew each other from the Malasaña neighborhood in Madrid. When Cimadevilla asked the music entrepreneur if he wanted to collaborate on a new Jess Franco film, Galán brought the band Killer Barbies on board, founded by musicians from the Galician Movida like Miguel Costas (one of the front men of Siniestro Total) and the exuberant singer Silvia Superstar (the former singer for Aerolíneas Federales).[14] Apart from recurrent Jess Franco

Jess Franco, knife in hand, setting the scene for Silvia Superstar in *Killer Barbys*. (Civic Producciones S. L., Emilio-Miguel Mencheta Benet, and Jacinto Santos Parrás. Courtesy of Tomás Cimadevilla.)

collaborators such as Lina Romay, the most well-known cast member was Santiago Segura, who was awarded the Goya for Best Young Actor for *El día de la bestia* (*The Day of the Beast*, 1995) while he was filming *Killer Barbys*. The plot was highly influenced by the cult movie *La matanza caníbal de los garrulos lisérgicos* (*Cannibal Massacre*, 1994), codirected by Antonio Blanco and Ricardo Llovo. Starring musicians César Strawberry (from Def con Dos) and Julián Hernández (from Siniestro Total) and made for the VHS market, *Cannibal Massacre* attained a cult status in the underground world after the sudden death of its codirector Blanco. It is a mix of Galician commonplaces, explicit criticism of European policies, and the plot of Tobe Hooper's *The Texas Chain Saw Massacre* (1974), in which a group of lost youngsters meets a cannibalistic family. As Cimadevilla recalls: "We showed the film to Jess, because his original project was a little bit tacky: he wanted a flamenco fusion band. We convinced him that maybe it was better to choose something more modern, like the kind of music that we were listening to" (Romero Santos and Rodríguez Ortega, "Cimadevilla").

Once finished, *Killer Barbys* began a long process of promotion. As Galán recalls, "we did quite a good job with the marketing campaign. In fact, I think that it was the most publicized film in Jess' career. We even managed to get the cultural section of the conservative newspaper *ABC* to write about the film. Headlines said things like 'The Underground Rediscovers Jess Franco' or 'Indie Music Rescues Jess.' Problems began after its release though [when] we started receiving calls from angry journalists, complaining about 'that rubbish.' I mean, Jess had made over 120 films: it was not our fault if they didn't bother to watch any of his previous works. In the end, journalists had written a lot of articles but nobody did really care to go deep into his films and peculiar personality" (Romero Santos and Rodríguez Ortega, "Galán"). In this respect, it seems as though many people watched *Killer Barbys* because they were supposed to like Jess Franco but had little idea about what they would encounter on the screen (Romero Santos and Rodríguez Ortega, "Crespo"). Cimadevilla insists on this idea: "People were fans of Jess Franco without having watched any of his films. Jess Franco became trendy. Everybody talked about 'uncle Jess.' In that sense, the marketing operation that we had planned was a success. He became a phenomenon" (Romero Santos and Rodríguez Ortega, "Cimadevilla"). Signifying how times were changing in the Spanish cultural sphere, the release of *Killer Barbys* coincided with the first Festimad music festival, where a retrospective of Jess Franco's films took place.

CONCLUSION

Although *Killer Barbys* was a commercial disappointment, with a total of 28,328 spectators and €84,078.76 at the box office, the core of the film crew continued helping Jess Franco afterward. Never again would Jess Franco release a film theatrically, but Galán distributed Franco's next movies, *Tender Flesh* (1997) and *Mari-Cookie and the Killer Tarantula* (1998), on VHS

A photo from the set of *Killer Barbys*, the film on which veteran cult director Jess Franco teamed up with a new generation of Spanish "indie" talent. (Civic Producciones S. L., Emilio-Miguel Mencheta Benet, and Jacinto Santos Parrás. Courtesy of Tomás Cimadevilla.)

format through his label Video Nasties, which was devoted to gore and genre films. Galán wanted to build on the momentum since, "After *Killer Barbys*, we met a lot of new talents such as Manuel Romo or Pedro Temboury and Video Nasties was a sort of a continuation of the project. We decided to produce not only music, but also to support young filmmakers" (Romero Santos and Rodríguez Ortega, "Galán"). Galán also made a cameo in *Lust for Frankenstein* (1998), playing Frankenstein's ghost. Certainly, *Killer Barbys* contributed to the international revival of Jess Franco, as well as to the promotion of the eponymous band beyond Spain. According to Carlos Moral, "as a result of its repercussion, the band Killer Barbies would travel to New York as guests of the magazine *Draculina*, edited by Kevin Collins. Jess Franco was honored at the Chiller Theatre Convention in New Jersey, where the film was shown. . . . All these events gave Subterfuge a fantastic contacts agenda: people from cinema, fashion, journalism" (21).

The help of Joey Ramone, a big fan of Franco's, was crucial. Soon thereafter, Subterfuge would become a key player in the Spanish cultural scene, mostly as a music label.

Killer Barbys launched Cimadevilla as a successful film producer. To date, *El otro lado de la cama* (*The Other Side of the Bed*, 2002), directed by Emilio Martínez-Lázaro has been his biggest success at the box office. It is also worth noting that he done much to ensure the continuation of Franco's legacy. Through his production company Telespan, for example, he financed *Kárate a muerte en Torremolinos* (2003) and *Ellos robaron la picha de Hitler* (2006) by Jess Franco pupil and admirer Pedro Temboury. Alongside film features, he has also participated in documentaries about Franco, such as *La última película de Jess Franco* (Pedro Temboury, 2013). Cimadevilla and Telespan also produced what can be considered the best tribute to Franco: *Torremolinos 73* (Pablo Berger, 2003), a bittersweet comedy freely inspired by Jess Franco and Lina Romay's life.

As for the band Killer Barbies, they starred again in *Killer Barbys vs. Dracula* (2003). Santiago Segura, who when he starred in *Killer Barbys* was an unknown young actor, has become a national celebrity. More pertinent to this chapter, given his links to Franco's revival in the first half of the 1990s, Segura was chosen to hand Franco his lifetime achievement Goya Award in 2008. In his speech, the clearly moved and uncharacteristically earnest Segura stated: "Only between 1972 and 1973 Jess Franco made 20 films. In almost all of them he directed, produced, scripted, edited. . . . He has made movies with crisis and without crisis, with money and without money, with clothes on and naked. . . . He has done everything except giving up." Franco came onstage in his wheelchair, pushed by his inseparable partner Lina Romay. He thanked Juan Antonio Bardem, Lina, the Cinémathèque Française, and, "the 4,000 girls . . . and 4,000 boys that are now with their short films in their pockets looking for someone to help them filming." Certainly, this was a way of thanking young fans for their support over the last two decades of his career. At the same time, it was also a way of flagging his close collaboration with a new generation of artists and entrepreneurs trying to make it in early 1990s Spain and his perennial status as an outsider, someone who could only remain faithful to his artistic practice by making films far removed from any official institutional or industrial context.

ACKNOWLEDGMENTS

This chapter was written in the context of the Research Project I+D+i "Cine y televisión en España 1986–1995: modernidad y emergencia de la cultura global," for Spain's Ministry of Economy and Competitiveness. The authors would like to thank the staff at Filmoteca Española and especially Luis E. Parés for their help in providing archival material for the essay.

NOTES

1. The *Ley Miró* was passed by the Spanish socialist government through the *Real Decreto 3.304 /1983 de 28 de diciembre, sobre la cinematografía*. See Triana Toribio's *Spanish National Cinema* (111–13) and Lázaro-Reboll's *Spanish Horror Film* (175–76) for a brief discussion of the ways in which the Miró Law privileged the production of high-quality films, based mainly on literary or historical sources, bringing to an end a specific type of genre filmmaking.
2. La Movida was a Madrid-based countercultural movement that emerged during the Spanish transition to democracy in the late 1970s through the mid-1980s, and encompassed a variety of artistic disciplines. It comprised a mix of heterogeneous approaches to art unified by the rejection of dominant representational models and the desire to appropriate international tendencies according to the idiosyncrasies of the changing Spanish landscape.
3. According to INE (Spanish National Institute of Employment), in 1993 unemployment soared to 23.9 percent of the population. A year later, it was 24.1 percent.
4. RNE3 is part of the public broadcasting system and is mostly devoted to popular music. It specifically targets youngsters, playing, for the most part, alternative music.
5. Obviously, we are discussing a pre-internet era. Things have radically changed with the rise of blogs, fan pages, and similar websites as fundamental tools of exchange among communities of cultural consumers and creators.
6. In Spain, the penetration of VHS technology soared from 9 percent of households in 1985 to 50 percent in 1991 (Señán 91).

7. Scholars and film historians also conceptualize Franco as a deviant and idiosyncratic creator who questions canonical versions of Spanish film history. Pavloviç, for example, describes him in these terms: "he is a marginalized body that disrupted Spanish official cinema throughout his prolific career; the official body of cinema disregarded him, but he created his own extraordinary bodies" (110).

8. Santiago Segura's short *Evilio* (1992) follows a male pervert who abducts and tortures three young girls; Pablo Berger's *Mama* (1988) deals with a family locked in a cellar after a nuclear disaster, as the father is forced to make a bloody decision.

9. "Mercromina" means mercurochrome. It is a medical antiseptic typically used to prevent infections in minor wounds. Due to the red color of this medical solution, the term was used to name a generation of filmmakers—"Generación Mercromina"—headed by Santiago Segura and Álex de la Iglesia, whose works explicitly represented violence and bloodletting.

10. Jesús Llorente, founder of the music label Acuarela, also points out the heterogeneity of and interconnectedness between different artistic disciplines at these music festivals. He states: "All kinds of people came to the concerts, people who wanted to start a band, people who worked in labels, journalists, the fanzine crowd, music fans, *Melody Maker* readers, young people who had travelled abroad and knew the musical trends in London or New York. . . . And lastly, those who were disenchanted with mainstream radio and everything that was commercial" (Holguera).

11. To date, Los Planetas is undoubtedly the most successful and enduring band to emerge from the Spanish indie scene of the 1990s; since their initial EP, they have always worked in partnership with corporate, multinational companies. While using the term "indie" to describe Los Planetas strikes us as being artistically and culturally appropriate in the context of this chapter, their exposure and visibility stem, at least partially, from their belonging to a global company with financial resources to make them stand out in the highly competitive and often unpredictable music market.

12. At the 1995 FIB festival, Los Planetas was one of the most acclaimed live acts. By then, it was clear that they had gathered a legion of fans that would remain faithful for decades to come. Today, the music festival circuit in Spain is a multi-million-euro business. It all started in the mid-1990s with festivals such as Sónar, FIB, and Doctor Music, which came into existence between 1994 and 1996, and the slightly later Primavera Sound, which began in 2001 (see Manrique; APM; Prat Forga).

13. One of the defining features of the term "indie," according to David Hesmondhalgh, is a "deliberate muting of charisma" (38). In addition, the

lyrics of "Himno generacional #83": "Cuando todo esto haya terminado/y no importe demasiado lo que digan/ Cuando no/ estés ya,/ cuando no estés ya/ y no haya nadie más" ("When all this is over / and what they say doesn't matter any longer / when you're no longer here / and there's nobody else around") have a definitely nihilistic flavor that signals the influence of the grunge movement, more generally, and records such as Nirvana's *Bleach* (Sub Pop, 1989), more specifically.

14. Vigo was the epicenter of the Galician youth culture during the 1980s. The term "Movida," as noted in the introduction to this chapter, is typically applied to the cultural scene in Madrid; however, there's also a Vigo Movida.

WORKS CITED

Aguilar, Carlos. "Jesús Franco Retrospective Official Brochure." Madrid: Filmoteca Española, 1993. Print.

Aguilar, Carlos, et al. "Jesús Franco: Francotirador del cine español." *DeZine* 4 (1991). Print.

Ansola González, Txomin. "La producción del cine en España durante la década de los 90: una aproximación." *Área Abierta* 6 (2003): 1–14. Print.

APM. "Anuario de la música en vivo" IV (2013). Web. 20 Feb. 2015.

Buse, Peter, et al. *The Cinema of Álex de la Iglesia*. Manchester: Manchester UP, 2007. Print.

Crespo, Borja. "El lado oscuro del celuloide." *Subterfuge* 11 (1994):76–77. Print.

———. "Prólogo." *Papo el payaso exconvicto*. Murcia: Tres Fronteras, 2010. Print.

Franco, Jesús. *Memorias del tío Jess*. Madrid: Aguilar, 2004. Print.

Freixas, Ramón, and Joan Bassa. "El increíble hombre mutante (entrevista con el heterónimo Jesús Franco)." *Archivos de la Filmoteca* 2.8 (1990/1991): 39–51. Print.

García, Yago. "Hasta siempre, 'Tío Jess': Los amigos y 'fans' de Jesús Franco le rinden homenaje." *Cinemanía*. Oct. 2013. Web. 11 May 2017.

Gelder, Ken. *Subcultures: Cultural History and Social Practice*. London: Routledge, 2007. Print.

Heffernan, Kevin. "Art House or House of Exorcism? The Changing Distribution and Reception Contexts of Mario Bava's *Lisa and the Devil*." *Sleaze Artists: Cinema at the Margins of Taste, Style, and Politics*. Ed. Jeffrey Sconce. Durham: Duke UP, 2007. 144–65. Print

Hesmondhalgh, David. "Indie: The Institutional Politics and Aesthetics of a Popular Music Genre." *Cultural Studies* 13 (1999): 34–61. Print.

Holguera, Juan P. "Así empezó el indie español." *Rolling Stone*. May 2011. Web. 21 Feb. 2015.

Lázaro-Reboll, Antonio. *Spanish Horror Film*. Edinburgh: Edinburgh UP, 2012. Print.

"Los Planetas." *Spiral* 27 (Feb. 1996): 17–21. Print.

Lucas, Tim. "How to Read a Franco Film." *Video Watchdog* 1 (1990): 18–35. Print.

Manrique, Darío. "Los festivales de verano en datos." Oct. 2012. Web. 21 Feb. 2015.

Mateu, Marc. "Los Ramones." *Rockdelux* 71 (January 1991): 4–8. Print.

"Morpho Index." *Monster World*. May 2009. Web. 20 May 2017.

Moral, Carlos. "Simpatía por el Diablo: resumen histórico de los 25 años de Subterfuge." *Viaje al centro de Subterfuge 1989–2014*. Ed. Carlos Moral and Carlos Galán. Madrid: Subterfuge Records, 2014. 9–35. Print.

Muelas, Yolanda. "Los Planetas." *Vang* 1 (March 1996): 16. Print.

Pavlović, Tatjana. *Despotic Bodies and Transgressive Bodies: Spanish Culture from Francisco Franco to Jesús Franco*. Albany: State U of New York P, 2003. Print.

Prat Forga, J. M. "La estructura relacional de las organizaciones colaboradoras con los festivales de música en España." *Gran Tour: Revista de Investigaciones Turísticas* 7 (2013): 75–96. Print.

Riambau, Esteve. "El periodo socialista (1982–1995)." *Historia del cine español*. Ed. Román Gubern, Esteve Riambau and Casimiro Torreiro. Madrid: Cátedra, 1995. 399–445. Print.

Romero Santos, Rubén, and Vicente Rodríguez Ortega. "Álex Mendíbil." Feb. 2015. Web. 20 Mar. 2015.

———. "Borja Crespo." Feb. 2015. Web. 20 Mar. 2015.

———. "Carlos Galán." Feb. 2015. Web. 20 Mar. 2015.

———. "Tomás Cimadevilla." Feb. 2015. Web. 20 Mar. 2015.

Sanjek, David. "Fan's Notes: The Horror Film Fanzine." *The Cult Film Reader*. Ed. Ernest Mathijs and Xavier Mendik. New York: Open UP, 2007. 419–28. Print.

Señán, Gaspar Brändle. "Consumo y cambio social en España: evolución en el equipamiento doméstico (1983–2005)." *Revista Española de Investigaciones Sociológicas* 120.1 (2007): 75–114. Print.

Subterfuge, Carlos. Editorial. *Subterfuge* 1 (1989): 2. Print.

———. Editorial. *Subterfuge* 2 (1990): 2. Print.

———. Editorial. *Subterfuge* 10 (1993): 2. Print.

———. "20 Trash-Sexy Films Celtibéricos." *Subterfuge* 10 (1993): 75. Print.

Triana-Toribio, Núria. *Spanish National Cinema*. London: Routledge, 2003. Print.

Ward, Glenn. "Journeys into Perversion: Vision, Desire and Economies of Transgression in the Films of Jess Franco." Diss. U of Sussex. 2011. Print.

11

SHE KILLS IN ECSTASY AND DRIVES AT DANGEROUSLY HIGH SPEEDS

The Death Cult Stardom of Soledad Miranda
Xavier Mendik

And so began the "dead star" phenomenon, a complex series of events and circumstances that is crystallized in certain images and in certain films, many of which have subsequently attracted a cult audience. . . . In certain exemplary "cursed" movies . . . images and dialogue both reflect and illuminate all the issues surrounding the death of the human body.

—Mikita Brottman

The story comes to an end with dismaying abruptness: Mrs. Johnson steers her car into the sea, her dead husband strapped in at her side. The scene may be crude but it has terrible tragic resonance, prefiguring as it does the fate that would soon befall the film's intensely talented young star. . . .

—Stephen Thrower

Following her violent death in 1970, the actress Soledad Miranda posthumously established herself as a leading "dark star" of European exploitation cinema. Although she appeared in a variety of popular Spanish coproductions, from musicals and melodramas to muscleman movies, she is now best remembered for titles such as *Eugenie (Eugenie de Sade,* 1974), *Les Cauchemars naissent la nuit (Nightmares Come at Night,* 1970), *Sie Tötete in Ekstase (She Killed in Ecstasy,* 1971) and *Vampyros Lesbos* (1971). These paired her talents with the surreal creations of the maverick

Spanish horror director Jesús "Jess" Franco, whose wider output remains the key subject of this volume. In their collaborations, Miranda was cast as an undead, dying, or death-driven heroine who recounts past transgressions involving sex, violence, and incest-bound retribution.

For a woman whose most significant on-screen roles were devoted to these macabre acts and frenzied performances, perhaps a dramatic and violent demise—met speeding along a Lisbon highway—seems inevitable. Miranda's real-life death on August 18, 1970 as a result of a car crash was made even more unnerving by virtue of the fact that it was cruelly prefigured by the ending of one of her final films for Franco: *She Killed in Ecstasy*. This movie, in which she is cast as the vengeful Mrs. Johnson, closes on the image of the actress fatally driving the corpse of her dead husband over a cliff. The scene carries unsettling echoes of Soledad Miranda's own death, especially since she was accompanied in this tragic last journey by her own husband (who was, in fact, a race car driver). The coincidence of Miranda's real-life and fictional fatality relegates her to that class of star personality whose macabre performances would appear to prefigure an actual and untimely end. As a "cursed" cult film icon, she exemplifies the phenomenon of dead stars identified by Mikita Brottman's opening citation. The actress's ill-fated performativity, gestures, and attributes conform to a near mythical belief that some stars operate at the axes of "cinema, psychosis, celebrity and death" (Brottman 105), which allows inflections of their impending doom to be retroactively deduced from their final performances.

Writing in the study "Star Cults/Cult Stars: Cinema, Psychosis, Celebrity, Death," Brottman offers a convincing consideration of the cultural and psychic traumas of those American stars whose very public deaths provoke not only mourning in their fans but also the endless quest to uncover "clues" to a future fate within their most celebrated final fictions. For instance, in her case study of Nicholas Ray's *Rebel without a Cause* (1955), Brottman maps the near identical demises of not only James Dean but also other leading cast members whose deaths mirror key scenes of threat and potential annihilation within the narrative. By guaranteeing the burnout of its key players, *Rebel without a Cause* remains "'[u]nique in the annals of Hollywood's 'cursed movies'" (112). The search for impending tragedy becomes even more pronounced for fatal stars such as Marilyn Monroe, whose final feature, *The Misfits* (John Huston, 1960), can be read as a morbid precursor of her own impending death: "Today's cult of Marilyn Monroe sees her as full of tragic consciousness, a quality so at odds with her movie roles that, to the modern viewer, the contradictions threaten almost to fragment the image altogether" (106). Arguably, Soledad Miranda's death cult stardom is similar to the extent that her final performances replicate what Brottman would term an example of the "celebrity death rattle" (109). It has ensured that she is best remembered not for her beauty (namely as a former model during the mid-1960s) or her acting career (appearing in over thirty films in various genres between 1960 and 1970), or even her musical abilities (as evidenced by the recording of two Spanish pop albums completed in a parallel career as a singer), but rather for associations with death and violence that tragically transcended her performances for Jess Franco to doom even the star herself.[1] The blurring between Soledad Miranda's death-ridden characters and her own real-life demise provides a crucial insight into the key role that this cult film performer had in the creation of Franco's cinema of sexuality, excess, and annihilation. This chapter will explore the evolution of Miranda's death cult stardom through her performances for Jess Franco, and consider her legacy for the legions of fans who remain fascinated by her menacing and yet enduring image.

They Filmed in Ecstasy:
Soledad Miranda and Jess Franco

What needs to be stated from the outset is that Soledad Miranda's chilling and potentially "cursed" screen presence was entirely constructed via her work with Jess Franco, a fact that warrants further investigation. Indeed, it could be argued that the director's formative films provided a transgressive template that would later be perfected through his collaborations with the actress. Writing in her 2004 essay "Gender and Spanish Horror

Film," Tatjana Pavlović argues that the director consistently challenged the boundaries of "legitimate" Spanish cinema via moments of outrageous generic excess, which frequently gave rise to atypical representations of female sexuality of the kind he exploited with Miranda. In particular, his frequent conflation of erotic and horrific imagery created a series of iconic and deadly heroines who convey their sexual power by wreaking havoc on the ineffectual men that populate these often transgressive films.

Pavlović explores how the director's gender representations contributed to his marginalization in official discourses about Spanish film culture, while simultaneously unpacking how his unwieldy body of work subverted the ideological constraints of General Francisco Franco's regime:[2]

> Jesús Franco's interest in horror, in pornography, in the pulp imagery of superspies and musclemen, can be seen as an effort to represent all that the Fascist government had officially repressed. . . . Jesús Franco's films enact a return of Fascism's repressed, the playing out of the delirium from which that political order drew its energy, but had to disavow in the name of normality, Catholic morality, and political and familial order. (*Despotic Bodies* 146)

If Franco's work utilizes images of female sexuality as a key element of this ideological struggle, then it seems relevant that this tendency was present in his first feature film *Tenemos 18 años* (1961). The film proved transgressive at the time of its release for promoting tropes of female bonding outside of the domestic sphere, while its cross-genre fusion of road movie and paternal horror also disoriented contemporary reviewers. As the *ABC* newspaper review commented at the time of the movie's release: "what could have been a gentle but distracted film becomes confused, losing all naturalness and grace in the process" (qtd. in Thrower: 51). The film details the plight of two girls who leave the security of the family home for a trip that culminates in a monstrous encounter with the dark "father figure" of Lord Marian. For Pavlović, this confrontation conflates psychosexual and social horror, fusing "elements of the thriller and horror films," with a "focus on incestuous fears and desires" ("Gender" 138). The film's more unsettling elements also involve a set of historical inferences to Spain, where a "focus on paternal authority could also be read as an implicit reference to Francisco Franco, the dictator" (138).

While Pavlović identifies this early cross-genre production as a template for later Franco works, *Tenemos 18 años* also initiated the important theme of perverse paternal intent breeding female transgression that he would explore in a more explicit manner with Soledad Miranda in titles such as *Eugenie de Sade*. Here, the focus is on a sexually charged killing spree by the perverse stepfather Albert de Franval (Paul Muller) and his brooding female offspring Eugenie (Miranda). Another early template for the theme of perverse paternal intent and female transgression that Franco would later perfect with Miranda can be found in *Miss Muerte* (*The Diabolical Dr. Z*, 1966). This film uses a motif of female doubling in a story that revolves around a vengeful daughter who exacts revenge on the medical board that spurned the scientific advances of her late father, Dr. Zimmer. Using the process of "mind manipulation" he invented, Zimmer's daughter seizes psychic control of an alluring cabaret performer, Miss Muerte, who seduces and kills those responsible for his untimely death. In her analysis of the film, Pavlović notes the preponderance of castrative imagery, much of which derives from the performer's destructive use of her long, poisoned fingernails to blind, gore, and tear at her male victims. Confirming the vengeful power of Miss Muerte, whose real name is Nadia, the author notes:

> *Miss Muerte* explores female sexuality as monstrous . . . and illuminates anxieties about uncontrollable female power. The beautiful, sexually active woman is not the victim—she is the killer. At the same time we see Nadia's victims, professional men, coded as powerful and masterful, screaming, fleeing and dying. ("Gender" 139)

Both in its focus on male victimization, as well as its theme of a vengeful woman taking revenge on medical authorities responsible for the death/humiliation of a loved one, *The Diabolical Dr. Z* anticipates later Franco/

Miranda collaborations such as *She Killed in Ecstasy*. This film casts the actress as Mrs. Johnson, a vengeful bride who orchestrates a campaign of seduction, entrapment, and castration against the male-dominated medical board that wrecked her husband's career and provoked his suicide. As part of her murderous quest, Mrs. Johnson makes elaborate use of costumes and disguises to conceal her identity, thus replicating the notion of the doubled or split woman that Pavlović identifies in her analysis of *The Diabolical Dr. Z*. Beyond these similarities, both *The Diabolical Dr. Z* and *She Killed in Ecstasy* also highlight another feature that would be foregrounded in Franco's work with Soledad Miranda, namely the traumatic reduction of male power embodied by a radical loss of visual control. In the case of *The Diabolical Dr. Z*, "the focus shifts from the scientific, voyeuristic gaze of all three men (victims) to their threatened, frightened eyes" (Pavlović, "Gender" 139). This alteration between female sexual dominance and faltering male vision becomes even more marked in Franco/Miranda pairings such as *Eugenie de Sade*, *She Killed in Ecstasy*, and *Vampyros Lesbos*, which repeatedly use objects, obtuse angles, and even the actress's own hands thrust violently into the camera lens to connect the idea of sexually charged looking with impending punishment.

As well as sharing central elements with the director's foundational films, Soledad Miranda's work with Jess Franco also fits within more general trends identified within Franco's output between the 1960s and the 1970s. For instance, in her *Despotic Bodies and Transgressive Bodies*, Pavlović situates these subversive representations of gender and sexuality against three specific phases of Franco's career: the "Pop Art Body" as well as the "Horrific Body" and "Pornographic Body" stages. The author defines the first period of the director's work through the concept of the "Pop Art Body," which broadly correlates to his early to mid-1960s output. Here, narratives center on superheroes, detectives, and spies, revealing the director's fascination with pulp novels and European cult comics. Corporeality in these pop art creations is marked via a process of "hyper-masculine subversion," which undercuts dominant codes of nationally defined virility (via repeated connection of the masculine to the comedic), while also casting female performers in more potent roles as investigators and detectives (Pavlović, *Despotic Bodies* 111). This emphasis on female agency thriving outside of traditional familial and social bonds continues in the later "Horror Body" and "Pornographic Body" narratives that Pavlović analyzes. Here, Franco's output responded to loosening censorship constraints across Europe via a series of terror/titillation hybrids that include the iconic films he completed with Soledad Miranda.

For Pavlović, Franco's early to midcareer phase remains his most radical, with the pop art/horror stages containing "his most interesting and innovative features such as blending horror and eroticism" ("Gender" 140). Her position that his later productions "rapidly dissipat[ed] into soft porn and, eventually, into hard-core pornography" (140), however, seems complicated by the period in which the director worked with Soledad Miranda. Firstly, this position is in many ways complicated by the unique manner in which Franco worked, with projects frequently initiated only to be deferred or diverted into alternative projects that were often released several years after their inception. This complex system of production renders distinctions between "good" and "bad" Franco periods problematic. As Stephen Thrower has argued, "Franco's work is best seen as a borderless continuum rippling with recurring themes, individual films less important than the wider trends and currents passing through" (15). While Franco's exhaustive back catalog does render traditional filmic distinctions difficult, Pavlović's distinction between "body" phases seems to be a useful way of interpreting his work. However, as Thrower contends, all modes of physiology in Franco revert to the erotic, with "films re-edited and redubbed, recast and reshuffled, more sex, no sex, hardcore sex. . . . Franco's chief hallmark is sex, often perverse or sadistic, but his films are only occasionally 'porno films' per se" (15). As a result, the collaborations between Franco and Miranda not only conflate the "Pop," "Horror," and "Pornographic" stages outlined by Pavlović but also contain a series of features that add further complexity to the director's oeuvre. In particular, I would highlight three distinct tropes that provide further insight into the collaborations between the director and the female performer. These three features revolve around Miranda's associations with death and her manipulation of male-ordered systems of vision, as well as the frequent strategies of doubling that accompany her image.

SOLEDAD MIRANDA: THE FEMALE PERFORMER AS A SYMBOL OF DEATH

While earlier titles such as *Tenemos 18 años* and *The Diabolical Dr. Z* highlight Jess Franco's interest in the rebellious and potentially destructive female spirit, his later work with Soledad Miranda creates a more distinct and perverse embodiment for this trope. This was achieved by conflating the performer's allure with an overwhelming sense of impending doom and tragedy, which subsequently helped to cement the "death cult" aura that surrounded her demise. She is a "pinup" performer who exudes a very peculiar sex appeal that appears to unravel as soon as she disrobes. Despite slinky titles such as *Vampyros Lesbos* and *Sex Charade* (1972), Miranda's erotic scenes for Jess Franco remain curiously alienating, performed with all the passion of a woman who has just expired. Her corpse-like bouts of copulation have been described by Cathal Tohill and Pete Tombs as "lobster-like . . . where one body lies limply on another" (102).

Even in her supporting roles for the director, Miranda's connection to the living world is repeatedly rendered ambivalent. For instance, in *Count Dracula* (1970), she is cast as Lucy, one of the count's female victims. Importantly, as soon as Miranda is introduced into the narrative (in a scene where she and Mina visit the deranged Jonathan Harker at Van Helsing's clinic), she falls into a state of deathlike paralysis from which her living body cannot recover. Paradoxically, it is only when the character joins the ranks of the undead that she truly appears animated. Equally, the reassembled "lost" Franco film *Nightmares Come at Night* features the actress on-screen for less than ten minutes, yet continues the tradition of equating her performative style with macabre eroticism. In a narrative that focuses on the delusions of a murderous lesbian strip club performer, Soledad Miranda's cameo here functions similarly to her more central performances for the director: she strips, she gazes (aggressively into the camera), and then she dies.

Complementing these paradoxical performances, the director's camera frequently renders Soledad Miranda's physical form as an unstable entity with the potential to terrify as well as to entice the male victims who become her favored prey. For instance, in *She Killed in Ecstasy*, Miranda is represented as the ultimate threat to phallic potency, playing the vengeful wife who castrates male surgeons at the point of orgasm. The resultant fusion of soft-core iconography with scenes of penile mutilation ensured that *She Killed in Ecstasy* would be regarded by critics like Tohill and Tombs as "too serious to be entertaining. . . . Like a lot of Franco's work it's morbidly obsessed with oblivion, a fixation that's out of place in a lusty sex film" (102).

Rather than being an isolated exception, this overlap between erotic and horrific imagery became the motif that dominated Soledad Miranda's work for the director. The depiction of female sexuality as a symbol of death in *She Killed in Ecstasy* is echoed in other movies such as *Eugenie de Sade*. This film follows the incestuous adventures of the perverse patriarch Albert de Franval, with Miranda cast as Eugenie, the teenage girl in his charge. The film details how the couple draws inspiration from Sade's work to commit a series of sexualized killings across Europe. Although Eugenie is initially coded as the passive partner in the proceedings, her concealed aggressive nature increasingly comes to the fore during the course of the couple's killing spree. In one memorable scene, the pair travels to Brussels in order to commit a sex crime, which culminates in them murdering an erotic cabaret performer. Here, Albert initially appears to orchestrate proceedings, dictating how Eugenie should sensuously interact with the model while he begins to photograph the pair. However, when he instructs his female accomplice to dispatch their unwitting subject, Eugenie's nihilistic intentions suddenly emerge. She proceeds to strangle the performer with a pair of oversized tongs before emitting a piercing shrill of sexual pleasure, which evokes the extremes of suffering and arousal central to the performative style she developed for the director.

What such unsettling scenes point to is that despite her pinup looks and modeling past, Soledad Miranda carried a very different set of connotations than other Euro-glamour icons of the late 1960s and the 1970s. Frequently, cult actresses such as the Italian starlet Edwige Fenech or even Franco's long-term collaborator Lina Romay sought to infuse an air of fun-filled naughtiness into the most gruesome of their horror/exploitation films, often through the manipulation of comic performance styles or elaborate forms of costume. However, when such fanciful and excessive forms of display and decoration were used by Miranda, they failed to detract from the morbid films in which she factored. For instance, the opening flashback sequence in *She Killed in Ecstasy* features the actress kitted out in (near futuristic) metallic underwear—complete with cone-shaped breastplates that accentuate the appeal of her near nakedness. In other contexts, this kitsch costuming would represent a camp, carnal invitation. However, the fact that she wears this outfit at the point in the story where her character is enthusiastically inspecting her husband's fetus research laboratory serves only to heighten the incongruity between her physical presentation and the morbid scientific concerns that the narrative pursues.

Soledad Miranda: Black Stares and the "Interruptive" Porno Gaze

As indicated previously, the fictional characters that Miranda played for Jess Franco are marked by their repeated associations with annihilation, which have become a frame of reference through which to evaluate her untimely death. These unsettling productions are also marked by a disorientating film style, resulting from the ways in which Franco's camera frames and surveys its star, often with disturbing effect. As Pavlović has noted: "Besides the sexual act per se, Franco's camera angles, lighting, beautiful photography, and mise-en-scène center on questions of eroticism, voyeurism, fetishism, violence, and power and disempowerment, exploring its connection to bodies, sensations, pleasures, and affects"

Miranda in a publicity still from *The Devil Came from Akasava* that highlights the morbid, funereal quality that distinguished her from other Euro-glamour icons of the late 1960s and the 1970s. (Cooperativa Fénix Films and CCC Filmkunst. Courtesy of Photofest.)

(*Despotic Bodies* 116–17). The voyeuristic potential that a male director can project upon the body of an actress has long been documented by film critics and feminist theorists alike, and very much provides a starting point for Pavlović's analysis. Here, she draws on Laura Mulvey's now classic account of "Visual Pleasure and Narrative Cinema," which considers the ways in which the cinematic apparatus produces systems of spectatorship that privilege the male subject. In the course of this analysis, Mulvey examines the extent to which systems of cinematic looking reproduce "a world ordered by sexual imbalance," where the articulation of a male gaze ensures that the "pleasure in looking has been split between active/male and passive/female" (62). For the author, classical cinematic mechanisms function to contain the threat of female sexuality and bodily difference by reducing women to "their traditional exhibitionist role," where they "are simultaneously looked at and displayed, with their appearance coded for strong visual and erotic impact" (62). As a result, these mainstream cinematic mechanisms function to marginalize the feminine, playing on the notions of lack and castration it evokes for the male viewer. While strategies of voyeurism (which Mulvey exemplifies via Alfred Hitchcock) limit the "threat" of female physiology by investigating and devaluing her sexual power, processes of fetishism (which she identifies in the cinema of Josef von Sternberg) glamorize and adorn the body of the female performer as an additional coping mechanism to diminish her implicit threat.

As critics of Franco's presumed voyeurism have long maintained, the director often went to elaborate ends to ensure that his camera captured *all*, particularly when it surveyed the female body caught in throes of extreme sexual passion. As recently as 2015, Stephen Thrower noted in his exhaustive overview of the director that Franco was above all else a voyeur who "gained sexual enjoyment from watching others, from conceiving and then filming sex between other people. His scopophilia is intense, his arousal predicated on gathering up the maximum visual harvest" (42). Representing this obsession to "see" is Franco's trademark zoom shot, which he uses to focus in extreme and fetishistic detail on actresses such as Soledad Miranda.

However, while Franco's work clearly features the key mechanisms of voyeurism and fetishism that Mulvey's study highlights, their projection upon Soledad Miranda appears to function in a markedly different manner vis-à-vis the "determining male gaze" (62) identified by Mulvey in "Visual Pleasure and Narrative Cinema." Specifically, because of the unique way in which the director filmed his star, as well as how she responded to his camera, Franco's collaborations with Miranda feature what I would call an "interruptive porno gaze" that complicates visual access to their titillating scenes. This gaze is partly ensured by Franco's distinctive use of photography, and in particular his much discussed use of the zoom shot. Thrower argues that the director's preoccupation with the zoom can be seen as an "essential part of his style" (22), and it has ramifications for the concept of the interruptive porno gaze in representations of Soledad Miranda. For Franco's detractors, the use of this mechanism is evidence of the "cheap, crude, ugly and unsophisticated" (22) nature of his work. For Thrower, however, the criticism Franco has received for his heavy use of the zoom shot is related to the way in which it suddenly jolts spectators out of the security of the fiction they are consuming. The "zoom lens, by doing something the human eye cannot, reminds us that what we are experiencing is not real but mediated by the hands of others" (22). While Thrower concedes that the director's use of this device had as much to do with budgetary restrictions as it did with ensuring an experimental feel to his productions, it does have ramifications for images of female sexuality portrayed in his cinema. If it is it is the case that, in Thrower's words, the "zoom is erotic!" (23), it also functions to ensure that such sensuality is diffuse, undefined, and beyond the control of any assumed male spectator.

If the zoom shot functions to disrupt the seamless pleasure associated with heterosexual pornography, this technological intervention is augmented by the threatening manner in which Soledad Miranda frequently returns the desiring gaze of her audience. Indeed, it seems significant that the title of Tim Lucas's foundational essay on the actress references her "black stare." More recently, Thrower has compared her unnerving gaze to that of "a gorgon, her dark brown eyes turning to black marbles of hostility . . . we see in her eyes a fury that's feral, intense and utterly convincing" (248). Both Lucas's and Thrower's observations indicate that rather than being a compliant object of sexual display, the performer possesses an overbearing and defiant gaze that not only seduces but also surveys and terrifies the male characters she encounters. Not strictly a horror device, this "black stare" is evident in Soledad Miranda's last role as the undercover agent/erotic dancer in Franco's *Der Teufel Kam aus Akasawa* (*The Devil Came from Akasava*, 1971). This film contains a number of examples where her threatening stare and austere performative style injects a sinister tone into otherwise titillating scenes. In particular, the star's gaze back at the camera in seduction scenes and nightclub performances contrasts starkly with her alluring costumes and movements, functioning to challenge the viewer's pleasure in surveying her. This provocative gaze is more challenging than inviting, especially when coupled with Franco's use of zooms and dissolves on extreme close-ups of the performer's face to further complicate visual access to her image. In such instances, the star image is degraded, because it subverts "cinematic techniques such as the close-up" (105) that Brotmann argues should ensure that the performer's "bodily movements and physical gestures are constantly subject to intense and ongoing public scrutiny" (105).

Soledad Miranda's disruptive gaze is arguably similar to that of other famous "Eurotrash" icons such as Barbara Steele. It is no coincidence that Lucas compares the actresses in his article "The Black Stare of Soledad Miranda," and this comparison is confirmed by wider theoretical studies on Steele. For example, Carol Jenks has noted the association between sex and death in a number of the actress's 1960s productions. In particular, the author concludes that Steele's influential work with Italian director Mario Bava is dominated by "an extreme violence toward the audience, an aggressive desire to wound the very site of vision, the eye" (154). The process of rendering the spectator "the owner of a violated gaze" (154) here is similar to the one that dominates *The Devil Came from Akasava*, as well as other Franco films like *Vampyros Lesbos*. Here she is cast as

Countess Nadine Carody, whose role oscillates between that of a melancholic member of the undead and that of an erotic nightclub performer. In the many club routines that punctuate the film, Miranda's stripteases repeatedly evoke an unsettling mood through both her staged seduction of an immobile female mannequin and the way in which she frequently confronts the nightclub audience that has assembled to contemplate her. *Vampyros Lesbos* even underscores the danger of Miranda's dark stare via the repeated use of low-angled shots of her thrusting her hands aggressively into the lens of the camera during the erotic performances. In so doing, the film confirms Pavlović's view that:

> Jess Franco's work often foregrounds ambiguities of gender and sexuality and suggests the instability of power relations implied by acts of looking. . . . Franco gave Spanish cinema many interesting female figures and created remarkable and unusual heroines: women detectives, female and lesbian vampires and women killers. ("Gender" 138)

Arguably, Soledad Miranda's performances for Jess Franco confirm Pavlović's view that the director's female characters function to destabilize patriarchal structures. More importantly, the prominence of the performer's "black stare" further connects these subversive qualities to unsettling scenarios of suffering and fatality.

SOLEDAD MIRANDA: FORMAL REPETITIONS IN THE REPRESENTATION OF "DARK STARDOM"

Underlying Soledad Miranda's morbid look and disruptive modes of looking in her final performances was the way in which her presence signified a kind of suffering and decay that seeped into the structure of the movies she made with Franco. What is remarkable in films such as *Vampyros Lesbos* and *She Killed in Ecstasy* is the extent to which Soledad Miranda's role as an agent of trauma also renders motifs of sexual violence and death as narrative problems: nihilistic elements that must be endlessly replayed and recounted through the use of montage sequences, flashback scenes, and melancholic voice-over narrations.

For instance, in its attempts to be both hip *and* horrific, *Vampyros Lesbos* reverses much of the iconography associated with the vampire genre (such as bats and wolves), to replace them with psychedelic shots of red kites and butterflies in flight. However, it is significant that the film repeatedly juxtaposes these vibrant inserts with images of blood-drenched drapes and a scorpion ready to deliver a venomous blow as if to reiterate Nadine's slippage between the boundaries of life and death. These juxtapositions represent a form of macabre montage that repeatedly halts the film's narrative flow in order to review the vampire's campaign of destruction.

Even when cast as a human character, Miranda's ambiguous link to the living becomes similarly recast as a form of narrative fixation. For instance, *Eugenie de Sade* is told via a "fatalistic" flashback in which the dying heroine recounts how a past incestuous infatuation with her stepfather resulted in their mutual destruction after the pair committed a killing spree. The frequent switches in temporality between Eugenie's past actions and her present-tense suffering indicate that the female body in an agonized state of near annihilation is ultimately caught in both a physical and a temporal bind.

Although Miranda is cast as a human for her emblematic performance in *She Killed in Ecstasy*, she is frequently referred to in supernatural terms. For instance, one of her male victims brands her "a devil" at the point at which he realizes her intent is vengeful castration rather than seduction. Given that the ending of the production provides a near mirror to the performer's actual car crash, it seems appropriate that the film also demonstrates one of the most complex forms of narrative repetition in all of her work with Franco. It opens with a past-tense sequence of shots from her husband's research laboratory (which is later destroyed by the medical panel that condemns his work), before shifting to present-tense narration that follows Miranda through the isolated villa that is now her home. Here, she begins to explain in voice-over the loss of her husband, triggering an extended flashback sequence that takes us from the beginning of their marriage to the moment of his suicide.

This extended flashback establishes a pattern whereby death and violence continually interrupt the smooth running of narrative progression, confirming that the film remains wedded to an exploration of past suffering. Even when the text does return from these prior scenes to follow Miranda tracking each of her potential victims, her fatal past still interrupts the filmic flow in the form of a series of "prior inserts." For instance, during Miranda's seduction and murder of one male medical figure, the film juxtaposes images of the couple kissing with similarly framed shots of her kissing her husband. In this respect, *She Killed in Ecstasy* exemplifies what Olga Cox Cameron has defined as the "type of narrative in which the forces of repetition . . . reflect the particular mode of inhibiting time, which . . . illustrates the death drive in action" (109). According to Cox Cameron's analysis, types of narrative repetition that remain fixated on loss, suffering, or trauma provide a link between fictional forms and the psychic construction of reality that lies behind them. Drawing on Sigmund Freud's work on the death drive and obsessive compulsives, Cox Cameron argues that the morbid fears that plague the adult mind are often revisions and repetitions of earlier infantile displeasure: "The basic trope of narrative is repetition of a prior event, an event which exists primarily in the telling, but repetition as Freud demonstrates is also that which provides the warp and wave of psychic life" (109). Although Freud was eager to utilize case study as a method of linking such compulsive repetitions to unresolved childhood and Oedipal dramas, he frequently made connections between the workings of the mind and the workings of narrative. As early as 1899, Cox Cameron notes, his work on "Screen Memories" discussed how disturbing childhood memories could become altered, recast, and characterized "almost like works of fiction" (101).

In terms of linking the fatal fictions of Soledad Miranda to the traumatic compulsions that Cox Cameron discusses, it is notable that her films reference death and impending doom through similar processes of repetition and doubling. Indeed, the notion of "split" female identity is itself underscored by the fact that Miranda herself endlessly doubled her true identity by using the pseudonyms Susan Korda, Susann Korda, and Susan Korday for her collaborations with Franco. The opening sequence of *Vampyros Lesbos*, where Miranda performs a strip routine before a full-length mirror (in what is later revealed to be an erotic stage routine), indicates that this is a character whose reflection and indeed very essence is literally doubled. Indeed, throughout the film, the heroine (and Miranda's on-screen love object) Linda Westinghouse (Ewa Strömberg) is unsure whether the seductive Nadine who performs erotic strip routines at an Istanbul nightclub is the same person as the countess whose estate she has been employed to catalog. These instances of repetition and doubling are themselves repeated in other Miranda performances, such as the one in *She Killed in Ecstasy*, where the female body comes to connote not only desire but also death, doubling, and mutilation. In her role as the castrating Mrs. Johnson, Soledad Miranda is literally everywhere: not only is her reflection endlessly doubled and reproduced by the mirrors in which she mysteriously appears and disappears but she also occupies an impossible spatial as well as temporal plane. For instance, one sequence depicts her chasing a victim through a network of buildings and passages before unexpectedly (and unrealistically) turning up in the surgeon's bed a moment later.

While these processes of narrative repetition and doubling serve to connect Soledad Miranda's collaborations with Jess Franco, they also function to fatally prefigure her own real-life demise on the road. Franco molded her on-screen persona as a female protagonist who strives for sexual gratification and emancipation only to have these desires thwarted by suffering, mutilation, and death. This scenario uncannily prefigures Soledad Miranda's own untimely death. After a succession of "B" movie roles, she died on the way to sign the contract that would have allowed her to become the kind of actress she dreamed of being. As Franco himself recounts in Lucas's "The Black Stare of Soledad Miranda":

The day before she died, she received the greatest news of her life. . . .
I visited her in her apartment in Lisbon with a German producer,

who came to offer her a two-year contract with CCC which would assure her of at least two starring roles per year in big budget films. She was going to become a major star in Germany. The next day, as her contract was being drafted, she had the accident. When the hospital called to break the news . . . I nearly passed out. (189)

Her accident was made even more bizarre by the way in which it was cruelly prefigured at the end of *She Killed in Ecstasy*, where the vengeful widow drives her car (along with her husband's corpse) off a cliff. According to Tohill and Tombs, the film's frenzied finale confirms that, "deprived of sex and genuine affection she embraces annihilation" (102). The fact that Miranda's real-life husband (and the driver of the doomed vehicle) escaped the incident relatively unscathed only adds further weight to the perception that she was fated to die.

REPETITIONS BEYOND A ROLE:
OR HOW TO READ DEATH INTO ONLINE LIFE

Although Soledad Miranda worked with a number of other filmmakers (completing 31 movies before she died), her curious affiliation with Jess Franco's morbid obsessions functions to index her fictional roles to her real-life demise. The movies she starred in for the director included porn potboilers, lesbian vampire narratives, and female revenge melodramas, but they were all marked by a macabre similarity in both theme and performance style. At the level of content, Miranda's roles were governed by an overpowering sense of doom and impending (and repeated) peril, a mood that appears incongruous when set alongside her characters' craving for eternal love and sexual plenitude. As Franco observed in a *European Trash Cinema* interview, "she had a personality which translated to the screen a lot of the things that she felt deep inside. But it was translated in an unconscious way. She was a funnel" (qtd. in Collins: 17).

In terms of her on-screen persona, this mode of performative "funneling" sees the actress oscillate between wild, uncontrollable gestures of sexual desire and a near entranced approach to scenes of death and suffering.

In these works, it is as if the performer's body becomes possessed by a greater and otherworldly force when she is exposed to Franco's constantly zooming and penetrating voyeuristic lens. If Miranda's output with Franco does fulfill the function of fatalistic fiction, then it is also worth assessing the impact of her death on him. According to Tohill and Tombs, the director remained haunted by Miranda's memory and would frequently alter shooting schedules and request location changes after being "consulted" by the dead actress during his sleep. Equally, the process of doubling and traumatic repetition identified previously in Miranda's films became the basis for continued modes of replication in Franco's work beginning in 1973, when he met his late partner and long-term collaborator Lina Romay.

Given Franco's interest in doubling and repetition, it seems appropriate that Romay, with her long flowing dark hair and slender frame, resembled Miranda and was cast in nearly identical roles by the director. In the words of Tohill and Tombs, "it seemed that Lina was a projection of Soledad. She moved like her; it was uncanny, almost as if she was trying to live up to the image of Soledad" (103). What is even more unnerving than Franco finding his "double" of Miranda in Romay is the fact that her first film for him, titled *La Comtesse noire* (*Female Vampire*, 1973), was a virtual remake of *Vampyros Lesbos* (even down to the image of the heroine's suicide in a blood-filled bath). As if to underscore Tohill and Tombs's view that Romay represented "a lusty reincarnation of Soledad" (103), it seems significant that when she appeared in her 1980s porn films for Franco under the pseudonym Candy Coster, he had her don a blonde wig identical to the one worn by Miranda in *She Killed in Ecstasy*. Filming these works—which included *Die Marquise von Sade* (1977), where Romay is literally doubled as a pair of twins exploring the limits of violent sexuality—Franco was well aware of the influence that his former star continued to exert over his work:

> After the first two or three films with Lina . . . strange things happened. . . . We were shooting in Madeira for instance, and it was like Soledad was there . . . in those first two or three films, Lina too had the feeling that Soledad was vampirising us (Collins 18).

Beyond the fatalistic impact that Soledad Miranda had on Franco's later career, it is also interesting to note how the contradictions surrounding her "dark star" persona and demise have affected her subsequent reception by critics and fans of Eurotrash/horror cinema. For instance, Amy Brown's website, *Sublime Soledad*, features a number of striking fan portraits, paintings, and collages of the star that emphasize the melancholy qualities linking her collaborations with Jess Franco to her untimely demise. Stephen Abel's artwork for the site manipulates shots from the pair's collaborations with startling compositions and colorings that clearly connote the star's deathly qualities. These images include "Blood Queen" (featuring a publicity still from *The Devil Came from Akasava*) and "Psycho" (adapted from a still from *She Killed in Ecstasy*), both of which distort the actress's otherwise glamorous appearance via saturated, blood-red backdrops to convey her more sinister qualities. The fatal connections between Miranda's roles for Franco and her later death also seem to permeate other paintings produced by this artist. For instance, images such as "Soledad Transcending," "Death Mask," and "Immortal Clay" effectively split or multiply images of the cult star's face and body in a manner that recalls the unnatural processes of female doubling that mark her work for the director.

Equally, titles such as "Soledad Ghost," "Soul of the City," and "Huge Shades" (also by Abel) draw attention to the near demonic gaze that the actress used to seduce and then torture the predominantly male victims featured in these works. What such fan-based artifacts point to is the fact that at the level of pop iconography, Soledad Miranda remains one of Europe's first fully fledged scream queens, a label that ensures her immortality. Indeed, her screen persona as a "cool," kitsch, and kinky femme fatale seems confirmed by the plethora of contemporary internet sites and fanzines serving as shrines to the dead star beyond Amy Brown's exhaustive resource. These ancillary resources explore Miranda's biography and influence from a number of different perspectives that include her use of fashion/costume, questions of her national heritage, and the connections between her early roles and later career.[3] However, as this chapter has considered, the reasons for fans' identification with and adoration of the

A work of fan art by Stephen Abel from Amy Brown's tribute website *Sublime Soledad*, "Blood Queen" uses saturated color and other effects to distort an image of Miranda from *The Devil Came from Akasava*, emphasizing the glamorous star's sinister side. (Courtesy of Amy Brown and Stephen Abel.)

dead star remain as complex and troubling as the roles and performative strategies undertaken by the actress herself.

By virtue of her sudden demise in a manner so close to that staged in one of her final films, Soledad Miranda epitomizes what Mikita Brottman has termed the "dead star phenomenon" (112). As Brottman notes, it is little wonder that "the death of a celebrity (particularly if public, tragic, untimely, accidental or self-inflicted) should arouse such violent emotion, such voyeurism, such curiosity, such alarm" (111). It is precisely these unsettling qualities that index Miranda's final performances to her death, and that remain the basis for the fascination with which she is regarded by the fan sites and online communities dedicated to her work. The legend of Soledad Miranda ultimately highlights the point where the cult of Jess Franco and death cult stardom meet.

ACKNOWLEDGMENTS

My thanks to Amy Brown from *Sublime Soledad* for her assistance with the preparation of this article. The image "Blood Queen" is courtesy of Amy Brown and the website *Sublime Soledad* and remains the property of artist Stephen Abel.

NOTES

1. For further information, see Amy Brown's site *Sublime Soledad*, which out-
   lines the actress's range beyond her more morbid entries for Jesús Franco.
   As Brown notes, Soledad Miranda's initial film performances were in
   light-hearted musical comedies such as José María Elorrieta's *La bella Mimi*
   (1960), where her role revolves around a number of musical routines. While
   other musical performances dominate Miranda's early repertoire (including
   a minor role in Franco's *La reina del Tabarín* [1960]), her expressive qualities also ensured her entry into other European cycles popular during the
   decade, including historical adventure dramas such as Carlo Campogalli-
   ani's *Ursus* (1960) and the 1967 release *Cervantes* (Vincent Sherman). She
   also appeared in "spaghetti" westerns such as *Sugar Colt* (Franco Giraldi,
   1966). The majority of her roles during the 1960s, however, were in comedies, which traded on her quirky and nonthreatening persona. Importantly,
   when she appeared in horror productions during this decade (such as Julio
   Coll's *Pyro* from 1963), Miranda was presented as as a love interest, rather
   than the destructive female figures that she would later perfect with Franco.
   Also, Brown points out that the two records that Soledad Miranda completed in 1964 and 1965 function as a counterpoint to her more melancholic collaborations with Franco. As Brown notes: "Most of us know
   Soledad as the dark, mysterious icon of Franco's movies. But when Soledad
   sings, we experience a whole other side of her: flirty, bubbly, happy, and
   cute, as well as seductive" (http://www.soledadmiranda.com/records.html,
   accessed 18 Sept. 2016).
2. This essay was, in fact, expanded from the author's earlier monograph *Despotic Bodies and Transgressive Bodies: Spanish Culture from Francisco Franco to
   Jesús Franco* (2003).
3. See www.anothermag.com/fashion-beauty/1697/soledad-miranda;
   http://asketchofthepast.com/2015/08/18/young-rebel-the-exploits-of-soledad
   -miranda; and https://robbinsrealm.wordpress.com/2012/09/28/the-all-too
   -short-life-of-soledad-miranda.

WORKS CITED

Brottman, Mikita. "Star Cults/Cult Stars: Cinema, Psychosis, Celebrity, Death."
   Unruly Pleasures: The Cult Film and its Critics. Ed. Graeme Harper and Xavier
   Mendik. Guildford: FAB, 2000. 105–19. Print.
Collins, Kevin. "Interview with Jess Franco." *European Trash Cinema* 1 (1996):
   2–36. Print.

Cox Cameron, Olga. "Narrative Form and the Freudian Death Drive." *The Death Drive: New Life for a Dead Subject?* Ed. Rob Weatherill. London: Rebus, 1999. 97–120. Print.

Jenks, Carol. "The Other Face of Death: Barbara Steele and *La maschera del demonio.*" *Popular European Cinema.* Ed. Richard Dyer and Ginette Vincendeau. London: Routledge, 1992. 149–63. Print.

Lucas, Tim. "The Black Stare of Soledad Miranda." *Obsession: The Films of Jess Franco.* Ed. Lucas Balbo and Peter Blumenstock. Berlin: Graf Haufen and Frank Trebbin, 1993. 183–96. Print.

Mulvey, Laura. "Visual Pleasure and Narrative Cinema." *Feminism and Film Theory.* Ed. Constance Penley. London: Routledge, 1988. 57–69. Print.

Pavlović, Tatjana. *Despotic Bodies and Transgressive Bodies: Spanish Culture from Francisco Franco to Jesús Franco.* Albany: State U of New York P, 2003. Print.

———. "Gender and the Spanish Horror Film." *Gender and Spanish Cinema.* Ed. Steven Marsh and Parvati Nair. Oxford: Berg, 2004. 135–50. Print.

Thrower, Stephen, with Julian Grainger. *Murderous Passions: The Delirious Cinema of Jesús Franco.* London: Strange Attractor, 2015. Print.

Tohill, Cathal, and Pete Tombs. *Immoral Tales: Sex and Horror Cinema in Europe, 1956–1984.* London: Primitive, 1994. Print.

CONCLUSION

Finding Franco: A Quixotic Filmography
Will Dodson

f Jess Franco's films, Tim Lucas famously wrote, *"You can't see one until you've seen them all"* ("How to Read" 23). Lucas, who more than anyone has spurred cult interest in Franco as an auteur, surely (?) did not mean to suggest it's *possible* to see them all, given that various sources list Franco as having directed anywhere between 140 and over 200 feature-length films and videos in a career spanning more than fifty years. Researching and compiling a comprehensive, much less complete, filmography of Jess Franco's work is a gargantuan, multilingual, multinational, quixotic project. So, when I was invited to do just that for a book of essays on Franco, I pictured myself tilting at windmills whose vanes were fluttering strips of film.

Which would be the greater deed, raising a dead man or killing a giant?[1] I've as much chance of either as I do of cataloging Franco's corpus. No published Franco filmography agrees on how many films Franco actually made. *Il caso Jesús Franco* (2010), a multilingual collection of essays from a 2009 conference on Franco at the University of Venice, lists 180 films (Totaro). Tim Lucas's 2013 elegy to Franco in *Fangoria* notes 194 films, and claims that more than 140 are available worldwide on DVD or Blu-ray ("Jess Franco: The Undying Legend" 47).[2] Volume 1 of Stephen Thrower's massive two-volume critical filmography registers 173 films (2015).[3] As of this writing, the crowdsourced *Internet Movie Database* (*IMDb*) lists 203 directorial credits, though a handful of those feature the disclaimers "uncredited" or "unconfirmed," and the count includes some unfinished films, like *Juliette* (1970), which he began with Soledad Miranda but abandoned upon her death. No doubt, any filmography I could assemble would almost instantly be rendered obsolete.

Not only obsolete but overwhelming. If I condensed nearly 200 short plot synopses with cast and crew lists and production notes, it would say little of Franco's work but that it's prolific; that it primarily traffics in pulp genres; that it tends toward the erotic, particularly scenes of voyeurism and light S&M; and that actors and crew reappear on multiple projects. It might also indicate that Franco gravitated toward serials, and that characters and character names tend to recur often.[4] Carlos Aguilar's *Jess Franco: El Sexo del Horror* (1999) offers a nearly complete career overview, detailing the production of almost all of Franco's known films up to its publication date.[5] Stephen Thrower's aforementioned mammoth tome *Murderous Passions: The Delirious Cinema of Jesús Franco* (2015) covers in 432 pages only the first fifteen years of Franco's career, from 1959 to 1974. Volume 2 is forthcoming as of this writing, and faces the enormous prospect of tracking down Franco's work in the video and digital era. Thrower's project will, no doubt, be the definitive such work, the result of years of research. I will not duplicate his efforts here, but assume the infinitely easier tasks of reflecting upon the idea of a comprehensive, chronological filmography and sketching an alternative approach fans and scholars might take toward such a project.

The sheer number of films Franco made contributes to his cult mystique, but he is not unique with respect to prolificity. Franco's output is vast, but he's hardly the only director to have made over 100 films. Many Hollywood directors during the studio era approached such an output. Mihály Kertész, for example, made about fifty films in Europe and, as Michael Curtiz in Hollywood, somewhere between 160 and 180 overall. John Ford directed over 100 films. William "One Shot" Beaudine has over 400 credits, counting television. Roger Corman acolyte Jim Wynorski and Japanese agitator Takashi Miike, both still active, have directed over 100 pictures each. Italian cult director Joe D'Amato (Aristide Massaccesi) was credited with 195 titles when he died in 1999. What distinguishes Franco from masters and hacks alike is the unique interaction of the filmmaker and his cult fans through his filmography. In the context of this collection of scholarship, it might be productive to think of Franco's filmography in terms of his approaches to filmmaking and how his cult fans now experience his cinema, in meandering, improvisational, affective terms. Franco's "strategic auteurship," as Antonio Lázaro-Reboll argues, aligned his work with pulp fiction and genre cinema, expressing "his desire to be linked to a set of US and European cultural histories far removed from the Spain of the 1950s" (170). At the same time, Franco's cosmopolitan rootlessness has enabled the strategic viewing practices adopted by fans who arrange his films—those they've seen and those they haven't—in a variety of ways, developing different understandings of the director that shape how they engage with his work.[6] This sort of "performative spectatorship," a term coined by Ian Olney to refer to the unique viewing attitudes and interactions of fans of European horror films, combines home media sleuthing, personal narrative, and critical consideration of Franco's work as a *continuum* (Thrower 41–44), the work of a unique auteur obsessed with jazz and serial narratives.[7] Any appreciation of Franco's films involves a metafilmography, and plotting that metafilmography requires a cinephiliac immersion. As metafilmography, then, reception of Franco involves understanding his strategic auteurship and one's own performative specatorship, an ongoing interplay between film viewer, filmmaker, and home media distributors. Fans' idiosyncratic and incomplete arrangements of Franco's filmography offer various rhetorical constructions of his work and personal mythology, of which I will briefly sketch two examples at the end of this chapter. Franco cultivated an image of himself as a cineaste and auteur, but the cinephiles who trace his filmography ultimately craft that image with him.

Compiling Franco's filmography, to the extent that it's possible, has led to multiple readings of Franco's life and career, most prominently in the work of Tim Lucas. Lucas has published in print and online about Franco for decades, and has categorized Franco's filmography at least three times (1990, 1993, 2010), each time offering a revised declaration of principles for appreciating Franco. Lucas's evolving appraisal of Franco's work illustrates the paradox of Franco's career as an exploitation genre film-maker. In "How to Read a Franco Film," the line following "*You can't see one until you've seen them all*," is, "A degree of immersion is essential" (23). The word "until" is a hugely important qualifier, as is "degree." One might watch individual Franco films and enjoy or dismiss them as low-grade exploitation fare, but to watch them in concert and continuum with his entire filmography reveals that Franco's work is as intertextual and densely layered with visible influences and references as that of the most highly regarded postmodernist filmmakers.

Like the work of any postmodernist, Franco's cinema demands partic-ipatory immersion from its viewers. There is no casual Franco fan. Joan Hawkins invokes Marshall McLuhan's notion that all "cool" media invite a high degree of audience participation to suggest that Franco's films, which she says are often "clumsy," require audience immersion in his film-ography and therefore enjoy a "cool" factor (201–2). To watch Franco's films, to "get" them, is a lot of work. As Hawkins puts it, "The idea that viewers have to learn to like Franco's style, have to learn how to watch his movies removes the director's work from the arena of what Theo-dor Adorno would call true 'mass culture.' Here, as in [Pierre] Bourdieu's descriptions of mainstream elite culture, the viewer has to be educated into the system" (215). Olney, extending Hawkins's point, argues that Franco, in particular, and European horror and sex cinema in general, "encourages spectatorship-as-performance by transgressing the norms of sex and gender representation" (153). Franco's fans, in order to become fans, have to put forth effort to locate editions of his films to view, then learn to "like" Franco's style, which requires them to critically consider Franco's eroticism, voyeurism, and violence. Performative spectatorship of Franco requires filmographies-as-experience in individual, idiosyncratic ways. Additionally, to "like" Franco's style is to identify as a member of a particular cult community. To scour through films that even ardent Fran-cophiles qualify as slipshod, if not totally inept, for moments or images that seem to indicate the filmmaker's unique vision is, further, to position oneself as a viewer not of individual films but of films as phases of a larger personal quest.[8]

Availability conditions perception. Locating various distributors, identifying various producers, and comparing various cuts and home media editions has become much easier than when Lucas published "How to Read a Franco Film." Global networks of cult film fans provide an active market that effectively finances the archival research and production of dozens of niche media companies like Blue Underground, Image, Mondo Macabro, Redemption, Severin, Synapse, and various imprints, like Mondo Macabro's Shriek Show and Severin's Intervision.[9] These companies curate Franco's output, untangle copyrights and distribution deals, locate prints and negatives to assemble definitive editions, and restore Franco films with the care and presentation one would associate with Criterion Collection editions of high-profile films. Smaller independent companies like SRS Cinema distribute Franco's microbudget video and digital films, several of which he made in his own home. (I mention here only home media distributors who cover North America, and so the adventures of Francophiles outside the United States and Canada must span farther afield.)

As I emphasized in acknowledging Lucas's multiple arrangements and readings of Franco, individual filmographies lead to particular understandings of Franco's work. For example, Lucas categorizes Franco in terms of chronological periods and associations with various producers. Thrower aims for absolute completion, and recognizes a certain futility to categorizing the films by genre or theme, even as he does just that (15–16). Thrower traces recurring character names, lines, motifs, and scenarios, while at the same time noting Franco's purported uninterest in dialogue. Alain Petit evaluates films based on Franco's perceived passion for the project, and divides them into "films made on command," "quickies," and "films of the heart." Francesco Cesari, citing Petit, looks for evidence of Franco as a "Trickster" figure by sifting through the filmography (qtd. in Totaro). Bloggers like Robert Monell conduct ongoing assessments of home media releases and theatrical releases, crowdsourcing fans' filmographic research.[10] These alternate approaches perhaps put us on the difficult terrain of determining authorial intent, though Franco's generous interviews in his later years reveal much about his experiences and modest ambitions, if he's to be trusted.[11] Any Franco filmography, finally, must combine an objective delineation of chronological periods and thematic obsessions, and the personal reception of Franco's work as a continuum of improvised serial filmmaking. Such a cinephiliac approach, then, is filmography as fandom, immersing oneself in groups of films to establish points of overlap and conversation and to trace avenues of serial-dom. In other words, the filmographer strikes channels in the swirling current and follows their branches and brooks.

The labor of the fan filmographer leads to immersion points, groups of films linked by some designated criteria. The idea of "immersion points" for Franco merges Lucas's and Thrower's rhetoric, recognizing any such point as an arbitrary dive into Franco's themes, icons, and obsessions that could include any number of films. In the limited space of this chapter, I compile two clusters, one organized around Franco's brief but legendary involvement with Orson Welles, and the other around his underappreciated and often dismissed late-period digital films. These two clusters represent an alpha and omega of Franco's filmography.

Fans and critics have been much fascinated by Franco's brief association with Welles, variously to frame Welles's patronage as validation of Franco's maverick talents or to dismiss Franco as a parasitic hack benefiting from a moment in the sun. Alternatively, Franco's connection with Welles, and the subsequent contradictory myths and legends that followed, suggests Franco was a kindred spirit, an obsessive *bon vivant*, idealistic but, like Sancho Panza, somewhat more uncouth.

Compiling and watching Franco's late microbudget video and digital films is a decidedly more challenging project, as even Franco's most ardent defenders have criticized them as shoddy, lazy, and boring. Yet these films are also arguably Franco's most personal and political, for they are truly his "Spanish" films, shot at home, free of producer interference or government censorship. They recast Franco's earlier work in a recursive meditation on his life in cinema at a time when he had become "Uncle Jess," the familial appellation favored by his cult fans.

Other chapters in this book and previous works on Franco expand on these and more immersion points—for example, clusters of Franco's films starring Soledad Miranda or Lina Romay, his most iconic stars. Or groupings that include his Gothic films, Sadeian films, Orlof(f) films, Fu Manchu or Red Lips serials, and so on. Each allows for consideration of Franco's varied working styles and narrative obsessions. Any immersion point will necessarily include important gaps, which mark the ongoing filmographic project of the Franco fan or scholar. Each new streaming or home media release necessitates the revision and extension of Franco's legacy, even as that legacy remains riddled with unconfirmed claims, legends, and myths. In their allusions to *Don Quixote* and extended references to Orson Welles, my two immersion clusters contribute to that mythology and perhaps meander around certain quiddities. They also revisit well-trodden ground from a different perspective—that of cinephiliac experiences of Franco's filmography—and offer alternative understandings of Franco's cinema.

These clusters, historically and aesthetically, could not be farther apart, yet they offer a chronological and cinephiliac beginning and end point of immersion into Franco's career. The Welles cluster casts Franco as an apprentice auteur, and the included films have as their association their proximity to *Chimes at Midnight* (1966), on which Franco served as a second-unit director, as well as their direct homage to Welles. Immersion in these films confers a critical legitimacy (or not) on Franco that colors how we look at his career from then on, including his retroactive (self) fashioning as an auteur. Starting from Franco's experience with Welles leads us to explore Franco's other formative influences: serials and comics, jazz and architecture, Sade and kink. Like Welles, Franco became an itinerant, though pulp, artist. In the decade following his time in Welles's orbit, Franco enjoyed his largest (relative) budgets and made his most well-known and regarded films.

His late period, microbudget digital video productions, on the other hand, test the resolve of even the most fervent Francophiles. But contrary to its reputation as dull and crude, Franco's late video work, which is both experimental and intertextual and should be approached as such, offers another perspective on Franco's auteurism. The digital video group—a group that is far larger than could be coherently discussed in this essay—have as their connection location, budget, and the period of life in which Franco made them, and are best viewed after having seen many of his films. Considering both of these immersion points foregrounds an understanding of Franco as a filmmaker not through the finished films but through their cult mythology and intertextuality. The Welles association offers a biographical position from which to consider Franco as a filmmaker, while the digital and video work offers an intertextual coalescence of Franco's obsessions.

The Welles Films

Rififí en la ciudad (1964); *La muerte silba un blues* (1964); *Chimes at Midnight* (1966); *La isla del tesoro* (Unfinished [?], 1965); *Le Journal intime d'une nymphomane* (*Sinner: The Secret Diary of a Nymphomaniac*, 1973); *Don Quijote de Orson Welles* (1992).[12]

It is tempting and perhaps appropriate to cast Orson Welles as Don Quixote and Franco as Sancho Panza. Welles is deservedly famous for his artistry and genius, as well as his petulance and propensity for tall tales. Franco, too, was prone to self-mythologizing, but at the same time insisted he had no pretensions.[13] A Welles cluster allows an opportunity to reflect on what Franco may have learned from the master and to speculate about the ways in which Franco exploited the association to develop his own auteur persona. Conversely, one might suggest that Welles's influence overwhelmed and possibly even restrained Franco's development as a filmmaker.[14] Where, then, to start with what we might provocatively call Franco's "Welles films?" Although Franco directed only three of the

Jeanne Moreau and Orson Welles in *Chimes at Midnight*, a film on which Franco famously worked with Welles as a second-unit cameraman. (Alpine Films and Internacional Films. Courtesy of Jerry Ohlinger's Movie Materials.)

films included here, the group contributes much to his history and legend, coloring interpretations of other clusters. While in Spain to work on his *Chimes at Midnight*, as well as other projects, including *Don Quixote*, Welles reportedly saw Franco's *La muerte silba un blues (1964)* and *Rififí en la ciudad* (1964) and liked them enough to invite Franco to work as second-unit director on *Chimes*.[15] Franco is in various places credited as director or assistant director on *La isla del tesoro* (1965),[16] an unfinished adaptation of *Treasure Island* written by Welles, with Welles as Long John Silver.[17] The film may have been a ruse by Welles to secure financing for *Chimes at Midnight*, or *Don Quixote*, or both.

Franco, at least in retrospect, seems to have had no illusions about his mentor even as he idolized him. Of *Chimes at Midnight*, Franco said it "was a total mess, not because the film was too expensive, but because Orson lied with the budget and the film was ten times more expensive [than he had claimed it would be]" (Wisniewski). Franco made the comment with affection, impressed with Welles's chicanery and devotion to cinema. One story of *Chimes at Midnight*, possibly apocryphal, emphasizes their quixotic pairing:

> Welles started to run out of money on the shoot . . . so Franco stepped in to help. He sent a rough cut of the project to producer Harry Saltzman to entice him to put up funds. Saltzman liked what he saw, and agreed to invest. Welles was furious that Franco had done this behind his back. Although he accepted Saltzman's money, Welles reportedly attacked Franco physically and had his credit removed from the picture. (Kalat 237)

Could this be true? Harry Saltzman did invest in the film, but other sources say Welles sought Saltzman out. Franco's name appears in the credits of every version of *Chimes* I've seen. It's an attractive story, but more than likely untrue, as are so many attractive stories.

Whatever the case, Franco was effusive about Welles's influence, and nearly a decade later, completed *Le Journal intime d'une nymphomane* (*Sinner: The Secret Diary of a Nymphomaniac*, 1973), a strange and tawdry tribute to *Citizen Kane* (1941). Its narrative follows Rosa, the wife of a man charged with the murder of a woman named Linda, as she investigates Linda's life. Linda turns out also to have killed herself and framed Rosa's husband, and Rosa puts together the story through interviews with people who knew Linda. The film is psychedelic sleaze, and its narrative is structured as *Kane*'s, with an investigator piecing together the life of a dead person through interviews with various figures from her history. It's a prime example of Bill Landis and Michelle Clifford's assessment, "Some of Franco['s] fans believe he is a genius, citing as proof [his] brief association with Orson Welles in making the penny-dreadful Shakespeare adaptation *Chimes at Midnight* in the mid-1960s. One can more realistically see Franco as a talented, imaginative filmmaker who is self-aware enough to know he functions best in exploitation modes" (179). That self-awareness is on display in *Sinner*, as Franco pays stylistic homage to Welles while also deflating Welles's artistic stature with his subject matter.

Chimes and *Sinner* are interesting to those who might wonder about Welles's influence on Franco, and in the case of *Sinner,* as a rather bizarre homage. Most interesting, though, is the unfinished *Don Quixote,* which Welles worked on in fits and starts between 1957 and his death in 1985. Franco, commissioned by the Andalusian government, acquired some of the extant footage and completed a version of the film for Seville's Expo '92, to mostly negative reviews. Jonathan Rosenbaum lamented that Franco was chosen to assemble this version because "[he] was Spanish, and . . . supposedly he was a friend of Welles. Maybe he was, but they didn't factor in that he's also the biggest hack in all of Spanish Cinema!" (French, "Interview with Jonathan Rosenbaum"). Welles had in his will bequeathed footage to various parties, primarily to his partner, Oja Kodar, and Costa-Gavras had assembled a 40-minute cut, exhibited at Cannes in 1986. Franco was given footage by producer Patxi Irigoyen, and completed a 114-minute cut. Rosenbaum and the Spanish critical establishment excoriated it. Franco did not at the time enjoy cult status, which came later, and the fact that he was commissioned at all is surprising, even given his previous association with Welles. True, the film is missing some of the best footage Welles shot (much of it is available on YouTube), the film elements are damaged, and the dubbing is crude. For Francophiles, though, the editing effects, including various jump cuts and trippy fades, are unmistakably Franco's. Franco did not make his own quixotic journey in trying to reconstruct a faithful *Don Quijote de Orson Welles,* which is as much an impossibility as assembling a complete Franco filmography. Rather Franco, like Panza, followed his master on his own terms and created a feverish film experience that is, well, like watching a madman wander through modern Spain.

Franco's assemblage—probably the most accurate thing to call it—is compelling if framed as a tribute to Welles as a Quixote figure. Welles said to Peter Bogdanovich, "what interests me is the *idea* of these dated old virtues [of idealism, grace, and gallantry]. And why they still seem to speak to us when, by all logic, they're so hopelessly irrelevant. That's why I've been obsessed so long with *Don Quixote*" (96). Could any statement better describe Welles himself? Is it better, finally, to be a friar or a knight errant? Julian Grainger argues that Welles's double-dealing may have made the most significant impact on Franco's career. Welles's attempt to make two films simultaneously failed, but Franco subsequently succeeded in similar schemes many times. Grainger suggests Franco's experience taught him "how he really wanted to make films: shooting with a small crew, with whatever means came to hand . . . surrounded by trusted friends and colleagues" (99). Is it coincidental that Franco's working methods changed so drastically around this time? Previous to working on *Chimes,* Franco had made several traditional genre films, and his first two "real" Franco films, *Gritos en la noche* (*The Awful Dr. Orlof,* 1962) and *La mano de un hombre muerto* (*The Sadistic Baron Von Klaus,* 1964), under somewhat stable production conditions. After working with Welles, Franco struck out on his own, shooting fast and constantly, seemingly no longer concerned with method or means.

Immersion in the Welles films can offer new perspectives on Franco's approaches to filmmaking in other filmographic clusters, some of which lead far afield of Franco's best known erotic and horror work, like his serial crime capers. From *Rififí en la ciudad* and *La muerte silba un blues,* Franco fans might explore Edgar Wallace's influence on the exploits of the Red Lips Agency in *Labios rojos* (1963), *Küss mich Monster* (*Kiss Me Monster,* 1969), and *El caso de las dos bellezas* (*Two Undercover Angels,* 1968); or Sax Rohmer's influence on *The Blood of Fu Manchu* (1968) and *The Castle of Fu Manchu* (1969). Perhaps one might branch off from *Sinner: The Secret Diary of a Nymphomaniac* to trace the "Linda" films, each of which features a so-named character who enters into an erotic Sadeian relationship, such as *Vampyros Lesbos* (1971), *Die Nackten Superhexen vom Rio* (*Linda,* 1981), and *Les Nuits brûlantes de Linda* (*The Hot Nights of Linda,* 1974). Another fascinating tangent to explore is the films Franco shot simultaneously, with trusted (and not-so-trusted, in the case of producer Harry Alan Towers) companions, such as *Die Sieben Männer der Sumuru* (*The Girl from Rio,* 1969), *99 mujeres* (*99 Women,* 1969), and *Justine* (*Marquis de Sade's Justine,* 1969).[18] As boundaries between film projects vanished, Franco more and more frequently returned to symbols, stories, and themes that linked even his most slapdash films into pulpy mosaics. Welles loomed as a mythical influence as Franco immersed himself in cinema as a "low-art" inverse of Welles, and, in retrospect, we can see in this cluster of films the beginnings of Franco's self-fashioned auteurist mythology.

THE VIDEO AND DIGITAL FILMS

Tender Flesh (1997); *Mari-Cookie and the Killer Tarantula* (1998); *Dr. Wong's Virtual Hell* (1998); *Vampire Blues* (1999); *Red Silk* (1999); *Broken Dolls* (1999); *Helter Skelter* (2000); *Blind Target* (2000); *Vampire Junction* (2001); *Incubus* (2002); *Snakewoman* (2005); *Paula-Paula* (2010); *La cripta de las condenadas* (2012); *La cripta de las condenadas 2* (2012); *Al Pereira vs. The Alligator Ladies* (2012); *Revenge of the Alligator Ladies* (2013).[19]

Here we can plunge our hands all the way up to our elbows into this thing they call adventures. Franco's most perplexing, vexing, and frustrating immersion point may be the two dozen or so microbudget video and digital films made over the last twenty years of his life. All of these films are surreal, slowly paced, and often antinarrative, yet remain familiar as remakes or serializations of his earlier work. Truly, the last two decades of Franco's career, beginning with *Tender Flesh* (1997), constitute his own metafilmography, and thus another way to think of Franco as an auteur. *Tender Flesh* was the first film produced and distributed by One Shot Productions, a U.K./Spain-based microbudget company owned and operated by Franco fans.[20] Among them were Kevin Collins and Hugh Gallagher, formerly of *Draculina* magazine; writer Tim Greaves of 1-Shot Publications; and Peter Blumenstock and Christian Kessler, both contributors to *Obsession: The Films of Jess Franco*, the first book on the director. The group formed the company to help Franco produce *Tender Flesh*. One Shot Productions worked with Franco on twelve more features, from *Mari-Cookie and the Killer Tarantula* (1998) to *Snakewoman* (2005).[21] After questing for so long, Sancho Panza came home. In the last two decades of his life, Franco worked almost exclusively with his own fans in making his films, most of which were shot in Spain near his home or in his own apartment.

All of them comment on Franco's previous work, on aging, dying, and filmmaking.

Carlos Aguilar speaks for many fans and scholars in his assessment of Franco's time with One Shot, referring to *Tender Flesh* as amateurish and "a disaster" (*Jess Franco* 143), and completely dismissing his output from then on, save for a few moments here and there.[22] I would not dare argue that this cluster represents Franco at his most entertaining or conventional, but that is part of my point, and part of the reward of immersion in this grouping. These films are "disastrous" when viewed out of the context of Franco's previous work. But they may, in fact, be his purest and most personal, made by "Uncle Jess," surrounded by his "family" of Francophiles. Even more so than in his previous work, Franco uses comic strip imagery and sketches of genre plots as stepping-stones for free-flowing images evoking his longtime obsessions—voyeurism, erotic performance and play, sadism, rootlessness, and ennui. The latter theme Lucas has explored at some length ("How to Read" 26–28), as has Thrower in a meditation on Franco's filmic relationship with time (39–43). Franco's recurring images of the coast, the ocean, and hotels, as well as his disruption of continuity and location, unmoors his subjects from time, which "itself tends not to exist" ("How to Read" 27).

Lucas's and Thrower's observations focus on Franco's earlier work, but apply equally to his video and digital films. This immersion cluster leads viewers backward and sideways and around in time to earlier Franco films and further immersion clusters. *Snakewoman*, for example, remakes *Vampyros Lesbos*, muting its color palette and playing with in-camera digital effects to create a more claustrophobic psychological state for its heroine, Carla (Carmen Montes). It includes a new awareness of mortality and despair over lost youth, in the familiar genre form of a snake woman who replenishes her vitality with the blood of her prey.

To outline briefly the group and their most prominent links to past Franco: *Tender Flesh* offers a retread of *La Comtesse perverse* (*Countess Perverse*, 1973) and several other of Franco's jungle films, all of which owe a genre debt to Richard Connell's 1924 short story "The Most Dangerous

Game." Franco adds some sadistic sex slavery, in the vein of Pasolini's *Salò o le 120 giornate di Sodoma* (*Salò, or the 120 Days of Sodom*, 1975), and the specter of fascism here offers fresh ways to review his previous jungle adventure and cannibal films. *Incubus* (2002) reimagines *Necronomicon* (*Succubus*, 1968) and *Lorna . . . l'exorciste* (*Lorna the Exorcist*, 1974), with a striking mirror sequence that once again recalls Welles, but in the context of a Faustian bargain between a man and a succubus. *Mari-Cookie and the Killer Tarantula*'s motifs call back to the Spider Woman character in one of his early Spanish comedies, *Vampiresas 1930* (1961),[23] and *Miss Muerte* (*The Diabolical Dr. Z*, 1966). *Red Silk* (1999) revisits the sexy detectives of *Labios rojos* as semi-retired private eyes. *Helter Skelter* (2000) dispenses with narrative and presents images and scenarios inspired by Sade. *Paula-Paula* (2010) is similarly almost plotless, sketching a version of the Jekyll and Hyde story as its foundation. The film is essentially a procession of

An appropriately dizzying image from *Incubus*, which, like many of the films Franco shot on video late in his career, revisits and remakes his earlier work—in this case, *Succubus* and *Lorna the Exorcist*. (One Shot Productions. Screen capture.)

images that fold into themselves, and is aptly subtitled "An Audiovisual Experience." Franco's in-camera effects and, of course, his ever-present zoom characterize each of the digital films.

Most of these films prominently feature sequences that recall the erotic cabaret set pieces of the Soledad Miranda films and the masturbatory sequences of earlier Lina Romay films—*Vampyros Lesbos* meets *La Comtesse noire* (*Female Vampire*, 1973), or *Der Teufel Kam aus Akasawa* (*The Devil Came from Akasava*, 1971) meets *Macumba Sexual* (1982). These exhibitions are, if I may stretch the point a bit, erotic jazz improvisations themselves, playing the body to see where it takes us. Watching the videos from this perspective, the in-camera effects function similarly to the mise-en-scène in Franco's earlier cabaret set pieces, which typically feature Miranda, Romay, or other actresses performing with mannequins, mirrors, sheer fabrics, and other props that soften the borders of their bodies.[24] Franco's penultimate films, *La cripta de las condenadas* and *La cripta de las condenadas 2* (both 2012) revisit his surrealist erotic obsessions: a group of women cursed with living death are locked in a crypt, where they pass the time indulging in sexual pleasures and performances.

Franco's final films, *Al Pereira vs. The Alligator Ladies* (2012) and *Revenge of the Alligator Ladies* (2013), revive the titular private eye from at least ten prior Franco films, ranging from *Cartas boca arriba* (1966) to *El tesoro de la diosa blanca* (*Diamonds of Kilimandjaro*, 1983), not to mention Lina Romay's turn as "Alma Pereira" in *Paula-Paula*. The diptych appropriately caps Franco's career, as both are metafilms in which Franco, playing himself, intervenes to direct the actors. The nonlinear "plot" of the former culminates in Pereira giving the Alligator Ladies a tongue lashing for their lusty behavior while they, in turn, chastise him for not joining in the fun. As is the case with Pereira, the Alligator Ladies themselves reference such previous Franco icons as the daughters of Fu Manchu, or, for that matter, any female duo, of which there are many, in the Franco filmography.

This immersion point requires prior immersion, which takes Lucas's maxim to its logical conclusion. Franco's late films require complete immersion, total obsession. To watch these digital experiments is to experience the recursiveness of Franco's filmography, the "swirling current" that constantly destabilizes attempts to categorize it. Part of the intellectual and affective enjoyment comes from connecting these films to Franco's earlier work and watching how he explores the same themes that have always obsessed him, free of producers' restrictions but without the resources of even a low budget. These films ruminate on all that has always been political about his work. As Tatjana Pavlović writes in a summary of Franco's career, his "interest in horror, in pornography, and in the pulp imagery of superspies and musclemen can be seen as an effort to represent all that the Fascist government had officially repressed" (120). His final films, like many of his earlier films, deconstruct masculine superhero fantasy in pursuit of "pure, excessive, and unlimited enjoyment, so alien to the sensibilities of [Fascist Spain and conservative cultures anywhere], especially in regard to womanhood" (Pavlović 113). This immersion point throws Franco's politics, intuitive as they may have been, into high relief and recontextualizes the radicalism of his entire body of work.

Thrower argues that Franco is a "genre artist," one who works "not just with the clay but the mould itself" (15). Franco's late movies fold back into sixty years of genre filmmaking as Franco reflects on and even parodies his filmography. Several times, I have highlighted the fact that this rootless cosmopolitan made all of his late period films at home, in Málaga, the place of his birth and his death. Are these his true "Spanish" films? Finally rooted, he remade his entire corpus. Watching one truly means watching them all.

WHEN ARE YOU GOING TO FINISH DON QUIXOTE?

There are some who exhaust themselves learning and investigating things that, once learned and investigated, do not matter in the slightest to the understanding or the memory. This chapter argues that a traditional, truly comprehensive filmography of Jess Franco is impossible, even though, as evidenced in the brief exploration of Franco's video and digital work, such a project cannot help but emerge as one sees more Franco films. All Francophiles are quixotic in a sense, necessarily questing on their own filmographic immersions, aware of their contributions to Franco mythology. I have seen seventy-seven Franco films, which by any measure is less than half of his output. Every time I watch a "new" Franco film, I find two or six more that extend that film as a serial, or remake that film. There is, as Thrower writes, "no fixed centre" (16). No doubt my thinking about Franco, like Lucas's, will change and evolve further in the years to come (see chapter 9). The videos, DVDs, and Blu-rays pile high on my desk, stacked like a filmstrip windmill.

The permanence of these home media editions (whether or not the technology becomes obsolete) is paradoxical. Once theatrical distributors got Franco's "finished" films, they inevitably altered the products, inserting hard-core scenes here, deleting violence or exposition there, reassembling narratives. Outside of the video work of his later years, it's hard to call any release a "definitive" cut. Franco's position as a genre filmmaker enabled him to keep making films about his personal obsessions, but he rarely had complete control of his vision. *Erotikill*, *The Bare Breasted Countess*, and *Female Vampire* are the same movie—or are they? Which one is Franco's? All of them? Franco is an auteur, but his artistic "statement" isn't really the films themselves but his constant improvisatory filmmaking. As Olney and Lázaro-Reboll suggest in the introduction to this volume, Franco's auteurism, much like Welles's, is not in the films but in their making. Franco is the filmography, and the filmography demands much of his fans. You can't watch one until you watch them all, but immersing oneself demands (guarantees?) obsession. To read a Franco film, you must be obsessed with Franco films. Cinephilia is the only lens through which to understand the rituals of Francophiles, the way we dive into (and embrace) even his shoddiest, most tedious movies in search of special moments here and there, connections to a dozen other movies, instances of Uncle Jess winking.[25]

What does any of this tell me about Jess Franco's many faces? What would have been Franco's 87th birthday (May 6, 2017) and Orson Welles's 102nd (May 11, 2017) passed during production of this book. In at least one way, Welles and Franco were similar filmmakers. Welles said "I'm not interested in . . . posterity, or fame, only in the pleasure of experimentation itself. It's the only domain in which I feel that I am truly honest and sincere" (qtd. in Heylin: 335). Franco said similar things his entire career, and truly we cannot examine Franco's work by any conventional measure, certainly not mere chronology. Franco lived cinema unpretentiously but with some sly illusions of grandeur.

NOTES

1. All allusions to and quotations from *Don Quixote* reference Edith Grossman's translation of Cervantes.
2. As of 2017, I count at least 79 titles available on Region 1 DVD or Region A Blu-ray to North American Franco fans, including forthcoming Blu-ray releases announced by Blue Underground, Mondo Macabro, Redemption, and Severin. No doubt there will be more by the time this sees print.
3. Yet even here there remains a question about Franco's output. Thrower claims Franco directed 173 feature films (15), but his feature film appendix lists only 171 (427–30).
4. See Tim Lucas, "Jess Franco's Declaration of Principles," 19.
5. The filmography lists 158 feature-length films and seven short documentaries, as well as 34 films for which Franco served as assistant or second-unit director.
6. As Tatjana Pavlović argues, Franco's "cult followers scattered around the world problematize the notions of the national, the nation, foreign, local, and their interplay. International circulations of Franco's low-budget, cult, trash, B production, and sexploitation films have transnational implications posing questions about co-productions, market, and movements across national borders" (119).
7. In an interview with David Gregory for the Blue Underground releases of his Fu Manchu films, Franco noted his appreciation for the pulp serial writer Sax Rohmer, creator of the Fu Manchu series, and comic strips and comic books, saying "I love all things related to series." Understanding Franco's predilection for series-based entertainment is key to an appreciation of his filmmaking.
8. See chapter 2 for a discussion of how fan writing on Franco's films involves the cinephiliac celebration of singular moments from his oeuvre.
9. As Lázaro-Reboll argues, "The making of [Franco's] cult reputation is the result of both localized cult responses in the United States, Europe, and Spain since the 1960s and the more recent emergence of the 'cult movie' and 'cult

director' as niche markets for global consumption" (171). Franco's auteurism, again, developed retrospectively as fan obsession led to academic interest.

10. *I'm in a Jess Franco State of Mind*, http://www.robertmonell.blogspot.com, and, in collaboration with Álex Mendíbil, the English-Spanish *El Franconomicon*, https://franconomicon.wordpress.com. The two blogs are comprehensive and vital sources of fan scholarship on Franco, but of course there are many others.

11. For example, Franco's claim that he was the inspiration for Yoda has, amusingly, excited some controversy. (An extra feature devoted to the myth is included on the 2015 Severin Blu-ray release of *Vampyros Lesbos*.) Franco says that he worked with the young makeup artist Stuart Freeborn on a few of his Harry Alan Towers pictures. Years later, Franco claims he ran into Freeborn, who sheepishly told Franco that he'd based the design of Yoda on him. This is a rather dubious claim, given that all of Freeborn's published accounts state that Freeborn himself was the model. In fact, both men bear a striking resemblance to Yoda, though Freeborn more so and Franco only later in life. As appealing as the story is, let us heed Yoda's advice and not be reckless . . .

12. *Rififí en la ciudad* and *La muerte silba un blues* are not yet available on Region 1 DVD or Region A Blu-ray, but can be found on various international streaming services. *Chimes at Midnight* was released on DVD and Blu-ray by the Criterion Collection in 2016. *Sinner: The Secret Diary of a Nymphomaniac* is available on DVD from Mondo Macabro, and *Don Quijote de Orson Welles* from Image.

13. In a 2008 interview at the Sitges festival, Franco said, "for me . . . cinema is not: 'Here I am, the marvelous Jess Franco giving the dwarfs who encircle him a tiny masterpiece. I have not done any masterpiece nor do I think it should be very usual for a film maker to make a masterpiece, seriously. Those who say they make masterpieces, I think they do it mostly due to a lack of culture, since I think that cinema, which I love and is my life 100 percent, is a pseudo-artistic-commercial expression, whose aim is to entertain and amuse folks." Franco simultaneously affects humility while puncturing the pretensions of "better" filmmakers. He professes a veneration for cinema while insisting it is as commercial as it is artistic.

14. As Carlos Aguilar argues (2011). I am indebted to Antonio Lázaro-Reboll for sharing this resource, which is not yet available in an English translation.

15. Cathal Tohill and Pete Tombs share the potentially apocryphal story that producers then showed Welles *Rififí en la ciudad*, thinking Welles would see how terrible a filmmaker Franco was and drop him from the project. On the contrary, Welles was happy to see an homage to his own *The Lady From*

Shanghai (1947) and proceeded with the hire. See Tohill and Tombs, 87. The anecdote is repeated by Joan Hawkins, 216n. Carlos Aguilar, however, suggests a more conventional connection. Juan Cobos, a friend of Franco's who worked with him previously, including on *Rififi*, was also Welles's personal assistant in Spain, and brought Franco into Welles's orbit (*Jess Franco* 54).

16. The *IMDb* has two listings for the film on Franco's page, one in Spanish and one in English. He's apparently the director of the Spanish title, and assistant director of the English. Robert Monell claims that "Franco was set to helm Welles in an adaptation of *Treasure Island* but the two men parted ways" ("Orson Welles and Jess Franco"). Julian Grainger disputes this, arguing it more likely "that Franco was announced as the film's director as cover for the uninsurable [Welles], and furthermore, Franco himself has stated that it was always the intention that Welles would direct the film" (98).

17. He reprised the role for the Harry Alan Towers–produced 1972 adaptation.

18. Franco denied in interviews that he used footage featuring Shirley Eaton shot for *The Girl from Rio* in *The Blood of Fu Manchu* without Eaton's knowledge. Eaton states in an interview with David Gregory that she thought producer Harry Alan Towers was responsible for repurposing footage. Towers allowed that Eaton was probably correct. According to several accounts, because shooting for *The Girl from Rio* wrapped early in 1968, Franco and Towers immediately conceived and shot *99 Women*, rather than releasing the cast and crew early. Franco completed *99 Women* later in the year while also shooting *Marquis de Sade's Justine* (Thrower 165).

19. All of the above are available on DVD from SRS Cinema, except *Paula-Paula*, which was released by the Severin imprint Intervision.

20. The company is still active at the time of this writing, at www.oneshotproductions.bizland.com/movies/index.html, and has a large catalog of microbudget features, shorts, and web projects.

21. Aguilar, *Jess Franco* 143; One Shot Productions website.

22. For example, Aguilar rates a cabaret sequence in *Tender Flesh* as among the best sequences Franco ever produced (*Jess Franco* 143).

23. Unsubtitled versions are available on various streaming services.

24. As I have mentioned elsewhere, many critics cruelly, and with more than a hint of sexism, note that Lina Romay's own aging softened her body. Aguilar refers to her as "fattened up and prematurely aged" (*Jess Franco* 143). Lucas, in his elegy to Romay no less, writes "As the years passed, Lina changed and her body changed, but it never mattered to Franco, who continued to star her and film her *as if* she was the most desirable woman on earth" ("Franco's Muse," my emphasis). Yet Franco and Romay refused this

ageist evaluation of female beauty and sexuality, incorporating aging as just another challenge to conventional limitations placed on pleasure seeking. See Dodson, "The Sapphic, The Sadean, and Jess Franco."

25. Again, see chapter 2 for more on reading Franco through the lens of cinephilia.

Works Cited

Aguilar, Carlos. *Jess Franco: El Sexo del Horror*. Ed. Carlos Aguilar, Stefano Piselli, and Riccardo Morrocchi. Florence: Glittering Images, 1999. Print.

———. *Jesús Franco*. Madrid: Cátedra, 2011. Print.

Balbo, Lucas, Peter Blumenstock, and Christian Kessler. *Obsession: The Films of Jess Franco*. Ed. Lucas Balbo and Peter Blumenstock. Berlin: Graf Haufen and Frank Trebbin, 1993. Print.

Cervantes, Miguel de. *Don Quixote*. Trans. Edith Grossman. New York: Harper-Collins, 2003. Print.

Cesari, Francesco, ed. *Il caso Jesús Franco*. Venice: Granviale, 2010. Print.

Dodson, Will. "The Sapphic, The Sadean, and Jess Franco." *International Horror Film Directors: Global Fear*. Ed. Danny Shipka and Ralph Beliveau. Bristol, UK/Chicago: Intellect, 2017. 115–29. Print.

Franco, Jesús. "Jesús Franco Manera documental dirigido por Kike Mesa." *You-Tube*. 7 Apr. 2016. Web. 20 Aug. 2016.

French, Lawrence. "An Interview with Jonathan Rosenbaum." *Wellesnet*. N.d. Web. 20 Aug. 2016.

Grainger, Julian. "Welles, Shakespeare, Stevenson & Franco." *Murderous Passions: The Delirious Cinema of Jesús Franco*. With Stephen Thrower. London: Strange Attractor Press, 2015. 96–99. Print.

Gregory, David. "My Friend, Jess Franco." *Fangoria* 325 (August 2013): 42–45. Print.

Hawkins, Joan. "The Anxiety of Influence: Georges Franju and the Medical Horror Shows of Jess Franco." *The Horror Film Reader*. Ed. Alain Silver and James Ursini. New York: Limelight, 2000. 190–222. Print.

Heylin, Clinton. *Despite the System: Orson Welles Versus the Hollywood Studios*. Chicago: Chicago Review, 2005. Print.

Kalat, David. *The Strange Case of Dr. Mabuse: A Study of the Twelve Films and Five Novels*. Jefferson, NC: McFarland, 2005. Print.

Landis, Bill, and Michelle Clifford. *Sleazoid Express*. New York: Simon & Schuster, 2002. Print.

Lázaro-Reboll, Antonio. "Jesús Franco: From Pulp Auteur to Cult Auteur" *A Companion to Spanish Cinema*. Ed. Jo Labanyi and Tatjana Pavlović. Oxford: Wiley Blackwell, 2015. 167–71. Print.

Lucas, Tim. "Franco's Muse: Lina Romay (1954–2012)." *Tim Lucas Video Watch-Blog.* 23 Feb. 2012. Web. 16 Oct. 2016.

———. "How to Read a Franco Film" *Video Watchdog* 1 (1990): 18–34. Print.

———. "Jess Franco's Declaration of Principles: How to Read the Early Films 1959–67." *Video Watchdog* 157 (July/Aug. 2010): 16–49. Print.

———. "Jess Franco: The Undying Legend." *Fangoria* 325 (Aug. 2013): 46–48. Print.

Monell, Robert. "Orson Welles and Jess Franco." 6 May 2015. Web. 8 Aug. 2016.

Olney, Ian. *Euro Horror: Classic European Horror Cinema in Contemporary American Culture.* Bloomington: Indiana UP, 2013. Print.

Pavlović, Tatjana. *Despotic Bodies and Transgressive Bodies: Spanish Culture from Francisco Franco to Jesús Franco.* New York: State U of New York P, 2003. Print.

Thrower, Stephen, with Julian Grainger. *Murderous Obsessions: The Delirious Cinema of Jesús Franco.* London: Strange Attractor, 2015. Print.

Tohill, Cathal, and Pete Tombs. *Immoral Tales: European Sex and Horror Movies, 1956–1984.* New York: St. Martin's Griffin, 1995. Print.

Totaro, Donato. "The Case of Jesús Franco." *Offscreen* 15.2 (Feb. 2011). Web.

Welles, Orson, and Peter Bogdanovich. *This Is Orson Welles.* New York: De Capo, 1998. Print.

Wisniewski, John. "Jess Franco: Sex, Horror and All That Jazz." N.d. Web. 8 Aug. 2016.

ACKNOWLEDGMENTS

Antonio Lázaro-Reboll

ittle did I know when I invited Ian to participate in a symposium on "Euro horror" I organized at the Institute of Contemporary Arts in London on Halloween 2013 that our encounter would lead to this coedited volume on the films of Jess Franco. Our shared interest in European horror film has also extended to an article he published for a special issue I edited on the topic in the journal *Film Studies* in 2016. I have lost count of the emails I exchanged with Ian over the last four years, but every one of them demonstrated the scholarship, rigor, and passion I had already found in his excellent 2013 book *Euro Horror: Classic European Horror Cinema in Contemporary American Culture.* That book was the reason why I brought Ian across the Atlantic. It has been a real pleasure to work with him. This book would not have been possible without our contributors, whose individual projects and takes on Jess Franco have allowed us to present incisive, innovative, and fascinating readings of the many faces of such an iconoclastic director. A very special thanks to Annie Martin, the editor-in-chief at Wayne State UP, whose encouragement and firm steering has been terrific throughout the whole process. Her colleagues Ceylan Akturk in the Rights and Permissions Department and Emily Nowak in the Marketing Department have been extremely helpful whenever we have had any queries. The careful, thorough, and valuable responses of the Editorial Board and the anonymous readers to the volume were the best we could wish for. My colleague Peter Stanfield at the Centre for Film and

337

Media Research at the University of Kent has been, as always, a trusted (unofficial) peer-reviewer of my work. The School of European Culture and Languages at Kent via its Research Development Fund facilitated research trips to the British Film Institute and the Spanish Filmoteca. I would like to thank particularly Anastasia Kerameos at the BFI Reuben Library for sourcing material. Tim Lucas and Stephen Thrower have been truly generous for allowing me to use covers of *Video Watchdog* and *Eyeball*. Álex Mendíbil, Francophile supremo, went beyond the call of duty to source some visual material for the volume. (Best of luck with your thesis on Franco, Álex.) On a more personal note, I want to thank my partner, Donna, and my children, Elsa and Noah, for their continued love, support, and sense of humor.

ACKNOWLEDGMENTS

Ian Olney

T his book underwent a lengthy gestation prior to its publication, and there are a number of people I wish to thank for their contributions to its development. First and foremost, I am indebted to my coeditor, Antonio Lázaro-Reboll, without whom the book would not exist at all. It has its origins in an international symposium on "Euro horror" organized by Antonio on behalf of the Centre for Film and Media Research at the University of Kent and held at the Institute of Contemporary Arts (ICA) in London on October 31, 2013. As one of the invited speakers, I gave a talk on the cycle of 1970s Euro horror possession movies made in the wake of *The Exorcist*, with a special focus on Franco's 1974 film *Lorna the Exorcist*. In conversation over the course of the day, Antonio and I found ourselves circling back again and again to Franco. He was such a fascinating figure—why hadn't there yet been a scholarly volume devoted to his cinema? The time for a reconsideration of his contributions to popular European cinema over the decades seemed ripe with his passing earlier that year. Finally, I proposed to Antonio that we coedit such a book ourselves; he immediately agreed, and the rest, as they say, is history. Throughout the production of this volume, he has been the ideal partner—diligent, conscientious, and enthusiastic, with a wealth of knowledge about the material covered herein: Spanish cinema, cult film production and reception, and, of course, the movies of Jess Franco. I am also grateful to our eleven contributors, whose essays on Franco form the backbone of the book. From the start, Antonio and I shared the aim of assembling an international cadre of scholars—comprising both established figures in cult film studies and those just entering the field—who would bring a range of fresh and exciting perspectives to bear on the most unconventional of directors. I think we have succeeded in this aim, and it is largely thanks to our authors, who have demonstrated not only great acuity and innovation in their analyses of Franco and his films but also exemplary professionalism and patience as we worked with them on the different drafts of their essays. We have been very fortunate to find a home for our book at Wayne State UP. The entire staff has been wonderful to work with, but we owe special thanks to editor-in-chief Annie Martin; promotions manager Kristina Stonehill; marketing and sales director Emily Nowak; rights and permissions manager Ceylan Akturk; senior designer Rachel Ross; editorial, design, and production manager Kristin Harpster; and copyeditor Sandra Judd. The book's inclusion in the Press's Contemporary Approaches to Film and Media Series, edited by the estimable Barry Keith Grant, is an honor. I would like to express my gratitude to the staff at Photofest and Jerry Ohlinger's Movie Materials Store who helped us source the rare public domain publicity stills that illustrate this volume. Tim Lucas, Stephen Thrower, Tomás Cimadevilla, Amy Brown, and Stephen Abel were kind enough to allow us to use their personal photographs and artwork as illustrations. I am grateful for a research and publication grant from the Faculty Development Committee at York College of Pennsylvania that helped pay for the book's illustrations. I would also like to acknowledge the assistance provided by CaseyAnn Salanova and the staff at York College's Schmidt Library who helped me source research materials for this project from as far afield as the University of Salamanca. Above all, however, I want to thank my family—my wife, Jill, and my children, Ethan and Emma—who were forever ready with a sympathetic ear or a word of encouragement when the going got tough. As always, my work is dedicated to them.

CONTRIBUTORS

ALBERTO BRODESCO earned his PhD in audiovisual studies—cinema, music, communication from the University of Udine, Italy. He works as a research assistant at the Department of Sociology and Social Research, University of Trento. He is the author of *Una voce nel disastro. L'immagine dello scienziato nel cinema dell'emergenza* (Meltemi, 2008) and *Sguardo, corpo, violenza. Sade e il cinema* (Mimesis, 2014) (French translation by Editions Rouge Profond, 2017). His publications (see http://unitn.academia.edu/AlbertoBrodesco) focus on the limits of representation (violence, death, pornography, freaks) and the image of technoscience in film and TV. His articles have appeared in *Cinergie—Il cinema e le altre arti, Nuncius—Journal of the Material and Visual History of Science, Scienza & Politica. Per una storia delle dottrine*, and *Porn Studies*.

WILL DODSON, PhD, teaches rhetoric, literature, and film at the University of North Carolina at Greensboro, where he is the coordinator of Ashby and Strong Residential Colleges, liberal arts programs focused on ethical communication, sustainability, and global engagement. His research focuses on rhetorical theory and education, film/video studies, and transgressive cinema. He has published articles in *Quarterly Review of Film & Video* and *Film International* and contributed chapters to various edited collections.

FINLEY FREIBERT is a PhD candidate in visual studies at the University of California-Irvine. He currently researches in film and media studies at the intersections of industry studies and queer history.

ANTONIO LÁZARO-REBOLL is senior lecturer in Hispanic studies at the University of Kent (UK), where he teaches Spanish and European film. He is the author of *Spanish Horror Film* (Edinburgh UP, 2012) and coeditor with Andy Willis of *Spanish Popular Cinema* (Manchester UP, 2004). His essays on the cross-cultural dialogue between Spanish horror and international traditions of the horror genre have been published in journals such as *New Review of Film and Television Studies* and *Film Studies*, and in such edited volumes as *A Companion to Spanish Cinema* (Wiley-Blackwell, 2012), *Spanish Erotic Cinema* (Edinburgh UP, 2017), and *Tracing the Borders of Spanish Horror Cinema and Television* (Routledge, 2017).

XAVIER MENDIK is professor of cult cinema studies at Birmingham City University, U.K., from where he runs the *Cine-Excess* International Film Festival (www.cine-excess.co.uk). He is the author/editor/coeditor of nine volumes that explore international cult film traditions. Some of his publications in this area include *Bodies of Desire and Bodies in Distress: The Golden Age of Italian Cult Cinema* (Cambridge Scholars Publishing, 2015), *Peep Shows: Cult Film and the Cine-Erotic* (Wallflower Press, 2012), and *The Cult Film Reader* (Open UP, 2008), coedited with Ernest Mathijs. Mendik has also completed a number of documentaries on cult film traditions, most recently *Tax Shelter Terrors: The Real Story of Canadian Cult Cinema* (2016).

IAN OLNEY is an associate professor of English at York College of Pennsylvania, where he teaches film studies. He is the author of *Zombie Cinema* (Rutgers UP, 2017) and *Euro Horror: Classic European Horror Cinema in Contemporary American Culture* (Indiana UP, 2013). His essays on European cinema and the horror film have appeared in such journals as *Quarterly Review of Film and Video* and *Film Studies*, and in such edited volumes as *A Companion to the Horror Film* (Wiley-Blackwell, 2014) and *Recovering 1940s Horror Cinema: Traces of a Lost Decade* (Lexington Books, 2014).

TATJANA PAVLOVIĆ is professor of Spanish at Tulane University in New Orleans. She is author of the monograph *Despotic Bodies and Transgressive Bodies: Spanish Culture from Francisco Franco to Jesús Franco* (SUNY Press, 2003) and coauthor of the comprehensive survey *100 Years of Spanish*

Cinema (Wiley-Blackwell, 2009). Her monograph *The Mobile Nation (1954–1964): España cambia de piel* (Intellect, 2011) focuses on a crucial period of transition in the history of Spanish mass culture, examining the publishing industry, the expansion of the television network, popular cinema, the development of mass tourism, and the national automobile manufacturing industry. Pavlović is also coeditor of *A Companion to Spanish Cinema* (Wiley-Blackwell, 2012) with Jo Labanyi. Her research and teaching interests center on twentieth-century Spanish intellectual history, literature, cultural studies, and film theory.

VICENTE RODRÍGUEZ ORTEGA is a visiting professor at the Universidad Carlos III, Madrid. He is the coeditor of *Contemporary Spanish Cinema and Genre* (Manchester UP, 2013) and the author of *La ciudad global en el cine contemporáneo: una perspectiva transnacional* (Shangrila, 2012). He has published articles in *New Media & Society*, *Studies in European Cinema*, *Transnational Cinemas*, and *Soccer & Society*, and has written chapters for *A Companion to Spanish Cinema* (Wiley-Blackwell, 2012), *A Companion to Pedro Almodóvar* (Wiley-Blackwell, 2013), *Gender meets Genre in Postwar Film* (U of Illinois P, 2012), *Sampling Media* (Oxford UP, 2014), and *Transnational Stardom: International Celebrity in Film and Popular Culture* (Palgrave Macmillan, 2013), among others. His interests include cinema and globalization, digital technologies and representation, and film genres. He is member of the research group "Cine y televisión: memoria, representación e industria" (TECMERIN).

RUBÉN ROMERO SANTOS is a PhD researcher at the Department of Journalism and Media Studies at the Universidad Carlos III, Madrid, and has an MA in mass media research. His essays have appeared in *World Film Locations: Barcelona* (Intellect, 2013), *Ficcionando en el siglo XXI: La ficción televisiva en España* (Fragua, 2016), and *Tracing the Borders of Spanish Horror Cinema and Television* (Routledge, 2017). He has worked as a film and television journalist for almost two decades. He started his career at the counterculture publication *Ajoblanco*, from where he jumped to editor-in-chief of the film magazine *Cinemanía*. He currently combines his academic work with contributions to magazines like *Rolling Stone*, *ELLE*, and *Icon/El País* and television platforms such as Canal +. He is member of the research group "Cine y televisión: memoria, representación e industria" (TECMERIN).

NICHOLAS G. SCHLEGEL is an assistant professor of communication studies at Alfred University in New York and the author of *Sex, Sadism, Spain, and Cinema: The Spanish Horror Film* (Rowman & Littlefield, 2015). Schlegel has written broadly about international film, including essays on Japanese and Mexican horror films. His current book project is titled *Monster of London City: Edgar Wallace, New German Cinema, and the Krimi Phenomenon* (Lexington Books, forthcoming).

AURORE SPIERS holds masters degrees from the École Normale Supérieure in Lyon, France, and Columbia University. She is currently a PhD student in the Department of Cinema and Media Studies at the University of Chicago. She is also working as the country coordinator for France for the Women Film Pioneers Project at Columbia University. Her research interests include American and French silent cinema, early women filmmakers, slapstick, African American cinema, the representation of gender on screen, and French exploitation cinema.

GLENN WARD is a senior lecturer in visual culture at the School of Humanities, University of Brighton. He was awarded a PhD for his thesis on Jess Franco from the University of Sussex in 2011. He is the author of numerous pieces on aspects of exploitation and fantastic cinema.

ANDY WILLIS is a professor in film studies at the University of Salford and Senior Visiting Curator: Film at HOME (Greater Manchester Arts Centre). He is the coauthor of *The Cinema of Álex de la Iglesia* (Manchester UP, 2007) with Peter Buse and Núria Triana Toribo; editor of *Film Stars: Hollywood and Beyond* (Manchester UP, 2004); and coeditor of *Spanish Popular Cinema* (Manchester UP, 2004) with Antonio Lázaro-Reboll, of *East Asian Film Stars* (Palgrave Macmillan, 2014) with Wing-Fai Leung, and of *Chinese Cinemas, International Perspectives* (Routledge, 2016) with Felicia Chan.

INDEX

Page numbers in *italics* refer to images.

The Diabolical Mr. Franco, 49

Diamants pour l'enfer. See Women Behind Bars

Diamonds of Kilimandjaro, 329

Diary of a Chambermaid, 57

Dietrich, Marlene, 99, 217

direct-to-video horror films, 211–34

La dolce vita, 79, 259

Don Quijote de Orson Welles, 23–24, 321, 324, 333n12

Don Quixote (Cervantes novel), 320, 332n1

Don Quixote (unfinished Welles film), 23, 322, 324

Der Doppelganger. See The Double

Dor, Karin, 105

The Double, 108n3

Dracula, 149, 156

Dracula (Horror of Dracula), 90

Draculina, 214, 215, 216, 326

Dr. Mabuse, der Spieler. See Dr. Mabuse, the Gambler

Dr. Mabuse, the Gambler, 91

Dr. Orloff's Monster, 14, 71, 75, 76

Dr. Wong's Virtual Hell, 214, 326

Dr. Z and Miss Death, 137n2. See also The Diabolical Dr. Z

Dr. Zhivago, 124

Eaton, Shirley, 334n18

Ellos robaron la picha de Hitler, 285

Elorrieta, José María, 312n1

Ema, E. W., 108n3

Ercole a la regina di lidia. See Hercules Unchained

The Erotic Rites of Frankenstein, 259

Erotikill, 21, 136, 138n8, 138n11, 331. See also Female Vampire

Erotikiller, 138n8. See also Female Vampire

Eugenie. See Eugenie de Sade

"Eugénie de Franval," 186, 188, 200

Eugenie (Historia de una perversión). See Wicked Memoirs of Eugenie

Eugenie . . . the Story of Her Journey into Perversion, 13, 75–76, 188, 189, 203–4

Eugenie de Sade, 140, 141, 187, 188, 189, 200–202, 202, 290, 294, 295, 298, 305

Eurociné, 49, 134, 135, 171, 236n9, 251, 252

European art cinema: and cinephilia, 67, 68, 70–71, 72, 73, 79–80, 84; features shared with European exploitation cinema, 55, 60, 121; Franco's relationship with, 28, 32, 55, 60, 61, 68, 70–71, 72, 73, 79–80, 84, 98, 170–71, 182–83

European exploitation cinema: audience for, 8–9, 168; censorship of, 21–22, 140; features shared with European art cinema, 55, 60, 121; film variants in, 22; Franco's contributions to, 32, 49, 56, 72, 113, 140–65; on home video, 130, 184n2; industrial context of, 19–20, 57, 72, 73; international coproductions in, 31, 57, 88, 89, 95, 105, 106, 114–15, 116, 122, 123, 124–25, 134, 212, 234, 270, 290; pornography and, 142–43, 147, 150; and sexology, 140–65; spectacle and excess in, 8; theatrical distribution of, 21–22, 121–22; theatrical exhibition of, 8–9, 121, 242; transnationality of, 31, 60, 94, 123, 125, 137, 171, 211, 212, 213, 214, 234, 243, 245, 332n6

European Trash Cinema, 5, 114, 244, 245, 256, 259, 261n2, 269, 308

78–80; and the cinephiliac gaze, 31, 68, 71–76, 80–82, 84–85; compared to Marquis de Sade as artist, 33, 189–92, 202–5; "countercinema" of, 32–33, 169–76, 180–83; critical reputation of, 10–11, 42–43, 74–75, 80, 168–69, 324; cult reputation of, 4–5, 43, 75–76, 80–82, 114, 168–69, 213–14, 271, 314, 332–33n9; diversity of his cinematic output, 24, 68; ennui in the films of, 16, 102, 224, 254, 327; and European art cinema, 28, 55, 60, 61, 68, 70–71, 78, 79–80, 84, 98, 170–71, 180, 183; and European horror cinema, 5, 7, 8–9, 84, 171, 176, 221, 255, 256, 269; excess in films of, 8–9, 12, 118, 168, 191, 292, 293; as exploitation filmmaker, 1, 19–20, 21–22, 42, 43, 68, 72, 78, 84–85, 134, 140–65; 317; fan collaboration with, 11, 213–14, 265, 266, 276, 278–86; 326–27; fan writing on, 4–5, 31, 68, 75–76, 81–82, 84–85, 115, 315, 316–17, 318–19, 332n8; fanzine connoisseurship of, 5, 33–34, 243, 249, 261, 318; female spectatorship and the films of, 184n5, 211, 235n3; femininity in the films of, 29–30, 82–84, 116, 118, 140–65; 169–76, 180, 182–83, 192–95, 229, 235n2, 238n24, 293–304, 330; film criticism by, 4, 70; filmography of, vii–viii, 2, 19–24, 34–35, 244, 246, 253, 261, 314–32; film performances of, 16, 98, 149, 173, *187*, 329; in Francoist Spain, 28–29, 77, 95, 170–71; Gothic sexology of, 32, 140–65; Goya Award for lifetime achievement, 6, 285; home video distribution of his films, 3–4, 14, 21, 184n2, 211, 216–17, 236–37n13, 247–49, 260, 271, 318, 320, 332n2, 333n12, 334n19; immersion points in the work of, 23, 34–35, 223, 232, 244, 253, 319–30; improvisatory filmmaking of, 9, 17, 41, 72, 73, 319, 329, 331; incoherence in the work of, 24–26; institutional recognition of, 4, 5–6, 275; and Jean Rollin, 168–71, 176, 180–83; and the *Kriminalfilm*, 31–32, 50, 88–108; late video and digital work of, 35, 211–34, 238n27, 315, 318, 319–20, 321, 326–30; legends surrounding, 1–2, 4, 70, 77, 319, 320, 322, 323, 333n11, 333–34n15; and Lina Romay, 15–16, 17, 20, *21*, 108n6, 115, 134, 135, 136, 144, 147–48, 184n3, 197, 213, 214, 220–33, *226*, *231*, 234, 237n17, 237n19, 282, 285, 299, 309, 320, 329, 334–35n24; masculinity in the films of, 142, 147, 159, 173, 295, 330; *Memorias del tío Jess*, 4, 265; montage in the films of, 13–15, 305; music in the films of, 16–18, 98–99, 119, 128, 133, 254, 258, 270; number of movies made by, 19, 22–23, 68, 168, 314–15, 332n3, 332n5; obituaries for, 2–3, 19; and Orson Welles, 23–24, 28, 35, 56, 57, 58, 70, 71, 104, 234, 275, 319, 320, 321–26, 331, 333–34n15, 334n16; periodization of his work, 24–25, 249, 253, 261n4, 262n6, 316, 318, 319; perversity of his work, 2, 30–35; place in the films of, 15, 128, 131–32, 197–98; pornography in the films of, 1, 2, 7, 20–21, 24, 140, 150, 151–52, 164, 191,

Franco, Jesús (Jess) (*continued*)
212–34, 237n19; prolific production
of, 1–2, 68–69, 168, 211, 314, 315;
queerness in the films of, 9, 10, 13, 33,
127, 132, 141, 144, 145, 149, 151–52,
154, 156, 157, 158–59, 160–61,
162–64, 169–76, 180, 182–83, 186,
190, 194, 199–200, 211–34, 235n2;
queer spectatorship and the films of,
33, 184n5, 211–34, 235n3; repetition in the films of, 10, 187, 190–91,
227–28, 238n23, 304–8; "respectable"
early career of, 31, 41–61; retro-
spectives of his films, 5–6, 244, 266,
275; revival of in the 1990s, 211,
233, 265–66, 269, 270–71 284–85;
Sadeian adaptations by, 33, 140, 144,
186–205, 320, 328; scholarly writing
on, 30–31, 44–45, 211–12, 220, 221,
233–34, 235n2, 287n7; scream queen
films of, 212–34; serial filmmaking
of, 10, 315, 316, 319, 320, 332n7;
and Soledad Miranda, 15–16, 17, 34,
89, 99, *100*, 105, 115, 122, 126, 127,
129, 130, *131*, 133, 134, 136, 137,
163, 184n3, *202*, 290–311, *300*, *311*,
312n1, 314–15, 320, 329; as Spanish filmmaker, 1, 28–29, 31, 33, 34,
44–59, 170–71, 319–20, 330; and the
Spanish "indie" scene, 34, 265–86;
spectatorship theory and, 211, 220,
221, 235n2, 316, 317; strategic
auteurship of, 4, 316, 320, 321, 326;
theatrical distribution of his films,
14, 22, 78, 331; theatrical exhibition
of his films, 78, 120, 121; themes in
the films of, 9–10, 318, 319, 325–26,
327, 330; as transnational filmmaker,
1, 29, 31–32, 77, 95, 123, 137, 171,
212–34, 243, 316; as "Uncle Jess,"
271, 319–20, 327, 331; unevenness
of his work, 25, 68, 72–73, 74–76, 78,
80–82; variants of his films, 19–22,
23–24, 136, 137n2, 138n8, 331; and
videophilia, 249, 251; voyeurism in
films of, 172–73, 195–98, 225, 232,
299–304, 315, 327; "Welles" films of,
35, 319, 320, 321–26; working on set,
29, 282; and the zoom lens, 11, 12,
41–42, 61, 191, 195, 204–5, 302. *See
also* Francophiles; horrotica
El Franconomicon, 246, 271, 333n10
Francophiles: as cinephiles, 73–76,
80–81, 84–85, 331, 335n25; communities of, 75–76, 216, 317, 327;
interacting with Franco's filmography, 34, 81, 89, 315–16, 317–18,
321, 330–31; as producers of
Franco's late direct-to-video work,
11, 213–14, 265, 266, 276, 281–86,
326–27; as videophiles, 251, 254
Franju, Georges, 44, 50, 51, 53, 54, 71
Freda, Riccardo, 66
Freeborn, Stuart, 333n11
Free Jazz, 181
French New Novel (*Nouveau Roman*),
180
French New Wave (*Nouvelle Vague*), 3,
33, 68, 70, 180
Fric, Mac, 108n3
Le Frisson des vampires. See *The Shiver
of the Vampires*
Des Frissons sur la peau. See *Tender and
Perverse Emanuelle*
Der Frosch mit der Maske. See *Face of
the Frog*
Fuchsberger, Joachim, 105
Fulci, Lucio, 18

Mastroianni, Marcello, 79

*La matanza caníbal de los garrulos lisér-
  gicos*. See *Cannibal Massacre*

Matarazzo, Raffaello, 66

May, Karl, 123

Mayans, Antonio, 16

Melville, Jean-Pierre, 57, 71

Memorias del tío Jess, 4, 265

Mendíbil, Álex, 30, 246, 261n2, 266,
  271, 333n10

Le Mépris. See *Contempt*

Merino, Manuel, 104, 128

Metropolis, 91

Meyer, Russ, 279

Miike, Takashi, 315

Miller v. California, 137n4

Mil sexos tiene la noche. See *Night Has
  a Thousand Desires*

Miranda, Soledad (Soledad Rendón
  Bueno): accidental death of, 16, 34,
  89, 105, 122, 134, 307–8; "black
  stare" of, 16, 302–3; in contrast to
  other Euro-glamour icons of the
  1960s and 1970s, 299, *300*; death
  cult stardom of, 34, 290–311; and
  erotic cabaret set pieces, 17, 297,
  329; fan art devoted to, 310–11;
  fandom of, 34, 310–11, *311*; Franco's "discovery" of, 15–16, 115, 129;
  as Franco's muse, 34, 320; "interruptive porno gaze" of, 299–304;
  performances for Franco, 16, *100*,
  131, 136, 137, *163*, 184n3, *202*,
  290–311, *300*, *311*, 312n1, 314–15,
  320, 329; pop music career of,
  312n1; pseudonyms of, 307; range
  of her film roles, 99, 122, 126, 127,
  130, 133, 308, 312n1; repetition
  and doubling of in Franco's films,
  304

Miró Law (*Ley Miró*), 286n1

The Misfits, 292

Miss Death and Dr. Z, 137n2. See also
  The Diabolical Dr. Z

Miss Muerte. See *The Diabolical Dr. Z*

Modot, Gaston, 183n1

Mona, 120

Monell, Robert, 22, 30, 75, 76, 97,
  245, 246, 261n2, 318, 333n10,
  334n16

Monroe, Marilyn, 292

Montés, Elisa, 103, 105

Morpho, 269–70

Morrissey, Paul, 129

"The Most Dangerous Game," 327–28

La Movida, 267, 268, 272, 273, 279,
  286n2, 288n14

La muerte silba un blues, 57, 321, 322,
  325, 333n12

Muller, Paul, 16, 98, 126, *202*

Murnau, F. W., 69, 91, 131

Die Nackten superhexen vom Rio. See
  Linda

Naschy, Paul, 273, 281

Necronomicon. See *Succubus*

Newfield, Sam, 184n1

Newman, Amber, 214, 216, 219, *226*,
  237n19

Newman, Serge, 48, 49

New Spanish Cinema (*Nuevo Cine
  Español*), 33, 70, 170

Night Has a Thousand Desires, 9

Nightmare Sisters, 236n7

Nightmares Come at Night, 14, 290,
  297

Night of the Living Dead, 138n7

99 mujeres. See *99 Women*

99 Women, 14, 105, 120, 121, 325,
  334n18

queerness: and camp sensibility, 213, 221–22, 234, 238n26; definitions of, 212; in Franco's films, 9, 10, 13, 33, 127, 132, 141, 144, 145, 149, 151–52, 154, 156, 157, 158–59, 160–61, 162–64, 169–76, 180, 182–83, 186, 190, 194, 199–200, 211–34; in Jean Rollin's films, 169–71, 176–80, 182–83; and queer collectivity, 223, 224, 226–27, 233, 238n21; and the queer gaze 212, 220, 223, 230, 232, 234; and queer labor, 213, 236n8; and queer monotony, 33, 224, 227–33, 234, 238n22; in queer studies, 235n4, 235n6; and queer zoning out, 33, 220–27, 230, 234; in scream queen cinema, 212–13, 217, 220–34, 237n16; in scream queen film production, 215, 217, 236n7, 237n15, 237n18; in scream queen film reception, 213, 215, 217, 220–34, 237n15, 237n18, 237–38n20

Quigley, Linnea, 214, 215–16, 217, 226, 234, 237n18

Radio Nacional de España 3 (RNE3), 268, 278, 286n4

"Raga," 17

Una rajita para dos, 20

Ramírez Ángel, Antonio, 17

Ramone, Joey, 272, 275

The Rape of the Vampire, 33, 168, 170, 176–77, 177, 178, 179–81, 182–83, 183–84n1, 184n2, 184n6

Rauger, Jean François, 5–6

Ray, Fred Olen, 216

Ray, Nicholas, 70, 291

Rear Window, 196

Rebel without a Cause, 291

Red Lips, 216

Red Silk, 326, 328

La reina del Tabarín, 17, 49, 312n1

Reinl, Harold, 105

Renoir, Jean, 72, 73

Residencia para espías, 71

Resnais, Alain, 70, 79, 259

Revenge in the House of Usher, 266, 270

Revenge of the Alligator Ladies, 326, 329

Reynaud, Janine, 16, 80, 83

Rialto Films, 54, 88, 89, 95, 96, 102, 104

Rififi, 71, 334n15

Du rififi chez les hommes. See Rififi

Rififi en la ciudad, 56, 57, 70, 321, 322, 325, 333n12, 333–34n15

"The Rising of the Akasava," 97

A ritmo de Jess, 41, 62n1

Rivette, Jacques, 70

Robbe-Grillet, Alain, 61, 71, 79

Rohm, Maria, 16

Rohmer, Éric, 70

Rohmer, Sax, 88, 325, 332n7

Rollin, Jean: alternative sexualities in films of, 169–70, 176–80, 182–83; auteur status of, 18, 168–69; "countercinema" of, 33, 168–71, 176–83; critical reputation of, 168–69; early career of, 183–84n1; formal distortion in films of, 180–82; and French commercial cinema, 33, 170–71, 180, 183; and the French New Wave, 33, 170–71, 180, 183; home video distribution of his films, 184n2; and Jess Franco, 20, 33, 168–71, 176, 180–83; narrative subversion in

films of, 176–80; and paracinema, 169, 182–83; transgressive femininity in films of, 169–70, 177–80, 182–83
roman policier film, 116
Romay, Lina (Rosa María Almirall Martínez): acting style of, 16, 229, 309; ageist responses to her late-career performances, 237n17, 237n19, 334–35n24; cult status of, 16, 213, 226–27, 234; as director, 16, 20; Franco's "discovery" of, 15–16, 108n6, 135; as Franco's muse, 135; as Franco's partner, 16, 108n6, 115, 134, 136, 213, 285, 309; performances for Franco, 15–16, 17, 20, *21*, 136, 144, 147–48, 184n3, 197, 214, 220–33, *226*, *231*, 234, 237n17, 237n19, 282, 299, 309, 320, 329, 334–35n24; as "reincarnation" of Soledad Miranda, 108n6, 115, 134–35, 309
Romero, George, 138n7
Rooyen, Jerry van, 77
Rossellini, Roberto, 72, 73
Der rote Kreis. See *The Crimson Circle*
Rue Morgue, 234

Sade, Marquis de: approach as writer, 189; "Augustine de Villeblanche," 186, 199; compared to Franco as artist, 33, 189–92, 202–5; desire in the works of, 140, 190, 200, 201, 204–5; "Eugénie de Franval," 186, 188, 200; incest in the works of, 191, 200; isolation (*isolisme*) in the works of, 33, 197, 206n7; *Juliette*, 186, 205n4; *Justine*, 186, 188, 193, 202; mechanisms of his writing, 190; *The 120 Days of Sodom*, 190,

205n4; *Philosophy in the Bedroom*, 186, 188, 197, 203, 204; philosophy and sex in the works of, 191, 202–4; Sadeian woman in the works of, 193–94, 199; sadism and masochism in the works of, 33, 191, 192, 196–97; tropes in the work of, 33, 186, 188–89, 191, 192, 193–94, 195, 196–97, 199, 200; queerness in the works of, 199; voyeurism and exhibitionism in the works of, 33, 191, 195, 206n6; works of as sources for Franco's films, 10, 33, 140, 144, 186–205, 320, 328
El sádico de Notre-Dame. See *The Sadist of Notre Dame*
The Sadistic Baron Von Klaus, 17, 58, 188, 325
The Sadist of Notre Dame, 21, 188, 255, 256
Sadomania, 13, 188
Sadomania—Hölle der Lust. See *Sadomania*
Safra, Michel, 116
Die Säge Des Todes. See *Bloody Moon*
Saint, Eva Marie, 65
Salamanca Conversations, 46
Salò, or the 120 Days of Sodom, 196, 328
Salò o le 120 giornate di Sodoma. See *Salò, or the 120 Days of Sodom*
Saltzman, Harry, 323
San Martín, Conrado, 51
San Sebastián Horror and Film Festival, 270, 274
Los santos inocentes. See *The Holy Innocents*
Schwab, Siegfried, 98, 128, 133
Scream franchise, 236n10

scream queen cinema: as American direct-to-video phenomenon, 213, 214–15, 234; and Brinke Stevens, 215, 237n18; camp dimension of, 213, 214–16, 217, 223–26, 228–30, 232–33, 236n7, 237n15; casting in, 213, 214, 216; cult following of, 214, 215, 216, 217; figure of the scream queen in, 214–15, 217, 220, 223, 234; and Franco's late direct-to-video work, 212–34; heterosexual male reception of, 213, 215, 217, 218–20, 236n7; home video distribution of, 211, 216–17; and Lina Romay, 214, 220–33, *226*, *231*, 234, 237n17, 237n19; and Linnea Quigley, 214, 215–16, 217, *226*, 234, 237n18; mainstreaming of, 236n10; marketing strategies of, 213, 215–16, 217, 218–20, 236n7, 237n14; and Michelle Bauer, 214, 215–16, 217, 219, 223, *226*, 228, *231*, 234, 237n18, 237n19; misogyny and ageism in reviews of Franco's scream queen films, 213, 218–20, 229, 233, 237n17, 237n19, 238n24, 238n25; origins of term, 214–15; performances in, 213, 217, 220, 223, 228, 232, 233; production strategies of, 213, 236n7; queerness of, 212–13, 217, 220–34, 237n15, 237n16; queer production of, 215, 217, 236n7, 237n15, 237n18; queer reception of, 213, 215, 217, 220–34, 237n15, 237n18, 237–38n20; and soft-core spectacle, 217, 218–20, 224, 229, 237n19; transnationality of, 212–14, 234; twenty-first-century legacy of, 234

Scream Queens, 236n10

Scream Queens Illustrated, 215

Secret of the Black Trunk, 102

El secreto del Dr. Orloff. See *Dr. Orloff's Monster*

Segura, Santiago, 266, 273, 274, 276, 282, 285, 287n8, 287n9

Serie-B, 270

Serra, Koldo, 274

7 Women, 27

Seville Expo '92, 24, 267, 324

Sexadelic, 133

Sex Charade, 297

sexology: clitoris in, 149, 154–56; cross-genre and cross-media overlaps with, 142–44, 147; and female pleasure, 33, 142–43, 144, 146–47, 154–56, 156–57, 159–60, 161; and feminism, 142, 149, 155, 159–60, 161; and Franco's Gothic sexploitation films, 33, 140–65; frigidity in, 33, 145, 152, 160–61; heteronormativity of, 159; lesbianism in, 145, 160–61; literature of, 33, 143; marriage in, 142, 146, 150, 155–56, 156–58; masturbation in, 146, 148, 149, 151, 154, 155; and modern femininity, 142–43, 144, 149, 156–57; nymphomania in, 33, 145, 152–53, 160, 161; oral sex in, 149–51; and patriarchy, 146, 149, 154–56, 159; phallocentrism of, 155, 158; and pornography, 142–43, 146–47, 149–50; and the "repressive hypothesis," 145–46, 148–49; and rhetoric of liberation, 33, 142–43, 145; and rhetoric of maladjustment, 152, 153, 156–57, 161; and sexual modernity, 33, 142, 144, 145, 157–58, 163, 164; and sexual stereotypes, 143, 145, 146, 152–53, 155, 158, 159

Van Husen, Dan, 105, 106, 108n7
Vent d'Est, 180
Venus in Furs, 13, 15, 17, *18*, 74–75, 120, 143, 242, 256, 258, 259
Vernon, Howard, 16, 51, 52, *53*, 57, 69, 71, 98, 116, 126
Vertigo, 79, 105
VHS: and censorship, 5, 14; early 1980s boom of, 3, 41, 211; and fanzines, 3, 211; Franco's films on, 21, 30, 33, 211–34, 243, 244, 251, 264; and niche markets for home distribution, 211, 216–17, 236–37n13; penetration of in Spain, 286n6; and video stores, 211, 269
"video nasties," 5, 14, 262n8
videophilia, 249, 254
Video Times, 247
Video WatchBlog, 260
Video Watchdog: cataloging of Franco's work in, 5, 33–34, 249, 251; consumer focus of, 247; creation and development of, 245, 247; critical construction of Franco's work in, 245, 246–55, 261; Franco as cornerstone of, 246; global emphasis of, 248, 255; interviews in, 182; oppositional stance of, 249; periodization of Franco's work in, 249, 261n4; philosophy of, 246
Vidor, King, 70

Le Viol de vampire. See *The Rape of the Vampire*
A Virgin among the Living Dead, 251
Vitti, Monica, 99
Viva Maria!, 57
Vohrer, Alfred, 93, 105
Le Voleur, 57

Wakamatsu, Koji, 86
Wallace, Bryan Edgar, 89, 96, 102
Wallace, Edgar, 31, 71, 88, 89, 90–96, 104, 108n3, 123, 325
Welles, Orson, 23–24, 28, 35, 56, 57, 58, 70, 71, 104, 234, 275, 319, 320, 321–26, *322*, 328, 331, 333–34n15, 334n16
Wendlandt, Horst, 105
White, Daniel, 17, 119, 137n3, 153–54
Wicked Memoirs of Eugenie, 188, 189, 196–97
Wiene, Robert, 91
Witch Academy, 216
Women Behind Bars, 12, 262n8
Wood, Ed, 18
Wynorski, Jim, 315

Les Yeux sans visage. See *Eyes without a Face*

Der Zinker. See *The Squeaker*
Zombie Lake, 20
Zulueta, Iván, 273

CPSIA information can be obtained
at www.ICGtesting.com
Printed in the USA
BVHW04s1459310718
522868BV00007B/6/P

9 780814 343166